The Rhetorical Act
Second Edition

■ ■ ■

About the Author

Karlyn Kohrs Campbell is professor and chair of the department of speech communication at the University of Minnesota. She is the co-author of *Critiques of Contemporary Rhetoric* and of *Interplay of Influence: News, Advertising, Politics, and the Mass Media* (Wadsworth Publishing Company). She is also the author of *Man Cannot Speak for Her,* co-author of *Deeds Done in Words: Presidential Rhetoric and the Genres of Governance,* and author of articles appearing in such journals as *Philosophy and Rhetoric* and the *Quarterly Journal of Speech.* She is editor of a two-volume reference work, *Women Public Speakers in the United States.*

She received the Woolbert Award for scholarship of exceptional originality and influence (1987), the Winans-Wichelns Book Award (1990), and the Ehninger Award for outstanding scholarship in rhetoric (1991). In 1992 she was selected as one of the first five distinguished scholars honored by the Speech Communication Association. She was awarded a fellowship at the Barone Center of the John F. Kennedy School of Government at Harvard University in the fall of 1992. She has served on the editorial boards of *Communication Monographs, Quarterly Journal of Speech, Philosophy and Rhetoric, Communication Education, Communication Quarterly, Communication Studies,* and *Critical Studies in Mass Communication.*

The Rhetorical Act

Second Edition

Karlyn Kohrs Campbell

University of Minnesota

Wadsworth Publishing Company

I(T)P™ An International Thomson Publishing Company

Belmont ▪ Albany ▪ Bonn ▪ Boston ▪ Cincinnati ▪ Detroit ▪ London
Madrid ▪ Melbourne ▪ Mexico City ▪ New York ▪ Paris
San Francisco ▪ Singapore ▪ Tokyo ▪ Toronto ▪ Washington

Communication Editor: Todd Robert Armstrong
Editorial Assistant: Laura A. Murray
Production Services Coordinator: Debby Kramer
Production: Scratchgravel Publishing Services
Designer: Anne Draus, Scratchgravel Publishing Services
Print Buyer: Barbara Britton
Permissions Editor: Robert Kauser
Copy Editor: Meg Korones
Cover Designer: Jeanne Calabrese
Compositor: Scratchgravel Publishing Services
Printer: Quebecor Printing/Fairfield

Printed in the United States of America
 2 3 4 5 6 7 8 9 10—01 00 99 98

For more information, contact Wadsworth Publishing Company:

Wadsworth Publishing Company
10 Davis Drive
Belmont, California 94002, USA

International Thomson Publishing Europe
Berkshire House 168-173
High Holborn
London, WC1V 7AA, England

Thomas Nelson Australia
102 Dodds Street
South Melbourne 3205
Victoria, Australia

Nelson Canada
1120 Birchmount Road
Scarborough, Ontario
Canada M1K 5G4

International Thomson Editores
Campos Eliseos 385, Piso 7
Col. Polanco
11560 México D.F. México

International Thomson Publishing GmbH
Königswinterer Strasse 418
53227 Bonn, Germany

International Thomson Publishing Asia
221 Henderson Road
#05-10 Henderson Building
Singapore 0315

International Thomson Publishing Japan
Hirakawacho Kyowa Building, 3F
2-2-1 Hirakawacho
Chiyoda-ku, Tokyo 102, Japan

Library of Congress Cataloging-in-Publication Data

Campbell, Karlyn Kohrs.
    The rhetorical act / Karlyn Kohrs Campbell. — 2nd ed.
       p.   cm.
    Includes bibliographical references and index.
    ISBN 0-534-16752-7
    1. Rhetoric   I. Title.
PN187.C3   1995
808—dc20   95-5414

*To all those who have struggled
for the right to speak,
in the hope that what this book contains
will help to give them voice*

Preface

More than thirteen years have passed since the first edition of *The Rhetorical Act*. Much has occurred in our intellectual life to complicate and expand our understanding of discourse and rhetoric, including the works of postmodernists and students of cultural studies and the impact of theorists such as Michel Foucault. I continue to believe that in spite of those developments, the necessary starting point is a traditional humanistic approach to rhetoric. Accordingly, although I have incorporated more recent research into the chapters that follow, my approach still draws from the classical works of Aristotle and the more contemporary writings of Kenneth Burke. In addition, the book still reaffirms the ancient Ciceronian relationship between art and practice—that you cannot master rhetorical skills without understanding the theory, the ideas on which such skills are based.

Consistent with the first edition, this second edition of *The Rhetorical Act* departs from traditional textbooks in several ways. Of greatest importance is that this book treats rhetorical action as the joint effort of rhetor and audience, emphasizing the audience's active, collaborative role. In Aristotelian terms, it treats enthymemes, arguments produced cooperatively by rhetor and audience, as "the substance of persuasion." Buttressing that perspective, the second edition shows how the elaboration likelihood model is further evidence of the power of that ancient idea.

Second, *The Rhetorical Act* approaches rhetoric as "a strategy to encompass a situation" (Kenneth Burke) and as "that art or talent by which discourse is adapted to its end" (George Campbell). Consistent with that approach, this second edition explores the rhetorical obstacles that arise out of the audience, the subject/purpose, and the rhetor, and then examines the resources available to overcome them.

The purpose of this book is to help students become critics or analysts who can assess situations, conceive of rhetorical possibilities, examine actual rhetorical action, and compare their efforts and those of fellow students with the discourse of journalists, politicians, and other public persuaders.

Third, *The Rhetorical Act* treats all forms of rhetoric as points on a single continuum of influence rather than as measured by success or failure in altering belief or attitudes. As considered here, rhetoric ranges from discourse that affects perception to ritualistic reaffirmation of community membership. There is no separate treatment of listening or of informative speaking or explanatory writing. Thus, the book minimizes distinctions between oral and written rhetoric except in recognizing the special role of nonverbal elements in oral persuasion.

What is new? Relevant research materials published in the interim between the first and second editions have been incorporated into sources. Chapter 8 on the resources of argument now includes an exercise on fallacies that mimic other rhetorical strategies. What was formerly Chapter 3, instructions for a beginning speaker or writer, has been moved to the appendix in recognition that this book is used primarily in advanced public speaking, composition, and speechwriting courses or in classes that introduce students to rhetorical criticism. The appendix still includes suggestions to beginning public speakers about delivery and the strategy report that is such an important tool in teaching students to become critics of their own rhetoric.

In addition, all the chapters except the first and second include new material for analysis by students. Briefer examples within chapters also are drawn from more contemporary materials. Materials for student analysis include such diverse rhetoric as testimony at the Anita Hill–Clarence Thomas hearings, an essay on Israeli–P.L.O. negotiations, Governor Bill Clinton's speech to the American Legion, Judge Ruth Bader Ginsburg's acceptance speech for nomination to the Supreme Court, California Chief Justice Rose Bird's speech on her experiences with breast cancer, a theologian's argument on the feminism of Jesus, a model sermon, a column incorporating an interview with a women's rights activist, and essays on the nonverbal rhetoric of flag burning and the Statue of Liberty. It is hoped that these varied examples will stimulate the kind of critical discussion so essential to developing analytical skills.

My profound thanks to the readers who reviewed this manuscript and made helpful suggestions that have improved this book in many ways: Dr. Nancy Mitchell, Kent State University; Betty Zane Morris, Shorter College; Richard J. Johannesen, Northern Illinois University;

Dana Cloud, University of Texas at Austin; Bonnie Dow, North Dakota State University; and Edward Schiappa, Purdue University. My thanks also to my fine Minnesota students and to my speech/communication colleagues whose work continually enlarges my understanding of our field. Finally, my boundless thanks to Paul Newell Campbell who is a constant source of joy and support and whose conversation keeps my critical faculties sharp.

Karlyn Kohrs Campbell

Contents

PART TWO
The Rhetorical Problem

CHAPTER 9   The Resources of Organization   243

CHAPTER 10   The Resources of Language: Style and Strategy   285

PART ONE

Rhetorical Action

CHAPTER 1

A Rhetorical Perspective

Through its title, *The Rhetorical Act*, this book boldly announces that it is about rhetoric. Because mass media commentators often use *rhetoric* to mean "hot air" or "lies," you may well ask why you should study rhetoric in a class or read a book about rhetorical action. One way to answer this question is to define *rhetoric* properly and to show the possible value of a rhetorical perspective on human action.

A "perspective," literally, is a way of looking through (*per* = through; *specere* = to look), an angle of vision, a way of seeing. All perspectives are partial and, in that sense, distorted or biased: each looks at this rather than that; each has its particular emphasis. Because someone is always doing the looking and seeing, it is impossible to avoid taking some point of view.

Just what is a rhetorical (as opposed to a philosophical or scientific) perspective? Whereas scientists would say the most important concern is the discovery and testing of certain kinds of truths, rhetoricians (who study rhetoric and take a rhetorical perspective) would say, "Truths cannot walk on their own legs. They must be carried by people to other people. They must be explained, defended, and spread through language, argument, and appeal." Philosophers and scientists respond, rightly, that whenever possible, assumptions should be tested through logic and experiment. In fact, they would argue that you and I should pay more attention to how conclusions are reached and tested. Rhetoricians reply that unacknowledged and unaccepted truths are of no use at all. Thus, the bias of a rhetorical perspective is its emphasis on and its concern with the resources available in language and in people to make ideas clear and cogent, to bring concepts to life, to make them salient for people. A rhetorical perspective is interested in what influences or persuades people.

3

Those strongly committed to a rhetorical perspective argue that some scientists and philosophers delude themselves, claiming that they are not persuaders and do not use rhetorical strategies in their writings. In a review of two books reporting research on Neandertals, for example, Stephen Jay Gould, who teaches biology, geology, and the history of science at Harvard, says that humans are storytelling creatures and comments on "the centrality of narrative style in any human discourse (though scientists like to deny the importance of such rhetorical devices—while using them all the time—and prefer to believe that persuasion depends upon fact and logic alone)."[1] When objectivity is highly valued, some feel that any hint of subjectivity must be denied. Similarly, feminist challenges to traditional philosophy call attention to possible sources of bias in modes of philosophizing, pointing to rhetorical impulses in the works of great philosophers.[2] In other words, rhetoricians can identify persuasive elements in all discourse, including scientific and philosophical communication.

A rhetorical perspective, then, focuses on social truths, that is, on the kinds of truths that are created and tested by people in groups and that influence social and political decisions. These truths represent what a group of people agrees to believe or accept; such truths become what the group takes to be "common sense." Among the important social truths a rhetorical perspective might teach you to examine are the processes by which taxpayers, parents, congressional committees, school boards, and citizens respond to issues that cannot be resolved solely through logical analysis and experimental testing. For example, should affirmative action programs be used to rectify past discrimination against minorities and women? Early acceptance of affirmative action as an appropriate remedy for past discrimination has shifted as doubts arise about "quotas" or "reverse discrimination." What constitutes discrimination? What remedies for past discrimination are fair to all those who compete for jobs and admission to educational pro-

---

[1]Stephen Jay Gould, "So Near and Yet So Far," *New York Review of Books,* October 20, 1994, p. 26.

[2]In "Feminists and Philosophy," *New York Review of Books,* October 20, 1994, pp. 59–63, Martha Nussbaum, a professor of philosophy, classics, and comparative literature at Brown University and a visiting professor of law at the University of Chicago, reviews a collection of essays by feminist philosophers who write in defense of reason; yet she comments, "Feminists note that males who wish to justify the oppression of women have frequently made a pretense of objectivity and of freedom from bias in sifting evidence and have used the claim of objectivity to protect their biased judgments from rational scrutiny" (pp. 60–61).

grams? As another example, should air quality standards be set high enough that cars must be redesigned to use alternative energy sources, gasoline reformulated, and industries converted to use less polluting fuels? How can we balance our concern for healthy industries that create good jobs with the impact of pollution on the environment and on human health? Still another example: Will harsh penalties for convicted rapists provide better protection for women, or will such penalties increase the reluctance of juries to convict? For social questions such as these, philosophers can point out contradictions in our thinking and spell out the implications of a given position. Researchers can give us the best available data about the lack of women and minorities in categories of employment, about available pools of minority applicants for jobs, about causes and effects of pollution, and about the low conviction rates of accused rapists. When we have looked at the data and examined the logic of the conclusions drawn from them, we still must make decisions that go beyond the facts and make commitments that go beyond sheer logic.

From its beginnings, this emphasis on social truths has been the distinctive quality of a rhetorical perspective. What fragmentary historical records exist seem to indicate that rhetoric was first studied and taught early in the fifth century B.C.E. by Corax and his pupil Tisias in the Greek city-state of Syracuse located on the east coast of Sicily. A despot came to power and seized much of the privately owned land. When he was overthrown, former landowners went to court to recover their holdings by pleading their cases. It soon became apparent that those more skilled in arguing were the more successful, and Corax and Tisias began to teach rhetoric—or how to be more skillful in pleading one's case in court.

WHAT IS RHETORIC?

The first major treatise on the art of rhetoric that still exists was written by Aristotle in fourth-century-B.C.E. Athens. The Greek word for rhetoric comes from *rhêtorikê, -ikê,* meaning "art or skill of," and *rhêtor,* meaning an experienced political/public speaker. Both in *On Rhetoric* and in his other works, Aristotle distinguished among kinds of truth. He believed that there were certain immutable truths of nature, which he designated as the province of metaphysics or science (*theoria*). He recognized a different sort of wisdom or social knowledge (*phronêsis*) as needed to make choices about matters affecting communities or a whole society. These truths, not discoverable through science or analytic logic, he described as contingent, that is, as dependent on cultural values, the situation, and the nature of the issue. They were the special concerns of the area of study he called "rhetoric."

The contingent qualities of social truths can best be illustrated by looking at what it means to say that something is "a problem." Put most simply, a problem is the gap that exists between what you think ought to be (value) and what is; it is the discrepancy between the ideal and the real, between goals and achievements. By this definition, a problem for one person may not be a problem for another person. For example, some students are satisfied with C's in most courses. Their goal is to get the "ticket" represented by a college degree with a minimum of inconvenience. They plan to exert their energies after they begin work at an occupation or position of their choice. Other students are devastated by anything less than an A in any class. Their goal is graduate school or highly specialized study and work. They need very high averages and the best possible preparation and achievement now. For these different students, the same fact—a grade of C—can be a big problem or no problem at all. In other words, a problem can literally be defined out of existence!

For you as students and for society as a whole, defining problems depends on goals and values, and these can change. In this same sense social truths—and thus rhetoric—are "subjective" and "evaluative"; rhetoric addresses issues that arise because of people's values.

Rhetoric is, of course, also concerned with data that establish what exists and with logical processes for drawing conclusions from facts and implications from principles and assumptions. Indeed, Aristotle considered rhetoric an offshoot of logic, and a rhetorical perspective is characterized not only by an emphasis on social truths but also by an emphasis on reason-giving or justification in place of coercion or violence. This distinction can be subtle. In general, rhetorical efforts seek to affect the free choices of groups or individuals, whereas coercion creates situations in which only one choice seems possible—the costs of any other option are too high, the pressure too great, the threat too awful. Violence coerces by threatening bodily harm or death if any choice but that desired is made. Reason-giving assumes that by presenting the implications of the available options, one can persuade an audience to choose one of them freely, based on the justifications and evidence offered. Rhetoric presumes that audiences have some real freedom of choice.[3]

---

[3]Some behaviorists argue that all choice is an illusion; if so, all efforts at influence are pointless.

Of course, not all of the reasons used by rhetors (those who initiate symbolic acts seeking to influence others) will make sense to logicians or scientists. Some rhetorical reasons are grounded in facts and logic, but many others are grounded in religious beliefs, history, or cultural values, in associations and metaphors, in hunger, resentments, or dreams. A rhetorical perspective is eclectic and inclusive in its search for what is influential and why. In fact, rhetoric's concern with justification grows out of its focus on social truths tested by people in their roles as voters, property owners, consumers, workers, parents, and the like. In other words, reasons are presented to the decision makers and evaluators to whom the rhetoric is addressed, the audience.

Obviously, in some situations you can say, "Do this and don't ask any questions—just trust me," but these situations are rare. Reasons can be ignored only where your relationship to those addressed is so close and strong that the relationship itself is the reason for action or belief.

In most cases, then, even those involving your nearest and dearest, you must give reasons, justify your views, explain your position. And you must do so in terms that will make sense to others. Rhetors must "socialize" their reasons. It is more acceptable, for example, to explain that you run several miles every day to maintain your weight and protect your health than to say that you run for the joy of it, for the sheer physical pleasure it gives you. "Socialized" reasons are accepted by society and by most people. U.S. culture is strongly pragmatic; therefore, "good" reasons tend to show that an act is useful. Other societies and some U.S. subcultures place greater emphasis on the sensual and aesthetic; for them, "good" reasons affirm behavior that is pleasurable and expressive, such as precision ice-skating, acrobatic skateboarding, skillful hang gliding, dancing the tango really well, losing oneself in musical sound, singing in close harmony, rapping, or savoring and preparing unusual foods.

Because rhetoric is addressed to others, it gives reasons; and because it is social and public, it uses as reasons the values accepted and affirmed by a subculture or culture. In this way, rhetoric is tied to social values, and rhetors' statements will reflect the social norms of particular groups, times, and places.

Because it is addressed to others, providing justifications that they will understand and feel, rhetoric is a humanistic study, and, as such, it examines all kinds of human symbol use, even the bizarre and perverse. From the beginnings of rhetoric in classical antiquity, rhetoricians have understood that persuasion occurs through both argument and association, through the cold light of logic and the white heat of passion, through explicit values and subconscious needs and associations. Accordingly, the field of rhetoric examines all of the available means by which we are influenced and by which we can influence others.

In summary, rhetoric is the study of what is persuasive. The issues it examines are social truths, addressed to others, justified by reasons that reflect cultural values. It is a humanistic study that examines all the symbolic means by which influence occurs.

RHETORICAL ACTS

As I have described it, a rhetorical perspective takes note of the rhetorical or persuasive dimension in all human behavior. Although all human actions can be considered implicitly persuasive, I do not wish to define "the rhetorical act" so broadly. The lines separating rhetorical acts from other acts are difficult to draw, however, and in this book I shall treat the concept of rhetoric in both its broad and its narrow senses.

The broadest view of rhetoric is expressed in the statement, "You can never not communicate," meaning that whatever you do or say (or don't do or say) can be observed and interpreted. For example, an unsmiling expression can be interpreted as evidence of sadness (rather than thoughtfulness); a young African American man walking home from work is perceived by some as menacing; or a woman walking home late from work is sometimes assumed to be extending a sexual invitation. Any behavior can become rhetorical when someone interprets it and is influenced by that interpretation, whatever the actors' intentions may have been.

Of course, many acts are intentionally rhetorical—advertisements, music videos, editorials, book and movie reviews, and films, essays, sermons, and speeches that declare a position and seek to defend it or make it attractive to others. When I address you as speakers or writers, I talk about rhetorical acts as intentional, deliberate attempts to influence others. When I function as a critic or analyst and address you as critics and analysts, however, I comment on all possible persuasive effects, both intentional and unintentional. To understand rhetoric, you must fathom all the processes of influence, and, as a rhetor, you must come to terms with unintended and accidental effects—especially because some of them may work against your purpose.

In other words, defined most broadly, *rhetoric* is the study of all the processes by which people influence each other through symbols, regardless of the intent of the source. A *rhetorical act,* however, is an intentional, created, polished attempt to overcome the obstacles in a given situation with a specific audience on a given issue to achieve a particular end. A rhetorical act creates a message whose shape and form, beginning and end, are stamped on it by one or more human authors with a goal for an audience. If you study all forms of influence, you will become aware of all the available resources for persuasion. Similarly, when you analyze your rhetoric and that of others, you must consider persuasive effects that may not have been fully under the control of or consciously intended by the source.

RHETORICAL PURPOSES

Because intention and impact are so important to a rhetorical perspective, I want to consider the range of meanings included in the words *persuasion* and *influence.* From the persuader's point of view, these meanings describe a range of purposes or intentions, not simply agreement or opposition. From the point of view of a reader, listener, or viewer, they reflect processes that constantly engage us as we experience the world, try to understand it, and decide what actions, if any, would be appropriate as responses. In other words, *rhetorical purposes* are conscious attempts to influence processes that are occurring in us all of the time as we come in contact with the world and the people in it.

Creating Virtual Experience

Through their use of symbols, rhetors call up ideas, pictures, and experiences in those they address. If I write, "The burning sun beat down on the stubble in the oat field, and through a haze of sweat, the stalks suddenly seemed to be hair sprouting in a crew cut from the scalp of a red-haired giant," you can draw on past sensations and experiences to re-create your own mental picture. Although each reader's picture will be different, and each will reflect the reader's unique past, most will concern summer in a rural area. Fundamentally, to act rhetorically is to communicate or to initiate an act—to express something in symbols—that someone else can translate into virtual experience. When something is virtual, it does not exist in fact; it is *as if* it existed. There is no sun, no stubble, no sweat, no scalp, no red hair, no giant on this page. But if I write about them vividly enough, you can imagine them; it is as if you saw and heard and felt them here and now. That re-creation in your mind is virtual experience. In response to my words, you imagine a scene, create a mental picture; what you experience is virtual experience, called forth and shaped by your response to the symbols produced by someone else. Effective communication creates an image or idea in your mind that approximates the image or idea that the speaker or author wished to convey.

In other words, the fundamental rhetorical purpose, the most basic kind of influence—communicating—requires you to initiate a rhetorical act that can be translated into virtual experience by others. The most basic question in rhetoric is how to do that.

One kind of rhetorical action is intended primarily to produce virtual experience. Most works of literature, for example, are written to expand and shape our experience. In them, one sees, hears, smells, tastes, and touches vividly and concretely and feels intensely, and these sensations are shaped and formed into a satisfying and complete experience. When such works are transformed into dramas presented on stage or in film or television, the words become lived experience incarnated in actors' dialogue, movements, and feelings. In such processes, producers, directors, and actors do what all of us do each day as we translate the symbols we encounter into units of meaning based on our own experiences; the greater the range of our experiences, the greater our potential for imagining these dramas on the stages of our minds, of comprehending and identifying with the messages of others.

In Larry McMurtry's novel *Lonesome Dove,*[4] for example, the reader tastes the dust stirred up on the prairie by the feet of herds of cattle, smells frying meat, hears pigs snore, and feels the warm neck of a horse. These sensations re-create the experience of a cattle drive in the U.S. West of the past.

Altering Perception

Literary works can also have political effects. Charles Dickens's *Oliver Twist*[5] re-created the experiences of orphans in English poorhouses so movingly that readers demanded reform. Harriet Beecher Stowe's *Uncle Tom's Cabin*[6] depicted scenes of slavery so vividly that the book

---

[4]New York: Simon & Schuster, 1985.
[5]Or, *The Parish Boy's Progress* (London: R. Bentley, 1838).
[6]London: J. Cassell, 1852.

became a major force for abolition. The same sensory or aesthetic stimuli that enliven good literature are a major means of persuasion. In other words, by creating virtual experience—the more vivid the better—literature can contribute to the second rhetorical purpose I want to discuss: altering perception.

George Washington wrote, "The truth is the people must *feel* before they will *see*." Whether or not you must experience something before you can comprehend it, it is surely true that vivid experience improves our capacity to understand.

For an example of how an author can change the meaning of an experience for an audience—that is, alter perception of that experience—consider what Corlann Gee Bush does to one's experience of a series of paintings by the famous Western artist and sculptor, Charles M. Russell. In her essay "The Way We Weren't: Images of Women and Men in Cowboy Art" she writes about how cowboy art has influenced viewers to believe in "the romantic West, the West of myth and legend."[7] She is particularly concerned with how women were depicted, and uses five portraits of a Keeoma woman by Russell as illustrations. In these paintings, an American Indian woman is shown in either a reclining or a hip-slung pose as a highly sensual and spirited person. As ordinary viewers, we are likely to assume that these are portraits of a real person and take them as indications of the character of Keeoma women in the nineteenth century. To alter such a perception, Corlann Bush tells us:

The truth is that Russell's wife, Nancy, was the model for the paintings. To pose, she dressed in buckskin and surrounded herself with artifacts. Russell painted the objects realistically; he painted her as an Indian. In this way he was able to paint his wife as the sensual women he knew her to be while preserving her place within the moral code of white society. . . . This repressed sexuality was transposed onto an Indian woman who did not exist but who lived, nonetheless, deep in the subconscious of white American males (p. 27).

Once we have this information, we see the paintings differently; they become a visual record not of a Keeoma woman of the past but of the stereotypes of white and American Indian women in the nineteenth century that persist in the paintings.

---

[7]*The Women's West,* ed. Susan Armitage and Elizabeth Jameson. (Norman: University of Oklahoma Press, 1987), pp. 19–33. Cited material is on p. 21.

Our impressions of the U.S. West have also been influenced by popular culture, including the novels of Louis L'Amour, John Wayne Westerns, television series such as *Bonanza* and *Gunsmoke,* and by miniseries based on McMurtry's novel. If your images of the West come from such sources, your perceptions may be altered by information provided by historians. For example, although African Americans rarely have appeared in the West of popular culture, I was surprised to read that "George W. Saunders of the Trail Drivers Association, as valid an authority as there is, estimated that about 25 percent of all cowhands were black." Although they constituted only a small percentage of Western settlers, Robert Haywood explains why such a large percentage of cowhands were African Americans:

> In an age when blacks were stereotyped as either foolish or primitive and where their opportunities to advance, either socially or economically, were limited, ranch-related jobs offered more dignity and more opportunity for self-expression than any other employment available. Whites in the ranching business realized the importance of the contributions of all cowboys— black, white, or Mexican—and adjusted their prejudices accordingly. . . . The mutual interdependence left little room for arrogant displays of racial superiority or overt discrimination, no matter how ingrained.[8]

If we accept it as true, Haywood's information may alter our perceptions of the popular culture portrait of the West, and he makes his rather surprising data more plausible by explaining why African Americans tended to congregate in this somewhat unlikely occupation.

To recapitulate, the most minimal rhetorical purpose, the smallest effect produced, is to add to the sum of your audience's experiences. If you can frame such experiences, you may be able to influence how those virtual experiences are interpreted.

---

[8]J. Marvin Hunter, ed., *The Trail Drivers of Texas: Interesting Sketches of Early Cowboys* (Austin: University of Texas Press, 1985, p. 453), cited in C. Robert Haywood, " 'No Less A Man': Blacks in Cow Town Dodge City, 1876–1886," *The Western Historical Quarterly,* May 1988, pp. 161-82, cited material on p. 169. See also Kenneth W. Porter, *The Negro on the American Frontier* (New York: Arno Press, 1971), pp. 521–522; William Loren Katz, *The Black West* (Garden City, NY: Doubleday, 1971), p. xi.

Explaining

If we evaluated rhetorical acts by how much they altered beliefs, nearly all would be failures. Normal, healthy human beings whose physical environments are under their own control do not change their beliefs in response to a single message—whether the message lasts five minutes or five hours. If people are influenced to alter their beliefs, they do so over weeks, months, or even years, and in response to many different messages.

The need for explanation is most strongly felt when we encounter an intense, apparently irrational experience. Let us suppose, for example, that you read news reports about an investment banker jogging in Central Park in New York City who is attacked by a gang of youths who rape and beat her and leave her for dead. Or you read of an African American youth from the Bronx going to look at a used car in Brooklyn who is attacked and shot by a gang of local Euro-American youths. In response to these events, many editorials appeared trying to explain why these events happened and what they meant, often accompanied by statements about how we should respond to them. Like these editorial writers, rhetors often provide explanations for events that have disturbed those they address. Note, however, that an encounter with a disturbing event precedes the felt need for explanation. As a result, rhetors sometimes begin by creating that kind of experience through vivid language and disturbing information and then offer and justify what they believe is the most plausible explanation.

Linda A. Fairstein, director of the Sex Crimes Prosecution Unit in the Manhattan District Attorney's Office, has been prosecuting rape cases since the mid-1970s and is the author of a book called *Sexual Violence: Our War Against Rape*.[9] Much of the book describes the changes that have occurred in rape laws, which no longer require corroboration of an alleged victim's testimony, for example. Because it is partly a memoir of her career and partly a series of real-life crime stories, the book's vivid virtual experience of how the criminal justice system treats rape victims describes the experiences of individuals with whom we can identify. This evidence is obviously intended to alter perception. However, Fairstein goes beyond the data to explain and to argue that rape is different from other violent crimes because it is so much more intimate, which emphasizes the significance of the

---

[9]New York: William Morrow & Company, 1993.

sexual element in this crime. Her views will find a ready audience because women, particularly the millions of rape victims, have found rape to be a special kind of outrage whose impact often persists for years in nightmares and sleeplessness. Fairstein's book provides much evidence about rape and about its treatment in the criminal justice system; it documents the horrors that occur but gives hope that legal changes have made the system better able to understand the crime and to punish those who commit it.[10]

Formulating Belief

By this time it should be apparent that rhetorical action is not a one-shot event, but a process. Although there is a somewhat orderly progression from enlarging audience experience to altering perceptions, which, in turn, leads to a search for explanations, followed by efforts to determine which interpretation is most satisfactory, these are not discrete, separable processes for coming to terms with experience, nor are they discrete rhetorical purposes. Virtual experience occurs within some kind of framework; new experience can alter a framework to change perception. When perceptions change, we seek explanations; sometimes we demand explanations before we consider altering our perceptual framework, perhaps even before participating in the creation of virtual experience. As these other processes overlap and intersect, so, too, do the processes by which we formulate a belief or discard one belief for another. Similarly, the processes by which a rhetor urges us to believe arise out of prior experience and conceptualization.

As an illustration, let us return to the nineteenth-century U.S. West. Virtual experience might be created by the autobiography of Nat Love, "the Deadwood Kid," one of the West's most notorious African American cowboys,[11] or by reading the memoir of Charlie Siringo, the "cowboy detective" who wrote of experiences on the trail with African American trail riders,[12] or from the biography of Print Olive, one of

---

[10]Another example of rhetorical explanation is *Reproducing Rape: Domination Through Talk in the Courtroom* (Chicago: University of Chicago Press, 1993), in which Gregory Matoesian analyzes transcripts of rape trials to show how courtroom talk by lawyers can shape or socially construct the victim's testimony to fit male standards of legitimate sexual practice, transforming the experience of rape into routine consensual sex.

[11]*The Life and Adventures of Nat Love . . .* (1907; Baltimore: Black Classic Press, 1988).

[12]Charles A. Siringo, *Riata and Spurs* (Boston: Houghton Mifflin, 1927), pp. 17–18, 28.

Dodge City's toughest ranchers, whose life was saved by James Kelly during a shootout in a saloon.[13] The experiences they provide would challenge those in most popular culture. Before prior perceptions were abandoned, however, you might seek out historical works, such as *The Negro on the American Frontier* by Kenneth W. Porter or *The Black West* by Loren Katz (both cited earlier), testing whether the experiences depicted were accurate and typical and seeking explanations of why African Americans were disproportionately represented among cowhands in the West.

Once that was completed, new questions might arise. Why haven't Western novels, films, and television programs reflected this reality? At this point, you are an audience member prepared to consider the claims of a rhetor who attempts to convince you that these omissions were no accident, but a result of the racism that is a heritage of the history of slavery in the United States. Such a rhetor might have gone through the process I've described to reach a point at which everything seemed to fall together and a belief emerged. Many rhetorical acts attempt to produce such a "precipitating moment" in which the audience agrees, "That's it. That's the way it is." Few rhetorical acts succeed, however, in taking members of an audience through all these stages to transform their attitudes. At best, most serve to confirm a position already being considered (somewhere between the search for explanation and the choice of one interpretation) or to reinforce an explanation the audience has pondered and considers plausible. Indeed, those who achieve such modest goals have been resounding successes as persuaders.

Initiating Action

Let us suppose, however, that you are present at a rhetorical event that formulates the beliefs of a group about the misrepresentation of African American cowhands in the West. The pleased rhetor now urges action—but finds that most of the audience is not ready to do anything about it. Those who share this belief may not write novels or produce films or television programs; indeed, they may not have the resources to do any of those things. Even if they share this attitude, they may not believe that action is needed; concern about misrepresentation may be a low priority.

---

[13]Harry E. Chrisman, *The Ladder of Rivers: The Story of I.P. (Print) Olive* (Denver: Sage, 1962), p. 122.

As this example suggests, shared belief is not necessarily linked to a willingness or an ability to act. At such a moment, doubts arise about whether beliefs have really been formulated, and such doubts have merit. But a survey of rhetorical processes suggests that the situation is normal. Even when beliefs are formulated, action will not follow unless that belief is reinforced, rendered salient, and then channeled so that action seems appropriate, possible, and necessary.

While the audience in this case might not include writers or television or film producers, it may well include parents, perhaps even members of school boards. A skillful rhetor might want to urge the inclusion of more material about African American history in elementary and secondary schools and suggest that this misrepresentation is just one example of the lack of such material, an example that is particularly telling because it reflects a distortion that reduces the African American past to slavery, ignoring the diverse, positive images that all students need to encounter in order to form a more accurate picture of U.S. history.

The chances of success in initiating action would increase if other messages reinforced such proposals. The 1993 film *Posse,* which was about African American cowboys and was directed by Mario Van Peebles, an African American, attempted to correct the distorted impressions created by past Westerns.[14] The killings of African Americans in Howard Beach and Brooklyn, New York, call attention to contemporary evidence of racism among young whites, suggesting the importance of teaching more African American history. Television specials on racism, produced in response to these killings, included studies demonstrating that many African American children still have negative self-images, first identified in earlier studies by Kenneth Clark that formed part of the basis for the 1954 Supreme Court desegregation decision in *Brown v. Board of Education* (347 U.S. 483).[15] Buttressed by such reinforcing messages, a rhetor who proposed action to change curriculum and textbooks would have a better chance of succeeding.

If messages and events support each other and are publicized, beliefs will be strengthened, and concerned individuals will form or join groups to formulate plans for influencing the school board and textbook publishers. Rhetorical acts aimed at initiating action will appear. An editorial will urge that units on African American history be developed and included in the curriculum; a parents' group will press the

---

[14]See William Loren Katz, author of *Black People Who Made the Old West* (Trenton, NJ: Africa World Press, 1992) and of *The Black West,* letter to the editor, *New York Times,* June 2, 1993:A10.

[15]Kenneth B. Clark, *Dark Ghetto: Dilemmas of Social Power.* New York: Harper & Row, 1965.

school administration to act and formulate a committee to coordinate efforts to modify textbooks.

Maintaining Action

And then, when the intense interest generated by dramatic events lessens, rhetorical acts will be needed to ensure that the new units remain in the curriculum, that as history texts are revised they continue to include such materials, that teachers continue to use them in classes, that African American teachers and principals are hired, retained, and encouraged. Such rhetorical action perpetuates what has been institutionalized, as illustrated by the yearly report to the PTA on test scores and dropout rates that reaffirms the school's successes with its varied pupils; the Sunday sermon to the regular churchgoer, which urges continued support and attendance; the monthly ritual of prayer and reports of activities at the Phyllis Wheatley women's club that reinforces their motto of "lifting as we climb";[16] the singing of the national anthem before baseball games, which proclaims the patriotism of sport.

This progression reflects the rhetorical dimensions in all human behavior and links them to the purposes that emerge in rhetorical acts. It should suggest to you as a prospective persuader that your choice of a purpose should reflect the prior experiences of your audience and should be attuned to the events taking place in your environment.

THE DISCIPLINE OF RHETORIC

A discipline is a field of study, an area of expertise, a branch of knowledge. A discipline provides theory, application, and experimentation, and criticism to test them all. *Theories* are explanations that seek to account for processes and data. Rhetorical theories seek to account for the processes in language and people that influence belief and action. *Applications* are rules for action that are developed from theory. Rhetorical applications suggest how you can use rhetorical principles to

---

[16]Phyllis Wheatley (1753–1784), a West African slave from Boston, was bought by Quakers who opposed slavery and educated her and promoted her writing talent. A collection of her poetry, *Poems on Various Subjects,* was published in 1773. She was free but penniless after her mistress died. She married, but her husband first abused, then deserted her. Impoverished, she and her three children died in an epidemic. "Lifting as we climb" is the motto of the National Association of Colored Women and Girls' Club.

be an effective moral agent and to protect yourself as you participate in rhetorical action initiated by others. *Experimentation* seeks to isolate variables or elements in the persuasive process and to test theoretical explanations as carefully as possible. *Critical analysis* examines rhetorical acts in order to describe processes of influence and explain how they occur. Both experimentation and criticism (of theories, applications, experimental research, and rhetorical action) contribute to the modification and application of theory.[17] In the chapters that follow, I develop theory about the nature and application of rhetorical processes, which is supported by experimental research and critical analysis that qualify, refine, and illustrate these theoretical concepts.

In its theory, the discipline of rhetoric examines the symbolic dimensions of human behavior in order to provide the most complete explanations of human influence. This broad view is tested by critical analysis. Rhetorical application focuses more narrowly on rhetorical acts—written and spoken messages designed to achieve predetermined effects in an audience. Experimental studies of persuasion focus more narrowly on rhetorical acts and test the adequacy of prior explanations of them and the appropriateness of rules for application.

As a discipline, rhetoric is the study of the art of using symbols. This understanding is reflected in many well-known definitions of rhetoric: "that art or talent by which discourse is adapted to its end" (George Campbell);[18] "the use of language as a symbolic means of inducing cooperation in beings that by nature respond to symbols" (Kenneth Burke);[19] "Let rhetoric be [defined as] an ability, in each [particular] case, to see the available means of persuasion" (Aristotle).[20] Rhetoric provides theory, application, experimentation, and critical analysis. It studies the social use of words by people in groups, the political use of words to decide who shall make what kinds of decisions, and the ethical use of words to justify belief and action through cultural values. Rhetoric is related to logic and empirical validation because it uses these materials. It is different from philosophy and science because it studies all the available processes for influencing people, and it defines influence broadly. Accordingly, it considers how people use language to alter perception, to explain, to change, re-

---

[17]Karlyn Kohrs Campbell, "The Nature of Criticism in Rhetorical and Communicative Studies," *Central States Speech Journal* 30 (1979):4–13.

[18]*The Philosophy of Rhetoric,* ed. Lloyd F. Bitzer. Carbondale: Southern Illinois University Press, 1963, p. 1.

[19]*A Rhetoric of Motives* (1950; Berkeley: University of California Press, 1969), p. 43.

[20]*On Rhetoric: A Theory of Civic Discourse.* Trans. George Kennedy. New York: Oxford University Press, 1991. 1.2.1355b.26.

inforce, and channel belief, and to initiate and maintain actions. Put more traditionally, it studies all the ways in which symbols can be used to teach, to delight, and to move.

This book is based on the ancient idea of the relationship between art and practice—the belief that you cannot improve a skill such as speaking or writing unless you understand the theory, the concepts, and the ideas on which it is based. Conversely, you cannot under-stand the theory unless you use it and test it in practice. In my view, this ancient relationship demands that those who would learn about rhetoric must take the posture of a rhetor–critic. The rhetor is an ini-tiator of rhetorical action who tries to make the choices that will make her or him the most effective moral agent. As a rhetor, you come to understand all the forces at work in persuasion, some of which are outside your control. The critic analyzes, describes, interprets, and evaluates rhetorical acts to understand what they are, and how and for whom they work. As a critic, you learn to criticize your own rheto-ric to improve it, and as a critic–consumer you learn to analyze oth-ers' rhetoric in order to make decisions as intelligently as possible. The materials in Chapter 6 are designed to help you become a more effec-tive critic of the rhetoric of others, including public figures, as well as an ever more skillful critic of your own discourse.

Whether or not you aim toward a career in which writing or speak-ing plays a central role, you must function as a critic in order to cope in an age of information explosion that will require you to sift and evalu-ate massive amounts of discourse—in news, advertising, and entertain-ment programming as well as political debates and speeches at various levels of government. Think of learning how to be a critic as a form of consumer protection, protecting you as a consumer of persuasion.

CRITICISM IS FEEDBACK

Every book addressed to students of communication begins with a model of the process that looks something like this:

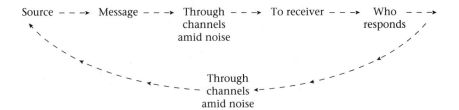

Most of you already know that the name for the receiver's response is "feedback," the kind of information used in guidance systems to keep a projectile on the correct path. When you speak or write, the immediate audience gives you useful but limited feedback. If you speak, they look at you intently, smile in amusement, frown in puzzlement, look away in annoyance or boredom, read the paper, sleep, take a note to check out a statistic, and the like. If you write a letter to the editor or an op-ed, your piece may be rejected or printed in an altered, edited form. If you are in a class and your instructor has other students discuss your speech or essay, you will discover that most reactions were not evident from facial reactions or movements. You will discover that the messages you could not see or misinterpreted or were only implied by editing are very important—perhaps the most important. Similarly, when your instructors discuss your speech or essay in class or write comments, you will discover that their observations are different—less superficial, more helpful, linked to concepts you have studied and discussed in class. Such feedback is criticism—the careful analysis and evaluation by an experienced student of rhetoric who has heard and read many rhetorical acts, pondered many critical analyses, studied available theories, and read many experimental studies. Ideally, you should aspire to be such a critic, and the aim of this book is to teach you to be one. If you understand rhetorical processes, you have the best chance of steadily improving your performance and of succeeding consistently. You will know how to evaluate your own work, and you will be prepared to consider carefully and learn from the rhetoric of others.

No one can teach you rules that will apply in all cases or even predict the occasions for rhetorical action that each of you will encounter. If you are to be an effective person, able to communicate your experiences, to place them in interpretive frameworks, to justify your interpretation as most plausible, and to initiate and maintain action consistent with your interpretation, you will need skills that enable you to find the words that will create virtual experience in your audience, to discover a framework that is intelligible in that particular time and place, to select justifications with salience on that specific issue, and so on. As a result, this book does not try to teach you universal rules (there are none!) but instead tries to teach you to be a critic. In each case, theory and application are related to critical analysis of rhetorical acts, with the goal of teaching you how to analyze your own and others' rhetoric. To the degree that I succeed in doing that, the process of learning that begins in this text and in your classes can continue outside the classroom and throughout your life.

▪ ▪ ▪

EXERCISES

1. Find a literary selection with vivid description that suggests an attitude, such as a poem by Nikki Giovanni or Susan Glaspell's short story "A Jury of Her Peers" or some other literary work with an apparent rhetorical purpose. Discuss how showing versus telling influences attitudes. Use material from such a source in a short speech, editorial, or letter to the editor.

2. Write a short essay about information that shocked you and caused you to rethink a perception or attitude, using your experience and reaction to invite audience identification.

3. Consider how some widely publicized events illustrate the processes described in this chapter. For example, how did the Anita Hill-Clarence Thomas hearings of 1991 affect attitudes toward sexual harassment? How did the O. J. Simpson case in 1994 influence attitudes toward domestic violence? Do these examples illustrate the movement from virtual experience to institutionalization and the need for maintenance rhetoric?

4. The history of rhetoric and of communication is embedded in and revealed by the meanings, usage, and origins of these terms. Both the history and the varied meanings of these words can be discovered this way: Ask each student or assign groups of students to look up rhetoric and communication (or communications) in one of the following:

The Oxford English Dictionary

Roget's Thesaurus or any dictionary of synonyms and antonyms

Encyclopedia Britannica (Compare the essay in the eleventh edition with that in the fourteenth; then look at the Macropedia and the Micropedia of the latest edition.)

Bartlett's Familiar Quotations or *The Oxford Dictionary of Quotations*

The Encyclopedia of Philosophy

A Dictionary of Contemporary American Usage

A Dictionary of Word Origins

The Oxford Classical Dictionary

The Dictionary of the Social Sciences

Black's Law Dictionary

M. H. Abrams, *A Glossary of Literary Terms*

Any other dictionary, encyclopedia, or reference work

William Safire, *Safire's New Political Dictionary* (New York: Random House, 1993). What is "bloviation"?

In class, share all the definitions, meanings, and information about word origins that were found. How old is the study of rhetoric? How old is the study of communication? What is the difference between communication and communications? How do their word origins reflect their meaning? What differences are there among these terms?

SOURCES

Aristotle. *Ethica Nicomachea.* Translated by W. D. Ross. (In *The Student's Oxford Aristotle*, Vol. V.) London: Oxford University Press, 1942. See Book Six for a discussion of the different kinds of knowledge.

Aristotle. *On Rhetoric: A Theory of Civic Discourse.* Translated by George A. Kennedy. New York: Oxford University Press, 1991. Aristotle's definitions of rhetoric used in this chapter and elsewhere are drawn from this source.

Burke, Kenneth. *Language as Symbolic Action.* Berkeley: University of California Press, 1966. See particularly the essays entitled "Definition of Man," "Terministic Screens," and "What Are the Signs of What?"

Clark, Kenneth B. *Dark Ghetto: Dilemmas of Social Power.* New York: Harper & Row, 1965.

Kennedy, George A. *Classical Rhetoric and Its Christian and Secular Tradition from Ancient to Modern Times.* Chapel Hill: The University of North Carolina Press, 1980. As its title indicates, this is a history of rhetoric. It is concise and readable.

Langer, Susanne K. *Feeling and Form: A Theory of Art.* New York: Charles Scribners Sons, 1953. This work is the source of the phrase "virtual experience," the phrase the author uses to describe the artistic form created by poesis or imaginative literature.

Langer, Susanne K. *Philosophy in a New Key: A Study in the Symbolism of Reason, Rite, and Art,* 3d ed. Cambridge, MA: Harvard University Press, 1957. This is one of the most important contemporary studies of human symbolization.

CHAPTER 2

The Rhetorical Act

In the first chapter, I discussed rhetoric, the rhetorical dimension in all human action, and rhetorical acts in general. In this chapter, I examine two rhetorical acts in some detail. Here I play the role of critic, analyzing and interpreting these rhetorical acts. As the analysis proceeds, I develop a lexicon or set of terms that can be used to talk about the elements of a rhetorical act.

The rhetorical acts I analyze appeared in the hearings held in September and October 1991 by the U.S. Senate Judiciary Committee to consider President George Bush's nomination of U.S. Court of Appeals Judge Clarence Thomas to be an associate justice of the Supreme Court.[1] The rhetorical acts were delivered not by a journalist or a politician but by a former assistant to Thomas at the Equal Employment Opportunity Commission (EEOC) and a former member of the staff of Senator John Danforth, R-MO, who was Thomas's chief advocate in the Senate. The first rhetorical act concerns affirmative action, an issue of continuing importance. The hearings on Judge Thomas's nomination were expected to end in September, although Anita Hill's allegations of sexual harassment already were known to some members of the committee. After two reporters, Timothy Phelps of *Newsday* and Nina Totenberg of National Public Radio, made those allegations public, the committee decided to hold hearings to assess them.

---

[1]*Nomination of Judge Clarence Thomas to Be Associate Justice of the Supreme Court of the United States.* Hearings Before the Committee on the Judiciary of the United States Senate, 102d Congress, 1st session, September 10, 11, 12, 13, 16, 17, 19, and 20, and October 11, 12, and 13, 1991. Four parts. (Washington, DC: GPO, 1993). J. C. Alvarez's testimony is found in 3:8–9 (prepared statement pp. 10–14) and 4:337–342.

Accordingly, the second statement by Alvarez addresses the controversial question of credibility: Who was telling the truth about the allegations of sexual harassment brought by Anita Hill—Hill or Thomas?

ELEMENTS OF RHETORICAL ACTION

The terminology I use allows critics and rhetors to describe the elements of rhetorical action. The terms name seven general categories of descriptive analysis as follows:

1. Purpose: the conclusion argued (thesis) and the response desired by the rhetor.

2. Audience: the rhetor's target; the listeners or readers selected by the act; the audience's role or the created audience.

3. Persona: the role(s) adopted by the persuader in making the argument (such as teacher, preacher, reporter, prophet, and the like).

4. Tone: the rhetor's attitude toward the subject (detached, emotional, satirical, and so forth) and toward the audience (personal/impersonal, authoritative/egalitarian/suppliant, and so on).

5. Structure: the way the materials are organized to gain attention, develop a case, and provide emphasis.

6. Supporting materials: different kinds of evidence for the argument.

7. Strategies: adaptation of all of the above, including language, appeals, and argument, to shape the materials to overcome the obstacles the rhetor faces (the rhetorical problem).

These categories (and their subcategories) of descriptive analysis provide a set of labels that permit critics and rhetors to talk about a rhetorical act in order to possess, understand, and analyze it (divide it into its parts) and describe it as fully and carefully as possible. Some of these categories are basic and are essential starting points. For instance, as a rhetor, you must decide your purpose and determine just whom you are addressing early in the process. You must select a method of organization and the supporting materials you will use, although as these acts indicate, there are many options. The simplest role would be to speak or write as a peer to your classmates (but there are always the problems of the teacher, who is not a peer, and of a subject on which you are more expert than your classmates). You may also try to treat tone simply by saying, "Oh, I'll be objective." But in most cases, you will find that you have beliefs, commitments, and personal involvements, and you must decide how to handle these. The category of strategy is the most difficult, requiring the greatest experience. You will need to read and hear many rhetorical acts to see the possibilities, and you will also need to use your instructor as a resource to get suggestions about approaches you might use to overcome special elements of the rhetorical problem.

As you will discover, these elements are always present and are almost always important in understanding how and why a rhetorical act succeeded or failed in its purpose. If you talk to yourself and to others about anything, you must share a common language. This chapter offers some crucial terms needed to talk about rhetorical acts.

Descriptive analysis provides a vocabulary for discussing rhetorical action and a method of identifying what is distinctive about a particular persuasive effort. Both a vocabulary and a method are needed if you are to become a sophisticated consumer of contemporary persuasion. Skillful rhetors understand both their own acts and those of others. Your ability to initiate rhetorical action and to control how others influence you depends in part on your accuracy in describing discourse.

Here is the first rhetorical act I describe and analyze, the first statement by Ms. Alvarez:

Statement of J. C. Alvarez

1   Let me tell you about the first time I met Clarence Thomas. It was 13 years ago in some cramped offices in an annex building that no longer exists today. I had been with Senator Danforth a few months, undoubtedly out of place in an industry that employed very few minorities. If there were a half a dozen of us on the Senate side at that time, that was too many.

2   Almost daily I heard comments about the fact that I had been hired only because of my minority background. It never occurred to me to flaunt my bachelor's degree from Princeton and my master's degree from Columbia in defense of my presence on the Hill. Affirmative action was like a cloud that kept people from looking directly at my abilities, and I bore it like a scarlet letter of shame.

3   I was young, 23 years old, and thought perhaps that they were right. I was almost apologetic that I wasn't a white Anglo-Saxon Protestant male or that my daddy had not made some

enormous financial contribution to some campaign. And then one day a big black guy with a booming voice comes into the office as the newest addition to Danforth's staff.

4   Although everyone in the office knew he had worked with Jack [Danforth] before and that he had degrees from Holy Cross and Yale, one cynical staffer decided to challenge him directly by saying, "Let's face it. The only reason you got here is because you went to Yale, and the only reason you got into Yale was not because of your ability, but because of affirmative action."

5   Clarence turned to him, took a deep breath that filled out his broad shoulders, looked at him straight on and said, "You know, I may have been lucky enough to get in, but I was smart enough to get out."

6   From that day forward, my life was changed. I would never be ashamed again to be a minority, to be a Hispanic. I had nothing to apologize for, I realized. Most importantly, Clarence that day gave me a confidence that I had never felt before. I realized that affirmative action was perhaps just a minority's version of the same nepotism that had gotten that staffer his job.

7   OK, perhaps I had been fortunate to have had doors opened for me, but I alone had been smart enough, capable enough to walk through those doors.

8   It has been 13 years, and to say that I know Clarence well is probably an understatement. Although politically and professionally Clarence has grown and developed over the years, the basic character of the man has never changed in all the time that I have known him. And this is critical to consider when reviewing his appointment to the Supreme Court.

9   Clarence is a brutally honest man, an independent thinker who is careful and deliberate in making decisions. He is not egotistical enough or presumptuous enough to think he alone knows everything. Far from it.

10   When making decisions, I can recall seeing Clarence surround himself with all types of people, from the book-smart people to the people with experience about those specific issues. He always wanted to be sure not just to get the fact[s], but to get some real-life perspective so that he could make the right decision.

11   Take, for instance, when Clarence was appointed to head the EEOC. He asked me to join his staff to address the issues of two particular protected classes who had long been neglected by the EEOC: the Hispanics and the handicapped. He pulled out all the stops. There was no limit to the communication or the meetings that he would hold to learn about the issues that were important to these groups.

12   I can recall at the time how bitter many Hispanic leaders were because they had been ignored or shut out by the EEOC under the previous administration. And they obviously expected no more from Clarence and the Republicans. I arranged meetings between Clarence and these Hispanic leaders, almost expecting to hand out flak jackets at each meeting because they came in loaded for bear, as we say in the Midwest; and they had a good reason to feel that way.

13   But in every instance I can recall, the Hispanic leadership was shocked and amazed at the reaction and the response of the chairman. He was genuinely sincere in his concern for their cause. He solicited their views and their experiences, shared his perspective, and ultimately responded to the recommendations to address the issues. In every instance, they walked into his office as his enemy and left as his ally.

14   I must admit that listening to the criticism levied [*sic*] against Clarence last week about his lack of commitment to the Hispanic community sort of shocked me, and I prepared this statement, which I ask be submitted as part of the record.

Descriptive Analysis

From the outset, Clarence Thomas was a controversial nominee. He was given the American Bar Association's lowest positive rating ("qualified"), and because of his administration of the EEOC and speeches that he had given, questions had been raised about his competence and his commitment to minority rights in general and to affirmative action as a policy in particular. He was nominated to replace Thurgood Marshall, who was resigning for reasons of ill health, and Marshall's outstanding career as a civil rights lawyer made such questions more acute. Alvarez's first brief appearance was part of testimony that responded to those issues.

The opening paragraph of Alvarez's statement of September 20, 1991, is an *introduction* that *narrows the subject* (**structure**) to the speaker's first encounter with the nominee (**tone**: personal—"Let *me* tell you about the first time *I* met Clarence Thomas") and prepares the audience for what follows by setting the scene in two ways: where the encounter occurred and the hostile climate found by minorities like her on Capitol Hill.

Paragraph 2 *elaborates* (**strategy**) the second scene, describing daily comments attributing her hiring for a position on Senator John Danforth's staff solely to her minority background (**persona**). The paragraph also states some of her credentials: "my bachelor's degree from Princeton and my master's degree from Columbia," as well as some of her attitudes. Apparently she is modest: "It never occurred to [her] to flaunt" her credentials. In addition, she was affected by the comments and ashamed to think that she might have had an edge in being hired because she was Hispanic. Her words are vivid and metaphoric (**tone**): "Affirmative action was like a cloud that kept people from looking directly at my abilities, and I bore it like a scarlet letter of shame." Notice that she has made an allusion (**strategy**) to Nathaniel Hawthorne's novel *The Scarlet Letter,* in which Hester Prynne is made to wear a scarlet A that brands her as an adulterer. There is an implicit conflict between the speaker and those making the disparaging comments, and because of the opening reference to her first meeting with Thomas, we anticipate (**strategy**: participation in form) dramatic developments (**structure**).

Paragraph 3 continues to present the speaker (**persona**) as she was at the time of that meeting—young and somewhat insecure ("almost apologetic that I wasn't a white Anglo-Saxon Protestant male"). Then Thomas appeared—"a big black guy with a booming voice comes into the office."

Paragraph 4 describes an incident (**supporting material**: example). She details Thomas's credentials—"degrees from Holy Cross and Yale"—but despite that knowledge, another staffer, a "cynical" person, challenges him with the same accusation that had shamed the speaker: "Let's face it. The only reason you got here is because you went to Yale, and the only reason you got into Yale was not because of your ability, but because of affirmative action." This becomes a dramatic encounter between a villain, the cynical staffer, and a hero, Thomas (**tone**: dramatic; **structure**: narrative–dramatic).

In paragraph 5, the incident unfolds. In effect, the conflict rises to a climax. Thomas becomes a champion who rises to the challenge. He looks his opponent in the eye and delivers the perfect riposte: "You know, I may have been lucky enough to get in, but I was smart enough to get out." In other words, affirmative action may have made entry possible, but intelligence and ability enabled him to complete a degree.

Paragraph 6 offers testimony (**supporting material**: example) that, from that first meeting, the life of the speaker changed. Thomas's words had reframed the issue for her. She stopped being ashamed and developed a new self-confidence. Now she draws an analogy (**supporting material**). Affirmative action is for minorities what nepotism (favoritism shown or patronage given to relatives or close friends by those in positions of power) is for advantaged white males like the staffer who challenged Thomas. If those with connections don't feel ashamed about using them to gain admittance, why should minorities be ashamed of a program that gives them access to opportunities that they would otherwise not have?

Paragraph 7 makes that even more explicit. Alvarez applies the lesson to herself. She may have been lucky to have doors opened for her by affirmative action, but it was her intelligence and talent that had enabled her to take advantage of the opportunities. Note that "doors opened" is a metaphor so familiar that it no longer seems to be one. Note the implicit argument that Thomas, who benefited from affirmative action, must support such policies.

The next paragraph (8) reflects chronological development (**structure**). The incident happened 13 years ago, identifying the length of time that Alvarez has known Thomas, time for her to learn what kind of a person he is and, hence, to be able to speak as a character witness. What she claims is that his character has never changed over that time, that he has remained the same person he was in the incident that she described. The speaker now puts into words (**strategy**: labeling) just what kind of a man she thinks he is: "brutally honest, an independent thinker . . . careful and deliberate in making decisions. . . . not egotistical enough or presumptuous enough to think he alone knows everything" (paragraph 9). These qualities presumably match the qualities we should want in a Supreme Court Justice.

Paragraph 10 offers a kind of evidence for these claims. There is no specific example, but a generalized description of how Thomas went about making decisions—seeking out different people ranging from the "book smart" to those with firsthand experience as well as getting the facts (**strategy**: description; **tone**: the label "book smart" underscores the value of testimony based on personal experience). We know that she was there to observe, which adds to her credibility.

The speaker becomes even more specific, offering an instance that involves herself: Thomas's asking her to join his staff at EEOC to address issues of Hispanics and the handicapped and, in her musical metaphor, "pull[ing] out all the stops" (paragraph 11). Note that the weakness of this example is that it is based entirely on her perceptions, which are somewhat self-interested.

Once again she generalizes (paragraph 12) about what presumably were many examples—meetings between Thomas and Hispanic leaders, who were bitter because they hadn't been treated well by the EEOC under the previous administration. Although these aren't detailed, she arranged the meetings, and her vivid descriptions of the atmosphere—"they came in loaded for bear" and she thought she'd have "to hand out flak jackets"—add to the credibility of her claims (**supporting material**: figurative analogies).

The aftermath of these meetings "in every instance that [she] can recall" involved amazement on the part of the Hispanic leaders and genuine, sincere concern from Thomas. She sums up vividly: "They walked into his office as his enemy and left as his ally" (**strategy:** labeling).

The last paragraph, a rather abrupt conclusion (**structure**) indicates that her testimony is refutative, a rebuttal (**strategy**) of criticism leveled in previous testimony about Thomas's lack of commitment to the Hispanic community. The speaker indicates her shock at such criticism and says that her statement was prepared in response.

Note how these elements fit together. The persona of the speaker is that of a Hispanic, someone for whom Thomas has been a model and who, as a former member of his staff, is in a position to offer testimony about the way he operates and his commitment to the concerns of Hispanics. That is directly related to her purpose, to convince the members of the Senate Judiciary Committee that the nominee is committed to the rights of minorities, in particular, Hispanics. At the very end, we discover that her testimony is offered as a rebuttal to the criticisms of others.

Consistent with her persona and purpose, her tone is personal and emotional; she speaks from personal experience. The supporting materials are all drawn from that experience—a vivid example to dramatize Thomas's role in her life followed by general summaries of his treatment of Hispanic leaders and their reactions, based on her experience in his office, rendered more vivid by figurative language and apt labels.

The structure is dramatic in the beginning but becomes generally chronological, moving from that first incident 13 years ago to the present.

There are two audiences. The primary audience is the committee, although hearings on any Supreme Court nomination attract the general public. She wants to persuade the committee, but equally, she wants to persuade the citizenry that Thomas, despite a record that has raised some questions, is committed to protecting minority rights, with Hispanics a special target audience.

Strategically, Alvarez's statement attracts attention through a dramatic incident designed (1) to create admiration for Thomas, (2) to explain how he might have been a model for her, and (3) to demonstrate his attitudes toward minorities. The incident she describes appears to answer doubts about his views and commitments. Her report about his treatment of Hispanic leaders and their response is direct refutation. Alvarez's personal testimony, a limited form of proof, is buttressed by her efforts to show that she was in a position to know what kind of a person Thomas was and what his commitments to minority concerns really were. The self-disclosure offered in the opening incident is a source of identification, first for Hispanics, then for minorities and women, and, ultimately, given the values praised, to all those who believe in equality of opportunity.

ELEMENTS OF DESCRIPTIVE ANALYSIS

The seven elements of descriptive analysis can now be outlined from this rhetorical act:

1. Purpose

   a. Thesis: the specific purpose, central idea, or major conclusion; in this case, to demonstrate that Thomas is committed to fighting for the rights of minorities and women and supports affirmative action, reasons to support his nomination to the Supreme Court.

   b. Narrowing the subject: the introduction focuses only on the speaker's first meeting with Thomas; the statement is limited to Alvarez's firsthand, personal experience.

   c. Response desired: the beliefs and actions the author seeks from the audience; in this case, confirmation of the nominee through votes of senators and support from the general public, which would make this more likely.

2. Tone

   a. Attitude toward the subject: This is reflected in the kind of language used and in the stance or perspective the rhetor assumes. In this case, the tone is highly personal; much of the statement is drawn from the author's personal experience. Alvarez dramatizes the opening incident and indicates her strong commitment to the nominee using vivid language.

   b. Attitude toward the audience: This varies, depending on the rhetor–audience relationship. Rhetors may approach the audience as peers, as inferiors (for example, as students to be taught), or as superiors (such as addressing God in prayer, a student addressing teachers, a layperson addressing experts, and so on). In this case, the speaker addresses an audience of superiors, the senators, and a

second audience, the general public, with whom she seeks to identify. Although her statement is personal, she is respectful of the
senators and of the public.

3. Structure

a. Introduction: gaining attention, introducing the subject or the
perspective to be taken, narrowing the subject, creating a relationship between rhetor and audience. Not all of these are done in every introduction. In this case, a dramatic story involving the
speaker attracts and holds our attention.

b. Body: the development of and justification for the purpose. Ordinarily, here is where one expects to find most supporting materials (some may appear in the introduction and conclusion), and
here is where the strategies become apparent. Usually, development and justification occur along one of these lines:

(1) Chronological development: This is development over time
(starting with the earliest and working toward the latest event)
or in sequence. In this case, the speaker compares the first incident 13 years ago, Thomas's continuing behavior at the EEOC,
and today.

(2) Topical development: This organizes material by its parts,
facets, or aspects. In this case, there is really only one topic:
whether Thomas is truly committed to fighting for the rights of
minorities, here explored in relation to Hispanics and, implicitly, women (Alvarez is female).

(3) Logical development: This type of organization examines
processes that are necessarily related, such as the relationships
between problems and solutions or causes and effects. In this
case, the speaker recognizes the problems of minorities like herself and presents Thomas as someone committed to solutions
such as affirmative action that he understands as necessary.

(4) Narrative–dramatic development: discourse that unfolds as
a story or drama. In this case, an extended story functions as an
important piece of evidence, but the details strongly invite listeners to identify with the speaker.

c. Conclusion: summarizing the major ideas and reinforcing the
purpose. In this case, the abrupt conclusion is the last paragraph,
which reveals that this is refutation.

d. Transitions, often internal summaries: These are explanations
and comments made to show relationships. They are reminders of
what has gone before and preparations for what is to come. Transi-

tions enable the audience to follow the author's structural plan. Here, paragraph 8 is a transition.

4. Audience

   a. Those selected by the act; the target group the rhetor seeks to influence. In this case, Alvarez addresses first the senators as the agents of change and as persons in a superior position, and second, the general public but particularly minorities, especially Hispanics and implicitly women.

   b. The role prospective audience members are asked to play; in this case, they are merely asked to be fair judges.

   c. Agents of change, that is, those who can do what the speaker wishes, in this case, the senators on the committee who can recommend confirmation and the other senators who can vote in its support.

5. Persona

   a. The role(s) adopted by the rhetor in making the case. Here the rhetor speaks as a Hispanic and a woman and as someone who was there and is therefore in a position to know about Thomas's attitudes toward minorities and his way of operating to reach decisions.

6. Supporting materials: evidence that describes, explains, enumerates, and proves.

   a. Examples: instances or specific cases that illustrate concretely and often in detail. In this act, the opening incident is a detailed example, and throughout the statement personal experience or testimony, which is a form of example, predominates. The personal testimony is strengthened because of the position Alvarez held, which would have given her special knowledge, and because of the length of time that she has known the nominee; it is the only form of authority evidence presented.

   b. Statistics: numerical measures of size, scope, or frequency of occurrence. In this case, no statistics appear; Alvarez implies that she is reporting many instances but uses no numbers.

   c. Authority: quotation of an opinion or conclusion drawn by someone with expertise and experience in an area relevant to the issue. Presumably, such a person has special abilities to interpret information. No specific authority is cited in this essay. The author relies on her own credentials, her position first in Danforth's office and then as an assistant to Thomas in the EEOC, to establish her qualifications as a character witness and to attest to Thomas's attitudes toward minorities and affirmative action.

d. Analogy

(1) Literal analogies, usually called comparisons, compare events, objects, persons, and so on that are obviously or literally (on the face of it) alike or in the same category, for example, comparing two field hockey players, four pies, six funerals, two sewage systems, or three modern poets. Here, Alvarez draws a literal analogy comparing herself as a minority to Thomas and suggesting their similar experiences in being challenged as incompetent because of the attitudes of dominant groups toward affirmative action. A pointed analogy is also drawn between nepotism, which gets jobs for the advantaged, and affirmative action, which opens doors for minorities.

(2) Figurative analogies are imaginative comparisons between things, events, and persons that are not obviously alike at all but that nevertheless resemble each other in some way. Such comparisons make ideas vivid and associate what is familiar with what is unfamiliar and alien. Only a few appear here. A figurative analogy is suggested between the stigma of affirmative action and the scarlet letter that was the stigma of an adulterer in Hawthorne's novel. Also, vivid figurative language is used to describe the hostility that Hispanic leaders initially felt toward the EEOC before they met with Thomas.

7. Strategies: the selection of language, appeals, arguments, and evidence and their adaptation to particular audiences, issues, and occasions.

a. Language: the selection of terms and labels for their appropriateness and impact. This is particular evident in the terms Alvarez uses to describe Thomas's character and mode of operation and in the clever summary, "They walked into his office as his enemy and left as his ally."

b. Appeals: to needs, drives, and desires; to cultural values. A strong appeal is made here to equality of opportunity (qualified women and minorities should have an opportunity to obtain top jobs) and to fairness (affirmative action is for minorities what connections and perhaps an "old boy's network" are for advantaged white males).

c. Selection of specific discursive and aesthetic techniques. Out of the many persuasive strategies available, the statement uses these, among others:

(1) Refutation: responding to an opposing argument and, ideally, showing its weaknesses in some detail. Here, that opposing views exist is apparent only from the final paragraph, which reveals that the statement is also a rebuttal.

(2) Enthymemes: presenting an argument in such a way that the audience participates in its completion. That Thomas supports affirmative action is not stated explicitly; readers must infer it from the examples. This risks misinterpretation, particularly when the issue is controversial, but readers who draw a conclusion themselves are more likely to accept it.

(3) Personalizing and dramatizing the issue: Affirmative action is made dramatic; readers are given a basis for identifying with the speaker and imagining themselves in her position. In addition, opposing views are dramatized so that we vicariously experience the hostility of advantaged white males toward those who gain opportunities through affirmative action. The allusion to Hawthorne's novel also dramatizes the stigma of affirmative action created by those like the cynical staffer.

Alvarez's statement of September 20, 1991, preceded the charges of sexual harassment by Anita Hill; her second appearance on October 13 responded to those charges. Here is the testimony she presented on that occasion:

Testimony of J. C. Alvarez

1   My name is J. C. Alvarez. I am a businesswoman from Chicago. I am a single mom, raising a 15-year-old son, running a business. In many ways, I am just a John Q. Public from Middle America, not unlike a lot of people watching out there and not unlike a lot of your constituents.

2   But the political world is not a world that I am unfamiliar with. I spent nine years in Washington, D.C. A year with Senator Danforth, two years with the Secretary of Education, a short stint at the Federal Emergency Management Agency, and four years as Special Assistant to Clarence Thomas at the EEOC.

3   Because of this past political experience, I was just before this committee a couple of weeks ago speaking in support of Clarence Thomas's nomination to the Supreme Court. I was then and I still am in favor of Clarence Thomas being on the Supreme Court.

4   When I was asked to testify the last time, I flew to Washington, D.C., very proud and happy to be part of the process of

nominating a Supreme Court Justice. When I was sitting here before you last time, I remember [sic] why I had liked working in Washington, D.C., so much—the intellectual part of it, the high quality of the debate. Although I have to admit when I had to listen to some of your questioning and postulating and politicking, I remembered why I had left. And I thought at that point that certainly I had seen it all.

5   After the hearings, I flew back to Chicago, back to being John Q. Public, having a life very far removed from this political world, and it would have been easy to stay away from politics in Washington, D.C. Like most of your constituents out there, I have more than my share of day-to-day challenges that have nothing to do with Washington, D.C., and politics. As I said before, I am a single mom, raising a teenager in today's society, running a business, making ends meet—you know, soccer games, homework, doing laundry, paying bills, that is my day-to-day reality.

6   Since I left Washington, D.C., I vote every four years for President and more frequently for other state and local officials. And I could have remained outside of the political world for a long, long time and not missed it. I don't need this. I needed to come here like I needed a hole in the head. It cost me almost $900 just for the plane ticket to come here, and then there is the hotel and other expenses. And I can assure you that especially in these recessionary times I have got lots of other uses for that money.

7   So why did I come? Why didn't I just stay uninvolved and apolitical? Because, Senators, like most real Americans who witness a crime being committed, who witness an injustice being done, I could not look the other way and pretend that I did not see it. I had to get involved.

8   In my real life, I have walked down the street and seen a man beating up a woman and I have stepped in and tried to stop it. I have walked through a park and a group of teenage hoodlums taunting an old drunk man and I have jumped in the middle of it. I don't consider myself a hero. No, I am just a real American from Middle America who will not stand by and watch a crime being committed and walk away. To do so would be the beginning of the deterioration of society and of this great country.

9   No, Senators, I cannot stand by and watch a group of thugs beat up and rob a man of his money any more than I could have stayed in Chicago and stood by and watched you beat up an innocent man and rob him blind. Not of his money. That would have been too easy. You could pay that back. No, you have robbed a man of his name, his character, and his reputation.

10   And what is amazing to me is that you didn't do it in a dark alley and you didn't do it in the dark of night. You did it in

broad daylight, in front of all America, on television, for the whole world to see. Yes, Senators, I am witnessing a crime in progress and I cannot just look the other way. Because I am John Q. Public and I am getting involved.

11   I know Clarence Thomas and I know Anita Hill. I was there from the first few weeks of Clarence coming to the Commission. I had the office next to Anita's. We all worked together in setting and executing the goals and the direction that the Chairman had for the EEOC. I remember Chris Roggerson, Carlton Stewart, Nancy Fitch, Barbara Parris, Phyllis Berry, Bill Ng, Allyson Duncan, Diane Holt—each of us with our own area of expertise and responsibility, but together all of us a part of Clarence Thomas's hand-picked staff.

12   I don't know how else to say it, but I have to tell you that it just blew my mind to see Anita Hill testifying on Friday. Honest to goodness, it was like schizophrenia. This was not the Anita Hill that I knew and worked with at EEOC. On Friday, she played the role of a meek, innocent, shy Baptist girl from the South who was a victim of this big, bad man.

13   I don't know who she was trying to kid. Because the Anita Hill that I knew and worked with was nothing like that. She was a very hard, tough woman. She was opinionated. She was arrogant. She was a relentless debater. And she was the kind of woman who always made you feel like she was not going to be messed with, like she was not going to take anything from anyone.

14   She was aloof. She always acted as if she was a little bit superior to everyone, a little holier than thou. I can recall at the time that she had a view of herself and her abilities that did not seem to be based in reality. For example, it was sort of common knowledge around the office that she thought she should have been Clarence's chief legal adviser and that she should have received better assignments.

15   And I distinctly remember when I would hear about her feeling that way or when I would see her pout in office meetings about an assignment she had gotten, I used to think to myself, "Come on, Anita, let's come down to earth and life in reality." She had only been out of law school a couple of years and her experience and her ability couldn't begin to compare with some of the others on the staff.

16   But I also have to say that I was not totally surprised at her wanting these assignments because she definitely came across as someone who was ambitious and watched out for her own advancement. She wasn't really a team player, but more someone who looked out for herself first. You could see the same thing in her relationships with others in the office.

[There was an interruption here because Alvarez's testimony was going well beyond the time she had been allotted. After some discussion, she was allowed to continue.]

You could see that Anita Hill was not a real team player, but more someone who looked out for herself. You could see this even in her relationships with others in the office. She mostly kept to herself, although she would occasionally participate in some of the girl-talk among the women at the office, and I have to add that I don't recall her being particularly shy or innocent about that either.

17   You see, Senators, that was the Anita Hill that we all knew and we worked with. And that is why hearing her on Friday was so shocking. No, not shocking. It was so sickening. Trust me, the Anita Hill I knew and worked with was a totally different personality from the Anita Hill I heard on Friday. The Anita Hill I knew before was nobody's victim.

18   The Clarence Thomas I knew and worked with was also not who Anita Hill alleges. Everyone who knows Clarence, knows that he is a very proud and dignified man. With his immediate staff, he was very warm and friendly, sort of like a friend or father. You could talk with him about your problems, go to him for advice, but like a father, he commanded and he demanded respect. He demanded professionalism and performance, and he was very strict about that.

19   Because we were friends outside the office or perhaps in private, I might have called him Clarence, but in the office he was Mr. Chairman. You didn't joke around with him, you didn't lose your respect for him, you didn't become too familiar with him, because he would definitely let you know that you had crossed the line.

20   Clarence was meticulous about being sure that he retained a very serious and professional atmosphere within his office, without the slightest hint of impropriety, and everyone knew it.

21   We weren't a coffee-klatching group. We didn't have office parties or Christmas parties, because Clarence didn't think it was appropriate for us to give others the impression that we were not serious or professional or perhaps working as hard as everyone else. He wanted to maintain a dignity about his office, and his every behavior and action confirmed that.

22   As his professional colleague, I traveled with him, had lunch and dinner with him, worked with him, one-on-one and with others. Never did he ever lose his respect for me, and never did we ever have a discussion of the type that Ms. Hill alleges. Never was he the slightest bit improper in his behavior with me.

In every situation I have shared with Clarence Thomas, he has been the ultimate professional and he has required it of those around him, in particular, his personal staff.

23   From the moment they surfaced, I thought long and hard about these allegations. You see, I, too, have experienced sexual harassment in the past. I have been physically accosted by a man in an elevator who I rebuffed. I was trapped in a xerox room by a man who I refused to date. Obviously, it is an issue I have experienced, I understand, and I take very seriously.

24   But having lived through it myself, I find Anita Hill's behavior inconsistent with these charges. I can assure you that when I come into town, the last thing I want to do is call either of these two men up and say hello or see if they want to get together.

25   To be honest with you, I can hardly remember their names, but I can assure you that I would never try and even maintain a cordial relationship with either one of them. Women who have really been harassed would agree, if the allegations were true, you put as much distance as you can between yourself and the other person.

26   What's more, you don't follow them to the next job—especially, if you are a black female Yale Law School graduate. Let's face it, out in the corporate sector, companies are fighting for women with those kinds of credentials. Her behavior just isn't consistent with the behavior of a woman who has been harassed, and it just doesn't make sense.

27   Senators, I don't know what else to say to have you understand the crime that has been committed here. It has to make all of us suspicious of her motives, when someone of her legal background comes in here at the eleventh hour, after ten years, and having had four other opportunities through congressional hearings to oppose this man, and alleges such preposterous things.

28   I have been contacted by I think every reporter in the country, looking for dirt. And when I present the facts as I experienced them, it is interesting, they don't print it. It's just not as juicy as her amazing allegations.

29   What is this country coming to, when an innocent man can be ambushed like this, jumped by a gang whose ring leader is one of his own protégés, Anita Hill? Like Julius Caesar, he must want to turn to her and say, "Et tu, Brutus? You too, Anita?"

30   As a mother with a child, I can only begin to imagine how Clarence must feel, being betrayed by one of his own. Nothing would hurt me more. And I guess he described it best in his opening statement on Friday. His words and his emotions are still ringing in all of our ears and all of our hearts.

31   I have done the best I could, Senators, to be honest in my statement to you. I have presented the situation as it was then, as I lived it, side by side, with Clarence and with Anita.

32   You know, I talked with my mom before I came here, and she reminded me that I was always raised to stand up for what I believed. I have seen an innocent man being mugged in broad daylight, and I have not looked the other way. This John Q. Public came here and got involved.

Descriptive Analysis

Alvarez begins by introducing herself (**structure**), reflecting the wider public attracted by the sensational charges and the televised coverage of the hearings on the broadcast networks, but here she takes pains to present herself (**persona**) as a typical member of the U.S. public, an ordinary citizen rather than a Hispanic. She also describes herself as a businesswoman from Chicago and a single mother, which makes her a somewhat nontraditional woman but one whose circumstances are like those of many women and whose experiences should make her sympathetic to and concerned about the problems of women in the workplace.

Her introduction establishes her familiarity with the Washington scene and documents her government service, including four years as Clarence Thomas's special assistant at the EEOC. That experience constitutes her credentials for testifying (**evidence:** testimony/example) about Thomas's character as she remarks in paragraph 3. Note, however, that she omits any reference to her status as a minority, which would decrease identification (**strategy**) by the general public that she hopes to address and influence (**audience**).

Paragraph 4 recalls her earlier testimony and comments on the general process of nominating a Supreme Court Justice and the debate, questioning, and politicking that are involved. Implied here is that this is normal procedure. Again, she reiterates her identity as an ordinary citizen who has returned to an ordinary life, details of which she enumerates (**strategy**), a move designed to increase the chances of identification (**strategy**)—being a single mother raising a teenager, running a business, making ends meet, attending soccer games, helping with homework, doing laundry, paying bills—activities that much of the audience will have experienced. Note, also, that except for being "a single mom" who runs a business, this is traditional Americana, a kind of "Leave It to Beaver" existence that describes life as many would like it to see it lived (**audience:** created).

Paragraph 6 offers still more details to establish that she is an ordinary good citizen whose political involvement has become typical. That serves as a natural connection to an assertion of her disinterestedness (**strategy**: credibility), that she benefits in no way from doing what she is doing—"I don't need this. I needed to come here like I needed a hole in the head"—after which she reminds us of the costs she has incurred in coming—her plane fare and hotel.

The next paragraph (7) begins with a question that serves as a transition (**structure**) and then becomes a rhetorical question (**strategy**), that is, a question to which we all know the answer. She answers it, however, by saying, "like most real Americans who witness a crime being committed, who witness an injustice being done, I could not look the other way and pretend that I did not see it. I had to get involved." Quite a number of things are going on here. First of all, she identifies herself as a "real American" (**persona**), implying that there are false or unreal Americans who might shirk their duty. "Real Americans" are people who get involved, who do something when they see a crime happening or spot an injustice. Note that there is a figurative analogy (**supporting material**) at work here. Her testimony in support of Thomas's nomination is comparable to stepping in to stop a crime in progress or acting to prevent an injustice from being done.

Here she is also inviting her **audience** (created) to see themselves as like her, real Americans, who care and act when others are being victimized, an invitation that implies that they will respond as she has and resist believing Hill's charges. There is the echo of an allusion (**strategy**) here that probably was evoked in many listeners. It is the parable of the good Samaritan, a story told by Jesus to answer a lawyer's question, "Just who is my neighbor?" after Jesus had said that we should love our neighbors as ourselves (see Luke 10:29–37). That story deals with the victim of a crime (a man set upon by thieves) and contrasts the behavior of the uninvolved, a Levite and a Pharisee, to that of a caring Samaritan, a member of a group the Jews in Jesus's audience despised. The story epitomizes an unselfish Judeo-Christian ethic and rings with the golden rule, doing for others what we would hope that they would do for us. In this process, Alvarez greatly increases her ethos as a person with admirable values, and she increases the chances that listeners will identify with her—we want to be "real Americans" (and followers of the golden rule) who do the right thing even in difficult circumstances.

Viewers may be skeptical and cynical, however; so she offers two personal examples (**supporting materials**) to establish that Alvarez fights crime and injustice in real life as well as at Judiciary Committee hearings (paragraph 8). She claims that she has tried to stop a man beating up a woman and has jumped in when a group of teenage hoodlums were taunting an old man who was drunk, after which she reaffirms the analogy (**supporting material**; **strategy**: repetition) between what she did in those cases and what she is doing now and repeats that she is not a hero, just a real American, adding to the luster of that label (**strategy**: connotations). Moreover, not to do as she has done would lead to the deterioration of the nation and our society. Real Americans, then, are those who preserve national and societal values (**strategy**). Note that she is still enhancing her ethos and inviting viewers to identify themselves as "real Americans" who would do as she is doing and who see the world as she does (**audience**: created).

Paragraph 9 is a summary and transition (**structure**). She repeats the analogy (**strategy**) again, and then extends it: Thugs merely take money; "you [presumably, the committee] have robbed a man of his name, his character, and his reputation." This is a dramatic shift because she is now leveling a direct attack on the senators she is facing (**strategy**). They are abetting a crime and allowing an injustice to be done. The willingness to make such an attack may reflect the low esteem in which many Americans hold the Congress.

She renews her attack on the committee in paragraph 10 and extends the analogy. Unlike robbers who steal in the dark of night, the committee acts in daylight on television in front of everyone. She repeats (**strategy**) her theme that there is a crime in progress and that she is just John Q. Public getting involved. That claim labels (**strategy**) these hearings on Anita Hill's charges as a crime and presents Alvarez as the voice of ordinary citizens (**persona**) who won't let Hill or the committee get away with destroying Thomas's reputation.

Her **tone** has been personal from the outset; paragraph 11 highlights that her statement is personal testimony (**supporting materials**: example): "I know . . . I was there . . . I remember. . . ." She lists all the office personnel (**strategy**: enumeration) to authenticate the accuracy of her memory, a move that appeals to viewers who have seen or will see these people testify.

The colloquial language of paragraph 12 dramatizes the personal and emotional nature of her statement, "it just blew my mind. . . . Honest to goodness, it was like schizophrenia." The language stresses her shock and (mis)uses psychological terms (**strategy**: labeling) to heighten the difference between the Anita Hill she knew and worked with and the woman who testified: "On Friday, she played the role of a meek, innocent, shy Baptist girl from the South who was a victim of this big, bad man," language that turns the conflict between Hill and Thomas into a kind of melodrama. Her characterization of Hill also captures the qualities that made her testimony powerful and credible and that have to be called into question if her allegations are to be undermined, a process that begins in the next paragraph.

Alvarez describes the Anita Hill with whom she worked as "a very hard, tough woman" who was "opinionated," "arrogant," "a relentless debater," "who always made you feel like she was not going to be messed with, like she was not going to take anything from anyone," a sharp contrast to the person viewers had seen testifying. These comments suggest that before the committee Hill was an actress playing a role rather than a sincere person telling the truth. These are not terms of praise or approval, especially when applied to a woman; they make Hill appear unfeminine (**strategy:** labeling; characterizing).

The attack on Hill's character continues. Hill was "aloof," she "always acted as if she was a little bit superior to everyone, a little holier than thou." Alvarez claims that Hill had an overblown notion of her own abilities and buttresses her claim by saying, "it was sort of common knowledge around the office," and with an example, "she thought she should have been Clarence's chief legal adviser and that she should have received better assignments." Note that these claims are just her impressions and are unsupported by any external evidence. She offers more of her impressions: "I would see her pout in office meetings" although she had far less experience ("only been out of law school a couple of years") and ability than others on the staff (paragraph 15). These impressions become support for her characterization of Hill as "someone who was ambitious and watched out for her own advancement" who "wasn't really a team player" (paragraph 16). She adds that although Hill kept to herself, she sometimes participated in the girl talk in the office, and comments, "and I have to add that I don't recall her being particularly shy or innocent about that either," remarks that subtly belie Hill's innocence about sexual matters, which is related to her credibility.

The next paragraph (17) is a summary and transition (**structure**) that includes a clear statement of her **purpose:** "The Anita Hill I knew before was nobody's victim." That is what Alvarez is trying to demonstrate, and if that is accepted, it will debunk the impression Hill created in her statement and testimony.

In paragraph 18, she turns to a related **purpose**, to argue that the Clarence Thomas depicted by Hill is not the man with whom she worked. What follows is an attempt to characterize him and to indicate the grounds for her conclusions. She describes Thomas (**strategy:** labeling) in terms that contradict charges of sexual harassment, as "proud," "dignified," "like a friend or father." Moreover, "he commanded and he demanded respect. He demanded professionalism."

She now offers additional grounds for her conclusions—she knew Thomas outside the office; nonetheless, "in the office he was Mr. Chairman," and he didn't permit inappropriate familiarity. This and what follows in paragraphs 20 and 21 depict a person and an atmosphere in which the kind of sexual harassment that Hill described seems unlikely and implausible.

In paragraph 22, she offers still other grounds for believing her testimony about his character—she traveled with him and worked closely with him without any improper behavior of the kind alleged by Hill. The assumption is that if Thomas were a harasser, she would have been a target under these conditions.

Finally, in paragraph 23, she introduces still another support for her credibility, that she has been sexually harassed; thus, she says, "it is an issue I have experienced, I understand, and I take very seriously." Based on her own reaction to the experience, however, she finds Hill's behavior toward Thomas inconsistent and implausible. Unlike Hill, Alvarez never called up the men who harassed her or tried to maintain a cordial relationship. She says, "Women who have really been harassed would agree, if the allegations were true, you put as much distance as you can between yourself and that other person." Based on her personal experience, she is now presenting herself as someone who knows how women who have really been harassed behave (**persona**: authority).

As indicated in the next paragraph (26), this is refutation (**strategy**), an attempt to argue that Hill's behavior (remaining in contact with Thomas and trying to maintain a cordial relationship with him) toward Thomas was inconsistent with her accusations. Note that this assumes that the kind of harassment she allegedly experienced and the kind described by Hill were similar (**strategy**: literal analogy). Being harassed by one's boss, however, may be quite different from being harassed by someone in an elevator or a copying room; presumably, one would never need a recommendation for a future job from them.

Paragraph 27 is a summary and transition (**structure**). Alvarez repeats her claim that a crime has been committed and invites the audience to be suspicious of Hill's motives, not just because of what she has said but also because Hill has come forward late in the hearings process, after ten years have passed, and after having declined four earlier opportunities at congressional hearings on Thomas's appointments to come forward to make her allegations.

There is a shift in paragraph 28, which begins the conclusion (**structure**), an allegation that newspeople are all out "looking for dirt" to publish whereas they don't print the positives, such as her experiences. Hill's allegations of sexual harassment were revealed first on

National Public Radio by Nina Totenberg and in *Newsday* by Timothy Phelps. Accordingly, Alvarez implies that the charges are just "dirt" dug up by reporters.

The next paragraph (29) begins with a rhetorical question that stresses Thomas's innocence and makes Hill the traitorous head of a gang of thugs. Alvarez burnishes that image by adding a figurative analogy (**supporting materials**) comparing Hill to Brutus in the assassins' attack on Julius Caesar, which frames Hill's accusations as the villainy of someone attacking her mentor. The paragraph that follows offers an analogy (**supporting materials**) and a subtle allusion (**strategy**). As a mother, Alvarez says that she can imagine how Thomas must feel, implying that Hill's accusations are comparable to betrayal by one's child, an allusion to the line from Shakespeare's *King Lear*, "How sharper than a serpent's tooth it is/ to have a thankless child" (1.4.312). Note that this also recasts the relationship between Thomas and Hill, reframing it as a parent–child relationship, which presumably would make sexual harassment even less likely.

Alvarez then protests her honesty and reaffirms that she was in a position to know the characters of these two people. Finally, she returns to the opening theme, but with an addition. She is now a dutiful daughter (**persona**) who talked over this decision to return to testify with her mother, who reminded her that she had been raised to stand up for what she believed. Finally, she reiterates both the analogy between a robbery and the hearings and her status as an ordinary citizen, presumably a representative "not unlike a lot of your constituents" (paragraph 1), she tells the senators.

The contrast between Alvarez's earlier testimony and this statement should sharpen your skills as a careful descriptive analyst. Once again, however, first note how the elements of the second statement fit together and reinforce one another. Alvarez's persona has changed. She now presents herself not only as a representative citizen, a John Q. Public, but also as a special kind of citizen, a "real American" who is defined in terms consistent with the strategic way she wants to frame her purpose, as a courageous crusade against a crime being committed, against an injustice being done. Her purpose, of course, is to undermine the credibility of Anita Hill's testimony for the committee and the general public and to make the members of the committee, particularly the Democratic members, uncomfortable about their role in airing these accusations against a Supreme Court nominee.

As in her earlier testimony, her tone is highly personal, but here it is more consistently dramatic and emotional. While she declares herself disinterested—returning to testify only to see right done, not for any personal benefit—she is anything but impartial. She frames the entire issue in highly dramatic terms, as a crime being committed and an injustice being done, as a robbery of Thomas's good name and reputation, as a betrayal, an assassination. She describes herself as shocked and sickened.

As occurred earlier, her testimony unfolds somewhat chronologically, here a contrast between her earlier and present testimony but incorporating a dramatic contrast between the two Anita Hills that she describes.

Again, much of the supporting material is personal testimony, also with strong efforts to make her testimony credible by showing that she was in a position to know the characters of Hill and Thomas, that she was in situations that would enable her to judge whether Thomas was likely to commit acts of sexual harassment and to judge whether Hill's behavior toward Thomas, if she really had been harassed, was credible. Consistent with the dramatic, emotional tone are the analogies comparing the hearing to a robbery and comparing Hill's accusations of her mentor to Brutus's participation in the assassination of Julius Caesar or to the betrayal of a parent by a child. The allusions to Brutus and to the betrayal by a child are all part of efforts to redefine (**strategy**) the relationship between Hill and Thomas. This is no longer a male–female, employer–employee relationship; rather, it is a mentor–protégée or parent–child relationship, which makes Hill's accusations character assassination and a familial betrayal (echoing the view expressed in some opinion pieces that African Americans ought not accuse each other in public) rather than a courageous decision to come forward to reveal a major character flaw in a man nominated to sit on the highest court in the land.

Strategies are of great importance in this statement. There are powerful and obvious efforts to create identification with the public as an audience, to add credibility to her testimony by invoking her past heroics in fighting crime (for which we as auditors have no verification) and her past experience with sexual harassment (for which we also have only her word). There are evocative allusions to the story of the Good Samaritan and to Shakespeare's *King Lear* and *Julius Caesar*. Identification is heightened by enumeration of details of her life. Audience participation and involvement are increased by her language and the use of rhetorical questions. The attempt to create the audience in the image she desires is intensified by appeals to shared values. Repetition makes the themes unforgettable and unifies her statement into a coherent whole.

Finally, of course, Alvarez attacks the committee members as tools of the media, of reporters who are only out for dirt to sell papers, as abettors of a crime against the reputation of a good man. She implies that the senators may be punished by constituents who, she claims, feel about this as she does (**audience**: created—here a negative role she invites them to reject).

Now, once again in outline form, the elements of descriptive analysis are extracted from this second rhetorical act:

1. Persona: an ordinary citizen, a John Q. Public, a real American, an involved citizen, a dutiful daughter who stands up for what she believes.

2. Tone: personal, melodramatic, and emotional; accusatory toward the committee.

3. Supporting materials:

a. Example: Like her earlier statement, her testimony is predominantly based on her personal experience.

b. Authority: Again, no authority is cited, but she strengthens her testimony by emphasizing her ability to observe and report on the characters of Hill and Thomas and by claiming that she also has experienced sexual harassment, described in two undetailed cases.

c. Statistics: No numbers are used, except for the number of years she was in different positions, nor is frequency of occurrence at issue.

d. Analogies:

(1) In order to demonstrate difference, Alvarez draws a literal analogy between her own experiences of sexual harassment and her subsequent behavior and Hill's behavior toward Thomas after he allegedly harassed her.

(2) Figurative analogies are very important here. Throughout, Alvarez asserts an analogy between stepping in to stop a crime and returning to testify before the committee to prevent an injustice and to prevent the robbing of Thomas's reputation. Her willingness to involve herself is compared, via allusion, to the neighborliness of the Good Samaritan, which augments her ethos. She also compares Hill's accusations to Brutus's role in the assassination of Julius Caesar (the perfidy of a friend) and to the child who betrays a parent. She describes the relationship between Hill and Thomas as that of protégée to mentor and of child to father.

4. Audience:

   a. The target audience appears to be the general public, based on Alvarez's strong efforts to create identification with them and, through them, to threaten the senators whom she sees as abetting the dirty deed being done.

   b. In a sense, the agents of change continue to be the senators because they will vote on confirmation. In emphasizing her appeal to the general public, Alvarez recognizes the power of constituents to influence congressional votes.

   c. Alvarez labors to create or construct the audience, to offer them an inviting role to play that entails sharing her point of view and coming to the conclusion she desires. That role is labeled "real Americans," whose attitudes and behaviors are described in some detail and for whom Alvarez presents herself as a voice.

5. Structure:

   a. The introduction presents the speaker and lays the foundation for the identification with viewers that Alvarez seeks.

   b. As in her earlier statement, the body develops somewhat chronologically through her experiences. What unifies the act is the repeated theme comparing the hearings on Hill's charges to a crime being committed and her reiterated role as a John Q. Public who, like other "real Americans," has come to the rescue, has refused to be uninvolved.

   c. Paragraphs 7, 9, 17, and 25 contain summary/transition points; note that each of these returns to the central theme, which also works to unify this act.

   d. The conclusion starts in paragraph 26 and seeks to arouse additional outrage toward the role of the media in this proceeding.

6. Purpose:

   a. Thesis: in her words, "The Anita Hill I knew before was nobody's victim. The Clarence Thomas I knew and worked with was also not who Anita Hill alleges."

   b. Response desired: rejection of the charges and outrage at these hearings that are destroying a good man's reputation, which involves assuming the role of real Americans as she describes it.

7. Strategies: The personae that Alvarez adopts and the audience that she constructs are highly strategic. In addition, the personal history that she discloses, her attempts to stop crimes, her experience of sexual harassment, and her position as an observer as she reports it are

all important elements in making her credible for the audience. In addition, note the following strategies, among others:

a. Identification. Assuming that readers or listeners share experiences and have beliefs and values in common, the strategy of identification calls attention to these links and appeals to them. Alvarez labors mightily to prompt viewers to identify with her as a single mother, as a businesswoman, as an ordinary person struggling to pay bills and raise a teenager. She also presents herself as an ideal example of the real Americans that she invites her viewers to be, with a lifestyle and values that her target audience will admire and desire. By contrast, Anita Hill is described in terms that make her unappealing—difficult, arrogant, disloyal, and unfeminine. If viewers are to choose between these women as a way to decide Thomas's fate, Alvarez is trying to ensure that they will choose her.

b. Allusions. An allusion is a passing or brief reference to something familiar or commonly known. Usually allusions refer to religious or literary works, such as the Bible or Shakespeare's plays, or to elements of popular culture, such as long-running television programs. Alvarez alludes to the story of the Good Samaritan to strengthen our identification with her role. She uses allusions to *Julius Caesar* and *King Lear* to denounce Hill's accusations as treachery and betrayal by a nurtured intimate.

c. Repetition. The analogies between the hearing and a crime and between her role as a good citizen attempting to stop a crime and her coming to testify to the committee are reiterated again and again. That helps to fix them in our minds, and each repetition follows her efforts to reinforce the links she is creating. These repeated themes are the primary source of structure in this act, and they are particularly effective here because of the transience of oral rhetoric.

d. Labels and language are used strategically. Alvarez's dramatic language makes her claims vivid and frames our experience. The contrast between the Hill she knew and the Hill who testified "blew her mind," and watching "was like schizophrenia." Hill merely "played the role." The terms she uses to describe Hill are powerful and fit the pattern of the unwomanly woman who is selfish, cold, and ambitious. The terms describing Thomas are also powerful and form a pattern of competence, professionalism, and dignity modified by an appropriate warmth.

e. Like her earlier statement, this testimony is refutative. The chief target is character—to destroy the credible persona that was evident in Hill's testimony. Near the end, that refutation takes the form of an attack on consistency between the charges and her behavior and an assertion that these charges have surfaced merely because of the efforts of journalists to dig up dirt. Hence, they should not be taken seriously.

f. Finally, in an important sense, Alvarez invites us to see this event differently, to reframe it in her terms. The definition of the hearing was at issue with passionate disagreements over whether it was a trial or a hearing and whether it was an effort motivated primarily by political goals. There were also disputes over presumption of innocence (appropriate if there were a trial on charges of sexual harassment) or whether the burden of proof fell on Thomas and his supporters because no one is presumed to be qualified to be a Supreme Court Justice—that has to be demonstrated to the satisfaction of the Senate and the nation. Alvarez's testimony is part of this struggle. She redefines the hearing, over and over, as a crime, an injustice; she labels Hill's accusations as treachery and betrayal of the worst sort; she implies that the senators are the pawns of vile reporters and have succumbed to the media's desire for dirt. How one sees the event is an important factor in reaching a conclusion about whether Clarence Thomas should be confirmed.

As these examples illustrate, descriptive analysis puts you in possession of rhetorical acts, the first step in deciding how to interpret and evaluate what they contain.

■ ■ ■

EXERCISES

1. Select an editorial from your local or school newspaper, and describe it analytically. Write the results in an outline similar to the one in this chapter. What did you discover from your analysis that was not apparent from a casual first reading?

2. Read Letty Cottin Pogrebin's essay at the end of Chapter 4. Then apply the relevant and appropriate categories of descriptive analysis (purpose, persona, tone, structure, support materials, strategy, audience) to each of the following samples in order to explain its function in the discourse:

   a. "As Drora Kass, of the International Center for Peace in the Middle East, puts it, "To want to negotiate with Palestinians who are not identified with the PLO is like wanting to negotiate with Israelis who are not Zionists." (paragraph 9)

(sample analysis) This is authority evidence from an identified source that incorporates a literal analogy (supporting material) that functions to refute, even debunk (strategy), a position that the author is attacking. It is particularly well adapted to the target audience, who would recognize just how ridiculous it would be to try to seek out Israelis who were not Zionists. If such a search is analogous to the search for Palestinians not identified with the PLO, then that is also ridiculous and pointless (a kind of *a fortiori* argument).

b. "Although we may recoil at the idea of sitting down with the authors of so much terrorism and savagery, Abba Eban reminds us that, if we're keeping score, Egypt, Syria, and Jordan have killed far more Jews than the PLO visited upon us in 33 years." (paragraph 10)

c. "We can't trust them. That's true. In fact, we can't trust anyone. In 1975 the United States met secretly with the PLO while promising not to negotiate with Palestinians. Ronald Reagan calls himself a friend of Israel but, despite Jewish pleas, he sold AWACs to the Saudis and he went to Bitburg." (paragraph 18)

d. "We must learn from the mistakes in Vietnam, Lebanon, Algeria, Cyprus, Belfast, and South Africa. We must be aware of the follies of rulers. We must recognize that annexation brings disaster. Binationalism has proved a failure wherever it has been tried, and no nation has oppressed another people for long without poisoning a part of itself. History should teach us what we need from a peace treaty, not how to retreat from peacemaking." (paragraph 22)

3. Arrange for the class to attend a speech together, perhaps a chapel or convocation speaker or a lecturer who is brought to campus for a special event. Spend the next class period describing that event analytically. What does such analysis reveal that wasn't immediately apparent while you were listening to the speech?

SOURCES

Several published essays illustrate the use of careful descriptive analysis:

Black, Edwin. "Ideological Justifications," *Quarterly Journal of Speech* 70 (May 1984):144–150. An editorial published in the *New York Times* is subjected to textual analysis.

Slagell, Amy R. "Anatomy of a Masterpiece: A Close Textual Analysis of Abraham Lincoln's Second Inaugural Address," *Communication Studies* 42 (Summer 1991):155–171. This is a descriptive analysis and a fully developed piece of rhetorical criticism.

Stelzner, Hermann. " 'War Message,' December 8, 1941: An Approach to Language," *Communication Monographs* 33 (November 1966): 419–437. A detailed study of the language choices in Franklin D. Roosevelt's war message.

PART TWO

The Rhetorical Problem

CHAPTER 3

Obstacles Arising from the Audience

A problem is the gap between what you have and what you want. In rhetorical action, a rhetor confronts an audience that perceives, understands, believes, or acts in one way and wants that audience to perceive, understand, believe, or act in another way. The *rhetorical problem* is an umbrella concept that covers all of the obstacles rhetors face. In Part Two, I examine obstacles arising from the audience (Chapter 3), from the subject and purpose (Chapter 4), and from the rhetor's need to be credible (Chapter 5). In Chapter 6, I show how descriptive analysis and the rhetorical problem fit into evaluation and criticism.

In practice, of course, obstacles arising from audience, subject, and rhetor cannot be isolated so neatly. For example, suppose that your subject was the history of oats as a cash crop. Even if your purpose were merely informative (and not efforts to increase the acreage devoted to raising oats), you would have a fairly hard time holding the interest of audiences made up of teenagers or lawyers. But your rhetorical problem would be much smaller if your audience was a group of midwestern farmers, preferably sprinkled with dedicated horse breeders and trainers (oats is the best grain to feed horses). In other words, whether or not your subject and purpose create obstacles depends partly on the nature of your audience. In fact, obstacles are only obstacles if the audience perceives them that way.

Think of these three aspects of the rhetorical problem as forming a triangle:

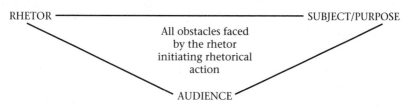

RHETOR ——————————————————— SUBJECT/PURPOSE

All obstacles faced
by the rhetor
initiating rhetorical
action

AUDIENCE

The interrelationships among the aspects symbolized by the triangle can be expressed in three questions: (1) What will be necessary to induce the audience to take part in rhetorical action? (2) What does the subject/purpose demand of the audience? (3) What demands are made on the credibility (ethos) of the rhetor by the subject/purpose and the audience?

Beginning rhetors tend to make two common errors in thinking about audiences. First, they assume that most audiences (particularly classmates, friends, colleagues) are just like themselves, with the same experiences, values, religious beliefs, political preferences, and life goals. They are shocked to discover wide divergences in belief within the same culture or community or even in the same rhetoric class. But people do differ. All audiences, even close friends, need explanation, adaptation, and effort to see the importance and significance of the issue and the purpose.

Your assumption that members of the audience are just like you, the rhetor, takes several specific forms. Sometimes, for example, you might take it for granted that those you address are, like you, rational, impartial, interested, informed, and concerned. Although people can be all of these some of the time, we are also creatures of deep feeling who are, at the same time, likely to be apathetic toward issues of great importance to others. And your audiences are people. As a rhetor, you must treat them as many-faceted and not assume they are well informed and curious unless you make an effort to provide information and arouse curiosity. In this sense, you create or construct your audience—you provide the materials that enable them to become the ideal respondents to your message.

The second common error rhetors make is to transform the audience into vicious monsters eagerly waiting to jeer at them and to discredit their messages. The sense that those for whom you write or speak are different from yourself can help you when you try to imagine yourself as a member of the audience. But this feeling can be carried too far. Audience members are like you. Although not identical, they have needs and fears similar to yours. You and they have many values in common. Generally, an audience can share your experience and come to understand a differing point of view.

To be successful as a rhetor requires that you induce the audience to participate, indeed, to collaborate in creating the rhetorical act. You and the audience must identify with each other and come to some kind of common understanding if the message you produce is to be a communication. With some experience, you will discover that one of your assets as a rhetor is your individuality—your special experiences, biases, and fallibilities, especially as you are able to recognize them and share them with the audience.

Your goal as a rhetor, then, is to avoid both these errors: to recognize differences between yourself and members of the audience and yet create common bonds between you from what you do share. In other words, prepare your rhetorical act to overcome the obstacles represented by these differences.

Beliefs about persuasion are also relevant to the rhetorical obstacles arising from the audience. At various times in U.S. history we have demonstrated our fears of the power of persuasion. We have banned certain books and movies as heretical or obscene and forbidden Nazis and Communists to speak in certain forums, as if exposure to a book, a movie, or a speech could cause loyal spouses to become licentious adulterers, or patriotic Americans to become traitors or Communists. As I hope this chapter will indicate, normal people are not transformed by a single rhetorical act. Audiences, in fact, show considerable resistance to persuasion in all forms. Indeed, considering all of the obstacles to persuasion that arise from audiences, you may well marvel that any persuasion ever occurs.

THE AUDIENCE

There are at least four ways to understand what is meant by an "audience." An audience can be (1) those exposed to the rhetorical act, the empirical audience; (2) the target audience, the ideal audience at whom the act is aimed; (3) the agents of change, those who have the capacity to do as the rhetor wishes, who can make changes; and (4) the role the audience is asked to play, the audience as it is created or brought into being by rhetorical action.

The Empirical Audience

In the simplest sense, the audience is all those exposed to the rhetorical act, whether in a face-to-face encounter or through the print or electronic media. Obviously, if people do not encounter the rhetorical act, nothing can occur. The channels through which rhetorical acts are transmitted select and limit the potential empirical audience. An essay printed in *Ms.*, a feminist magazine, reaches a relatively small audience of subscribers and others—at a friend's house or a women's clinic—

who pick up the magazine and read it. Those who read *Ms.* are likely to be different from those who read *Ebony,* a magazine targeted at African Americans, or *Road and Track,* a magazine for car lovers. A rhetor who wishes to reach the appropriate audience must try to find the channel that will expose her or his ideas to the ideal or target audience.

The Target Audience

Realistically, you cannot address everyone. All rhetorical acts are shaped and planned to reach people with certain characteristics. These people are the target audience. They are the ones most likely to be responsive to the issue and capable of acting on it. The target audience is likely to share basic assumptions with the rhetor; ideally, they have common experiences and shared longings. Patterns of television advertising illustrate this concept. For example, the demographic analyses of television viewers made by the Nielsen Company indicate that many viewers of network news are older (over age 45). Accordingly, if you watch the news on any broadcast network, you will see advertisements for such products as laxatives, tooth adhesives, and vitamins because older viewers are considered more likely to suffer from constipation, have loose false teeth, or need vitamin supplements. Similarly, razor blades and aftershave lotions are advertised during broadcasts of football games because Nielsen studies indicate that most viewers of such programming are male. In each case, the ads are targeted at audiences likely to have needs these products can fill.

In the case of J. C. Alvarez's statements and testimony analyzed in Chapter 2, there were two target audiences. One audience consisted of the senators on the Judiciary Committee and the Senate as a whole because they were the ones who would vote on Thomas's nomination. The second audience differed. In the first case, it was minorities and women and those concerned about their rights. In the second case, it was the public generally, particularly those who identify with the values that Alvarez identified as those of "real Americans." Presumably, if they as constituents were persuaded, they would have been able to influence the votes of the senators who represented them.

The Agents of Change

Alvarez's attempt to influence the Senate as a whole and the senators on the committee illustrates another important facet of the audience. You should target those who have the power to act, those with the political ability, the economic power, the numbers, or the social influence to alter the situation. In this case, the members of the Senate Judiciary Committee have the power to decide whether they will recommend confirmation of a nominee to the Senate, and all senators have the power to vote on whether a nominee will be confirmed. Effective rhetors aim their messages at those who can do what they desire—who have the political power (the vote), the economic power (the money), or the numbers (to march, petition, vote) or other resources (expertise, technology, or whatever) to act.

Such a description of the audience seems to make it a power elite, but other factors are also at work. Advertisers, for example, have learned that they can be effective if they reach those who can influence the agents of change. Teenage Mutant Ninja Turtles, monster-shaped vitamins, sugar-coated cereals, toys, and video games are advertised on children's television programs although few children make independent purchasing decisions. Children, however, can influence the decisions of their parents.[1] The agents of change are not only those with the power to act but also those who can influence them. In addition, the very process of participating in rhetorical action can create agents of change. Hence, Alvarez aimed her testimony at constituents who could influence the votes of the senators. Some analysts of the final, close Senate vote argued that Thomas's confirmation reflected the increased power of African American voters who pressured their representatives to support Thomas's nomination.

The Created or Constructed Audience[2]

Rhetorical action is participatory; it involves a reciprocal relationship between those involved in it. Just as the rhetor plays a role and takes on a persona, audiences are asked to play roles and take on one or more personas. For example, cosmetic ads invite the viewer to be a glamorous, seductive sex object with long, bouncy hair (buy our

---

[1]In 1993, children ages 4 to 12 had some $17 billion of their own money to spend, according to James U. McNeal, professor of marketing at Texas A & M and author of *Kids as Consumers* (New York: Lexington Books, 1992). According to the Nickelodeon/ Yankelovich Youth Monitor, a research service, youths ages 6 to 12 had $32 billion of disposable income last year. By contrast, children's influence resulted in their parents spending $155 billion in 1993, according to McNeal (*New York Times,* December 1, 1994, pp. B1, B4).

[2]Edwin Black, in "The Second Persona," *Quarterly Journal of Speech* 56 (April 1970):109–119, discusses the persona of the audience. See also Michael McGee, "In Search of 'The People,' " *Quarterly Journal of Speech* 61 (October 1975):235–249.

shampoo), glistening lips (buy our lipstick or lip gloss), and sultry eyes with long dark lashes (buy our eye shadow and mascara). In his 1988 campaign for the Democratic presidential nomination, Jesse Jackson invited Americans to form a rainbow coalition, and in his speeches to African American youth, he urged them to say to themselves, "I am somebody!"

The importance of creating the audience, of inviting them to play a role, is illustrated by the challenges posed by female audiences. An audience must not only have the power to act, it must also believe that it has that power. A number of studies seem to indicate that women, especially young women, have low self-esteem and lack confidence in their ability to succeed in areas not traditionally identified as female.[3] In fact, they can act as agents of change. As they have demonstrated, they can sue for admission to all-male institutions; they can use affirmative action to gain entry to areas from which women have been excluded; they can start businesses as well as vote, work as volunteers, and donate money to candidates; they can write letters to influential people and outlets; they can influence businesses through purchasing decisions; they can form groups that will influence school policy, television programming, and police actions. They can run for office and be elected. But they can do these things if and only if they come to believe that they can. For example, following the Hill–Thomas hearings, a record number of women ran for office, and women more than doubled their contributions to female political candidates. Their economic power to affect political campaigns had always been there, but the hearings mobilized many of them to exercise it. The so-called consciousness-raising groups in the women's liberation movement can be seen as transforming women into audiences, that is, into people who believe that they can act effectively to become agents of change.

The common kinds of audience-related rhetorical obstacles are

1. Inattention

2. Misperception and misinterpretation

---

[3]See K. K. Campbell, "The Rhetoric of Women's Liberation: An Oxymoron," *Quarterly Journal of Speech* 59 (February 1973):74–86, for evidence of some changes in women's self-images produced by contemporary feminism. See "The Glass Half Empty: Women's Equality and Discrimination in American Society," a report by the NOW Legal Defense and Education Fund, New York City, 1994, for data on young women's attitudes. In addition, a 1991 study by the American Association of University Women, "Shortchanging Girls, Shortchanging America," found substantial problems of self-esteem among teenage women. See also Peggy Orenstein, *School Girls: Young Women, Self-Esteem and the Confidence Gap* (New York: Doubleday, 1994).

3. Lack of motivation

4. Inertia

In other words, if a rhetorical act is to have any chance of succeeding, audience members must participate in it from beginning to end. They must perceive its ideas accurately and internalize the "virtual experience" presented. They must see the information and arguments as coming from an informed and trustworthy source[4] and the rhetorical act as relevant to their needs. In addition, the audience must see the purpose of the act and the means to achieve it as consistent with their values, and they must come to believe that they can take action, here and now, that can reasonably be expected to achieve the goal desired. These requirements suggest the dimensions and the facets of the obstacles that arise from the audience.

ATTENTION

Although you may not appreciate it, as a student you are in a rare and highly privileged rhetorical situation: You have a captive audience. Your teacher is paid to read and comment on your essays or to listen to and evaluate your speeches, and your classmates are required to attend class. Unlike most rhetors, you do not need to struggle to gather an audience, to have your name recognized, or to gain media coverage.

As a college teacher, I also have a more or less captive audience. Yet I compete directly in any given lecture with the university, throwaway, and Twin City newspapers, letters from parents and friends, and assignments for other classes.

And like all other rhetors I compete indirectly with the hundreds of eager persuaders my students encounter daily: newspaper editorials and letters to the editor; television, radio, and magazine advertising; telephone and door-to-door solicitors; billboards; political candidates; and family and friends. If this bombardment does not create resistance to persuasion by its sheer volume, it may outclass me in slickness or entertainment quality. Although I come in three dimensions and the mass media persuaders do not, and though we are both in "living color," I cannot make eight retakes, do a dissolve, edit the tape, or cut to an animated cartoon when attention flags.

---

[4]This part of the rhetorical problem is the subject of Chapter 5.

If my students could choose whether to come to class, I would encounter another audience-related obstacle. Let us call it *limited* or *selective exposure*. Audiences selectively expose themselves to messages and selectively attend to those they see or hear. In other words, audiences control their exposure to rhetorical acts. In general, we tend to expose ourselves to messages that meet our physical, psychological, or social needs. The young woman about to be married begins to seek out *Bride* magazine; the student faced with the need to buy a car seeks out *Consumer Reports* for information on reliability and repairs to maximize her purchase. We routinely read publications and watch programs that reflect our general interests and styles. The messages we encounter here are likely to be reassuring and reinforcing. If you are an investor or run a small business, you are likely to read the *Wall Street Journal,* and its editorial columns are likely to take positions congenial to people like you, for example, opposing an "employer mandate" in proposed health care reforms. If you are such a person, you are less likely to read *Mother Jones* and be exposed to editorials and articles with strong commitments to environmentalism, some parts of which may be costly to businesses. In other words, our patterns of viewing and reading are related to topics and subjects important to satisfying our needs for information and advice, and these patterns tend to expose us primarily to supportive or unchallenging viewpoints. When faced with a choice, however, especially an important choice, we seek out wider sources of information. We watch debates among prominent candidates and deliberately expose ourselves to conflicting views. In other words, our interests and needs limit our exposure to rhetoric, and to some extent, such limits filter in messages that are supportive or reassuring. You know this from your own experience. Although they hear both sides represented, committed conservatives are more likely to watch TV programs such as William Buckley's *Firing Line* where the conservative viewpoint is well and strongly represented. (If you want to avoid hearing opposing views, you can turn to Rush Limbaugh.) Such exposure is pleasant because it does not threaten our views, and it reinforces our sense that we have made the right choices. On the other hand, as these examples indicate, ordinarily we do not avoid exposure to alternative points of view.

As a rhetor, however, you need to know that under certain circumstances people actively seek out information that conflicts with what they know and presents views that challenge their own. At least three factors significantly modify the commonsense picture just presented: the audience's level of education, the usefulness of the information to be presented, and the audience's past history of exposure. One early study concluded, "Clearly the most powerful known predictor of voluntary exposure to mass communications of an information or public-affairs sort is the general factor of education and social class."[5] Put simply, people with more education and higher incomes choose to expose themselves to more news and information on public affairs in the mass media. They buy more magazines and newspapers; they watch more public affairs programs on radio and television (and can more easily afford cable hookups that give access to many of these programs); they are more likely to be active in groups that spread such information. In fact, education and social class may be a more significant factor in exposure than ideological agreement.

As just suggested, another factor influencing exposure is the immediate usefulness of the information to the recipient. In some studies, subjects preferred what they saw as more useful information to what they saw as less useful, regardless of which supported their previous beliefs.[6] Ideological differences or a lack of shared beliefs and attitudes are serious barriers, but ones that can be breached by relevance, that is, if the recipients see a direct, personal use for the information provided now.

Finally, past exposure to the issue influences exposure in ways that are not necessarily related to the compatibility of beliefs. Some studies have found that when individuals initially were exposed to one-sided or biased information, they later preferred opposing information whether or not it supported their initial position.[7] Such studies, along with others indicating tolerance for and interest in new and challenging data, suggest that it would be a mistake to assume that audiences will not read or listen to information that conflicts with their beliefs and attitudes.

---

[5]D. O. Sears and J. L. Freedman, "Selective Exposure to Information: A Critical Review," *Public Opinion Quarterly* 31 (1967):175. See also I. L. Janis and L. Mann. *Decision Making: A Psychological Analysis of Conflict, Choice and Commitment.* New York: Free Press, 1977.

[6]L. K. Canon, "Self-Confidence and Selective Exposure to Information," in *Conflict, Decision and Dissonance,* ed. L. Festinger (Stanford, CA: Stanford University Press, 1964); J. L. Freedman, "Confidence, Utility and Selective Exposure: A Partial Replication," *Journal of Personality and Social Psychology* 2 (1965):778–780.

[7]J. L. Freedman and D. O. Sears, "Selective Exposure," in *Advances in Experimental Social Psychology,* Vol. 2, ed. L. Berkowitz (New York: Academic Press, 1965); D. O. Sears and J. L. Freedman, "Effects of Expected Familiarity with Arguments upon Opinion Change and Selective Exposure," *Journal of Personality and Social Psychology* 2 (1965):420–426; D. O. Sears, J. L. Freedman, and E. F. O'Connor, "The Effects of Anticipated Debate and Commitment on the Polarization of Audience Opinion," *Public Opinion Quarterly* 28 (1964):617–627.

The first challenge you face as a rhetor in relation to an audience, then, is gaining and maintaining attention. As indicated here, the individual rhetor competes for attention with many other persuaders and meets obstacles having to do with the selection of messages by members of the audience. A tendency to be exposed to information compatible with our interests and needs and, hence, views we already hold is balanced by the generally high level of interest in information among the more educated and affluent, by a desire for useful information, and by a desire for opposing information if the initial exposure seems to have been one-sided or biased.

PERCEPTION AND INTERPRETATION

Selective perception names a second kind of audience-related obstacle you face. It refers to the human ability to function rather like a radio—to tune one channel in and another out, turn the volume down or up, fade the sound in and out, or turn the set off entirely. We do not perceive all the stimuli to which we are exposed—we would go crazy if we did. We sort out what we believe is relevant and ignore the rest. The basis for this ability remains largely a mystery. However, evidence suggests that our attitudes influence what we perceive and how we interpret it.

Attitudes

No one has ever seen an attitude. *Attitude* is a concept developed by researchers to describe some of the mental (emotional/affective and rational/cognitive) processes and behaviors of human beings. The concept is particularly difficult because it is complex, and not all researchers agree on how to define attitudes or on whether and how they can be distinguished from beliefs and values.

Attitudes are likes or dislikes, affinities for or aversions to situations (liking to speak publicly or hating to talk on the phone), events (weddings), objects (motorcycles), people (children), groups (Methodists), or any identifiable aspect of one's environment (humidity). Attitudes are a mental readiness or a predisposition to react that influences a fairly large class of one's valuative responses consistently or over a significant span of time.

Attitudes are expressed in statements like these: I don't like big parties; I love ice cream; I like assertive people; the *New York Times* is the best newspaper in the United States. Presumably, as a result of direct experience (at parties, eating ice cream, making choices, reading many newspapers) and of other kinds of learning (from school, parents, and peers, among others), people develop valuative categories so they are prepared to respond, favorably or unfavorably, with varying degrees of intensity to the items they encounter.

Attitudes are relatively generalized (they tend to refer to categories or classes rather than to individual items), and they are enduring (they persist over time). They also are learned. People probably learn likes and dislikes as they learn nearly everything else, and they categorize their valuative experiences in order to simplify the world. If you have an aversion to cats, for example, you were probably frightened or scratched by a cat as a child, had a reaction to cat dander, or have a parent, friend, or sibling with a strong dislike. In most cases, the attitude will apply to most or all cats, and if you dislike them today, you will probably continue to dislike them next week and next month, although change is possible based on new experiences and learning.

In addition, your aversion to cats would probably influence reactions to related areas: to cat shows, cat owners, prohibitions against pets in apartments, and so on. Obviously, the rhetor who tries to alter audience attitudes like this one or whose purposes run counter to intensely held attitudes of audience members will run into trouble. Attitudes are learned over time from experiences or credible sources; they are reinforced by later experiences; they are also patterns of response that make it easier to cope with the world. This rhetorical problem is compounded because attitudes influence what we perceive and how we interpret it.

A famous study of the influence of attitudes on perception used a particularly controversial football game between Dartmouth and Princeton as its raw material. The researchers showed students from both schools the same film of the game and tested their perceptions of who broke the rules how many times and in what ways. From the test results, you might have thought the two groups of students had seen two different events. For example, Princeton students saw the Dartmouth team break the rules more than twice as many times as the Dartmouth students saw their team do so. The researchers concluded that the same data transmitted in the same way create different experiences in different people, and that the significance of an event depends on the purposes different people bring to it and the assumptions they have about the purposes of other people involved. They wrote, "It is inaccurate and misleading to say that different people have different 'attitudes' concerning the same 'thing.' For the 'thing' simply is *not* the same for different people whether the 'thing' is a football game, a presidential candidate, Communism, or spinach."[8]

You can probably think of many similar examples from the sports world in which partisanship strongly influences what the fans see. And such responses are not surprising, given the nature of attitudes. For example, in the third inning of the second game of the 1991 World Series, Minnesota Twins first baseman Kent Hrbek tagged out Atlanta Braves center fielder Ron Gant at first base. Braves fans contended that the 258-lb. Hrbek used a "rasslin' move" to knock the 172-lb. outfielder off the base and record the inning-ending out. Hrbek himself expressed the view of the Minnesota fans: "I thought it was pretty obvious what happened. . . . He was the one with the momentum. If I wasn't there, he probably would have wound up in the dugout. I just held the tag on him."[9] The Twins fans wanted them to beat the Braves; the Braves fans wanted them to win; each team's fans perceived what happened through the lenses of their desires.

What happens in sports can easily happen in other areas. An attitude is a readiness to respond favorably or unfavorably. It represents an expectation of favorable or unfavorable qualities and behaviors. In other words, we tend to see the qualities and behaviors in objects, events, persons, and so forth that we expect to be there. Accordingly, our attitudes influence our perceptions and our interpretations of events.

Beliefs

The influence of attitudes on perception and interpretation suggests a close relationship between information and evaluation. A *belief* is a judgment about what is true or probable, real or likely. Beliefs may refer to the past (guns were involved in 11,832 murders in 1989, more than any other weapon), the present (rape is the fastest-growing violent crime in the United States), or the future (so many guns already are owned by Americans that gun control legislation cannot reduce their role in violent crime). They may assert a causal relationship (negative attitudes toward women are reinforced in televised entertainment programming) or evaluate the credibility of sources of information (seeing is believing; Alice Rivlin, head of the Office of Management and Budget, is an expert on the U.S. economy; Energy Secretary

---

[8]A. Hasdorf and H. Cantril, "They Saw a Game: A Case Study," *Journal of Abnormal and Social Psychology* 49 (1954):133.

[9]Jeff Lenihan, "South Riled About Hrbek's Push," *Star Tribune,* October 22, 1991, p. 6C.

Hazel R. O'Leary is knowledgeable about alternative sources of energy; the speaker knows what she's talking about).

Insofar as attitudes are learned from our own experiences or those of others, they are based on beliefs, on what we consider true or likely. For example, if you strongly dislike dogs, you probably believe that they bite many people each year, that they often bite without provocation, and that they are the source of some serious diseases of children. These beliefs not only describe dogs, as you may see them, but predict future situations.

Note that insofar as attitudes rest on beliefs, they can be influenced by future learning. Hence, the rhetor who wants to change attitudes tries to alter perception (and beliefs) through "virtual experience." Conversely, as the Dartmouth–Princeton and Twins–Braves examples show, attitudes influence perception in ways that undermine this process, and even conflicting information can be perceived as compatible with the perceiver's attitudes.

Decoding

Attitudes influence perception and interpretation so strongly that rhetors cannot be sure their audiences will perceive information as they do. In fact, the interpretation of information and argument is a problem with all audiences, however well intentioned they may be. *Decoding* refers to this interpretative process, by which listeners or readers translate and interpret messages from outside, assign meanings, determine relationships, and draw out implications.

Audiences find decoding difficult. Thus, much of the impact of a rhetorical act is lost unless rhetors make special efforts to organize material, to state conclusions, and to show the relationships among ideas. In one study, for example, an audience of bright college students became confused when conclusions were not stated explicitly. Other studies confirm this finding.[10] The rhetorical problem is that the audience resists or botches decoding unless claims are presented clearly and made explicit. At a minimum, the rhetor must state conclusions, organize materials clearly, and provide transitions that

---

[10]The original study was done by C. I. Hovland and W. Mandell, "An Experimental Comparison of Conclusion Drawing by the Communicator and the Audience," *Journal of Abnormal and Social Psychology* 47 (July 1952):581–588; its findings have been confirmed in subsequent studies. The results emphasize the importance of the thesis, organization, and transitions in your rhetoric; they are the subject of Chapter 9, on the structuring of a rhetorical act.

show relationships if the audience is to accurately interpret what is being said.

The Elaboration Likelihood Model (ELM)[11]   Researchers Richard Petty and John Cacioppo have developed a theory they call the elaboration likelihood model (ELM) because it emphasizes the central role of the audience in persuasion. Their theory, as its name implies, focuses on the likelihood that audience members will be stimulated not only to attend to and decode a message but also to develop or elaborate it, that is, to process or interpret it, to amplify, clarify, or embellish it, and to consider its implications. By this standard, the most effective rhetorical act is one that produces the greatest amount of cooperative message building by members of the audience. Under ideal circumstances, audience members collaborate with the rhetor in creating the discourse by which they are influenced.

ELM is useful in understanding the role of the audience in persuasion. As a theory, ELM postulates two routes through which persuasion occurs: a central route and a peripheral route. The *central route* is rationalist and argumentative; it is directly related to cooperative message building prompted by the quality of the argument and the evidence on which it rests. Many research studies indicate that changes in attitude that occur via this route require more work and thought on the part of the reader or listener; however, research also suggests that attitude changes resulting from this process last longer, are more resistant to counterpersuasion from opponents, and are more predictive of actual behavior. In other words, a good case can be made for the importance of argument and evidence if audience members respond to, participate in, and collaborate in creating a message that is initiated by a rhetor.

As its label suggests, the *peripheral route* is less direct; mostly, we use it for purposes of efficiency—we cannot investigate thoroughly all issues on which we must make decisions. Decisions made via this route are shortcuts; instead of the hard work involved in interpreting the argument and evidence, we use some element in the persuasive context or situation as a cue or sign by which to assess the message. It could be linked to the person who carries it—positively or negatively. It could be linked to a belief system with which audience members agree or disagree. Whatever the association, it allows audience members to make a relatively simple leap from the cue to the position be-

---

[11]Richard E. Petty and John T. Cacioppo, *Communication and Persuasion: Central and Peripheral Routes to Attitude Change* (New York: Springer-Verlag, 1986).

ing advocated; for example, someone who is intensely disliked supports a position that is rejected because of that association, that is, because of feelings about the source (for example, "If Phyllis Schlafly, a prominent antifeminist—or Gloria Steinem, a prominent feminist—favors it, it must be bad").

According to this research, the most important variable affecting audience members' willingness to work at this special kind of decoding—the motivation to actively participate in and interpret a persuasive message—is its personal relevance, that is, the belief that the topic or issue is vital and will affect them personally. The greater its possible personal consequences for the audience, the greater the importance of forming an opinion based on the most accurate and complete information. As the author can attest, younger women are less likely to work at understanding messages about osteoporosis, for example, but women in their early fifties who are entering menopause are likely to pay close attention to messages about the pros and cons of estrogen- or hormone-replacement therapy; in fact, they may even seek out such messages! That's unfortunate because younger women need to eat foods with lots of calcium (and do weight-bearing exercises) to build up their bone mass, which is the best protection against bone loss later in life. When there are immediate and vital personal consequences, people are likely to be motivated to engage in the mental work—the interpretation and decoding—necessary to evaluate the true merits of a proposal. This strongly suggests the importance of showing why your message is vital for those you hope to reach.

The willingness to collaborate in creating the rhetorical act is also affected by one's worldview. For example, those who view the world legalistically—such as lawyers—find messages justified on legalistic grounds more persuasive, whereas those who see the world in religious terms are more likely to be persuaded by messages that are justified on religious or moral grounds. The essay "Jesus Was a Feminist," found at the end of Chapter 8, is likely to be more persuasive to those with strong religious commitments who see the Bible as a primary authority and Jesus as a model for ideal behavior than to those who do not.

In sum, the ELM model suggests a tradeoff between the brainwork involved in participating in messages—exploring and evaluating arguments and evidence—and the importance of peripheral or external cues. In general, anything that reduces someone's ability or motivation to interpret and amplify issue-related arguments also increases the likelihood that external cues in the source, message, recipient, or context may affect response. On the other hand, all of us use such peripheral cues to make a great many decisions because we haven't the time or inclination to scrutinize all the arguments and evidence relevant to every choice we have to make. I sometimes buy bleach or laundry detergent, for example, impulsively by the color of the bottle or box, but I make a detailed study of car evaluations in *Consumer Reports* and other outlets before I spend thousands of dollars on a new one.

NEEDS AND VALUES OF THE AUDIENCE

Needs

People act for reasons. They pursue goals, they are motivated, they try to satisfy their needs. The significant role of needs and goals has already been indicated by people's willingness to expose themselves to messages containing information they believe will be useful to satisfy needs. What are these needs? Among the many catalogs of human needs, one of the most useful is Abraham Maslow's.[12] Maslow, a psychologist, postulates a hierarchy or ranking of human needs, suggesting that some needs may be more intense and basic than others. The most fundamental and intense needs are physiological—needs for food, water, sleep, and protection from exposure. Only when these are relatively well satisfied do needs for safety (stability, order, freedom from violence and disease) become predominant. When these, in turn, are relatively well met, needs for love and acceptance (affection, giving and receiving love, touching and being touched) emerge. And when these are satisfied, needs for esteem (recognition, respect from others and for ourselves) emerge. Finally, when all of these are relatively well met, the need for self-actualization—to be all that one is capable of being, to develop one's unique potential—becomes dominant. All humans experience all of these needs and seek to have them met.

This pyramid of needs can help us to understand the successes and failures of some kinds of rhetorical processes. We may wonder why parliamentary democracy has not attracted more Third World nations, but most citizens of these countries do not have their physiological and safety needs met. They need to find ways to meet the needs at the more basic levels of the pyramid, whereas democracy is an ideology that emphasizes satisfying individual needs for esteem and self-actualization, needs nearer to the top of the pyramid.

Likewise, the successes of charismatic and mystical religious movements should not be too surprising in our culture. We are a nation of

---

[12]Abraham Maslow, *Motivation and Personality* (New York: Harper, 1954).

transients (one of four families moves every five years) with a diminishing sense of community; our families are a less stable source of love and acceptance—one of every two marriages ends in divorce. In such a climate, a community of believers becomes very attractive; if no one else loves you or cares for you, God does. The vogue for books on self-development in the 1980s reflected a society in which the basic needs of many people were relatively well met so that interest focused on self-actualization; the changed conditions of the 1990s have shifted interest to books on how to cope with changing economic conditions or how to deal with stress.

Because the concept of needs focuses on deprivation and because it does not take into account the extent to which our needs are modified by socialization and acculturation, values also need to be considered.

Values

Attitudes, our predispositions to respond favorably or unfavorably to elements of the environment (including invitations to rhetorical action), are influenced not only by beliefs about what is true or probable but also by goals or values. Like *attitude* and *belief, value* is a construct describing a pattern of human behavior. It cannot be touched or seen. Values are usually defined as judgments about what is moral (good or right), important (worthy, significant), or beautiful (moving, expressive, pleasing), or as fundamental preferences for certain ends (such as equality, freedom, self-actualization) or for certain modes of conduct (such as honesty, courage, or integrity). In other words, values express strong, basic, and very general views of how one should act or what goals one should seek (what goals are worthy of seeking). The ideal of self-government, for example, strongly implies that all citizens should enter into policy deliberations and should involve themselves actively in discourse related to choosing those who represent them in government. These views positively value rhetorical action.

Values seem to arise from three sources: our biology, our culture, and our unique qualities as individuals. These sources suggest the relationship between values and needs. Some values arise from biological needs or genetic characteristics (birds need to fly; salmon need to swim upriver to spawn). Despite the many catalogs in psychological works or Maslow's hierarchy of needs (leading to a hierarchy of motives), there is no list of needs that satisfactorily describes human motivation. Consider Maslow's hierarchy. It cannot explain artists who are driven to paint or sculpt even though they cannot buy enough food to eat and are scorned by others. Nor can it explain religious figures, such as

Mother Teresa, who devote their lives to acting altruistically. Maslow himself recognized these exceptions and discussed the problems involved in establishing any needs as basic or in describing motivation as arising from deprivation. As he noted, rats seem to run mazes as fast out of curiosity as out of hunger, thirst, or sex drive. Obviously, human beings need nutrition, safety, shelter from exposure, and affection, but we have modified these needs culturally and socially. The Masai of Africa, for example, seem to thrive on a diet composed largely of the milk and blood of their cattle, a diet that would nauseate most Americans. Dwellers in tropical and even Mediterranean climates meet part of their sleep needs by the siesta, a practice unintelligible to those from more temperate climates. In other words, what begin as organic or biological needs are shaped by culture and society.

Every community has norms about what is good and proper to eat, and what is a delicacy to one group may be revolting to another. Values arise, then, not only from biological requirements, but also from the norms of the groups we belong to, groups ranging in size from the nation to the gang on the block. Group values are expressed in such statements as, "That is unpatriotic or disloyal." "This is the Chinese way." "Seventh Day Adventists are vegetarians." (Recall J. C. Alvarez's statements about "real Americans.") These values, affecting every facet of life, are so fused with biological needs that no one can say just where biology stops and socialization begins.

A third source of values is idiosyncrasies, the unique qualities of the individual. Each of us is physiologically different. Because I have an unusually acute sense of smell, I have a strong aversion to many perfumes; because tobacco smoke gives me headaches, I support strong regulations creating smoke-free areas. Epileptics place a special value on sleep (seizures are more likely if they are deprived of it). Some people have intense aesthetic needs, some have few sexual needs, some relish food, and others eat only to survive. As you will note from these examples, such individual values are refinements or modifications of cultural values and biological needs. Values arising from the special qualities of individuals may account for some unusual responses to rhetorical efforts. Individual values are also a source of variation in the importance or priority given to a particular social value.

Attitudes, our predispositions to respond, are a product of values and beliefs. The emotive and affective component of attitudes and goals (reflecting our desires) comes from our values; the cognitive component of values (based on information and inference) comes from our beliefs. Clearly, however, these concepts and the processes they represent are inseparable because evaluations are based on what we believe to be true, and our evaluations, in turn, influence what we perceive and how we interpret it.

SPECIFIC AND FEASIBLE ACTION

The concept of *inertia* is by now a familiar one. Inertia is the tendency of an object to continue doing whatever it has been doing—to rest if it has been resting, to move in a straight line unless disturbed by an outside force, and so on. When applied to people, it refers to an audience's resistance to the rhetor's purpose. Inertia is a complex psychological matter, but from a rhetorical viewpoint, it usually has to do with resisting demands on our time and energies or with a feeling of powerlessness. Audiences will resist changing their ideas and ignore calls to action unless proposed action is vital enough to engage their energies, is within their capabilities, can be done here and now, and has a reasonable chance of being effective.

The problem of persuading people to practice safer sex is illustrative. Many sexually active people have not used condoms in the past; as a result, safer sex involves a change in behavior. Condoms cost money, and buying them can be embarrassing and expensive, especially for many teenagers. Accordingly, those promoting safer sex provide condoms free of charge to make them easier to use and try to convince the sexually active not only that they face life-threatening dangers from unprotected sex but also that using condoms is easy, effective, and consistent with sexual pleasure.

Those who write about attitudes argue that they have three parts: cognitive (beliefs), affective (values), and behavioral. Attitudes do not exist apart from behaviors, but the relationship between them is complex. First, there is no simple correlation between an attitude and a particular behavior. For example, one can agree that unprotected sexual intercourse is dangerous and behave in various ways. One can act as if that belief had nothing to do with you—as if you are a special case, or as if only gay males were at risk, screening out data about increasing risks to heterosexuals and women. One can believe in the danger but also espouse the value that premarital sex is wrong. Taking precautions would contradict that value. In such instances, if sex occurs, pregnancy, a sexually transmitted disease, or exposure to the HIV virus (leading to acquired immune deficiency syndrome—AIDS) are risked, perhaps as punishment for flouting the value. Or one can carefully plan to enjoy sexual activity safely. Either attitudes and behavior correlate poorly, or people's reported attitudes differ from their actual attitudes.

Just as attitudes can influence behavior, so behavior can also influence attitudes. Studies have compared listening to a speech or reading an essay by someone else with composing one's own speech or essay or with recording the arguments made by others. In these illustrative studies, even for those hostile to the specific purpose of the speech or essay, greater participation brought considerable change in attitudes.[13] Advertisers who promote contests in which participants write "Why I like X in 25 words or less" are using behavior to influence attitudes. This process is sometimes called self-influence, and it may occur because the people involved try to make their attitudes consistent with their behaviors.

At a minimum, an action is a commitment, often a public commitment, to an attitude. It expresses the recipients' participation in the persuasive process and involves them in the process of influence. Participation in the rhetorical act may be a most effective way of influencing attitudes, and inducing a specific action may be just the reinforcement needed to ensure that a belief will persist. In all cases, as mentioned above, rhetorical acts that propose specific, feasible, and immediate actions for the audience will be the most successful.

These, then, are the rhetorical obstacles arising from the audience: inattention, misperception and misinterpretation, lack of motivation (different needs or values), and inertia. In the next section I offer examples to illustrate these facets of the rhetorical problem.

EXAMPLES OF RHETORICAL PROBLEMS

Consider, for a moment, why it is hard to mount a campaign to alter the status quo (what exists now) on these issues: state-sponsored lotteries, sex education and condom distribution in grade and high schools, and regulating the sale of automatic weapons and handguns.

If you have followed the persuasive histories of these issues, you will know that without dramatic incidents that call attention to them and arouse concern, it is hard to persuade an audience that there is any need for change. Even when such attention-getting incidents oc-

---

[13]O. J. Harvey and G. D. Beverly, "Some Personality Correlates of Concept Change Through Role Playing," *Journal of Abnormal and Social Psychology* 63 (1961):125–130.

cur, social change of this extent requires highly committed and sustained efforts that are costly for supporters. In each case, the successful persuader must find dramatic materials that will gain the attention of the audience, present convincing evidence, show that the needs and values of the audience are directly related to this proposal, and finally, show that action can be taken to produce the desired results at a cost that the community sees as feasible.

The status quo on all of these issues varies among the states; many have state-sponsored lotteries, some offer sex education beginning in elementary schools and distribute condoms in junior or senior high schools, and some jurisdictions have outlawed automatic weapons and require a waiting period before purchase of a handgun.

Sex Education and Condom Distribution

In July of 1993, the Board of Education of New Haven, Connecticut, approved a plan to provide condoms at school health clinics to students as early as the fifth grade.[14] The board's chair said, "Any time you have children at risk of dying, then I can't imagine anything more urgent than that. . . . If there is anything that you can do to prevent that, then it is your moral obligation to do so." There were strong objections. Some parents contended that educators had no right to meddle in family matters—sexual matters should not be discussed publicly, and sex education should take place only in the home. Others said, "It is inappropriate. . . . There are other reasons why our youngsters are becoming as involved in sexual activities. This is not necessarily going to be the answer. And unfortunately, it has the potential to create additional problems. It can and will send a message to our youngsters that we are sanctioning their activities." In other words, even informed teenagers with access to condoms and other forms of contraception often choose not to use them. Still others, especially local church leaders, object to contraception on religious grounds; some may believe that pregnancy and AIDS are punishments for sinful sexual behavior. Others may resist because of the costs of

---

[14]See Clifford J. Levy, "Distribution of Condoms to Include Fifth Graders," *New York Times,* July 28, 1993, p. B10. All quotations are from this source. According to this report, city officials said that in the first six months of 1993, New Haven accounted for 22 percent, or 202, of the newly identified AIDS cases in the state. In 1992, there were 201 cases of gonorrhea, 342 cases of chlamydia, and 14 cases of syphilis (sexually transmitted diseases) among New Haven residents aged 15 to 19.

providing sex education and contraceptives. Still others have no children or teenage friends or relatives and may see the issue as irrelevant to them, the fault of bad parents. What might an advocate do to respond to some of these bases for resistance?

Gun Control

Consider the difficulties that have faced efforts to regulate the sale and ownership of automatic weapons and handguns, although, based on polling data, a majority of Americans supports such regulation.[15] Part of the explanation may be that the public has ill-formed or loosely held beliefs about these controls, which are reflected in wide swings of opinion following sensational events, such as the attempted assassination of President Ronald Reagan.[16] In other words, most seem to think some control over guns is sensible; at the same time, they do not want to forgo the possibility of protecting themselves.[17] Most know that large numbers of guns are in private hands (over 120 million are estimated to be in circulation), and most believe that gun control efforts will be ineffective, that we can stop only law-abiding citizens, not criminals, from arming.[18]

The powerful lobbying group, the National Rifle Association (NRA), has been effective in preventing passage of most such legislation. In 1993, the so-called Brady Law was enacted, named for James Brady, President Ronald Reagan's press secretary, who was shot and disabled when John Hinckley attempted to assassinate President Reagan with a handgun he had purchased by mail. The Brady law requires a five-day waiting period prior to purchase, in which the purchaser's record is checked to prevent purchases by felons or by the mentally ill. The passage of that law was seen as evidence that controls on handgun purchases and ownership were becoming more acceptable politically. Support of some law enforcement groups for banning Teflon bullets that penetrate bulletproof vests and for other limited regulation has also influenced voters and politicians.

The NRA appeals strongly to such values as individual rights and interprets the Second Amendment of the U.S. Constitution as a guar-

---

[15]G. Kleck, *Point Blank: Guns and Violence in America* (New York: Aldine De Gruyter, 1991), pp. 368–370.
[16]Kleck, p. 367.
[17]D. Hook, *Gun Control: The Continuing Debate* (Bellevue, WA: Second Amendment Foundation, 1993), p. 127.
[18]Kleck, p. 370; G. Robin, *Violent Crime and Gun Control* (Cincinnati: Anderson Publishing, 1991), pp. 41–42.

antee of the right of individuals to own guns.[19] In 1994, it launched advertising that appealed to women with the slogan "Choose not to be a victim," echoing feminist appeals to the values of choice and empowerment, in ads that include a photograph showing a mother and daughter walking across a dark, largely empty parking lot, evoking the belief that a gun can protect women from predatory criminals. The NRA also argues that any regulation of guns or ammunition is the first step to greater control, evoking negative attitudes toward government regulation.

Finally, pro-gun voters, who are organized quite effectively by the NRA through pamphlets and mailings, have a powerful influence in U.S. politics. Some members of Congress from western states, for example, have remarked that reelection hinges on their stands on this issue.[20] A bloc of committed, single-issue voters can be a significant obstacle to change because the opposition, to be effective, needs to attain a similar level of commitment and organization.

In other words, beliefs about personal safety and protection, values related to individual rights, and attitudes about government regulation work against efforts for licensing gun ownership and increasing controls on purchase and ownership of some guns and ammunition. Moves toward greater control are affected by the commitment and organization of a core group of those with strong beliefs on one side of the issue. How might an advocate counter such beliefs, values, and attitudes? How might those seeking licensing increase feelings of control and efficacy among those who share their views?

State-Sponsored Lotteries[21]

At present, at least 34 states and the District of Columbia have state-sponsored lotteries; more are probably being instituted. Why have they become so widely accepted when only a short time ago most

---

[19]The Supreme Court and federal appellate courts consistently have interpreted the Second Amendment as a corporate or collective right, a protection of state-run militias only, not of individuals who may or may not organize on their own. Popular understanding, however, is that individuals have a right to "keep and bear arms" (W. Freedman, *The Privilege to Keep and Bear Arms* [New York: Quorum Books, 1989], pp. 20–23, 53–58).

[20]W. Freedman, *The Privilege to Keep and Bear Arms* (New York: Quorum Books, 1989), p. 3.

[21]A good general source of information on them is Charles T. Clotfelter and Philip J. Cook, *Selling Hope: State Lotteries in America* (Cambridge, MA: Harvard University Press, 1989).

Americans reportedly opposed legalized gambling? For the most part, lotteries have been promoted as a substitute for state income taxes, which most Americans resist and resent, probably more strongly than they disapprove of gambling. When states need to raise revenues and citizens resist higher income taxes or vote against bond issues that would raise property taxes, lotteries become attractive; in 1990, for example, state lotteries raised $7 billion in revenues.

As researchers have discovered, however, lotteries are a highly regressive form of taxation, even more regressive than sales taxes, which means that poorer people contribute much more than middle-class or wealthy people. They are regressive because poorer people tend to spend more per capita on lotteries than do middle-class or wealthy people; perhaps poorer people cannot see ways to improve their lot through more hard work, so they buy a chance hoping and dreaming that they will be lucky.

Even when they do not win, however, poorer people do not benefit equitably from their spending; revenues raised via the lottery for education, for example, merely replace other funding or tend to be distributed in greater amounts to more affluent districts. That happens because poorer people are less likely to be represented on the bodies that make such decisions, and often they find it more difficult to organize themselves to protest such inequities.

Lotteries clearly have undesirable social effects; for example, they increase compulsive gambling, and they do not extinguish illegal gambling games. In some cases, they have produced corruption; in others, the influence of organized crime has been felt. These effects and their costs, however, take time to develop, so voters may not take them into account when deciding whether a state lottery should be approved.

It is hard to overcome the feeling that lotteries are fun. Big prizes enable people to dream of vast riches. The stories of winners provide Americans with real-life soap operas complete with poignant, heart-rending tales of changed lives. It is hard not to participate in such stories. Moreover, when critics point out how regressive the tax benefits are, lottery proponents respond that nobody forces anyone to play and treat spending on lottery tickets as an example of the values of freedom and individualism.

The United States has a long history of applauding rags-to-riches tales, and the large winnings advertised in state lotteries fit into such stories. Lotteries raise revenues without compulsion as players choose to risk their money, consistent with values celebrating individualism and choice. Beliefs that lotteries are an inexpensive, noncoercive means to raise large amounts of revenue turn voters into supporters even though these beliefs are untrue. Negative attitudes toward turning state governments into "bookies" seem to be overwhelmed by resentment against increased taxes. Religious resistance to legalized gambling has been eroded by gambling games that have been used to raise money for charities. What would an advocate have to do to convince voters that state lotteries should be abolished?

Note that similar problems arise in all three of these examples: How can an issue be made salient for members of the audience? What beliefs will have to be challenged? What evidence might be credible? How can it be related to their needs? What values, if any, are in conflict? How can audience members be moved to act?

SUMMARY

In this chapter I have argued that certain rhetorical obstacles routinely arise from the audience, although their specific form depends on the particular topic, purpose, occasion, and audience. These obstacles, arising from the requirements every rhetorical act must meet, can be grouped under headings of inattention, misperception and misinterpretation, lack of motivation (different needs and values), and inertia. Every rhetorical effort must overcome these obstacles in order to reach the audience and have an opportunity to influence.

Obviously, rhetors need to understand their audiences: those exposed to a rhetorical effort, those chosen as the particular target for influence, and those able to produce change. The audience-related aspects of the rhetorical problem are also related to important psychological concepts: the human predisposition to react favorably or unfavorably to information encountered (attitudes), beliefs held about what is true or probable, and values that indicate goals and preferences. In every case, you must consider how to use the beliefs, attitudes, and values of the audience in order to reach them and induce them to participate in rhetorical action, and as a critic, you need to pay particular attention to such efforts.

Summary Outline

I. An important part of the rhetorical problem is made up of obstacles arising from the audience.

   A. There are four ways to understand what is meant by an audience:

      1. The empirical audience is composed of those exposed to the rhetorical act.

2. The target audience, an ideal audience at whom the act is aimed.

3. Agents of change, who can do as the rhetor desires.

4. The created audience, which is brought into being by rhetorical action, often by inviting members of the exposed audience to play a specific role.

B. Common kinds of audience-related obstacles are

1. Inattention, because potential audience members tend to limit their exposure except when they fear bias, when information has immediate usefulness, and when they are better educated.

2. Misperception and misinterpretation, which are affected by

a. Attitudes, which can affect perception by distorting what we see and hear.

b. Beliefs, which are formed from information and affect attitudes.

3. Lack of motivation to decode or respond to the message, which is affected by various factors:

a. The ELM model of persuasion suggests that self-interest is the key element in motivating audiences to collaborate in creating messages.

b. Basic needs for survival, safety, affection, esteem, and self-actualization affect motivation.

c. Values reflect the ways in which needs are socialized and acculturated.

4. Inertia, or unwillingness to change or act, unless audience members see a specific action or set of actions as within their ability and likely to be effective.

▪   ▪   ▪

MATERIAL FOR ANALYSIS

The kinds of obstacles that can arise from audience beliefs, values, and attitudes were among the obstacles faced by Anita Hill in her opening statement detailing the behavior of Clarence Thomas toward her, behavior she believed relevant to his fitness to sit on the U.S. Supreme Court. Before you read her statement, pause for a moment to list some of the attitudes, beliefs, and values related to issues of sexual harassment that might make an audience skeptical of her charges. In addition, consider that the incidents she described happened some ten years ago. You might also recall the efforts of J. C. Alvarez to create and arouse attitudes that would make it difficult to believe Hill. The following statement by Hill was presented on October 11, 1991, to the U.S. Senate Judiciary Committee and was televised on the broadcast networks and excerpted on CNN. The dramatic nature of her charges attracted much attention, which led to media coverage and commentary, and the importance of the Supreme Court in our system of government added salience to the issue. To what beliefs, values, and attitudes did she attempt to appeal in trying to present herself as a credible witness?

Testimony of Anita F. Hill, Professor of Law, University of Oklahoma, Norman, OK[22]

Ms. Hill. Mr. Chairman [Joseph Biden, D-NJ], Senator [Strom] Thurmond, members of the committee, my name is Anita F. Hill, and I am a professor of law at the University of Oklahoma.

1   I was born on a farm in Okmulgee County, OK, in 1956. I am the youngest of 13 children. I had my early education in Okmulgee County. My father, Albert Hill, is a farmer in that area. My mother's name is Erma Hill. She is also a farmer and a housewife.

2   My childhood was one of a lot of hard work and not much money, but it was one of solid family affection as represented by my parents. I was reared in a religious atmosphere in the Baptist faith, and I have been a member of the Antioch Baptist Church, in Tulsa, OK, since 1983. It is a very warm part of my life at the present time.

3   For my undergraduate work, I went to Oklahoma State University, and graduated from there in 1977. I am attaching to the statement a copy of my resume for further details of my education.

The Chairman. It will be included in the record.

Ms. Hill. Thank you.

4   I graduated from the university with academic honors and proceeded to the Yale Law School, where I received my J.D. degree in 1980.

---

[22]*Hearings Before the Committee on the Judiciary, U.S. Senate,* 102d Cong., 1st sess., 4:36–40 (her prepared statement follows on pp. 41–48). Thomas's statement is found on pp. 11–26.

5   Upon graduation from law school, I became a practicing lawyer with the Washington, D.C., firm of Wald, Harkrader & Ross. In 1981, I was introduced to now-Judge Thomas by a mutual friend. Judge Thomas told me that he was anticipating a political appointment and asked if I would be interested in working with him. He was, in fact, appointed as Assistant Secretary of Education for Civil Rights. After he had taken that post, he asked if I would become his assistant, and I accepted that position.

6   In my early period there, I had two major projects. First was an article I wrote for Judge Thomas's signature on the education of minority students. The second was the organization of a seminar on high-risk students, which was abandoned because Judge Thomas transferred to the EEOC, where he became the chairman of that office.

7   During this period at the Department of Education, my working relationship with Judge Thomas was positive. I had a good deal of responsibility and independence. I thought he respected my work and that he trusted my judgment.

8   After approximately three months of working there, he asked me to go out socially with him. What happened next and telling the world about it are the two most difficult things, experiences of my life. It is only after a great deal of agonizing consideration and a number of sleepless nights that I am able to talk of these unpleasant matters to anyone but my close friends.

9   I declined the invitation to go out socially with him and explained to him that I thought it would jeopardize what at the time I considered to be a very good working relationship. I had a normal social life with other men outside of the office. I believed then, as now, that having a social relationship with a person who was supervising my work would be ill-advised. I was very uncomfortable with the idea and told him so.

10   I thought that by saying "no" and explaining my reasons, my employer would abandon his social suggestions. However, to my regret, in the following few weeks he continued to ask me out on several occasions. He pressed me to justify my reasons for saying "no" to him. These incidents took place in his office or mine. They were in the form of private conversations which would not have been overheard by anyone else.

11   My working relationship became even more strained when Judge Thomas began to use work situations to discuss sex. On these occasions, he would call me into his office for reports on education issues and projects or he might suggest that because of the time pressures of his schedule, we go to lunch to a government cafeteria. After a brief discussion of work, he would turn the

conversation to a discussion of sexual matters. His conversations were very vivid.

12   He spoke about acts that he had seen in pornographic films involving such matters as women having sex with animals, and films showing group sex or rape scenes. He talked about pornographic materials depicting individuals with large penises or large breasts involved in various sex acts.

13   On several occasions Thomas told me graphically of his own sexual prowess. Because I was extremely uncomfortable talking about sex with him at all, and particularly in such a graphic way, I told him that I did not want to talk about these subjects. I would also try to change the subject to education matters or to nonsexual personal matters, such as his background or his beliefs. My efforts to change the subject were rarely successful.

14   Throughout the period of these conversations, he also from time to time asked me for social engagements. My reaction to these conversations was to avoid them by limiting opportunities for us to engage in extended conversations. This was difficult because at the time, I was his only assistant at the Office of Education or Office for Civil Rights.

15   During the latter part of my time at the Department of Education, the social pressures and any conversation of his offensive behavior ended. I began both to believe and hope that our working relationship could be a proper, cordial, and professional one.

16   When Judge Thomas was made chair of the EEOC, I needed to face the question of whether to go with him. I was asked to do so and I did. The work, itself, was interesting, and at that time, it appeared that the sexual overtures, which had so troubled me, had ended.

17   I also faced the realistic fact that I had no alternative job. While I might have gone back to private practice, perhaps in my old firm or at another, I was dedicated to civil rights work and my first choice was to be in that field. Moreover, at that time the Department of Education, itself, was a dubious venture. President Reagan was seeking to abolish the entire department.

18   For my first months at the EEOC, where I continued to be an assistant to Judge Thomas, there were no sexual conversations or overtures. However, during the fall and winter of 1982, these began again. The comments were random, and ranged from pressing me about why I didn't go out with him, to remarks about my personal appearance. I remember him saying that "some day I would have to tell him the real reason that I wouldn't go out with him."

19   He began to show displeasure in his tone and voice and his demeanor in his continued pressure for an explanation. He commented on what I was wearing in terms of whether it made me more or less sexually attractive. The incidents occurred in his inner office at the EEOC.

20   One of the oddest episodes I remember was an occasion in which Thomas was drinking a Coke in his office. He got up from the table, at which we were working, went over to his desk to get the Coke, looked at the can, and asked, "Who has put pubic hair on my Coke?"

21   On other occasions he referred to the size of his own penis as being larger than normal, and he also spoke on some occasions of the pleasures he had given to women with oral sex. At this point, late 1982, I began to feel severe stress on the job. I began to be concerned that Clarence Thomas might take out his anger with me by degrading me or not giving me important assignments. I also thought that he might find an excuse for dismissing me.

22   In January 1983, I began looking for another job. I was handicapped because I feared that if he found out he might make it difficult for me to find other employment, and I might be dismissed from the job I had.

23   Another factor that made my search more difficult was that this was during a period of a hiring freeze in the government. In February 1983, I was hospitalized for five days on an emergency basis for acute stomach pain, which I attributed to stress on the job. Once out of the hospital, I became more committed to finding other employment and sought further to minimize my contact with Thomas.

24   This became easier when Allyson Duncan became office director because most of my work was then funneled through her and I had contact with Clarence Thomas mostly in staff meetings.

25   In the spring of 1983, an opportunity to teach at Oral Roberts University opened up. I participated in a seminar, taught an afternoon session in a seminar at Oral Roberts University. The dean of the university saw me teaching and inquired as to whether I would be interested in pursuing a career in teaching, beginning at Oral Roberts University. I agreed to take the job, in large part, because of my desire to escape the pressures I felt at the EEOC due to Judge Thomas.

26   When I informed him that I was leaving in July, I recall that his response was that now I would no longer have an excuse for not going out with him. I told him that I still preferred not to do so. At some time after that meeting, he asked if he could take me to dinner at the end of the term. When I declined, he assured me that the dinner was a professional courtesy only and not a social invitation. I reluctantly agreed to accept that invitation but only if it was at the very end of a working day.

27   On, as I recall, the last day of my employment at the EEOC in the summer of 1983, I did have dinner with Clarence Thomas. We went directly from work to a restaurant near the office. We talked about the work that I had done both at Education and at the EEOC. He told me that he was pleased with all of it except for an article and speech that I had done for him while we were at the Office for Civil Rights. Finally he made a comment that I will vividly remember. He said that if I ever told anyone of his behavior that it would ruin his career. This was not an apology, nor was it an explanation. That was his last remark about the possibility of our going out or reference to his behavior.

28   In July 1983, I left the Washington, D.C., area and have had minimal contacts with Judge Clarence Thomas since. I am, of course, aware from the press that some questions have been raised about conversations I had with Judge Clarence Thomas after I left the EEOC.

29   From 1983 until today I have seen Judge Thomas only twice. On one occasion I needed to get a reference from him and on another he made a public appearance at Tulsa. On one occasion he called me at home and we had an inconsequential conversation. On one occasion he called me without reaching me and I returned the call without reaching him and nothing came of it. I have at least on three occasions been asked to act as a conduit to him for others.

30   I knew his secretary, Diane Holt. We had worked together both at EEOC and Education. There were occasions on which I spoke to her and on some of these occasions, undoubtedly, I passed on some casual comment to then-Chairman Thomas. There were a series of calls in the first three months of 1985, occasioned by a group in Tulsa which wished to have a civil rights conference. They wanted Judge Thomas to be the speaker and enlisted my assistance for this purpose.

31   I did call in January and February to no effect and finally suggested to the person directly involved, Susan Cahall, that she put the matter into her own hands and call directly. She did so in March 1985.

32   In connection with that March invitation, Ms. Cahall wanted conference materials for the seminar, and some research was needed. I was asked to try and get the information and did attempt to do so. There was another call about another possible conference in July 1985.

33   In August 1987, I was in Washington, D.C., and I did call Diane Holt. In the course of this conversation she asked me how long I was going to be in town and I told her. It is recorded in the messages as August 15; it was, in fact, August 20. She told me about Judge Thomas's marriage and I did say, congratulations.

34   It is only after a great deal of agonizing consideration that I am able to talk of these unpleasant matters to anyone, except my closest friends as I have said before. These last few days have been very trying and very hard for me, and it hasn't just been the last few days this week. It has actually been over a month now that I have been under the strain of this issue. Telling the world is the most difficult experience of my life, but it is very close to have to live through the experience that occasioned this meeting. I may have used poor judgment early on in my relationship with this issue. I was aware, however, that telling at any point in my career could adversely affect my future career. And I did not want, early on, to build [sic] all the bridges to the EEOC.

35   As I said, I may have used poor judgment. Perhaps I should have taken angry or even militant steps, both when I was in the agency or after I had left it, but I must confess to the world that the course that I took seemed the better as well as the easier approach.

36   I declined any comment to newspapers, but later when Senate staff asked me about these matters, I felt that I had a duty to report. I have no personal vendetta against Clarence Thomas. I seek only to provide the committee with information which it may regard as relevant.

37   It would have been more comfortable to remain silent. It took no initiative to inform anyone. I took no initiative to inform anyone. But when I was asked by a representative of this committee to report my experience I felt that I had to tell the truth. I could not keep silent.

Questions for Analysis

1. Until Anita Hill's allegations about Thomas's behavior became public, his nomination seemed secure. Why are Hill's charges so significant for this particular nominee's confirmation? What, other than sheer partisanship, might make audience members reluctant to believe her allegations? How are attitudes toward women and African Americans involved?

2. How does Hill attempt to make herself credible? What factors influence judgments of her credibility? How does she attempt to refute claims that might lessen her credibility?

3. What special problems are posed for audiences by issues for which only testimony is available as evidence?

4. The Hill–Thomas hearings sparked considerable interest in the issue of sexual harassment. Although laws had been passed and some key court decisions had been made, the hearings generated news stories of other harassment cases, interviews with experts and affected individuals, polls, and editorial commentary. Possibly the hearings, along with the related discourse, created public opinion about sexual harassment where little had existed before. Discuss how this process illustrates the ELM theory by considering how beliefs, attitudes, and values were affected by what occurred in the hearings and by the press reaction to them.

5. In the hearing record (vol. 4:443–551) are transcripts of telephone interviews of Angela Wright and Rose Jourdain by committee staff. These interviews indicate that Clarence Thomas made suggestive and inappropriate comments to Wright, who worked at the EEOC and was fired by Thomas, and that Wright, who was upset by them, reported these comments to her coworker and friend, Rose Jourdain. Neither Wright nor Jourdain was called as a witness by the Senate Judiciary Committee. In 1994 articles appeared in the *Washington Post* dealing with the content of Wright's testimony. Senator Paul Simon, D-IL, was reported as saying that "he didn't read Wright's testimony until after the hearings. That's when he was stunned to learn that a friend of Wright's at the EEOC, Rose Jourdain, had corroborated her account. Had he known this when the senators caucused, 'I would have insisted that she be called.' Simon says he thinks Wright's account, buttressed by Jourdain's, 'would have turned the situation around.'"[23] Read the telephone interviews and the articles. Then discuss the values, attitudes, and beliefs that might have influenced the reception of this testimony and its bearing on believing Hill or Thomas.

EXERCISE

Discovering Audience Beliefs and Attitudes

For this exercise, design an interviewing schedule (a series of planned and interrelated questions on a subject) and use it to interview seven to ten persons on the subject of your rhetorical act. The exercise has

---

[23]Florence George Graves, "Her Thomas Testimony Wasn't Heard," and "Wright's Story Added Heat to 'Cauldron of Recrimination,'" reprinted [Mpls.] *Star Tribune*, October 19, 1994:A4, A6, and October 20, 1994:A4, A10.

three purposes: (1) to give you experience with the problems involved in developing questions that accurately elicit what others know, believe, and feel; (2) to give you experience in creating an atmosphere in which others are willing to tell you what they know, believe, and feel; and (3) to provide you with information about the knowledge, beliefs, and attitudes of others to help you adapt a rhetorical act to a general or heterogeneous audience.

The intent of the interviews is to gather information that would help you, as a rhetor, prepare a rhetorical act more likely to be attended to and influential for a general audience. You are attempting to discover the causes of resistance to your purpose and the sorts of obstacles you might face. You are also trying to find out what bases there are for appeals that might cause this audience to give your point of view a fair and open hearing. In order to be an effective interviewer, you need to be well informed on the subject yourself.

A general audience is really a cross section or random sample of the population. For this reason, you should try to interview people representing diverse interests and situations. Ideally, those interviewed should differ in age, sex, ethnic group, socioeconomic level, occupation, and religious and political affiliation. Do not interview friends or roommates; in any case, seek to interview complete strangers.

You need to plan an opening that introduces you, indicates what you are doing and why, introduces the subject, and tells the person to be interviewed how much time will be involved and why it is important that he or she participate. Plan a series of questions that progresses through the areas of the subject you think most important. Begin with basic questions to determine just what the person knows. Plan a closing that expresses appreciation and that will end the interview comfortably.

Problems to be avoided include the following:

▪ not knowing the questions well enough or reading them mechanically
▪ lack of warmth and eye contact suggesting disinterest
▪ speaking too softly or too quickly
▪ rushing the interview so that answers are superficial
▪ apologizing
▪ asking biased questions
▪ suggesting answers if the person hesitates
▪ mentioning how others answered

■ taking too many notes

■ taking too much for granted (such as how much is known about the subject or familiarity with vocabulary)

1. Turn in a copy of the questions you used, together with an evaluation of them as a means of getting useful and accurate information about knowledge, beliefs, and attitudes.

2. Briefly evaluate your strengths and weaknesses as an interviewer and indicate what kinds of things were successful and unsuccessful in creating an atmosphere in which people were willing to be interviewed and to take the questions seriously. What places were the best for doing the interviews?

3. Briefly evaluate the information you obtained in terms of using it for a rhetorical act on this subject for a general audience. Indicate what assumptions were confirmed or disconfirmed; consider how your class differs from this wider audience; indicate some ways in which you might proceed that you think would be effective in gaining a hearing for your point of view.

SOURCES

A review and analysis of studies of selective exposure and perception is found in Daniel O'Keefe, *Persuasion: Theory and Research* (Newbury Park, CA: Sage, 1990), pp. 68–71.

Sources related to the Anita Hill–Clarence Thomas hearings include the following: Timothy M. Phelps and Helen Winternitz, *Capitol Games: Clarence Thomas, Anita Hill, and the Story of a Supreme Court Nomination* (New York: Hyperion, 1992); *Court of Appeal: The Black Community Speaks Out on the Racial and Sexual Politics of Thomas v. Hill,* ed. Robert Chrisman and Robert L. Allen (New York: Ballantine Books, 1992); *Race-ing Justice, Engendering Power: Essays on Anita Hill, Clarence Thomas, and the Construction of Social Reality,* ed. Toni Morrison (New York: Pantheon, 1992). See also Nancy Fraser, "Sex, Lies, and the Public Sphere: Some Reflections on the Confirmation of Clarence Thomas," *Critical Inquiry* 18 (Spring 1992):595–612. See also *Resurrection* by Senator John C. Danforth (New York: Macmillan, 1994) and *Strange Justice: The Selling of Clarence Thomas* by Jane Mayer and Jill Abramson (Boston: Houghton Mifflin, 1994).

CHAPTER 4

Obstacles Arising from Subject and Purpose

Although the audience is central in an analysis of rhetorical obstacles, subject and purpose are almost equally important. Actually, of course, the problems discussed here arise out of the interrelationship between the audience and the issue: the subject the audience must consider and the purpose, the response that the rhetor wishes to evoke from the audience. Again, no subject is without interest for some audience, and no subject interests everyone.

To give you a feeling for the kind of rhetorical problem discussed in this chapter, consider this paragraph from a review of books trying to make sense of the 1980s savings and loan crisis:

> The mosaic of disaster was complex in the extreme, mixing simple thuggery with subtle feats of financial and legal presti-digitation. This was a story in which good intentions knowingly served the cause of fraud, in which the line between the acciden-tal and the arranged became hopelessly blurred, and it was im-possible to distinguish between the good and the bad.
>
> It is also an extremely difficult story to tell in a fashion that would provoke the kind of outrage it deserves. . . . The problem is that the main lines of the sad story are woven from virtually innumerable threads. Both chronicler and reader risk at every turn being marooned in an acronymic quagmire: FICO (Financ-ing Corporation), FCA (Financial Corporation of America), FDIC (Federal Deposit Insurance Corporation), FSLIC (Federal Savings and Loan Insurance Corporation), FIRREA (Financial Institutions Reform, Recovery, and Enforcement Act), FHLBB (Federal Home Loan Bank Board, generally known as simply the "Bank Board"), FNMA (Federal National Mortgage Association, or "Fannie Mae"),

FHMLC (Federal Home Loan Mortgage Corporation, or "Freddie Mac"), and GNMA (Government National Mortgage Association, or "Ginnie Mae"). This is not a challenge most readers will find inviting. Indeed, I suspect that the business of simply chopping through this nomenclatural thicket so exhausted the bureaucrats and legislators charged with dealing with the collapse that they had scant energy left with which to confront the problem itself.[1]

The obstacles facing anyone writing about the collapse of the savings and loan institutions in the 1980s are indeed great—the audience's lack of personal experience, the formidable economic and financial vocabulary as well as the "acronymic quagmire," the similarity between the names of the various institutions and bureaucracies, and the mind-boggling statistics. Obstacles of this sort arise from the subject and from the rhetor's purpose.

SUBJECT-RELATED OBSTACLES

Two major obstacles are created by subjects or topics: resistance created by complexity and resistance created by the cultural history of the issue.

Complexity

Some subjects are complex or, more to the point, the audience sees them as complex. In such cases, you will meet a special kind of audience resistance that is definitely a barrier to joint rhetorical action. (Of course, there might also be an obstacle in your own ability to handle certain kinds of complex subjects. Even if you were speaking from personal experience, the preparation time would be far longer. But let's assume you can handle the subject.)

Subjects are complex or seem so (1) when they are remote from the audience's personal experience, (2) when they require technical knowledge or some other kind of special expertise, and (3) when they are bound up with many other difficult issues. That is, audiences resist participation in rhetorical acts for which they have no touchstone

---

[1]Michael M. Thomas, "The Greatest American Shambles," *The New York Review of Books,* January 31, 1991, pp. 30–31.

in their ordinary lives. They are uncomfortable with subjects demanding decisions that they do not feel competent to make, and they are often overwhelmed by subjects with broad ramifications.

Subjects that lie outside the personal experiences of the audience create special difficulties. The audience feels unfit to make judgments. This is the case with most foreign policy decisions. Despite a great increase in world travel by Americans, few of us have been in Bosnia or Haiti or have had experiences that would make us feel comfortable about deciding military or economic policies for those areas. By contrast, farmers have considerable experience with acreage allotments, storage facilities, insecticides, crop failure, and the like, and bring a good deal of familiarity to decisions on such issues. Women who have delivered children in hospitals have experience they bring to proposals for birthing rooms; parents have had personal experiences with teachers relevant to educational decisions; and so forth. But when a subject is outside our personal experience, we are at the mercy of others. We have to rely on data gathered by others and on interpretations made by experts. Because experts rarely agree, we face trying to decide who is more reliable. And because we have to rely on others, we are more vulnerable to manipulation: It is easier to fool those without personal experience because they have no basis on which to test the data or claims of others. That is one reason we feel helpless about foreign policy decisions and why we can be deceived about what really happened in 1989 in Tienanmen Square in Beijing, China.

Subjects are also complex when they require technical knowledge or a special kind of expertise. Subjects that demand a lot of economic knowledge from the audience are particularly dangerous. Making decisions about the S & L crisis, for example, demands many kinds of knowledge from audience members. People must know something about the regulations governing collateral, loans for mortgages, and rates of interest that can be offered by thrift institutions; "junk bonds"; money market accounts; the money supply; savings deposit insurance; and brokered deposits. They will also need to comprehend the meaning of $500 billion—the projected cost of the bailout to taxpayers over the next 30 years (the average length of a mortgage). Audiences faced with such demands are likely to resist participation—unless their savings were in thrifts that collapsed—because basic information is outside their personal competence. In such a situation, rhetors must become educators, and under such circumstances, they are likely to use the entire range of rhetorical purposes in a persuasive campaign. Rhetors will begin by creating virtual experience, including altering the audience's perception of its own competence. This will be followed by efforts to explain that link and interpret the data. Only then can rhetors try to formulate beliefs in the audience about such things as the degree to which fraud was involved, the responsibility of past administrations and congresses for the deregulation that contributed to the collapse, how the bailout should be paid for, and what kinds of regulation are needed to prevent this from recurring.

Subjects like banking regulation are even more complex because they are bound up with many other difficult issues with broad ramifications. Decisions on deposit insurance and banking regulation cannot be separated from issues of home construction, inflation, stimulating economic growth, and the comparative costs of these policies. The result is a sense that the problem is so large and its implications so extensive that no one can understand it or begin to solve it.

The history of the civil rights movement illustrates the complexity of a problem with broad ramifications. Initial efforts to attack the denial of civil rights involved eliminating clearly defined evidences of oppression—segregated waiting rooms, water fountains, and bathrooms, and barriers to voter registration, for example. But when these basic battles were largely won, other issues arose that were not so easy to define or solve: providing quality education, decent housing, and good jobs. Housing cannot be separated from employment nor employment from education. Hence, in order to solve one problem, all the problems apparently have to be solved. Such efforts take time and involve cultural dislocations (reflected, for example, in disputes over school busing and integration plans), and clear evidence of progress may be hard to see.

In summary, a subject may create obstacles because of its real or perceived complexity. A subject is complex when the audience has no firsthand experience with it, when technical knowledge or special expertise is required, and when the subject is part of an interrelated set of problems or issues.

Cultural History

The second set of obstacles arising from the subject has roots in events that happened long before you take the stage. Let us call them the subject's *cultural history* to indicate that the obstacles come from ideas or concepts about the subject formed during past discussions in your culture. Obstacles arising from cultural history include (1) boredom or indifference due to familiarity with existing arguments, (2) closed minds about public discussion of some taboo topics, (3) conditioned responses to emotionally loaded subjects, and (4) conflict with cultural values.

No subject exists in a void. Every subject has a context and mean-ing consisting of past experience with the subject and the issues sur-rounding it. This context is the residue of past rhetorical action. It is the subject's cultural history. If your topic has a long and rich cultural history, beware.

Take, for example, capital punishment. The death penalty for cer-tain crimes (usually murders) has been defended and attacked so often that the arguments on both sides have almost become clichés. Virtu-ally any audience will have been exposed to them before. Everyone has heard the argument that capital punishment deters people from committing murder (the deterrence argument), and everyone also knows the counterargument—that most murders are committed in the heat of passion when the part of the mind affected by deterrents is simply not in control. On and on go the arguments and counter-arguments—from cruel and unusual punishment, unequal protection of the law (many more nonwhites and poor people are executed than whites and the wealthy), the likelihood of rehabilitation, to the haunting possibility of executing the innocent. Death, as one anti–capital punishment argument reminds us, is so final.

Because everyone knows these arguments, the first obstacle you face may be boredom. Thus, unless you can find a fresh approach to the subject, you might be better off avoiding it. You might argue that the issues are far from settled, pointing out that in 1994, two Supreme Court Justices (Harry A. Blackmun and Lewis F. Powell, Jr., now both retired), who have supported opinions favoring the death penalty, publicly reversed their positions. The death penalty also was debated on *Firing Line* in the summer of 1994, in part because of allegations of unfairness. For example, in Georgia, "if the defendant is black and the victim is white, you are 22 times more likely to get the death penalty," say Bryan A. Stevenson and Stephen B. Bright, who are fighting capi-tal punishment in the southern states that account for 90 percent of executions in the United States.[2] Recent public argument about the death penalty reminds us that even much-argued, familiar issues can become lively once again.

Another rhetorical obstacle that may lurk in a subject's history is a taboo against discussing it. Consider, for example, almost any subject having to do with sexuality in the United States, dramatically illus-trated by public policy disputes over the prevention and treatment of

---

[2]Walter Goodman, "Debating Fairness of Capital Punishment," *New York Times*, July 1, 1994, p. B9. Since 1970, about 50 people have been freed from death row after their convictions were reversed or thrown out, a datum that suggests how real the possibility of executing an innocent person might be (Dirk Johnson, "Back to Family from Life on Death Row," *New York Times*, September 25, 1994, p. 10Y).

AIDS (acquired immune deficiency syndrome). The virus causing AIDS is spread primarily through sexual contacts, and AIDS cases in the United States initially appeared predominantly among the gay male community. As a result, AIDS involved two areas considered taboo by many—sexual acts and homosexuality. Consequently, policy makers and physicians found it hard to discuss, and actions to enhance prevention and to improve treatment were slow. Even now, with more detailed information about AIDS all over the world and an increasing number of cases caused by heterosexual contact, proposals to provide sex education in elementary schools and condoms to high school students in order to encourage safer behavior remain controversial. Many of us seem to want to deny that teenagers or subteens are sexually active and find blatant reminders of their sexuality deeply disturbing, even if providing condoms would help protect them from sexually transmitted diseases and AIDS and lower rates of abortion by preventing unwanted pregnancies. Discussion of issues such as pornography, venereal disease, rape, incest, and wife killing and wife battering arouse resistance among some audiences. Some of these taboos are breaking down; the subjects are beginning to be aired, and the victims are beginning to get help. But if you talk about these subjects, you must choose your audiences and your words carefully, or their minds will be so tightly closed against you that no rhetorical action can occur, not even the sharing of basic data.

The cultural history of a subject may also include highly charged emotional reactions. Most taboo subjects have such emotional loads. Arab–Israeli relations are highly charged subjects in Jewish and Arab communities. Racism and its remedies, general homosexual rights, or policies toward gays and lesbians in the military are hot-button issues in the United States. These topics produce intense emotional reactions in audiences. If you choose such a subject, you can expect to face several obstacles falling under the general headings of conditioned responses and closed minds.

One sure sign of a hot subject is a loaded slogan associated with it. In recent debates over legalized abortion in the United States, opponents have chanted "right to life." This slogan not only provokes a strong conditioned response and effectively closes minds to any discussion, but in any debate it labels abortion opponents as defenders of life and proponents of safe and legal abortion in the position of murderers. Thus, proponents have been forced to come up with a slogan of their own, "pro-choice" (or sometimes "voluntary motherhood"), which moves the debate to different ground. In 1992, Republicans associated their platform with "family values," but that phrase became tangled up with Vice President Dan Quayle's attacks on *Murphy Brown* as advocating single parenthood. Then, at the 1992 national convention, the phrase seemed to symbolize an attack on those who were not part of old-fashioned families or who favored reproductive choice and gay rights, partly because of the vivid language used by former Republican presidential candidate and CNN's *Crossfire* regular Pat Buchanan in a prime-time address. In 1994, Republicans abandoned that phrase and tried out a new one, "personal responsibility agenda." The advantage of such a phrase is that it sums up a body of values and beliefs, but as the 1992 experience illustrates, a phrase can develop undesirable connotations.

With any such emotionally loaded subject, your problem is to structure the discussion so issues can be treated apart from predictable and intense emotional responses—in short, to open closed minds, if only a little way.

Closely related to highly charged emotional reactions is the intense resistance created by subjects that conflict with revered cultural values. Anyone who chooses energy conservation as a subject will have to contend, for example, with the U.S. love affair with the automobile. Independence and personal autonomy have been ultimate goods in our culture for many decades, making the automobile's value part of our history. Bigger was better, greater speed and power were symbols of personal power and wealth, and driving bigger, faster, and more powerful cars that used more gas was a symbol of success. Faced with rising oil prices and greater dependence on foreign sources for petroleum, some voices argue that smaller is better, that policies need to encourage the construction and use of rapid transit systems. But until such energy-sensitive values establish themselves, efforts to persuade people to limit their energy consumption, to pollute less, and to protect the environment will run head-on into the value of independence and the long cultural history of the automobile as the symbol of success. And if minds are not actually closed to policies to conserve energy by reducing driving, they are certainly resistant, as reflected in rising sales of trucks and vans, most of which are gas guzzlers.

The second major set of rhetorical obstacles arising from your subject and purpose, then, lies in what I have called cultural history. Specifically, the obstacles are boredom, conflicts with cultural values, taboos, emotional loads, and the closed minds that can result.

PURPOSE-RELATED OBSTACLES

As a rhetor, you will not just deal with a subject; you will also try to induce a certain kind of participation from the audience. The kind of response that you seek may create obstacles. The two kinds of obstacles that arise from rhetorical purposes are resistance to the cost of responding and audience perception of having no control over the issue in question (audience members do not see themselves as agents of change).

Cost

Just what is the audience expected to do, and what is the cost in time, energy, money, inconvenience, or ridicule? The greater such costs to audience members, the smaller the chance that they will do what you ask. If you are typical college students, some of you smoke and few of you exercise enough, and many of you eat lots of junk food. In the face of medical evidence, no one argues that smoking is good for your health, that exercise is unnecessary, or that junk food will lengthen your life. Why, then, do so many Americans smoke, live sedentary lives, and eat junk food? The answer is that doing otherwise would cost them too much—too much agony or at least considerable discomfort to quit smoking, too much sustained thought and effort to fit exercise into their lives, and too much loss of pleasure from giving up Twinkies and french fries. Thus, if your purpose is to change any one of these habits, you will meet solid obstacles in the form of the costs the audience sees in what you are suggesting. In fact, no single rhetorical act is likely to achieve this kind of purpose, although Americans are extremely vulnerable to advertising for products that promise that you can stop smoking without discomfort, exercise painlessly, or lose weight without changing eating habits. Smoking clinics, exercise programs, and diet groups that succeed have long-term contact with participants and supply consistent support from people struggling with similar problems or toward similar goals.

Time is another cost that may obstruct your rhetorical purpose. For example, it is much faster (and easier) to write a check to a political candidate than to telephone all the Democrats, Republicans, or United We Stand, America, members in a precinct; this telephoning, in turn, is easier than going door to door to distribute literature and discuss a candidate. The greater the time, the energy, or the commitment demanded by your purpose, the greater the resistance you will meet.

Still other costs may be involved in your purpose—costs in money and expertise. Your audience may not have to contribute to either one directly but may feel the burden in other ways, such as higher taxes or smaller amounts of money or expertise available for other projects.

Finally, cost is closely related to cultural values; these are the social costs of some subjects and purposes. Some beliefs bring down ridicule and other social sanctions on the believers. Because all of us want to be liked and respected by our friends, neighbors, and family, a subject or purpose that would separate us exacts a cost that few are willing to pay, and then, only if the rewards are substantial. For example, nineteenth-century woman's rights activists recognized that what came to be called the "bloomer" costume was both healthy and comfortable. Its loose harem-style pants under knee-length skirts were far better for nurturing or housework than fashionably long dresses whose skirts trailed in the dirt and weighed up to 20 pounds and whose narrow waists, cinched by stays, cut off breath and circulation. Yet even the most stalwart gave up bloomers because the ridicule heaped on them was so consistent and so great that it threatened their cause. Similarly, it is hard for a Roman Catholic to espouse free choice on abortion, a car manufacturer to support rapid transit, or an evangelical Christian to endorse the Supreme Court decision outlawing prayer in public schools. There are exceptions, of course, but those who take such stances often pay a high social price.

The rhetorical problem of cost, then, measures the price the audience must pay in time, energy, inconvenience, commitment, money, expertise, or social pressure for going along with your purpose. The more your purpose demands from the audience in such costs, the greater will be your rhetorical problem.

Control

The second obstacle arising from purpose, *control,* is the audience's perception that it has no control over an outcome. Obstacles arise when members of the audience cannot see what they as individuals can do or do not believe that their actions will have any appreciable effect. For example, many Americans fail to vote because they think their votes make no difference—all politicians are alike, no one vote counts, they don't know how to nominate and elect officials who will do what they want, and so forth. Such feelings illustrate the rhetorical problem of control.

Lack of a sense of control can have other undesirable side effects. Some commentators, for example, have argued that because antiabortion activists have not been able to prevail through nonviolent tactics, some have come to accept violence, including the condoning of the murders or attempted murders of physicians who perform abortions. Deep commitment plus loss of control may lead to extremism.

Problems of control are closely related to problems of the audience—specifically, the audience as agents of change and as created through rhetorical action (see Chapter 3). If rhetors are to overcome obstacles to control, they must ensure that rhetorical action engages those who are or can be agents of change. But the obstacles to control that exist in audience perceptions are difficult to overcome. How does one convince women who are socialized to passivity and deference that they should take the initiative? How does one counteract generations of social influence that has taught African American children that they are inferior and ugly? Given the presidential power to deploy hundreds of thousands of troops prior to the vote, how does one convince members of Congress to vote against an authorization to invade Haiti or to defend Kuwait? The rhetorical efforts of feminists, of African Americans such as Jesse Jackson, and of politicians, protesters, and columnists writing and speaking about the war in the Gulf are examples of attempts to overcome the obstacle of control or, if you will, to empower the audience.

Obstacles related to control—and also to cost—exist for all audiences. It is easier to act once and be done with it than to commit yourself to a long-term course of action. If an audience feels unable to make a long-term commitment, it may refuse to act at all. Usually, it is easier to act alone than to organize a group. If a rhetorical act demands group action, individual audience members may not believe that others will join them in the effort. It is also easier to act if a problem is relatively limited and sharply defined than if the problem is complex and calls for varied and sustained actions.

Rhetorical obstacles arising from control are partly a function of audience characteristics. If rhetors are to overcome problems of control, they must not only target the audience carefully, but they also must see that the target audience includes agents of change or those who can influence such agents' decisions.

Obstacles arising from purpose are related to obstacles arising from the subject. For example, the problem of control will be greater if the issue is diffuse and complex, and if its ramifications are so great that achieving results requires the concerted and varied efforts of a large group of people over a long span of time.

ANALYSIS OF OBSTACLES

These four obstacles embedded in the subject (complexity, cultural history) and purpose (cost, control) can be illustrated by such topics as health care reform, gun control, and sex education and condom distribution.

Health Care Reform

In 1992, presidential candidate Bill Clinton made health care reform a central part of his platform. After some two years of speaking by representatives of his administration and debate by owners of small businesses, health insurance companies, and medical personnel and organizations, very few people felt that they fully understood the issues involved in health care reform, and even fewer were sure just what plan would be best. The complexity arose because of issues of financing (Should there be an employer mandate requiring businesses with more than 10 or 20 or 50 employees to pay the cost of health insurance? Should there be no such mandate? Would a single-payer plan financed by the government be the most efficient?), of coverage (Should the goal be universal coverage, despite its expense?), of access to medical personnel and services (Will patients be allowed to choose their physicians? Will medical care have to be rationed?), of regulation (How can costs be prevented from rising? How can quality medical care be assured?), and of encouraging competition (Are health care alliances or "managed competition" a way to hold costs down?).[3] Because there were so many issues, some argued that reforms should be introduced slowly because their effects would be hard to predict. Some argued that there was no health care crisis, an appeal to inertia and to the notion that changes might make the situation worse than it already was. In the Republican response to President Clinton's 1994 State of the Union address, Senate minority leader Robert Dole displayed an intricate chart that was supposed to reflect the complex layers of government bureaucracy that would be created by the plan that Clinton had proposed. One reaction to complexity is withdrawal from the issue, a decision to leave things as they are.

If you are a typical layperson, you've found the preceding material and this type of public discussion somewhat complicated. You may have found yourself skimming quickly to avoid all the detail. If so, you illustrate the rhetorical problem and its effect on an audience. Even the relatively limited question of whether "managed competition" is economically feasible is so complex that it is hard to talk about to an average audience. Note that complexity arises because you lack firsthand experience with the data, and that considerable expertise is required to evaluate the evidence and determine the assumptions on which it rests. The problem is compounded by conflicting

---

[3]See Robin Toner, "Streamlining the Ungainly" (On Language), *New York Times Magazine,* July 25, 1993, pp. 12, 14, for the problems political reporters faced in trying to convert this complex issue into digestible news bites.

evidence. Finally, the issue is complex because it is related to so many other issues—jobs, taxes, insurance, government regulation and control, and a whole host of medical questions.

Gun Control

Controversy over gun control is a relatively recent phenomenon. It was only after the 1968 federal Gun Control Act, which addressed interstate commerce, that the popular debate over rights and violence began. Subsequently, the National Rifle Association (NRA) began an intense campaign to prevent any further restrictions on gun ownership; in response, pro-control organizations formed, chiefly Gun Control, Inc. After some two and half decades of legislative effort, only modest restrictions were enacted—a partial ban on assault weapons and the Brady Law on the federal level and various waiting periods and buyer checks at the state level.[4]

Although the courts consistently have interpreted the Second Amendment as protecting only state-run militias, not individual gun ownership, it is popularly believed that individuals have a right "to keep and bear arms." That belief is grounded in a long-standing English tradition that people have a right to arm themselves,[5] which has been bolstered by nostalgic patriotic sentiment linked to the American Revolution.[6] Underlying it is the assumption that a well-armed citizenry is the last, best defense against governmental oppression. Overlaid on this belief is the cherished cultural history of the pioneers, whose personal armament was essential for self-preservation.[7] This cultural history is a rich source of anti-control appeals.

---

[4]A federal crime bill that bans 19 specific assault weapons as well as models altered slightly to skirt the ban and that makes it a federal crime to sell handguns to minors or for minors to possess a handgun under most circumstances stalled in Congress in summer 1994 in part because of these provisions (*New York Times,* July 29, 1994, p. A9), but eventually was passed and signed into law by President Clinton. Currently, some states are challenging the law. Connecticut also toughened its gun control laws, establishing a licensing system for buying guns that closed a loophole in the earlier law that allowed people to buy guns legally and resell them to felons and teenagers, who could not buy them legally. All handgun transfers, whether by sale or gift, must be reported to state and local police. Licenses are not required for guns already owned; it is estimated that in 1994 there were a million and a half handguns in Connecticut homes (George Judson, "Connecticut Toughens Gun Control Laws," *New York Times,* July 8, 1994, p. A12Y).

[5]W. Freedman, *The Privilege to Keep and Bear Arms* (New York: Quorum Books, 1989).

[6]S. Halbrook, *A Right to Bear Arms: State and Federal Bills of Rights and Constitutional Guarantees* (New York: Greenwood Press, 1989), p. ix.

[7]Richard Hofstader, "America as a Gun Culture," in *The Gun Control Debate,* ed. L. Nisbet (Buffalo, NY: Prometheus Books, 1990), pp. 25–34.

Building on this sense of a guaranteed right, the NRA and other pro-gun lobbies have mounted a "slippery slope" attack on any restriction on guns or ammunition. The argument is supported by the phrase "shall not infringe" in the Second Amendment. Any legislative control is painted as an unwarranted restriction on personal freedom, analogous to arguments that any restriction on free speech opens the door to a wholesale loss of rights. Consequently, the NRA has been absolutely intransigent, treating any form of control (waiting periods, licensure restrictions, partial bans, and the like) as the first step toward an eventual total ban. In addition, because of the wide availability of weapons on the black market, bans can be trumpeted as "disarming the citizenry" and favoring the criminals. For instance, the NRA successfully lobbied to protect Teflon ammunition (which pierces the bulletproof vests police wear) for sporting and target purposes on the grounds that a ban would set a dangerous precedent.[8]

Issues involved in gun control are also complex. Measuring the effect of guns on violence is extremely difficult because social scientific methodologies are highly manipulable.[9] Indeed, no consistent figures are available about guns and violence because of the varied and incommensurate methods used in different studies. Facts and figures, however, have a powerful, scientific appeal. As a result, the public is bombarded with a mass of contradictory quantitative evidence, all of relatively equal truth value, which gives no clear picture of the problem. Furthermore, police generally oppose control precisely because of the deterrence argument,[10] and because they are seen as authorities on law and order, gun control advocates seem, by comparison, to be favoring disorder.

Emphasis on the individual rather than the group is the basis for powerful fear appeals about personal security. Although even the most conservative estimates indicate that the risk of gun accidents and homicide are much greater from family and friends than from strangers, home protection against the evil intruder is a compelling issue for pro-gun lobbies.[11] Indeed, it is estimated that roughly half the homes

---

[8]D. Hook, *Gun Control: The Continuing Debate* (Bellevue, WA: Second Amendment Foundation, 1993), p. 105.

[9]W. Tonso, "Social Problems and Sagecraft: Gun Control as a Case in Point," in *The Gun Control Debate,* ed. L. Nisbet (Buffalo, NY: Prometheus Books, 1990), pp. 35–53.

[10]Hook, p. 153.

[11]A. Kellermann, and D. Reay, "Protection or Peril? An Analysis of Firearm-Related Deaths in the Home," in *The Gun Control Debate,* ed. L. Nisbet (Buffalo, NY: Prometheus Books, 1990, pp. 239–244, cited material on pp. 241–242; M. Yeager, J. Alviani, and N. Laing, "How Well Does the Handgun Protect You and Your Family?" *ibid.,* pp. 213–238, cited material on p. 218.

in the nation have guns on the premises.[12] Some evidence supports defensive gun use. For example, reports of defensive gun use are generally thought to be as common as actual arrests of those using guns in the commission of a crime, and in a widely publicized survey of convicted criminals, the majority indicated that they would be deterred by a potential victim with a gun.[13] Coupled with the appearance of crime at or near the top of public "worry lists," arguments for personal protection strike a responsive chord in many legislators and voters regardless of the quality of the evidence on which they rest.

Such risk analysis, however, is weighted in terms of individuals. If one shifts to a collective emphasis, the weaknesses of the emphasis on individuals become apparent. Few people are at risk from strangers, so disarming law-abiding citizens has little impact on individual risk. Limiting weapons in the home, however, directly reduces the availability of lethal weapons to the most common perpetrators of violence—friends and family. A study of homicides in three metropolitan areas reported in the *New England Journal of Medicine* found that instead of increasing protection, a handgun in the home almost triples the chances that someone will be killed there.[14] Such a shift in thinking is important to weighing the effectiveness of gun control measures, but it is a perspective largely absent from the gun control debate. To that extent the gun culture built around the armed individual fending off a dangerous world is a serious obstacle to gun control. In fact, restrictions that might do little good in the "showdown with

---

[12]Kellermann and Reay, p. 239.

[13]G. Kleck, "Crime Control Through the Private Use of Armed Force," in *The Gun Control Debate,* ed. L. Nisbet (Buffalo, NY: Prometheus Books, 1990), pp. 275–293, cited material on pp. 284–285.

[14]The researchers looked at homicides from August 1987 to August 1992 in Shelby County, Tenn., which includes Memphis, and in King County, Wash., which includes Seattle. Another team looked at murders in Cuyahoga County, Ohio, which includes Cleveland, from January 1990 to August 1992. Studying 420 homicides that occurred in the homes of the victims, about a quarter of the total, the researchers found that most victims, 76.7 percent, were killed by a spouse, family member, or someone they knew, and that in 85 percent of cases there was no forced entry into the home. Gunshot wounds were by far the most common cause of death, killing half, or 49.8 percent, of the victims killed at home. Even in the 14 percent of cases involving forced entry, a gun in the home provided little protection. Dr. Arthur L. Kellermann of Emory University in Atlanta, the lead researcher, said, "Guns were not found to be associated with decreased risk of homicide in any subset or subgroup that we studied, even when we just looked at cases involving forced entry or cases in which the victim actively resisted the assailant." Even when domestic violence and the use of illegal drugs were factored out, the researchers said, they found that the risk of being killed was 2.7 times higher, or nearly triple, in homes with guns than in homes without them (Warren E. Leary, "Gun in Home? Study Finds It a Deadly Mix," *New York Times,* October 7, 1993, p. A10).

criminals" scenario might be quite effective in reducing the numbers of gun deaths in other, more common scenarios—disputes between family members and friends.

Given the lack of clear and cogent data defining the problem, the way in which the debate is framed becomes crucial. That gun control is argued primarily in terms of individualism favors pro-gun lobbies. By focusing attention on individual risk, inconclusive and contradictory evidence linking guns and violence, coupled with appeals to constitutional rights, becomes sufficient to deter action. Further, the burden of proof falls on gun-control advocates who are the authors of various initiatives. When weighed against a vague sense of threat to constitutional rights and personal safety, evidence that is inconclusive, even contradictory, is seldom sufficient proof.

The cost of gunshot wounds to society is rarely considered in this argument. According to the National Centers for Disease Control, in 1988 the total national cost related to gunshot injuries approached $16.2 billion. At the Hennepin County Medical Center in Minneapolis, Minnesota, which admitted 165 patients with gunshot wounds in 1992, the average cost per hospitalization for a gunshot victim in 1992 was $15,390, which did not include physician charges, rehabilitation costs, follow-up visits, long-term care, legal fees, or lost work time.[15]

Sex Education and Condom Distribution

As noted in Chapter 13, cultural history is significant in debates over sex education and distribution of condoms in schools. Parents who feel uncomfortable talking about sexual matters are also unhappy at the thought of sex education in a public classroom. Parents would like to believe that their children are not sexually active, a belief that is challenged when condoms are distributed in schools. Some parents feel a loss of control over their children when such policies are proposed and strongly oppose them. Many have no personal experience of teens who have been infected with AIDS or other sexually transmitted diseases and wrongly believe that such illnesses pose no threat to their children, only to "bad kids." Some may feel that only the threat of pregnancy or serious disease can deter sexual promiscuity, which leads them to oppose such programs. Some fear that sex education in schools will be taught without consideration for moral issues or for the psychological impact of early sexual experiences on youngsters.

---

[15]Douglas D. Brunette, a physician at the Hennepin County Medical Center, "State Must Act to Halt Gun Violence," *Star Tribune,* July 13, 1993, p. 13A.

Some oppose sex education or condom distribution on religious grounds.

Dr. Joseph A. Fernandez, former Chancellor of Schools in New York City, for example, was committed to sex education and condom distribution in the schools in that city and defended them as ways to prevent illness and pregnancy. He and some of his vocal constituents disagreed on these issues, and his stance became a factor that led to his dismissal in the early part of 1993. A subsequent poll of parents revealed that many of them agreed with his opinions, but by then, he had already been dismissed. The controversy surrounding Fernandez's stance on these issues is a dramatic illustration of resistance to such proposals based on concerns related to cultural history and subjects that many treat as taboo.

SUMMARY

These brief analyses illustrate the four major obstacles—complexity, cultural history, cost, and control—and their relationship to the demands of subject and purpose on the audience. In preparing for rhetorical action, you will need to analyze your subject and purpose to consider the demands you will make on the audience. In this way you will be able to see in advance the obstacles you must overcome to achieve your goal.

All the problems I have described are directly related to the rhetorical purposes presented in Chapter 1. In terms of those purposes, the complexity of a problem like health care reform interferes with altering perception or providing an explanation the audience will consider. Cultural history—the beliefs, values, and attitudes of the culture and community—influences all the rhetorical purposes. Opening your mind to information that may force you to reconsider "how things really are" demands setting aside your past experience and preparing for new experience. Obviously, explanations and new beliefs may conflict with prior values, opinions, and attitudes, disrupting a settled pattern of beliefs. Thus, all rhetorical action exacts some price from the audience. The kinds of costs I have detailed, however, arise particularly from attempts to formulate or alter belief and channel it into specific action.

The problems of control arise most forcefully when an audience is asked to make a commitment that will inevitably lead to action. Audience members must believe that it matters whether they act; without such belief no reader or listener can be a member of the target audience or an agent of change.

To summarize the ideas in this chapter, here is an outline of the obstacles that arise out of subject and purpose. Use it as a checklist when trying to choose a subject and an approach.

Summary Outline

I. What sorts of demands does the subject make on the audience?

A. Does the complexity of the subject make special demands on the audience?

1. Do members of the audience have access to firsthand experience or must all data come indirectly from others?

2. Is special expertise required to interpret basic information on this subject?

3. Is evaluating the credibility and authority of secondary sources an inevitable part of this topic?

B. How does cultural history create resistance?

1. Do cultural values inhibit public discussion of this subject?

2. What problems are created by traditional, familiar arguments and by famous pieces of evidence?

3. Have past discussions created slogans or concepts that must be refuted or reformulated?

4. What beliefs, attitudes, or values held by the audience will conflict with the specific purpose?

II. What sorts of demands does the purpose make on the audience?

A. What special costs are exacted from the audience by the response desired?

1. How much inconvenience and discomfort must the audience undergo in order to believe or act as the rhetor desires?

2. How much time, energy, and commitment are required to achieve the desired goal?

3. How much money and expertise must be expended to achieve the goal?

4. How much social resistance from family, friends, and neighbors will the audience encounter in accepting the rhetor's claims?

B. How much control does the audience have in achieving the desired outcome? How much control does the audience perceive itself as having?

1. Is the audience that is exposed to the rhetorical act the group most directly involved in the issue or purpose?

2. Are those exposed the actual agents of change or do they have an influence on these agents?

3. Can one act alone or is concerted action required?

4. Is a single act enough or must one commit oneself to a series of actions to achieve the goal?

5. Is the needed action simple, obvious, and likely to produce an immediate reward, or is it complex, difficult to discern, and hard to evaluate?

▪ ▪ ▪

MATERIAL FOR ANALYSIS

Although the Israeli government and the Palestine Liberation Organization (PLO) headed by Yasser Arafat have signed a peace agreement that includes giving the PLO political control of the Gaza Strip and the city of Jericho, there is still much disagreement about whether such a peace process can work. In the summer of 1994, King Hussein of Jordan and Yitzhak Rabin, the prime minister of Israel, met to sign agreements leading to a peace treaty between their nations. Other issues of great importance remain to be settled. One of them, political control of the city of Jerusalem, has been addressed in a later essay by the same author.[16] This essay by Letty Cottin Pogrebin, which is adapted from an article that originally appeared in the journal *Tikkun*,[17] addresses the issues involved in negotiations between Israel and the PLO. Consider carefully how she addresses resistance based on cultural history, a particularly important source of resistance for the Jewish audience she targets, control (How does one negotiate with a sworn enemy?), and cost (balancing one kind of cost against others is an important part of her argument).

---

[16]Letty Cottin Pogrebin, "Two Forevers and a Maybe," *Tikkun* 8 (November/December 1993):72–74. Reprinted from *Tikkun* Magazine, **a bi-monthly Jewish critique of politics, culture, and society.** Subscriptions are $31.00 per year from *Tikkun*, 251 West 100th St., 5th floor, New York, NY 10025.

[17]"When Cant Becomes Can't—Or, How to Argue with Intransigents," *Tikkun* 3 (September/October 1988):56–59. This slightly edited version is from *Jewish Women's Call for Peace: A Handbook for Jewish Women on the Israeli/Palestinian Conflict*, edited and published by the Jewish Women's Committee to End the Occupation of the West Bank and Gaza (JWCEO) of New York City in 1990, pp. 49–53. This essay was brought to my attention by Sandra Berkowitz, now a professor at Wayne State University. For additional information on the JWCEO, see her Ph.D. dissertation, "Challenging Holocaust Ideology: Jewish Women Call for Peace," University of Minnesota, 1994.

When *Cant* Becomes *Can't*—
Or, How to Argue with Intransigents

1   Lately, when advocating peace in the Middle East, it seems necessary to establish one's Zionist credentials. So, first, some background: My grandparents made *aliyah*[18] in the 1930s; my grandfather was killed in Tiberias during an Arab raid; and I was raised to understand that the UJA [United Jewish Appeal], ZOA [Zionist Organization of America], JNF [Jewish National Fund], Pioneer Women [now known as Na'amat], Hadassah, and State of Israel Bonds[19] were as important to my parents as if these organizations were members of our own family.

2   My own commitments are those of a Jewish feminist. Among other things, this means that I look at Zionism and feminism as parallel movements of group liberation. I am a peace activist because I am a Jew and a woman, and I understand what it means to fear powerlessness and to want to secure one's safety and one's freedom.

3   Furthermore, I believe *anachnu am echad:* We are one people, and what happens to Israel happens to Jews everywhere. Therefore, I make no apology for saying *we*—not *they*—when I refer to Israel. *They* I reserve for our enemies. I know Israel has enemies, and I want us to come to terms with them—for our sake, not theirs.

4   All of this sounds logical and reasonable; so what is the problem? The problem is cant. Two kinds of cant. The first, *c-a-n-t,* is defined in the dictionary as the expression or repetition of stock phrases, opinions, or sentiments. This kind of cant feeds the second, *c-a-n-'-t:* intransigent negativism—i.e., we can't do this, we can't do that.

5   Cant statements, endlessly repeated, sound like this:

"There's no one to talk to."

"They always kill their own moderates."

"We can't trust them."

"We can't forget history."

---

[18]Literally, "going up," generally referring to being called up to the Torah to recite the blessings, but it also refers to immigrating to Israel.

[19]UJA and ZOA are U.S. organizations that provide a substantial amount of financial support to Israel as well as political support for U.S. lobbies; the JNF and State of Israel Bonds provide U.S. money to Israel for purchase and development of land; Pioneer Women and Hadassah are both organizations of U.S. Jewish women that support Israeli interests in the United States and abroad.

"We can't deal with people who want to destroy us."

"We can't give up the Territories because Israel needs them for its security."

6   There may be some truth to each assertion—but not the whole truth. The whole truth lies in subtleties and nuances; it must be coaxed out with sensitivity and skill. Instead, these cant statements are becoming doctrine in themselves. They are becoming calcified barriers to movement, the cant that leads to "we can't"—to utter hopelessness and chaos. And, more than the language of intransigence, these cant phrases are becoming code words for loyalty—which explains why I feel the need to present my Zionist credentials before I write or speak, and why so many Jews seem paralyzed.

7   Nevertheless, I think it is urgent to challenge the naysayers, to answer the cant and get at the whole truth.

"There's No One to Talk To"

8   As many have said, one negotiates with one's adversaries, not one's friends. Therefore, we must be willing to talk to any Palestinian or combined Arab–Palestinian delegation that can deliver a permanent peace. Our business is to police the results, not the delegates. Israel cannot choose its negotiating partners any more than the United States can choose the Soviet representatives at Geneva. At Camp David, [Anwar] Sadat would have preferred to talk to Ezer Weizmann, and [President Jimmy] Carter wanted to negotiate with Moshe Dayan. Both leaders had to accept that Israel was to be represented by Menachem Begin, and it was Begin who made peace because his people empowered him to do so. A check is meaningless without money in the bank.

9   At this point, it is clear that the conflict in the Middle East is first and foremost between Israel and the Palestinians, and, where the Palestinians are concerned, the PLO [Palestine Liberation Organization headed by Yasser Arafat] has money in the bank. We cannot bypass them. They have done hateful things to us, but in the eyes of their own people they symbolize self-determination and national identity. As Drora Kass, of the International Center for Peace in the Middle East, puts it, "To want to negotiate with Palestinians who are not identified with the PLO is like wanting to negotiate with Israelis who are not Zionists."

10   In any case, questions of Palestinian internal politics are their problem—or will be once we get the burden of the PLO off our backs and onto the backs of the Palestinians. But first we have to endure a transitional period during which they are our negotiating partners. Although we may recoil at the idea of sitting down with the authors of so much terrorism and savagery, Abba Eban

reminds us that, if we're keeping score, Egypt, Syria, and Jordan have killed far more Jews than the PLO visited upon us in 33 years.

11   The point is that the Jordanians killed more Jews than the PLO, yet we've been insisting that Jordan be a negotiating party. And the Egyptians killed more Jews than the PLO, yet we've made peace with Egypt—a peace that has been maintained through it all: Egypt's ostracism, Sadat's assassination, Israel's Iraqi raid, the Lebanon incursion, and the current uprising. Land for peace can work. Jewish lives can be spared. For that, we can give peace a chance.

12   Finally, if we could negotiate with the PLO for the release of 1,100 terrorists in return for two Israeli soldiers, why can't we negotiate with them for a settlement that will save the lives of hundreds or thousands of Israeli soldiers and civilians?

13   There *are* people to talk to on the other side. We may not like them, but they're there. And nobody dies from talking.

"They Always Kill Their Own Moderates"

14   Yes, the extremists murdered Hamami and Sartawi and Kawasi. And today Hanna Siniora[20] could be killed for advancing a compromise position, and Fayet Abu Rahme, the head of the Gaza lawyers' association, is probably in danger from his own far-right and far-left flanks for favoring a demilitarized state and for assuring the world that "Palestinian police will be unarmed and if necessary barefoot and in bathing suits."

15   One might comment that, given the deaths and intimidation, it is remarkable that there still are Palestinians willing to speak out. Yet again, at the risk of sounding insensitive, that's *their* problem. It only becomes our problem when we encourage Palestinian extremists by punishing their moderates for them. At this writing, we have deported 3,000 Palestinians, put 1,700 under "administrative arrest" without due process, arrested the lawyers who tried to defend them, and thrown 20 of their journalists in jail.

16   We cling to the fantasy that we can invalidate the Palestinian cause by eliminating the most viable Palestinian leaders. But punishing moderation doesn't soften one's opponents; it hardens them. In a sense, then, *Israel* has made the PLO the sole representative of the Palestinian people and left us with "no one to talk to."

17   Self-interest commands us to do just the opposite to create what David Grossman calls "bulletproof Palestinians," to validate

---

[20]Hanna Siniora is the moderate Palestinian Christian editor of *al-Fajr* who developed a 1988 plan that called for nonviolent civil disobedience; she is a close friend of Arafat.

the most reasonable voices and help make their extremists a threat to *their* self-interest. At the moment, the moderates seem to be holding sway. Remarkably, after the assassination of Abu Jihad, not one Palestinian disregarded the *intifada*'s rock-throwing strategy and took up guns. We need responsible Palestinian leaders to rise to positions of leadership—not for them, but because *we* need worthy counterparts with whom to negotiate.

"We Can't Trust Them"

18   That's true. In fact, we can't trust anyone. In 1975 the United States met secretly with the PLO while promising not to negotiate with Palestinians. Ronald Reagan calls himself a friend of Israel but, despite Jewish pleas, he sold AWACs to the Saudis and he went to Bitburg.

19   Reaching a peace settlement in the Middle East is not a question of trust. It's a question of negotiating a demilitarized Palestinian entity and creating protections and treaties based on vested interests and careful guarantees. Moreover, Israel is the fifth strongest military power in the world. If it can bomb atomic reactors in Iraq and get to Tunis in seconds, its early-warning systems and sophisticated armaments can deal with Palestinian encroachments. In the past, Israel has faced seven Arab armies. For 40 years it has had strong Arab countries on all of its borders. Why direct so much fear toward one small demilitarized state?

"We Can't Forget History"

20   I agree, but we must be informed by history, not captive to it. History is static, but we are in flux. What was, *was*—but we are responsible for what will be.

21   I am not willing to bequeath to my children a lifetime of insecurity and war. Since we are a state as well as a people, we must not look just at the history of the Jews but at the history of other nations.

22   We must learn from the mistakes in Vietnam, Lebanon, Algeria, Cyprus, Belfast, and South Africa. We must be aware of the follies of rulers. We must recognize that annexation brings disaster. Binationalism has proved a failure wherever it has been tried, and no nation has oppressed another people for long without poisoning a part of itself. History should teach us what we need from a peace treaty, not how to retreat from peacemaking.

"We Can't Deal with People Who Want to Destroy Us"

23   Yes, the PLO covenants of 1964 and 1968 contain an outright commitment to destroy Israel, and, yes, it would be a major breakthrough if the PLO leaders disavowed it. But they won't. First, they do not understand how the world's fifth most powerful military force can be afraid of their words. And, second, if we *are* afraid, then they will use words as a bargaining chip.

24   In any case, the covenant has already been superseded by 14 years of Palestine National Council meetings in which Palestinian leaders have recognized the need to make a political accommodation with Israel. (The last three PNC meetings have dropped all references to destroying Israel and to erecting a democratic, secular Palestinian state in its place.) Likewise, the Hussein–Arafat agreement of 1985, and the Arab summits at Fez in 1982 and Amman in 1987, recognized the principle of land for peace. And, at the Arab summit meeting in Algiers this summer, Bassam Abu Sharif, PLO spokesperson and Arafat adviser, affirmed the goals of lasting peace with Israel, mutual security, direct talks under international auspices, and political and economic cooperation.

25   Yehoshafat Harkabi, the former head of Israeli military intelligence who first translated the PLO covenant and brought it to the attention of the world, says it has no meaning. He distinguishes between the Arab "Grand Design" and real policy; that is, between cocky rhetoric and pragmatism. The rhetoric is to destroy Israel; the policy is evolving toward territory for peace.

26   Sure, they say they want Jaffa and Haifa; some on our side say we want Jericho and Nablus. One person's dream is another's nightmare. Lately, we too have a "Grand Design": the manifest destiny of the Bible and the rhetoric of a Greater Israel. We, too, have our inflammatory taunters: Begin, who called Palestinians "animals on two legs"; Shamir, who equated Palestinians with "grasshoppers"; and former general Rafael Eytan, who labeled them "drugged cockroaches." Just as we hear some Palestinians demanding Jaffa and Haifa, the Palestinians hear Yuval Neeman of Tehiya jeering, "Before we talk to them, we will deport 600,000 of them."

27   Jewish concern for the rhetoric of destruction boils down to one question: Will the Palestinians accept Israel's right to exist? I favor negotiations with no preconditions. I don't think we need anyone else to tell us that we exist. Israel has been recognized by the United Nations. The United States is its declared ally. Egypt signed a peace treaty with it. Syria signed a cease-fire agreement. You don't sign documents with a state that doesn't exist. In order simply to come to the table to negotiate, Israel doesn't need to be legitimated by the Palestinians. We know we're a nation and we know we're a people. We must not let ourselves be defined from without; we must define ourselves from within.

"We Can't Give Up the Territories Because
Israel Needs Them for Its Security"

28   On the contrary, the Territories are a liability, and Israel's security would be best served by a negotiated withdrawal. This conclusion has been reached not only by Joseph Alpher of the Jaffee Center for Strategic Studies, but by two of Israel's former directors of military intelligence, Harkabi and Aharon Yaariv. Harkabi says that it is easier to defend against bad borders than a hostile population in one's midst, and he asks us to imagine the United States trying to control 120 million angry Russians inside our borders. Yaariv says our failure to negotiate a Palestinian settlement could bring about a rapprochement among the Arab countries, inspire a military coalition, and lead to war.

29   Trading territory for security is favored by almost every former general of the Israel Defense Force; by 1,700 of the highest-ranking reserve officers; by Motti Hod, former commander of the Israeli Air Force; by Benjamin Ben Eliezer ("Fuad"), the former military governor on the West Bank; and by Ze'ev Schiff, the security affairs expert for the Israeli newspaper *Ha'aretz.*

30   These people are not bleeding hearts or renegade American Jews. They are Israel's top security strategists and military heroes, and they favor the exchange of land for peace.

31   The right does not have a monopoly on concern about security; our side, too, cares desperately about the survival of the state. But we see the threat differently. We see the status quo as the threat—militarily, demographically, morally, and economically.

32   The unrest has cost three-quarters of a billion dollars in nonmilitary costs because the Occupied Territories are Israel's biggest export market besides the United States. It has cost $300 million in military expenses. It has damaged tourism and hit the construction industry hard. Low-paying service jobs go begging. Arab job attendance is down 30 percent. The economy is suffering. The *intifada* is radicalizing the Israeli Arabs. The army is demoralized as a result of having to defend fanatic settlers and respond to rock-throwing children.

33   There are 1.7 million Palestinians in the Territories. However complicated the current situation may be, our options are really quite simple:

a. Give them equal rights and imperil the Jewish state;

b. Continue to dominate them, and imperil democracy by denying their rights or by annexing the Territories and transferring large portions of their population, thus eroding Israel's moral foundations and prolonging internal hostilities;

c. Withdraw unilaterally without negotiating any treaties;

d. Negotiate our withdrawal from most of the Occupied Territories and support some form of Palestinian self-determination.

34   Clearly (a) and (b) are untenable. I believe a unilateral solution (c) offers no long-term strategy for coexistence, precisely because it satisfies Jewish conscience without directly acknowledging the humanity and aspirations of the Palestinians. For the sake of a future relationship between our two peoples, process is as important as product. We cannot just disengage. We must sort out our competing interests and build a new reality based on mutual recognition and mutual guarantees.

35   The fourth option strikes me as the only realistic one. Ideally, Palestinian self-determination would be achieved as part of direct bilateral negotiations among all parties in the area. These negotiations would take place under international auspices, although no country would have the right to impose solutions or to veto agreements. The great powers, however, would buffer potential humiliation for those who make concessions. Ultimately, like many other people, I envision a Benelux situation with Israel living next to Jordan and a demilitarized Palestinian entity with which it has open borders and diplomatic, cultural, and economic exchanges.

36   Right now, such a political solution is possible. Soon it may be too late. Arafat is mending fences with Syria. Jordan has left the Territories to the Palestinians. Pan-Arabism could underwrite a war against Israel. Syria and Jordan in solidarity with the Occupied Territories could force a collapse of the peace with Egypt. The cease-fire between Iraq and Iran may free both countries to pay attention to Israeli–Palestinian tensions. Escalation of hostilities could fuel the fundamentalist elements throughout the Arab world and trigger a religious war between Judaism and Islam. And, as MK Shulamit Aloni has warned, "The God of the Muslims has many more soldiers than the God of the Jews."

37   Harkabi worries that Israel will have to give up the Territories in the future anyway, and at that point our failure would be seen not as misguided national strategy but as a failure of Zionism and the Jewish faith. That is too great a risk—too great a price to pay for the settlers' expansionism and the hard-liners' dreams of glory.

38   I am not sure that our way leads to eternal tranquility, but I am sure that the other way leads to national suicide. If there is even a small chance for negotiations without bloodshed, how dare we ignore it?

Questions for Analysis

1. This essay is targeted to U.S. Jews in order to refute major arguments used in opposition to a peace process that involves withdrawal from the Occupied Territories including some kind of Palestinian self-determination. Describe the rhetorical problem the author faces by identifying the objections she addresses. She never mentions "Holocaust theology," but it is an important factor in Jewish and Israeli resistance. What are the tenets that make up Holocaust theology? How they conflict with her proposal?

2. In addition to refutation, what are the primary strategies the author uses and how do they help her to be persuasive?

3. What are the values to which the author appeals? What ethical principles does she use to warrant her conclusions? How would you evaluate this essay on ethical grounds?

4. A significant motive in contemporary feminism and in twentieth century Zionism is empowerment. Discuss what that concept means and how it functions in this essay. How is this related to the problem of control as it affects this essay?

5. How does the author reduce complexity? How does this essay treat issues related to cultural history? How does she make cultural history work for her?

6. Read the author's subsequent essay on the problem of the city of Jerusalem, "Two Forevers and a Maybe," *Tikkun* 8 (November/December 1993):72–74; then compare and contrast the arguments she makes and the values she upholds in the two essays.

EXERCISE

Coping with Boredom and Hostility

Divide the class into two groups. One group will prepare a list of topics that they think most of their classmates would find uninteresting, such as technical or specialized subjects. The other group will prepare a list of topics that they think will arouse intense hostility from two or more class members, probably highly controversial issues. Each group should compose three or four introductions for their list of topics to be presented by speakers designated by the group.

The introductions for the uninteresting topics should seek to arouse interest, perhaps by presenting a novel point of view, a startling fact, or the like. However, the subject of the speech should be clear to the audience from the introduction.

The introductions for the highly controversial topics should seek to gain a fair and open hearing for a disliked point of view, perhaps by an appeal to self-interest or to the threat of biased or limited exposure, or the like. The controversial point of view should be clear to the audience from the introduction.

Present the introductions from each group. Discuss the strategies that were used, and suggest other possibilities. Discuss which approaches seemed to be more effective, and why.

CHAPTER 5

Obstacles to Source Credibility

Ideas do not walk by themselves; they must be carried—expressed and voiced—by someone. As a result, we do not encounter ideas neutrally, objectively, or apart from a context; we meet them as *someone's* ideas. The relationship between people and ideas is reflected in the way we talk. We speak of Thatcherism, by which we mean the economic ideas associated with former British Prime Minister Margaret Thatcher, ideas she articulated and promoted. We speak of the Elizabethan or Victorian Ages to refer to the periods dominated by the ideas and the leadership of those reigning British monarchs. Similarly, we tend to link qualities to people; for example, particularly courageous women reformers such as abolitionist and woman's rights advocate Anna E. Dickinson and antilynching activist Ida B. Wells were each referred to as a "Joan of Arc." Early advocates heightened the appeal of the woman suffrage amendment by calling it the "Susan B. Anthony Amendment," and when the equal rights amendment was first introduced in 1923, activists followed the earlier precedent by calling it the "Lucretia Mott Amendment" to link it to that intrepid Quaker activist who advocated abolition of slavery, peace, woman's rights, and separation of church and state. Even though science is popularly regarded as impersonal, we speak of Darwin's theory of evolution, Einstein's theory of relativity, Heisenberg's uncertainty principle, and curies of radioactivity (named for Nobel prize–winning chemist Marie Sklodowska Curie). Such language reflects what we all know—that ideas are linked to individuals and that an idea as carried by one person is not the same idea when it is interpreted and defined by another.

The importance of the rhetor in the persuasive process has been recognized since people first began to think and write about the discipline of rhetoric. In the treatise on rhetoric he wrote in the fourth century B.C.E., Aristotle described three paths through which ideas were made persuasive for an audience. One of these he called *ethos,* the character of the rhetor:

> [There is persuasion] through character whenever the speech is spoken in such a way as to make the speaker worthy of credence; for we believe fair-minded people to a greater extent and more quickly [than we do others] on all subjects in general and completely so in cases where there is not exact knowledge but room for doubt . . . character is almost, so to speak, the controlling factor in persuasion. (1.2.1356a.4.)

In other words, one way we are influenced is through our impressions of the rhetor—we accept the idea or believe the claim because we trust and respect the person who presents it. Moreover, says Aristotle, this is particularly true of rhetoric because it deals with social truths, what people in groups agree to believe and value, where certainty is impossible and controversy is likely. Aristotle even suggests that the character of the rhetor may be the most potent source of influence, even more powerful than the arguments and evidence or the needs and motives of the audience.

The power of the rhetor's character or ethos becomes more understandable if we comprehend the meaning of the ancient term. The Greek word *ethos* is closely related to our terms *ethical* and *ethnic.* In its widest modern usage, ethos refers not to the character or personality of an individual but to "the disposition, character, or attitude peculiar to a specific people, culture, or group that distinguishes it from other peoples or groups."[1] When understood this way, its relationship to the word *ethnic* is obvious, for ethnic means "characteristic of a religious, racial, national, or cultural group." Understood this way, ethos refers to the distinctive culture of an ethnic group, and the ethos of an individual depends on how well she or he reflects the qualities valued in that culture. In other words, your ethos refers not to your idiosyncrasies as an individual but to the ways in which you mirror the characteristics idealized by your culture or group. Similarly, *ethics* is "the study of the . . . specific moral choices to be made by the individual in his [or her] relationship with others." In other words, we judge the character of another by the choices that person makes about how he or she will live with other members of the community. What is ethical is right conduct in relation to other persons in one's community

---

[1]The definitions used in this chapter are taken from the *American Heritage Dictionary of the English Language* (Boston: Houghton Mifflin, 1969).

or society. (Ethical principles are the norms or values in a culture that describe what its members believe are the right relationships between persons. The ethos of a rhetor refers to the relationship between the rhetor and the community as reflected in rhetorical action.)

When he described what contributed to the ethos of a rhetor in a rhetorical act, Aristotle wrote that it arose from demonstrated wisdom about social truths (*phronêsis*), from moral excellence (*aretê*), and from evidence that rhetors were well intentioned (*eunoia*) toward their communities. In other words, he believed that members of the community were influenced by evidence of good sense on practical matters of concern to the community, by indications of the rhetor's ethical principles, and by manifestations that the rhetor had the best interests of the community, not just self-interest, in mind. In more contemporary terms, your good sense is a measure of your expertise or competence on an issue, your moral excellence is a measure of your trustworthiness, and your goodwill is a measure of your concern for the community's interests, not just how much you or your family and friends will gain.

Consider how these concepts have affected attitudes toward recent presidents. Carter, for example, is viewed as a person of high moral principles who is dedicated to the good of others. Despite his high intelligence, his wisdom on social matters came to be doubted as he fumbled efforts to influence members of Congress; his diplomatic efforts in North Korea and Haiti in 1994 were questioned for similar reasons, a sense that he was too trusting of those whose past behavior raises questions. Based on a variety of allegations, many had doubts about President Clinton's moral excellence. Those doubts strongly affected approval ratings of his performance even though during his administration the economy was strong and created many jobs, and his foreign policy moves in Haiti, against Saddam Hussein in Iraq, and in relation to North Korea were quite successful. Reagan was seen as well intentioned toward the community, but, especially in retrospect, he was seen as lacking in social wisdom, particularly in delegating too much to subordinates, as illustrated by the problems that arose in relation to what is called the Iran–contra affair. Consider how you would evaluate former President Bush in these terms.

Modern research has demonstrated that Aristotle's views of ethos were remarkably apt. In contemporary studies, ethos is usually defined as the attitude a member of the audience has toward the rhetor (the source of the message) at any given moment. Experimental studies demonstrate that the source of the message has considerable effect on its impact. The earliest studies compared the effects of messages attributed to different sources, and they found that sources with high prestige for an audience had a significantly greater effect. Thus, for example, similar audiences were more favorable toward a message supporting group health care when it came from the surgeon general of the United States than when it was attributed to a Northwestern University sophomore. Studies like these focused on prior ethos, or the attitude that members of the audience have toward the rhetor (the source) before the rhetorical act. Note, however, that ethos is affected by elements of the rhetorical problem. For example, when the original surgeon general's report on the evils of smoking first appeared in 1964, it had little immediate impact on behavior. The decrease in smokers in the United States from over 46 percent of the population to some 25 percent in 1994 occurred slowly. Moreover, no decline has occurred in the percentages of teenagers who smoke despite increasing evidence of the dangers of doing so.

PRIOR ETHOS

Attitudes toward the rhetor before the rhetorical act originate in (1) the rhetor's reputation or track record, (2) the rhetor's appearance, (3) how the rhetor is introduced to the audience, and (4) the context in which the rhetorical act occurs. Because the attitude of the audience toward the source is so important, it is worth noting how each of these can create problems.

Reputation

Although you may not be famous, you have a reputation and a track record that can be as troublesome as that of a famous athlete, politician, or scholar. Two stories about the problems that Jesus had in his hometown of Nazareth are illustrative. On one occasion, Jesus went home and preached in his local synagogue. According to the reports in three gospels, he did a superb job, but those in his local community were not impressed. In effect, his neighbors asked how a local boy could know and do such things—wasn't this the carpenter's son, the son of Mary, whose brothers and sisters they knew? They were offended that an ordinary person whom they knew well should preach and teach so. When Jesus heard what they said, he responded, "A prophet is not without honor, except in his own country, and in his own house" (Matthew 13:54–58; Mark 6:1–6; Luke 4:16–24).

As in this story, you probably will initiate rhetorical action in your local community or in a place in which you are personally known well. One of my students reported a difficult and embarrassing experience he had when he returned from a year of study abroad and was asked to speak at a convocation at his high school. As he walked to the podium, his friends laughed. This was little Andy Smith with whom they had grown up. What could he know about the world? The student described his struggle to gain attention and to be taken seriously, and he admitted that he never quite succeeded. As his story illustrates, you face a serious rhetorical problem when you try to establish your competence to speak to an audience in your local community, club, place of work, or neighborhood.

The second story is similar. The Gospel of John describes the process by which Jesus chose his disciples. One of them, Philip, tells another man, Nathaniel, how wonderful Jesus is. But Nathaniel responds, "Can any good thing come out of Nazareth?" And Philip answers, "Come and see" (John 1:46). Many of us come from places that, like Nazareth, are unknown and undistinguished. For example, I grew up on a small farm near Blomkest, Minnesota, a metropolis of some 147 residents. Audiences may well ask, How can someone from a little town in Minnesota know anything about rhetoric or criticism or the analysis of discourse? In other words, when you are outside your local community you will have the problem of establishing your credentials and of convincing audiences that people from unusual places or small places or unknown places or places with bad reputations do have the knowledge to discuss an important subject.

Both ordinary and famous persons encounter another problem—the difficulties that arise from inconsistent behavior. We trust those whose behavior demonstrates a systematic commitment to principles, and we are wary of those who make dramatic shifts of position. For example, some doubted Manuel Noriega's conversion to Christianity because of his record of highly unethical and ruthless actions as head of the Panamanian government. Such skeptics view his conversion (a word that literally means a turnaround) as a calculated decision to appear repentant and to lessen his punishment. But if he continues to behave as a Christian would, he may confound the skeptics and convince some, at least, that this was a sincere change of heart. Your track record as a rhetor (what you have said in the past) and as a citizen (what you have done on social issues) are analogous to your driving record or credit record. Just as you will pay higher insurance premiums if you've had accidents or will have difficulties getting credit if you have not paid your bills in the past, as a rhetor you must make a greater effort if your past statements or your past actions cast doubt on your sincerity or commitment. If what you urge appears to conflict with your past record, you will encounter a serious rhetorical problem.

In rare instances, however, deviation from the past can be an asset. When a person deviates from a lifetime of commitments, his or her message is important and becomes informed criticism by an insider. Former U.S. Ambassador to the Soviet Union George Kennan once said, "It is hard to understand how the Soviet system could produce a man such as Mikhail Gorbachev." Europeans and Americans found Gorbachev's moves to open up the Soviet Union to change and to allow divergent opinions particularly noteworthy and credible because those moves were so unexpected. Such action is called *reluctant evidence* because it is given reluctantly, against one's apparent interests. In such a case, inconsistency—deviation from what would be expected—can create positive ethos.

Appearance

Research on how humans form impressions of others indicates that we make initial decisions about an individual in a matter of seconds based on clothing, movement, posture, and facial expressions. Obviously, if the appearance of the rhetor (or of her or his discourse) creates negative impressions in the audience, an obstacle has been created that the rhetor must overcome to be heard, much less to influence. As a result, I believe that rhetors need to make careful choices about appearance. Like you, I am many different people or, if you will, I play many different roles. As a feminist, I try to be the "me" that will create the least resistance in an audience. When I talk to students in a dormitory lounge about the film *The Emerging Woman* on a weekday evening, I wear my favorite pair of jeans and a comfortable shirt, sit casually on the floor, and talk informally. When I give a speech at a scholarship dinner at a sorority, I put on a favorite fashionable outfit that I feel particularly attractive wearing, I stand straight, and I speak more formally. When I moderate a debate before students, faculty, and townspeople between a local anti-ERA activist and a psychiatrist on the one hand and a gay rights leader and a psychologist on the other, I wear a neat, relatively unobtrusive dress, and I try to speak, stand, and move with an authority and formality that bespeaks my desire to be fair. Recognize that I am all of these people—these are not false fronts that I put on. But if I shift them around, I will have problems. If I go formally to the dorm lounge, students will not feel free to talk easily and ask questions. If I am casual at the sorority, I will not do honor to the occasion and will disappoint and offend. If I go casually to the debate, my dress will be taken as a visual sign that I favor one side, and I shall be suspected of bias and expected to be unfair. (See Chapter 11 for further discussion of the nonverbal dimensions of rhetorical action.)

Appearance is less of an issue for writers, although the different looks of student papers also create impressions. A paper written in pencil suggests a first draft, not a finished product. Handwriting that is hard to decipher suggests a rather casual approach and minimal concern for the reader. Numerous spelling and typing errors suggest that the author didn't care enough to proofread; malapropisms, such as a "feudal attempt" that was not "worth wild," call your command of your subject into question; tiny margins suggest a refusal to edit down to the specified length. It is no accident that those who make presentations in person or on paper in commercial situations try hard to have them look as professional as possible—reports are in sleek covers, nicely bound, and professionally printed; visual aids are large, printed, and colorful. The impression created is of careful planning, great concern for the result, and considerable care for the comfort of the audience.

The special styles of some famous writers illustrate the impact of the visual. For example, bell hooks, an African American feminist, uses no capital letters in the name under which she writes, and the decision affects the way one interprets her words and imagines her persona. Some imagist poets have laid out their work to make the visual form resemble the content. Most poetry is laid out in a special kind of format that facilitates how one understands it, although it may make it harder to read well aloud.

As an alert and sensitive rhetor, you must consider the demands of the situation, the subject, and the audience. You must consider which is most appropriate and choose from your repertoire of selves you so that you will not create unnecessary obstacles that prevent your message from reaching the audience or that violate the occasion. Unless you are making a rhetorical point, as activists sometimes wish to do, you should choose a style of dress, posture, and speech that is appropriate to the occasion and the subject, one that will not prevent the audience from approaching your speech with interest and a willingness to listen. Note that such choices should be closely related to the persona or role that you adopt in your speech.

Your Introduction

The famous French philosopher Jean-Paul Sartre commented that one of the terrifying things about human life is that when we die, our lives become the property of others to do with as they will. If you have listened to the eulogies given at funerals you will understand how frightening that can be. In a less permanent but no less fearful way, the rhetor's ethos becomes the property of the person who introduces her or him to the audience, raising a potential rhetorical problem. The person who introduces you creates the climate in which you will begin to speak and can be significant in determining the initial attitude of the audience. Consider carefully what you would like to have said about yourself, and if the introducer asks you, be sure to be prepared to tell her or him. Similarly, when you introduce someone else, think about the climate you will create. A really thoughtful introducer tells the rhetor what she or he plans to say or write and asks if the rhetor would like any changes or additions. You, as a rhetor, will not be able to control all the possible problems that may arise, but you need to be aware of them.

The Context

Our initial impressions of a rhetor are influenced by context. We are likely to assume, until contrary evidence appears, that those whose articles appear on the op-ed page of the *New York Times* are knowledgeable and interesting and that those who write for *Ms.,* a feminist magazine, are feminists expert in some aspect of life of particular significance for women. In such cases, and in many others, audiences will form initial impressions from the process by which you came to be speaking or writing at this time and in this place. Although you may be totally unknown, you will have positive prior ethos if you participate in the DePauw University Undergraduate Symposium in Speech Communication because participants are selected competitively. If one of my students who is a well-liked member of a sorority invites me to speak at a scholarship dinner, the audience, to whom I am unknown, will probably assume that I am a professor who is often dynamic and interesting and who may be so on this occasion.

The context can also create a significant problem, however. An example of this involves the circumstances under which early women speakers such as Sojourner Truth (ca. 1797–1883) spoke. Truth was a freed slave who attended a regional woman's rights convention held in Akron, Ohio, in 1851. Because she was a former slave, the convention organizers were reluctant to allow her to speak—her very presence would link the controversy over the abolition of slavery to the already controversial movement to give women, especially married women, such basic legal rights as ownership of their earnings or of property, to sue and bear witness in court, and to make a contract. The controversy over woman's rights was reflected in the fierce resistance offered by members of the clergy, who were disrupting the meeting, using the Bible to argue that women should stay in their homes, modestly listening to their husbands rather than agitating on these issues. When Truth rose to speak, then, she faced reluctant conventioneers and extremely hostile clergymen. She was aided by her appearance—she was tall, almost six feet in height, she held her turbaned head erect, she had a powerful presence that hushed the audience, and she spoke in deep tones. Here is what she said:[2]

> Well, children, where there is so much racket there must be something out o' kilter. I think that 'twixt the Negroes of the South and the women of the North all a-talking about rights, the white men will be in a fix pretty soon.
>
> But what's all this here talking about? That man over there says that women need to be helped into carriages, and lifted over ditches, and to have the best place everywhere. Nobody ever helps me into carriages, or over mud puddles or gives me any best place (*and raising herself to her full height and her voice to a pitch like rolling thunder, she asked*), and aren't I a woman? Look at me! Look at my arm! (*And she bared her right arm to the shoulder, showing her tremendous muscular power.*) I have plowed, and planted, and gathered into barns, and no man could head me—and aren't I a woman? I could work as much and eat as much as a man (when I could get it), and bear the lash as well—and aren't I a woman? I have borne 13 children and seen them almost all sold off into slavery, and when I cried out with a mother's grief, none but Jesus heard—and aren't I a woman? Then they talk about this thing in the head—what's this they call it? (*"Intellect,"*

---

[2]The original text is from the *Narrative of Sojourner Truth* by Truth with Olive Gilbert (1878; New York: Arno Press, 1968), pp. 133–35, as recorded by Mrs. Frances D. Gage, who presided at the Akron woman's rights convention. Because Truth grew up speaking Dutch in upstate New York and had no contact with Southerners, white or African American, until her teens, it is unlikely that, although illiterate, she spoke in what is called substandard southern dialect, the form in which the speech was recorded by Mrs. Gage (see Arthur Huff Fauset, *Sojourner Truth: God's Faithful Pilgrim* [Chapel Hill: University of North Carolina Press, 1938]). Truth herself saved an article in her scrapbook of an interview in which it was reported that she "prides herself on fairly correct English. . . . People who report her often exaggerate her expressions, putting into her mouth the most marked southern dialect, which [she] feels is rather taking an unfair advantage of her" (cited in Suzanne Pullon Fitch, "Sojourner Truth" in *Women Public Speakers in the United States, 1800–1925*, ed. K. K. Campbell [Westport, CT: Greenwood Press, 1993], p. 421). Hence, all purely dialectical indicators have been removed. Note that Gage's decision to record this in substandard southern dialect is an illustration of the power of others, in this case the recorder, over the ethos of the rhetor.

whispered someone near.) That's it honey. What's that got to do with woman's rights or Negroes' rights? If my cup won't hold but a pint and yours holds a quart, wouldn't you be mean not to let me have my little half-measure full? (*And she pointed her signifi- cant finger and sent a keen glance at the minister who had made the argument. The cheering was long and loud.*)

Then that little man in black [a clergyman] there, he says women can't have as much rights as men, 'cause Christ wasn't a woman. Where did your Christ come from? (*Rolling thunder could not have stilled that crowd as did those deep, wonderful tones, as she stood there with outstretched arms and eye of fire. Raising her voice still louder, she repeated,*) Where did your Christ come from? From God and a woman.[3] Man had nothing to do with him. (*Oh! what a rebuke she gave the little man.*)

(*Turning again to another objector, she took up the defense of mother Eve. I cannot follow her through it all. It was pointed, and witty, and solemn, eliciting at almost every sentence deafening applause; and she ended by asserting that*) If the first woman God ever made was strong enough to turn the world upside down, all alone, these to- gether (*and she glanced her eye over us*) ought to be able to turn it back and get it right side up again; and now they are asking to do it, the men better let them. (*Long-continued cheering.*)

'Bliged to you for hearing on me, and now old Sojourner hasn't got anything more to say.

Note that Truth acknowledges the context and the disruptive scene. Note, too, that part of her adaptation to the scene involves a dialogue with the audience. She speaks in an oral style that makes the most of repetition and uses the powerful strategy of enactment—she is the proof of what she is saying—as she bares her muscled arm and testi- fies to her experience. She also uses vivid descriptive language that speaks to the experience of the audience in using the sizes of cups as a way to distinguish between depriving people of basic rights and ac- knowledging their differences. Such language and style contributes to her ethos because it is consistent with her background. She also adapts to the religious character of her opposition by reminding the clergy- men of the virgin birth as well as of the theology that the redemptive force of Christ's sacrifice erases the curse described in Genesis 3 after the fall. What we know of Truth's short speech is a model of adapta- tion to context, indeed, of encompassing the situation.

---

[3]Theologically, Mary's child wipes out Eve's curse: "Christ hath redeemed us from the curse of the law" (Gal. 3:13); "And there shall be no more curse" (Rev. 22:3).

The Occasion

Still other difficulties can arise from the event of which a rhetorical act is a part. Every rhetorical act is limited by the occasion, by the kind of happening or place in which it occurs. Effective rhetorical action, which reaches the audience, must be appropriate to its context. The problem of the rhetor is to select a purpose that is consistent both with her or his beliefs and desires and with the time and place in which it occurs. Think for a moment about inappropriate rhetorical acts you have experienced. I remember a long sermon at a cousin's wedding that no one could hear because they were angry that the clergyman could keep a nervous bride and groom standing in the front of a church for so long. I remember a highly partisan political speech given in a campus chapel that was so offensive that about half the students finally walked out. Just as audiences have purposes (the needs they wish to satisfy), occasions have functions or purposes, and an effective rhetorical act must be consonant with that purpose. If the purpose of the occasion is entertainment, your rhetorical act must be entertaining—among other things, perhaps. If the purpose of the occasion is to do honor, your act must be consistent.

For example, a scholarship dinner at a sorority is an occasion to honor women who have unusually fine academic records. As a feminist, I should like to have sorority sisters acutely aware of the problems of women and the injustices they suffer, but such a purpose is not entirely appropriate to a dinner of this kind. When I spoke on such an occasion, I tried to merge my purposes and theirs. I told the women that 200 years earlier, no women had scholarship dinners, and none of them had an opportunity for higher education that was comparable to that of males. I told them about the struggle of women to gain the right to an equal education, but I ended by honoring them and their school by telling them that from its beginning the University of Kansas had admitted women and that its first freshman class was composed almost equally of men and women. As a feminist, I accomplished my purpose by raising consciousness about the history of women's education; as a rhetor, I was heard because my purpose was consistent with the purpose of the occasion.

The rhetor is limited by the context of the occasion, and a rhetorical problem arises if the rhetor's purpose is not consistent with that of the occasion.

In sum, rhetorical problems may arise even before the rhetor begins to produce a message. These may arise from your past, from your appearance or the role you choose to play, from the way in which you are introduced to the audience, and from a conflict between your purpose and the purpose of the occasion.

ETHOS FROM THE RHETORICAL ACT

Ethos is an attitude—the impressions or images persons have of the source of a message. Like all attitudes, those about the credibility of a rhetor (or the source of the message, whether it is an individual or a medium or an institution) are general and evaluative. Unlike most other attitudes, which are unidimensional (that is, determined by only one factor), ethos is multidimensional, affected by at least two distinct factors. One of these is authoritativeness and the other is trustworthiness.[4] For a rhetor to be authoritative for an audience means that he or she is perceived as informed, expert, qualified, intelligent, and reliable. This cluster of attributes is similar to those characterizing a person who, in the classical sense, showed practical wisdom on matters of social concern. For a rhetor to be trustworthy means that she or he is perceived as honest, friendly, pleasant, and more concerned with the good of the community than with personal goals. This second factor seems to combine the Aristotelian views that a rhetor must be perceived as having moral excellence and as being well-intentioned toward the community. A third factor appears in some studies: dynamism. This means that, in some cases, the attitude toward the rhetor is affected by the degree to which he or she is emphatic, aggressive, forceful, bold, active, and energetic, but this factor functions less predictably and uniformly in diverse situations, and it may work either positively or negatively for women speakers depending on the audience.

The rhetor's ethos and the message do not have fixed, unchanging meanings for the audience; they interact. Once it was presumed that only the evaluation of the message was influenced by the prestige of the source from which it supposedly comes. S. E. Asch criticized this assumption and argued that authorship functions not as a source of prestige but as a context that influences the meaning statements have for members of the audience. Such a perspective holds that meaning is in people, and that when the context of a message is changed, its meaning will be interpreted differently.[5] A statement about revolution attributed to Thomas Jefferson, for example, has a different meaning than if it were attributed to Karl Marx. In other words, the source of an act, the rhetor or the medium in which a rhetorical act appears, are

---

[4]Admittedly this is an oversimplification. Using factor analysis as a technique, a number of other factors have been found, but these two are the most stable and generalized across studies.

[5]S. E. Asch, "The Doctrine of Suggestion, Prestige, and Imitation in Social Psychology," *Psychological Review* 55 (1948):250–278; see Wallace Fotheringham, *Perspectives on Persuasion* (Boston: Allyn and Bacon, 1966), pp. 90–92, for a discussion of this research.

contexts that influence how the audience decides what the message means. The nature of the message itself will be influenced significantly by the source, because the source is a major part of its context.

Identification

The importance of the rhetor for the determination of meaning is related to two processes with special significance for persuasion: identification and participation. *To identify* means "to establish the identity of; . . . to consider as identical, equate; . . . to associate or affiliate (oneself) closely with a person or group." The word is related to identity— "the set of characteristics by which a thing is definitively recognized or known" or "the quality or condition of being exactly the same as something else."[6] If you look closely at these definitions, you will notice that they are apparently contradictory or at least ambiguous. On the one hand, these words refer to the set of characteristics that make something or someone unique, distinctive. On the other hand, these words refer to what is alike, even identical, about two or more things or persons. In other words, they are terms about the relationship between similarities and differences. Identification is possible because of similarities—we are both students and Americans interested in understanding how to use communication in order to be effective moral agents. These are possibilities for identification despite the many ways in which we may be different—I am a woman, married, a professional, over 50, raised on a small farm in the Midwest in a community dominated by the Dutch Reformed Church. You can identify with me if my behavior as the author of this book consistently embodies our shared goals and interests, but I can become a real person for you, rather than an impersonal author, only as you become aware of the qualities that make me different, even unique.

The characters in highly successful television programs are illustrative. Dr. Quinn is a successful general practitioner on *Dr. Quinn, Medicine Woman,* but the program appeals to women viewers because it's about relationships more than it is about medicine, and Dr. Quinn is appealing because like many of us, she struggles with challenges that arise out of loving and trusting others. Murphy Brown is a nationally known television newscaster, but her appeal arises from her struggle to deal with the problems of being a highly competitive and successful woman. Put differently, we identify not with generalities but with

---

[6]*The American Heritage Dictionary of the English Language,* ed. William Morris. Boston/ New York: American Heritage Publishing Co. and Houghton Mifflin, 1969.

general characteristics as embodied in specific ways in an individual. Persons identify with each other, and it is as an individual that the audience will respond to you, specifically as an individual who illustrates and represents general qualities and characteristics you and they share.

Research that has been done on the development of trust helps explain this further. Trust arises out of a reciprocal pattern of interrelationships. We learn to trust by sharing, by mutual exchange, and by sensitivity to the other person. Trusting and risk-taking are two sides of the same coin because a trusting relationship requires a willingness to engage in trusting acts of self-disclosure. Thus, within limits, others trust us to the degree that they know details about us; we are trusted as we emerge for them as unique individuals. There are limits, of course, but they are often broader than you may think.

For example, in Rita Mae Brown's best-selling novel *Rubyfruit Jungle*,[7] the protagonist, Molly Bolt, is a young woman with a strong commitment to independence and a lot of artistic talent. She is an all-American girl who embodies values most Americans cherish—a sense of humor, a desire to develop her talents fully, a sense of fair play, loyalty. She is also a lesbian. As readers, we may or may not identify with lesbians, but as the novel's sales attest, many of us can identify with the Molly Bolt who makes us laugh, who expresses our ambitions, who gets angry at unfair treatment, and who can be trusted to stick by her friends. Like Molly Bolt, rhetors need to emerge as real and distinctive individuals to audiences. The rhetorical problem is not to become a bland amalgam of the attitudes of the audience; the rhetorical problem is the risks involved in disclosing yourself as a distinctive individual to the audience.

Similarity is important in persuasion. Kenneth Burke, a contemporary rhetorical theorist, wrote, "Only those voices from without are effective which can speak in the language of a voice within."[8] At its simplest, this statement recognizes that we are most influenced by those whose voices are most like the voices we use in talking to ourselves, and the more the rhetor shares with the audience, the greater the chance he or she will have of being able to speak in ways the audience will hear and understand and feel. Empirical studies reveal that rhetors increase their influence when they announce at the outset

---

[7]1973; New York: Bantam Books, 1977. In 1994 it was available from Book of the Month Club.
[8]Kenneth Burke, *A Rhetoric of Motives* (1950; Berkeley: University of California Press, 1969), p. 39.

that their personal views (attitudes) are similar to those of the audience, that members of the audience more readily accept a rhetor's view of an issue if common ground has already been established on previous issues, and that the audience is more susceptible to influence if its members decide that the intentions of the rhetor are consistent with their own self-interests.[9]

A cynical view of such findings would suggest that the rhetor should lie—tell the audience what they want to hear in order to gain the effects desired. That is good advice for only one kind of rhetorical situation: the one-shot effort at a quick payoff. The unscrupulous seller of, say, imaginary cemetery plots, who plans to hit town once, then take the money and run, may use this effectively. But most of us act as rhetors in quite different circumstances. You will be in a class for a quarter or a semester, and some of your classmates will know you in other contexts; so, even as nomadic students, it is difficult to wear a false face easily. It becomes even more difficult in a community in which you live and work over a period of time—the consistency of your behavior will be a test of your trustworthiness. In addition, most rhetorical acts are parts of persuasive campaigns. In such cases, you will be judged over time in different rhetorical actions with different audiences, and it would be not only difficult but also most unwise to try "to fool all of the people all of the time."

The moral of the story is to find real areas of similarity that you share with the audience. Do not try to be what you are not, but make sure that they know what you share with them. If you are to be effective, you must find common ground—yet you must also remain a unique individual who is, in fact, different from anyone else.

Social Power

Ethos is also influenced by the relationship between the rhetor and the audience. In a rhetorical context, *power* refers to the rhetor's potential for social influence, that is, influence that arises from the degree to which the audience depends on the rhetor and the rhetor depends on the audience. The classroom is a good example. As students, you depend on your instructor in significant ways; your instructor has power, and your relationship is between unequals. Your ability to graduate and your grade point average depend in part on your teacher, and this

---

[9]Ellen Berscheid reviews this research in "Interpersonal Attraction" in *Handbook of Social Psychology,* 3d ed. (New York: Random House, 1985), vol. 2, pp. 413–484.

additional power may increase her or his ability to influence your attitudes—at least for the duration of the class. An instructor, however, also depends on the students. Any one of you can disrupt the class so it cannot continue, and the course continues period after period because you as a group permit it to do so. Because of this power, you have the ability to influence your instructor or, at least, limit her or his behavior. The rhetorical acts of students and professors are influenced and limited by their relative power. These limits are evident in any relationship involving the potential for social influence—between spouses, partners, employer and employee, homeowner and plumber, landlord and tenant, dean and department head, coach and player, sorority member and pledge, parent and child, and so on.

Obviously, such interdependent relationships are a facet of identification. As employees we may dislike the boss but recognize that our livelihood depends on the health of the business. As students we may dislike a teacher but recognize that the class must continue if we are to learn what we need and get essential credits.

Participation

The ethos of the rhetor is also related to participation by the audience in the rhetorical act. To understand this process, we must return once again to the wisdom of Aristotle. In *On Rhetoric* he described a species of argument that he called the *enthymeme,* a form of argument that he believed was peculiar to rhetoric. This form of argument is unusual because it assumes a collaborative effort by the rhetor and audience. In effect, the audience fills in details, makes connections based on their experiences, or draws conclusions based on knowledge and understandings they share with the rhetor. Sometimes they do that because of a common context, from what they know of a particular time or place. Sometimes they do it because of assumptions or values they share. The perceived character of the rhetor influences whether audience members will collaborate in creating the rhetorical act because such perceptions function as signs of shared experience, attitudes, and values, which, in turn, lead to identification, which facilitates active participation in creating and elaborating the arguments offered by the rhetor. Note how similar these concepts are to the ELM theory discussed earlier.

An enthymeme is relatively easy to describe but harder to illustrate because it relies on audience participation and requires a good bit of adaptation. In general, an enthymeme is an argument that rests on what is already known and accepted by those addressed. Accordingly, audiences can fill in details that are omitted or only alluded to in passing, or the argument evokes not just assent but elaboration because it fits their personal experiences or speaks to what they believe is likely or probable. Many jokes based on current events illustrate the process. For example, when George Bush chose Dan Quayle for his running mate in 1988, some detected an inconsistency in Quayle's statements about military service and his service in the National Guard to avoid being drafted and sent to Vietnam. One wag asked, "What's the difference between Jane Fonda and Dan Quayle? Give up? Jane Fonda went to Vietnam." The humor, if any, arises out of audience knowledge about Jane Fonda, who aroused great controversy by traveling to North Vietnam and criticizing U.S. bombing of what were described as civilian targets. Without that knowledge, there is only puzzlement. Just who do you suppose might enjoy that joke particularly?

A more extended example comes from a senatorial campaign. In his 1990 race for the Senate against African American Harvey Gantt, Jesse Helms used a commercial that showed a pair of pale male hands reading, then crushing, a letter, presumably a letter of rejection, while a voice said, "You needed that job, and you were the best qualified. But they had to give it to a minority because of a racial quota. Is that really fair? Harvey Gantt says it is. Gantt supports Ted Kennedy's racial quota law that makes the color of your skin more important than your qualifications. You'll vote on this issue next Tuesday. For racial quotas: Harvey Gantt. Against racial quotas: Jesse Helms." The responses from people in focus groups who were asked about their reactions suggested that many white North Carolina voters had ready a scenario that they could link to the words of the ad, a racist scenario about unqualified minorities taking the jobs of needful blue-collar workers. The ad was powerful because it aroused that scenario in voters' minds and linked it to Gantt, which made them more likely to vote for Helms. Moreover, white males who could identify with the man in the ad were more likely to respond with that story line.[10] In addition, of course, it made those who responded well to the ad believe that Jesse Helms understood their problems and would act to ensure that they were treated fairly, thereby enhancing his ethos. Note that enthymematic argument is powerful because it uses self-persuasion and because it brings to consciousness ideas or feelings based on our own experiences and knowledge. Tony Schwartz, an advertising genius, wrote a book that argues that really powerful advertising

---

[10]Reports about focus group reactions to the ad are found in K. H. Jamieson, *Dirty Politics* (New York: Oxford University Press, 1992), 97–100.

works by prompting an enthymematic response, what he called a "responsive chord," in viewers or listeners.[11] In such cases, the rhetor produces cues that prompt members of the audience to collaborate or participate in creating the rhetoric by which they are persuaded.

The process by which the ethos of the source increases our participation is most evident in commercials made by well-known actors. Because we know little about them as individuals, we tend to believe they are like the characters they play. For instance, Bill Cosby is best known as a comedian and for his role as Dr. Huxtable on *The Cosby Show*. Cosby also appears in commercials for Jell-O. Dressed casually and usually shown with a group of children, he shows us how much kids love the yummy taste of Jell-O or Jell-O pudding. The advertiser hopes that we will confuse the actor Bill Cosby with Dr. Huxtable, the warm, caring father that he plays on *The Cosby Show*, a move made easier by books that Cosby has written on being a father. If so, we are more likely to accept his advice on what we should feed our children.

In sum, the character of the rhetor is directly related to two important rhetorical processes: identification based on perceptions of similarity and participation based on clues provided by the rhetor's words that suggest shared experiences and knowledge. Both of these influence the ways in which audience members interpret messages and the extent to which they are willing to fill in details or draw inferences based on statements in the rhetorical act.

These, then, are the kinds of problems that may arise in rhetorical action. Some of these problems arise out of the rhetor's background, appearance, the ways she or he is introduced, and the context or occasion. More important problems arise out of the relationship between the rhetor and the message. For an act to be effective, a rhetor must be perceived by the audience as competent and trustworthy. This is particularly significant because the rhetor is a context that affects how audience members will translate and interpret a message. Specifically, ethos influences audience identification—that is, the degree to which audiences see the rhetor as an individual is closely related to trust. In addition, as the rhetor emerges as a unique person, there is an association with and an affinity for those qualities, attitudes, and characteristics that form a common ground between rhetor and audience. This process is central to ensuring that the audience will hear the message and translate it with the greatest possible fidelity. In addition, ethos influences participation, the degree to which

---

[11] *The Responsive Chord* (New York: Doubleday, 1974).

the audience is willing to involve itself in rhetorical action, to draw conclusions, or to fill in details implied by the rhetor or to embellish the suggestions made.

THE RHETORICAL PROBLEM: INTERRELATIONSHIPS

By this time the interrelationships among the facets of the rhetorical problem should be apparent. For example, the decisions made by an audience member about the competence of the rhetor result from decisions that the rhetor makes about the treatment of the subject and the purpose selected. The problems the rhetor has in establishing credibility arise from the characteristics of a specific audience. The rhetorical problem on a given occasion will be a function of the interaction among these three elements: audience, subject and purpose, and rhetor. In the chapters that follow, I shall suggest ways to overcome these obstacles. Chapter 6 provides tools for analysis so the resources used by other rhetors to overcome rhetorical problems will be available to you. Part 3 explores the resources of evidence, argument, organization, language, and nonverbal action.

SUMMARY

Summary Outline

I. The rhetorical problems arising from the rhetor are issues of ethos, the rhetor's perceived character, or source credibility.

A. Prior ethos or impressions of the rhetor prior to the rhetorical act include

1. The rhetor's track record or reputation.

2. The rhetor's personal appearance or the appearance of the published/printed/written rhetorical act.

3. The way in which the rhetor or the rhetorical act is introduced.

4. The context or circumstances in which the rhetorical act appears.

5. The occasion and the role the rhetorical act must play in it.

B. The ethos or character of the rhetor is a product of the rhetorical act.

1. The rhetor as perceived by the audience is a context that affects the meaning of the rhetorical act.

2. Identification describes the recognition of similarities shared by the rhetor and the audience.

> a. Audiences respond positively to indications that the rhetor shares their attitudes and values.
>
> b. Audiences also respond positively to indications that the rhetor is a distinctive individual.

3. Social influence refers to reciprocal relationships between rhetors and audiences that make rhetorical interaction beneficial for both.

4. Participation refers to the willingness of audiences to collaborate in creating a rhetorical act by filling in details, recalling the specifics of an allusion, or calling up memories of personal experiences and knowledge that reinforce the rhetor's message.

> a. The Aristotelian rhetorical argument, the enthymeme, is an example of this kind of participation.
>
> b. Participation is facilitated by the associations a rhetorical act can evoke, the "responsive chord" prompted by skillful product and political advertising.

■ ■ ■

MATERIAL FOR ANALYSIS

A number of famous speeches illustrate the use of ethos as a powerful rhetorical resource. You might choose one of them, such as Edward Kennedy's speech on health care at the midterm Democratic convention in 1978,[12] John F. Kennedy's famous speech, "Ich bin ein Berliner,"[13] or Geraldine Ferraro's nomination acceptance address at the 1984 Democratic National Convention.[14] As a critic, you should consider how these well-known political leaders used their personal history, personal experience, roles, and enactment as resources for persuasion.

---

[12]See first edition of *The Rhetorical Act* (Belmont, CA: Wadsworth Publishing, 1982), pp. 142–145.

[13]*Presidential Rhetoric (1961 to the Present)*, 4th ed., ed. Theodore Windt (Dubuque, IA: Kendall Hunt, 1987), pp. 49–50.

[14]*Congressional Quarterly*, July 21, 1984, pp. 1794–1795.

On August 25, 1992, President George Bush and presidential candidate Bill Clinton both made speeches to the national convention of the American Legion. During the primary campaign, Clinton faced press reports of allegations of an extramarital affair with singer Gennifer Flowers. No sooner were these charges defused than new allegations surfaced about his conduct as a student at Oxford University during the Vietnam War. In February, during the New Hampshire primary campaign, the *New York Times* published the letter Clinton had written in 1969 to the ROTC commander at the University of Arkansas. According to the *Times* report, "The letter further rattles a candidacy already shaken by accusations from a supermarket tabloid about marital infidelity."[15] The issue became less whether Clinton had tried to avoid service during an unpopular war and more whether his statements about his actions in that period were inconsistent. He survived to win the nomination, but questions about this issue continued into the presidential election campaign, in part because the Bush–Quayle campaign kept the issue alive.

In August, after both national party conventions but before the official campaign began after Labor Day, both presidential candidates were invited to address the American Legion Convention in Chicago. Bush spoke first. Prior to his speech, the Bush–Quayle campaign released two scathing memos to the media. One charged that throughout 1992 there had been discrepancies in Clinton's statements about what occurred in 1969; the other attacked his policy positions as a threat to national security.[16] Both suggested that Clinton was not fit to be president, much less commander in chief.

Although Bush never mentioned Clinton by name, the entire speech invited listeners to compare an image of Bush as a young bomber pilot in World War II and as the hero of Desert Storm with the image of Clinton as a draft dodger. Bush appealed to his audience's shared experience of service and combat, and he referred repeatedly to his World War II experience to show how that had prepared him to be the nation's commander in chief during the Persian Gulf war and in Panama. The implication was, of course, that because his rival had no such experience, he did not have the credentials to be the commander in chief. On the other hand, the convention booed Edward Derwinski, Bush's secretary of veterans affairs, for his experiment in using veterans' hospitals for rural health care among other things, and there was

---

[15]*New York Times*, February 13, 1992, p. A25. I am indebted to Tom Burkholder, who presented a paper on these speeches at the Central/Southern Speech Association Convention, April 18, 1993, for much of this background material.
[16]*New York Times*, August 26, 1992, A18; *Chicago Tribune*, August 26, 1992, 1:10.

continued concern about Bush's unwillingness to pursue the Gulf War until Saddam Hussein was ousted.

This, then, was Bill Clinton's rhetorical problem. Charged with behaving improperly during the Vietnam War and possible duplicity in statements about what he had done, which raised questions about his fitness for the presidency and to serve as commander in chief, Clinton needed to repair his image and restore his credibility. Because his opponent's image had some flaws, however, he also had an opportunity to subvert Bush's image with the legionnaires. Here is what he said.[17]

Speech by Governor Bill Clinton
American Legion Convention
Chicago, Illinois, August 25, 1992

1   Thank you. Thank you Commander DiFrancesco.

Thank you Commander DiFrancesco, and thank you all [sic] legionnaires who have been so gracious in welcoming me here and inviting President Bush and me to address this convention.

2   I want to salute all my friends in the Arkansas department of the American Legion. And I promised Al Gore that I would also recognize the legionnaires from the Volunteer State of Tennessee.

3   I want at the outset to pay a personal tribute to two legionnaires: first, my good friend Hershel Gober, a Vietnam veteran, former adjutant of the Arkansas department of the American Legion, and current American Legion department service officer for Arkansas, who is my national campaign manager for veterans' affairs.

4   I also want to recognize Al Lynch, whose heroism in Vietnam earned him the Congressional Medal of Honor and who has volunteered for another tough mission: serving as my veterans' coordinator for Illinois.

5   I know it's become fashionable for some politicians to claim that they won the Cold War. But I know who won the Cold War—you did.

6   No American would be free today if it weren't for the heroic sacrifices of you and all the millions of men and women who have served America in times of trouble. I feel a special sense of gratitude. You not only gave me the freedom you won for all Ameri-

---

[17]The text of the speech was provided by the Clinton/Gore National Campaign Headquarters, P.O. Box 615, Little Rock, AR 72203.

cans on the field of battle. You gave me the opportunity to serve America myself in the arena of public service.

7   It is literally true that I might not be here today if it weren't for the American Legion. Without your dedication to the youth of America—which gave me the opportunity to attend American Legion Boys' State and American Legion Boys' Nation. If that hadn't happened, I might not be standing before you as my party's nominee for president.

8   I still remember that July afternoon in 1963, in the Rose Garden of the White House as I was waiting eagerly, a young 16-year-old, to shake the president's hand. I couldn't help thinking that only in America could someone like me be so fortunate as to meet the president of the United States.

9   I knew then that I wanted to answer President Kennedy when he said, "Ask not what your country can do for you, ask what you could [*sic*] do for your country."

10   Just three months before a lot of America's innocence died, when President Kennedy was assassinated, those warm and hopeful summer days, the American Legion taught me lessons I have tried to live by all my life. Lessons about the greatness of America, and the responsibility to stand up for what you believe.

11   The strength of our people and the durability of our Bill of Rights. The nobility of public service. That summer I learned from the American Legion that being a citizen involves responsibilities as well as rights—including the responsibility to love your country even enough to right its wrongs; the responsibility to get involved, to make a difference, to serve.

12   I am not the only American whose life has been made better by your continuing service here at home. From baseball to the Boy Scouts; from keeping veterans' hospitals open to keeping kids off drugs; from addressing homelessness to preventing child abuse to instilling a deep sense of patriotism into still another generation of Americans, a grateful nation owes you a debt of gratitude.

13   Like any adult I have to take full responsibility for the mistakes I've made in my life. But the American Legion deserves a large measure of credit for whatever successes I have enjoyed.

14   The first group I introduced Al Gore to as my running mate was the Arkansas department of the American Legion.

15   Because of my respect for the American Legion, I am here to speak to you as a candidate for the presidency. But before I can speak in that role, I have to tell you something very personal— not as a governor—but as a citizen.

16   You know that I never served in the military. You know that I opposed the war in Vietnam. But I want you to know this: I was never against the heroic men who served in that war. I honored your service then, and I honor it still.

17   Although I have discussed my conduct during the Vietnam War in great detail, I feel I owe you one final statement, to set the record straight.

18   In 1969, while studying at Oxford on a Rhodes scholarship, I received a draft notice, which arrived late. My draft board postponed the induction date to give me time to finish my first year of study. That summer, I agreed to join the ROTC program and attend law school at the University of Arkansas. But a few weeks later, I changed my mind and decided I should take my chances with the draft.

19   Not long after that, the lottery was initiated. My draft lottery number was 311. If it had been 3, or if my number had been called, I would have served, and gone to Vietnam if so ordered. But I won't lie to you: I was relieved when I saw my number was 311, not because I didn't want to serve my country, but because I believed so strongly that our policy in Vietnam was wrong. I still believe that. It weakened and divided America and made us reluctant to use our strength in other parts of the world. But I know many of you then and many of you today disagree with me. I respect that.

20   If you choose to vote against me because of what happened twenty-three years ago, that's your right as a American citizen, and I respect that. But it is my hope you will cast your vote while looking toward the future with hope, rather than remaining fixed to the problems of the past. For in this critical year, if all of us vote our hopes and not our fears; if we use this election to bring our country together instead of keeping it apart; if, in short, we all begin to behave like Americans again, then I know that the greatest country in human history will make itself greater still.

21   The other question that arises, of course, is perhaps inevitable, not just in this election, but in other elections to come, as the post–World War II generation comes to leadership. And it is: Can someone who has never served in the military serve as commander in chief?

22   Lincoln might have thought the question odd. He used to joke about his lack of military experience, saying the only blood he lost in defense of his country was to mosquitoes. As a congressman, he had been a passionate critic of the Mexican War, and the sum total of his military experience consisted of a few weeks as a militiaman called to service during the Black Hawk War, in which he saw no action. And yet he had the judgment and the wisdom and the strength of conviction to lead America through its bloodiest and most painful conflict.

23 In our own century, the professorial Woodrow Wilson—a governor who was never in the service—led America and its allies to "make the world safe for democracy" in the First World War, and another governor, Franklin Roosevelt, proved himself one of history's greatest wartime commanders, though he had never served in the military.

24 In 1980, still another governor, Ronald Reagan, was derided for having spent more time filming *Hellcats of the Navy* than actually serving in the armed forces during World War II. And yet he never wavered from the use of American might when he felt it was right.

25 In President Bush's administration, Secretary of Defense Dick Cheney, who had deferments during the Vietnam era, has served with genuine distinction, especially during the Gulf War.

26 Our history—and common sense—tell us that competent commanders draw their wisdom from the strength of our country—and our countrymen and countrywomen.

27 What makes a president fit to command is, in my view, faith in God, belief in the greatness of our country and the goodness of our people, a commitment to making and keeping America the strongest country in the world—militarily, economically, and morally—and an understanding of the essential character of the American people.

28 We Americans love peace. But we will not shrink from force of arms if arms are required to keep the peace and defend our interests. In the end, every decision must be guided by principle as well as experience. Just after his election, with the prospects of war appearing imminent, Lincoln told his neighbors in Springfield that defending the nation in a civil war was a task "more difficult than that which devolved upon General Washington. Unless the great God who assisted him shall be with and aid me," he said, "I must fail. But if the same omniscient mind and Almighty arm that directed and protected him shall guide and support me, I shall not fail, I shall succeed."

29 No one knows better than those of you in this room the solemn responsibility of the decision to use force to protect our nation's security and interests. When the American people choose a president, they want someone whom they can trust to act when those moments arise. Every president in the last half-century has had to confront the fateful decision to send Americans into combat. I do not relish this prospect, but neither do I shrink from it.

30   I know we must have the resolve constantly to deter, sometimes to fight, always to win. And as commander in chief, I will fight to ensure that our troops who must go to battle are the best trained, best equipped, and best supported in the world. Good people ensure victory on the battlefield.

31   As we scale back the force structure, we must restructure those that remain to meet the new, less predictable threats in the post–Cold War Era. Our forces must be ready and sustainable. They must be more mobile, more precise, and more flexible. And they must have the technologically advanced weapons they need to get the job done.

32   I will never allow a hollow army. My five-year defense budget over the next five years totals $1.36 trillion compared to the president's level of $1.42 trillion—a difference of only 5 percent.

33   There are differences between these proposals. This administration would keep more troops in Europe and spend more on SDI; I would shift the focus to real threats we are likely to face in the coming decade: aggressive tyrants like Saddam Hussein, new regional conflicts, terrorists, and the threat of nuclear proliferation. I would preserve a more limited SDI option and support more emphasis on some military weapons, including the V-22 and fast sealift ships.

34   I still believe we should strive for an *American,* not a Republican or a Democrat, but an American national security and defense policy. I supported President Bush's efforts in Desert Shield and Desert Storm. I support the tough line the administration has taken with Saddam Hussein recently. I urged the policies the administration has adopted in Bosnia and Somalia.

35   The American people do not believe either political party has a monopoly on love of country. Patriotism is not partisan.

36   Nor does patriotism require a blind devotion to the status quo. Indeed, the risk of staying put; the costs of standing pat; the dangers of the status quo are far greater: for economic decline, more defense cuts without a conversion plan to protect those who won the Cold War and promote growth, more skyrocketing health care costs.

37   From now on a large part of our national security policy must be found in economic strength as well as military might. A country that is not strong at home cannot be strong abroad.

38   My economic plan will create millions of new jobs for displaced defense workers, for veterans, for all Americans by reinvesting in our nation's infrastructure, civilian research and development, for the highway jobs of the future, in retraining our workers and our servicemen and women, and in redeveloping our communities.

39   As an American, I honor the service of every man and every woman who has served our country in uniform. As president, I will honor your service and sacrifice with deeds, not words. You've earned nothing less.

40   I will honor it first by giving veterans the kind of health care system your country owes you. I will work to ensure the VA—the Veterans' Administration—gets the funding it needs to provide the excellent and timely care our veterans deserve—*all* our veterans.

41   I will work to see that once again our veterans' hospitals work for veterans. As long as I am president, we will not merge the veterans' medical centers into the welfare system.

42   Instead, we will simplify and reform eligibility, and strengthen the VA's efforts to deal with the special problems veterans face—like post-traumatic stress disorder, complications from Agent Orange, drug and alcohol abuse. And we will honor America's unbreakable moral obligation to care for our veterans who were disabled in the service of our country.

43   And I will honor your service by appointing not a secretary [*of*] veterans' affairs, but a secretary *for* veterans' affairs—not someone appointed for political reasons, but a secretary I will choose after consulting with the American Legion and other veterans' groups.

44   Someone who will have your respect and esteem—and mine. Of course, sitting even closer to me than the secretary of veterans' affairs will be your fellow legionnaire and my running mate, Al Gore, so you know your voice will be heard.

45   I will honor your service by cutting the VA bureaucracy to make sure you get the benefits you've earned without a lot of red tape and delay. It shouldn't take longer to get your VA benefits than it took to liberate Kuwait.

46   I will honor your service by carrying on your tireless struggle to account for everyone who has ever served this country.

47   Back home I formed the Arkansas POW/MIA Verification Task Force to determine the status of the 26 Arkansans whose fates are still unknown. I do not know if there are still American POWs being held. But I do know this: When I am your president the files will be thrown open, the roadblocks will be torn down, and the truth will come out.

48   America must never leave its warriors on the battlefield. If there are men being held captive still, I will not rest until they are returned. And if they are not, at least we will know the truth, and the truth will set us free.

49   I will honor your service by moving swiftly to address the special needs of the veterans who have been left out and left behind. Too many homeless shelters are bursting with veterans—including veterans of last year's victory in Desert Storm. You[r] Family Support program is an important and helpful step—veterans helping veterans.

50   But all Americans should help their fellow Americans. The fact that the American Legion is doing so much should not be used as an excuse for the American government doing so little.

51   And I will honor your service by making sure the heroes who won the Cold War are not left out in the cold.

52   Our people in uniform are among the most highly skilled in the areas of expertise we need the most. As gradual, sensible defense cuts take effect, we must transfer their talents and hard work to the civilian sector, and ensure they receive the assistance to do so successfully.

53   For example, I support incentives for military personnel to earn military retirement by taking jobs as teachers and police, as Sen. [Sam] Nunn [D-GA] has recommended.

54   I want to add 100,000 police officers to help reduce crime and drug abuse.

55   I want to retrain defense industry technicians for work in critical civilian fields such as biotechnology, renewable energy, and environmental cleanup.

56   The Pentagon stands as America's best youth training program, and our most potent research center. It's time to put those assets to work at home in the battle to make America strong once again.

57   We ought to encourage as many as possible to serve as citizen soldiers in the National Guard and Reserves. Our talented men and women in uniform are the best equipped to help solve the problems of infrastructure, education, and rural health—offering the possibility to our military personnel to serve as role models here at home, to many young people who never have good role models here at home, but still, all the while still meeting their obligation to fulfill their primary military mission.

58   How do you know I will do these things? Just ask my good friends from the American Legion of Arkansas.

59   I am proud of what we've done to honor the service of veterans at home. I appointed the first Vietnam veteran as director of the cabinet-level Department of Veterans' Affairs. We have a County Veterans' Service Officer Program, which is the backbone of our statewide outreach system, which makes sure no veteran is left out or left behind.

60 I am proud of the fact that Arkansas ranks first in the per capita reimbursements we get for our veterans from the federal Department of Veterans' Affairs. And we were first last year too. And the year before that.

61 I signed executive orders ensuring veterans' preferences in hiring. And I helped find the money to upgrade and expand the intermediate nursing facilities of the Arkansas Veterans' Home; I balanced 11 budgets in a row, but never on the backs of the veterans of my state.

62 In 1989, when the flag-burning controversy arose, I joined with the American Legion in taking steps to react. I signed legislation making it a crime to burn or deface the flag. But I also wanted to stop flag burning before it starts. So together with the American Legion we established one of the finest flag education programs in the country. Volunteers from the American Legion launched an all-out assault in our grade schools, instilling in our young students the deep patriotism that gives you and I [*sic*] a lump in our throat and a stir in our hearts every time we see Old Glory go up the flagpole.

63 I am proud of my record of support for veterans. And I admire the American Legion's 74-year commitment to what's best about America.

64 For three-fourths of a century you've been advising presidents—from calling for the GI Bill in 1944 to opposing the IRS's shameful attempt to tax cost of living adjustments to veterans' disability payments.

65 I will be a good president for America's veterans. After all, I've been taking advice from the American Legion for 29 years.

66 Some of you may know, my father served in World War II. But he didn't die in the war. He was killed in a car accident three months before I was born, on his way home to Arkansas to see my mother.

67 He was killed just as he was about to start living for all the things he had risked dying for. And, when, many years ago, my mother showed me his service citation from World War II, I felt as proud as I've ever been.

68 I doubt he ever dreamed that, some day, the son he never knew would be standing here today as a candidate for president of the United States.

69   This could only happen in America. And in my case, it might never have happened without the encouragement and assistance of the American Legion.

70   I know you are unlikely to base this important vote on the fact that I was in American Legion Boys' State 29 years ago, or that I have a good record on veterans issues as a governor.

71   But I also hope you will not base your vote on the fact that I didn't serve in Vietnam 23 years ago.

72   This campaign must be decided on the future of our nation and on the issues—on jobs and health care and education and safer streets; on making the government work for all Americans, not just the special interests and the privileged few; on building a strong America at home and abroad.

73   In 1960, John Kennedy told the Greater Houston Ministerial Association that they should not oppose him just because he was a Catholic. He said, "If I should lose this election on the real issues I shall be . . . satisfied that I tried my best and was fairly judged."

74   Much changes. But much remains the same. What Abraham Lincoln called the "mystic chords of memory" preserve from generation to generation our hopes and dreams for our country. We have a chance, right here, right now—the chance of a dozen lifetimes—to fulfill those hopes, realize those dreams, and create the finest America yet.

75   For the next 70 days I *will* try my best. And I have confidence that you and all Americans will judge me fairly—on the real issues. Because that's the American way.

76   Thank you, God bless you, and God bless America.

Questions for Analysis

1. How does Clinton try to create identification with the audience? How does he attempt to ingratiate himself with the audience of legionnaires?

2. What is the implicit argument in telling the audience about Vietnam veterans, one a Medal of Honor winner, who had volunteered to serve in the Clinton campaign?

3. Some critics have seen this speech as an *apologia,* that is, a speech of self-defense in which charges are not refuted but the person's character is presented and detailed as a response. How does Clinton respond to charges about his draft evasion or explain discrepancies in what he had said? What does he do to counter such charges?

4. Some critics view this address as an example of campaign rhetoric, in which audience members are judges of a future event but are urged to act by voting for a particular candidate. How does Clinton try to present himself as the better presidential alternative? Why should one vote for him, based on this speech?

5. The Bush–Quayle campaign had claimed that Bush was responsible for the fall of the Soviet Union. How does Clinton try to counter that claim?

6. How does Clinton attempt to exploit weaknesses in Bush's image? What issues does he use?

7. Clinton recalls a speech that President Kennedy made to the Houston Ministerial Association during the 1960 campaign defending himself against charges that a Roman Catholic could not be president because of his commitments to the church. What kind of an analogy is Clinton trying to draw between that campaign and the campaign of 1992?

SOURCES

Delia, Jesse G. "A Constructivist Analysis of the Concept of Credibility." *Quarterly Journal of Speech* 62 (1976):361–375.

Infante, Dominic, K. R. Parker, C. H. Clarke, L. Wilson, and I. A. Nathu, "A Comparison of Factor and Functional Approaches to Source Credibility." *Communication Quarterly* 31 (1983): 43–48.

CHAPTER 6

Understanding the Rhetorical Problem: The Resources of Analysis

The efforts of past rhetors are a resource that can be tapped both to understand rhetorical obstacles and to discover ways of overcoming them. Speeches and essays appearing in the mass media are excellent models of strategies designed in recognition of and in response to specific barriers. You must become an analyst and critic if you are to learn from the rhetorical efforts of others, including experts, political figures, and your classmates and friends.

Two methods of analysis have already been presented: descriptive analysis, outlined in Chapter 2, and the rhetorical problem, outlined in Chapters 3, 4, and 5.

Descriptive analysis is basic to the study of all rhetoric. As a critic, your first task is to understand a discourse as fully as possible. That requires a close reading of the act. Here is an outline of descriptive analysis specifically devised for your use as a critic:

Descriptive Analysis[1]

I. What is the rhetor's purpose?

    A. What is the thesis or central idea?

    B. How is the subject limited or narrowed?

    C. What response is desired?

II. Who composes the target audiences?

    A. What must you know, believe, or value to participate in this act?

---

[1]Some rhetors use ghostwriters. As part of your analysis, you may need to determine what persons played a major role in the creation of the rhetorical act and how they affect the character of the text.

  B. Who are relevant agents of change?

  C. What evidence is there of efforts made to create a role or roles for the audience?

III. What role(s) or persona(s) does the rhetor assume?

IV. What is the rhetor's tone?

  A. What is the rhetor's attitude toward the subject?

  B. What is the rhetor's attitude toward the audience?

   1. Is the rhetor a subordinate of those addressed?

   2. Is the rhetor a peer of those addressed?

   3. Is the rhetor a superior of those addressed?

 V. How is the discourse structured?

  A. What does the introduction do?

  B. What kind of organization is used to develop ideas?

  C. What does the conclusion do?

  D. What efforts are made to create relationships among ideas?

 VI. What kinds of supporting materials are used?

  A. How is evidence adapted to the audience?

  B. How is the selection of evidence adapted to the purpose?

  C. What evidence is evoked from the audience?

VII. What strategies are used?

  A. What is the rhetor's style?

   1. How does language reflect the rhetor's role?

   2. How does language reflect the relationship between rhetor and audience?

   3. How is language adapted to the complexity of the subject?

  B. How does the rhetor appeal to the needs, drives, desires, and cultural values of the audience?

  C. What strategies are used to assist in proof?

  D. What strategies are used to animate ideas?

  E. What strategies are used to alter associations and attitudes?

These categories apply equally to speeches or essays by classmates and to essays, editorials, speeches, or statements in the mass media or presented live. If you work with visual rhetoric, these categories will need to be adapted to reflect its added dimensions.

The rhetorical problem is the second method of analysis. It goes beyond the text to look at a discourse in relation to its context. The obstacles that may arise can be outlined this way:

The Rhetorical Problem

I. What demands do subject and purpose make on the audience?

    A. Is the subject's complexity an obstacle?

        1. Do audience members have firsthand experience of the subject?

        2. Is special expertise required to interpret essential information?

        3. Is evaluation of the credibility and authority of secondary sources inevitable?

    B. Is the subject's cultural history an obstacle?

        1. Is there a taboo against public discussion?

        2. Are available arguments familiar and boring?

        3. Has past discussion created slogans and symbols that have to be refuted and reformulated?

        4. Does the purpose conflict with beliefs, attitudes, and cultural values of the audience?

    C. What will it cost the audience to participate?

        1. How much inconvenience and discomfort are involved?

        2. How much time, energy, and commitment are needed?

        3. How much of the audience's resources, money, and expertise must be expended?

        4. How much social resistance can be expected from family, friends, and neighbors?

    D. What control does the audience have over the outcome?

        1. Are the agents of change in the exposed audience?

        2. Is concerted action required?

        3. Is a series of actions needed?

        4. Is needed action simple, obvious, and likely to produce immediate rewards, or complex and difficult to evaluate?

II. What kinds of obstacles arise from the audience?

    A. Can the rhetor reach the target audience?

    B. Are misinterpretation and misperception likely?

   C. Is the subject salient for the audience?

   D. Does the audience believe that it can take effective action?

III.   What obstacles are created by the rhetor's character?

   A. What obstacles exist prior to rhetorical action?

   1. What is the rhetor's reputation and track record?

   2. How was the rhetor introduced?

   3. How do the setting and occasion limit the rhetor's choices?

   a. What expectations are created by the occasion?

   b. What expectations are created by the setting or environment?

   c. What preceding or subsequent events affect audience response?

   d. Who are the competing persuaders?

   e. How do the media of transmission select the audience and create expectations?

   B. How can the rhetor demonstrate competence, trustworthiness, and dynamism?

   C. What is the rhetor's relation to the audience?

   1. Are there bases for identification?

   2. What is the social power of the rhetor?

   3. What shared experiences and knowledge may prompt participation?

The rhetorical problem is a critical device to set up a fair basis for evaluation. For example, a novice tennis player probably cannot beat such top players as Steffi Graf or Monica Seles, and we would be most unfair if we judged her a failure merely because she lost. We have to assess her efforts in terms of the obstacles she must overcome.

Applying these questions to the testimony by J. C. Alvarez in Chapter 2 illustrates how the rhetorical problem can be used as an analytical device to locate the obstacles a rhetor faced and discover the strategies she or he used to overcome them.

The subject of Alvarez's first testimony is a problem, the claim by some that Clarence Thomas does not support affirmative action for minorities and women. The actual audience, those exposed, are the senators on the Judiciary Committee and in the Senate as a whole and those attending the hearing or interested enough to watch the hearings on C-Span. The senators on the committee and in the Senate as a whole are the primary agents of change, but secondary agents of change who can influence their votes are minority and women constituents, who need to be convinced that Thomas understands their problems and will support programs to alleviate them.

Because many people will testify, Alvarez's time is brief. Accordingly, she chooses to personalize the issue and to rely on her experience to attest to Thomas's commitment to minority rights. That choice allows her to present her credentials for testifying as an integral part of her testimony to the committee. On the one hand, it is limited proof; on the other hand, it is presented in a dramatic way designed to provoke identification from minorities and women like her. Because her time is short, Alvarez cannot be expected to make a detailed, fully documented case for Thomas's views on affirmative action, and it would be unfair to demand that she do so. Her experience with Thomas is both a plus and a minus. As a plus, she was there on the scene to have detailed familiarity with his behavior; like him, she is a minority who needed the help of such programs to gain an entree. Thus, she should be a good person to know and judge his record. As a minus, she is Thomas's close friend, and that may make us wary of accepting her evaluation—we may fear that she is somewhat biased toward her friend and a boss who helped her to advance in her career. Moreover, as a Hispanic, she is in an ideal position to respond to the complaints of other Hispanics.

Note that here the issues are not cost, control, complexity, or cultural history in a simple sense. There are potential costs to the senators if their constituents disapprove of the votes they cast, but they are very much in control—their votes will determine the outcome. The complexity arises out of conflicting testimony about Thomas's record, with some minority group members, older Americans, and women testifying that he was not responsive to their problems and did not enforce the law vigorously while others, such as Alvarez, testify to his commitments to such efforts. Cultural history is involved in conflicting views among the public about affirmative action—the value of individualism and judging solely by merit versus righting the past wrongs done to the disadvantaged by ensuring that when they are qualified, they have equal access to education and employment. Those conflicting values were reflected in the election of Ronald Reagan in 1980, who appointed Thomas to head the EEOC because his views about affirmative action were similar to those of the president. President George Bush shared those views and nominated Thomas to the Supreme Court, leaving senators in the difficult position of trying to balance electoral majorities for Reagan–Bush and Bush–Quayle against the voting power of women and minorities among their constituents. In other words, the rhetorical problem helps to place the rhetoric in context, to point to the limits created by the occasion, and to focus attention on the relationship between the rhetor's strengths and limitations and the decisions made by the rhetoric in the piece of discourse.

STANDARDS FOR EVALUATION

Four general standards or criteria can be used, alone or in combination, to judge rhetorical discourses. They are (1) achieving desired effects, (2) presenting as truthful, complete, and accurate an account of the issue as is possible, (3) producing an artistically satisfying discourse, and (4) using ethical means and advancing ethically desirable ends for society and for rhetorical practice. Each is relevant to rhetorical action. Each has important strengths and limitations.

The Effects Criterion

The effects criterion, the evaluation of a rhetorical act in terms of the response that it evokes, reflects the demand that every rhetorical act communicate, induce participation from an audience, and affect perceptions, beliefs, and attitudes. Unless some reaction occurs, the act initiated by a rhetor must be judged a failure.

But effects are difficult to isolate and verify. It is difficult to separate responses to one act from responses to other rhetoric that precedes and follows it. Most influence is the result of a campaign or of a series of experiences. Similarly, it is hard to measure just what the audience response was. Clapping may be a matter of relieved courtesy; questionnaires report only what people say occurred; the size and nature of the response may be greatly affected by the medium in which an act is presented. For these reasons, it is usually difficult to determine accurately the effects of a given rhetorical act.

The effects criterion also raises ethical problems. Applied strictly and in isolation, it would applaud rhetoric without regard for its accuracy or social consequences. By such a measure, the finest rhetorical works would be the speeches of Adolf Hitler, advertising that persuades teenagers to smoke despite serious health hazards, and the come-ons of particularly savvy con artists. Clearly, the effects criterion cannot be used alone; other criteria need to be used with it. The starting point of much analysis, however, is an attempt to explain why and how demonstrable effects were produced.

The Truth Criterion

The truth criterion measures the similarity between the "reality" presented in a speech or essay and "reality" as presented in other sources. In this case, the critic tests the accuracy and typicality of evidence in the discourse against other sources known to be well informed and compares the arguments selected against the pool of arguments available. Rhetoric is a part of social decision making. If we are to make good decisions, we need the best evidence available, and we need to examine all the relevant arguments. For this reason, considerations of adequacy and accuracy always are important.

But this criterion also has limitations. As noted in Chapter 1, the truths of rhetoric are social truths, truths created and validated by people. There is no simple way to verify all rhetorical claims or to validate all rhetorical arguments. The occasions best suited to rhetorical deliberation are those in which well-intentioned, informed people disagree. A good critic has to acknowledge conflicting evidence, varying interpretations, and competing perspectives, and recognize that no simple judgment about the truth of most acts can ever be made. In addition, no discourse is ever long enough to tell the whole truth, and the constraints of space and time, which are inherent to rhetoric, complicate strict application of this standard.

In one respect, this criterion conflicts with concerns for effects. Discourses that tell the whole truth, as far as that is possible, and adhere to strict, technical accuracy, are likely to be suitable only for experts. In fact, if the truth criterion were applied strictly, nearly all rhetorical acts would be judged inadequate, and the finest pieces of rhetoric would be those directed to an elite group of specialists. Given rhetoric's popular character and its role in social and public decision making, this criterion alone would not be an appropriate basis for evaluating rhetorical action.

The Artistic Criterion

The artistic or aesthetic criterion focuses on means, on how effects are produced. The word *aesthetic* comes from the Greek word *aisthêtikos*, which means "pertaining to sense perception." This original meaning is retained in the word *anaesthetic*, which refers to a substance like chloroform or novocaine that causes total or partial loss of sensation. The artistic or aesthetic criterion is a measure of how well a rhetorical act succeeds in altering perception, creating virtual experience, and inducing participation and identification. It is a measure of how well an act achieves its purpose, of how creatively a rhetor responds to the obstacles faced, of how inventively a rhetor fulfills the requirements of form.

For example, I rate Sojourner Truth's speech (see Chapter 5) high on artistic grounds because I think she was highly creative in responding to a difficult situation. In her case, there is only Frances Gage's testimony about the impact of her presence and her words. In this case, the critic must recognize how many obstacles existed and anticipate limited response. Despite that obstacle-filled situation, however, one can applaud the skill with which Truth responded to her rhetorical problem. Moreover, the capacity of her speech to arouse our admiration attests to its enduring power, a strong indicator of aesthetic merit.

The Ruth Bader Ginsburg nomination acceptance speech, reprinted at the end of this chapter, also deserves high artistic ratings. Bader Ginsburg not only fulfills the requirements of the occasion, discussed below, but she tailors this form to the occasion and to herself, and she produces a moving speech that has the capacity to endure as a model of its type. In this case, however, there is some evidence of effect. The text of the speech was printed in the *New York Times,* and a major segment from it was shown on the *MacNeil/Lehrer NewsHour.* President Clinton and many others were so moved that they had tears in their eyes afterward, but even without such evidence a critic can judge Bader Ginsburg's skills as a rhetor. The artistic criterion demands analysis of techniques, means, and strategies. These can be assessed with or without external evidence that a discourse achieved its goal. The artistic criterion also reveals those works that have the capacity to endure through time as models of rhetorical action because they are deeply moving, eloquent, and original.

The limitations of the artistic criterion are evident when we turn our attention to advertising and admire the skills of those who exploit the strategic resources of verbal and nonverbal language in order to manipulate us politically or commercially. Such uses of artistry may trouble us, but the artistic criterion does not provide standards to judge the purposes or ends of rhetorical action.

The Ethical Criterion

The ethical criterion judges the long-term effects of the ends espoused and the methods used. It evaluates the social consequences of rhetorical action—both its purposes and the means by which they are achieved. It judges the long-term effects of rhetoric both for society (What happens to a political system in which voting decisions are made on the basis of 30-second television commercials?) and for future rhetorical action (How can we communicate about complex issues if norms for rhetorical action are limited to the short segments typical of commercial and cable television programming?) as well as how these are affected by new technology (How can we vote intelligently if political advertisers exploit the visual capacities of television to prompt us to draw false conclusions?). Obviously, such judgments are highly controversial, and in some cases, they are directly related to the truth criterion. In recent history, the conflict in government between limiting press coverage during the war in the Persian Gulf on the one hand, and the requirements of national security on the other, illustrates this kind of problem. Ethical judgments require us to balance legitimate competing claims. There are limits on First Amendment freedoms, for example, but we ought to fight to see that only absolutely essential limits are set.

In this regard, the essay by Cottin Pogrebin in Chapter 4 is ideal for ethical evaluation. She advocates a controversial position while trying to take moral questions into account. In evaluating it, you might ask whether the principles she develops are defined clearly enough to be good standards by which to judge the arguments for negotiating with a hated enemy. Ethical evaluation requires that you take a close look at opposing views and at the social consequences of the policies she advocates. You might contrast the ethical dimensions of her essay with the more intransigent positions advocated by Jewish settlers in the Gaza Strip.

CONTEXT AND OCCASION

Rhetorical evaluations must be modified in terms of the special pressures created by the context and the occasion. These special pressures or constraints (a *constraint* is something that limits, restricts, or regulates) include (1) competing rhetorical action, (2) preceding or subsequent events, (3) the media of transmission, and (4) expectations and requirements created by the occasion. Each of these should be examined to see if it leads us to qualify or refine our judgments about effects, truth, artistry, and ethics.

Competing Rhetorical Action

Very few rhetorical acts occur in isolation, and many are part of campaigns and movements. But campaigns include competition from other persuaders—political candidates or advertisers—and movements are protests against the status quo, which will be defended by its supporters. In other words, much rhetoric occurs in a competitive environment, and it has to be judged in relation to its competition. It's nice to receive an award for excellence in advertising, for example, but it's equally important to know how well you did against competing products.

Political campaigns illustrate how competition modifies judgments. For example, Bill Clinton's performance in the 1992 presidential debates had to be assessed in comparison to those of George Bush and H. Ross Perot and in relation to each debate's format and time limits. Effective rhetoric is responsive to the specific context: It refutes precisely those charges made by the opposition; it reacts to issues of concern to this audience; it takes account of the stands of competing advocates. And what might be highly praised in one situation might be inappropriate for another.

Comparison is an integral part of assessing rhetorical acts. As you evaluate, consider the choices available and then examine the ways in which those choices were limited by opponents, by competing positions, or by events and issues. Ask yourself what was possible, given the situation. Given the opposition, what was the best strategy? Given competing persuaders, what role was possible, what purpose was reasonable? Pay special attention to attempts to respond to issues, charges, and opponents. These should help you notice one kind of constraint that limits rhetorical action.

Preceding or Subsequent Events

A rhetorical act is always one in a series of events. The meaning of a rhetorical act is not an absolute or a given; it is always, in part, a function of the context in which it occurs. Evaluation needs to include an awareness of events that preceded and followed it, for these may explain the act and modify its meaning.

Many examples of rhetorical acts illustrate these principles. In 1948, Margaret Chase Smith of Maine was elected to the Senate after four terms in the House of Representatives. As her career in the Senate began, Senator Joseph McCarthy, R-WI, was fanning the flames of the "Red Scare" by announcing that Communist spies had infiltrated the highest levels of the government, including the State Department. Although she was concerned about the issue, Chase Smith began cautiously to ask McCarthy for specific details, names, and numbers; McCarthy repeatedly avoided answering her questions. After seeking the advice of journalist friends, she drafted a speech that objected to McCarthy's tactics, but that never mentioned his name. She added a final statement of principles that was signed by six other Republican senators. On June 1, 1950, she addressed the Senate and delivered what came to be known as her "Declaration of Conscience" asking her Senate colleagues to "do some soul-searching . . . on the manner in which we are using or abusing our individual powers and privileges."[2] Unless the reader knows about these prior events, the meaning of her words is not clear, and the excited reaction to her speech is unintelligible.

Similarly, one needs to know the background of the ten-month Smith Act trial in 1952–1953 of labor activist Elizabeth Gurley Flynn in which she acted as her own attorney.[3] The Smith Act made membership in the Communist Party illegal, in effect criminalizing people's political beliefs. The "Red Scare" fanned by Senator Joseph McCarthy and reflected in the Smith Act are essential to understanding Flynn's appeals to constitutional rights and her attempts to persuade the jury to put aside its fears in order to render a just verdict.

What has come to be called Richard Nixon's "Checkers Speech" (named for his children's dog Checkers, who was mentioned in the speech) is another example.[4] Unless you know that Nixon had been accused of misusing funds given by wealthy supporters and was being pressured to resign as the vice-presidential candidate by the Republican National Committee, and that presidential candidate Dwight Eisenhower withheld his support even after Nixon was cleared of the charges by an audit and a legal opinion, and that his entire political future hung on whether he could generate an extraordinarily massive response from the audience, you are likely to view the speech as highly emotional and sentimental, a tear-jerker. But when you know the events that preceded it, the speech takes on a slightly different hue.

Political campaigns also illustrate the role of surrounding events in rhetorical evaluation. For example, it is often forgotten that the first Kennedy–Nixon debate in 1960 took place very early in the campaign, on September 26. Americans were highly interested in the 1960 presidential race, and the first debate, given its date, was able to frame issues and create impressions because very little of the campaign (which traditionally begins on Labor Day) had preceded it.[5] By contrast, because the debate between Jimmy Carter and Ronald Reagan occurred so late in the 1980 campaign (the Thursday night before the election

---

[2]"Declaration of Conscience," U.S. Senate, June 1, 1950, in *Declaration of Conscience* (New York: Doubleday, 1972), pp. 12–17; cited material pp. 13–14.

[3]"Statement at the Smith Act Trial," February 2, 1953, with headnotes. *We Shall Be Heard: Women Speakers in America,* ed. Patricia Scileppi Kennedy and Gloria Hartmann O'Shields (Dubuque, IA: Kendall Hunt, 1983), pp. 235–244.

[4]For a detailed discussion of the events leading up to this speech, see Garry Wills, *Nixon Agonistes* (New York: Signet, 1969), pp. 93–114.

[5]See *The Great Debates, Kennedy vs. Nixon, 1960.* Ed. Sidney Kraus (Bloomington: Indiana University Press, 1962), pp. 224–231, 319–329.

on Tuesday), it was the culmination of the campaign and cannot be understood or assessed apart from what preceded it. Similarly, disappointed Carter supporters pointed to preceding events as a way of explaining his defeat, particularly to events just prior to the election that raised and then dashed hopes that the American hostages held by Iran would be released. Even the most skillful rhetorical efforts might be ineffective in such a context.

As discussed earlier, the obstacle of cultural history is a long-term view of the problem of preceding events. In light of the past, a rhetor may be expected to develop a new argument, take a new perspective, develop a new role, or respond to unforeseen events. The problem of long-term cultural history, as well as that of immediate happenings, needs to be considered in making assessments.

Subsequent events can have a variety of effects that complicate assessment. For example, it is difficult to assess the final speech of Dr. Martin Luther King, Jr., without being affected by what now seem to be his prophetic statements about his own death. Similarly, the Thanksgiving Day Proclamation prepared by President John Kennedy before he traveled to Dallas took on special poignancy after his assassination. Subsequent events transformed these statements into "last words," which we treat with special significance.

Subsequent happenings can also become a truth criterion against which to measure the claims of speakers, and the passage of time is the ultimate determinant of ethical judgments. Similarly, the ability of some rhetoric to withstand the test of time is clear evidence of artistic excellence. Thus, Lincoln's Gettysburg Address is no longer merely a speech made to honor those who died in the battle of Gettysburg; it remains an enduring commemoration of all those who have given their lives in battle for this nation.[6] As time passes, you may be forced to take account of two different judgments: that of the immediate audience and that of history.

Media of Transmission

Rhetoric is disseminated in many different ways: by direct mail, E-mail, the Internet, newspapers, magazines, books, radio, television, in face-to-face encounters, and through a microphone system in an auditorium or rally. Like all elements in rhetoric, these media create opportunities and generate constraints.

---

[6]For an analysis of its enduring significance, see Garry Wills, *Lincoln at Gettysburg* (New York: Simon and Schuster, 1993).

The great opportunity provided by the mass media is, of course, the chance to reach large audiences quickly and simultaneously. The ability of President Franklin Roosevelt to reach millions of Americans through radio in his "Fireside Chats" and to explain policies and raise morale in periods of crisis illustrates this opportunity. His success reflects his understanding of the immediacy and intimacy of radio as a medium and his skill in adapting to it—he "chatted" with Americans as citizens, peers, and members of a common national family united in their efforts. The continued use of radio and television by presidents, presidential candidates, and those representing particular ideological views reflects the importance of media that permit a message to be widely distributed. The use of talk show formats by presidential and vice-presidential candidates and their wives in 1992 exploited formats that permitted them to reach large audiences while presenting their views with little chance of being challenged as they would be by journalists in a press conference or on *Meet the Press*.

But the mass media also create problems. Gone are the days when public figures can speak privately to some part of the electorate; somehow, government leaders must find ways to speak to all of the nation all of the time. If you have understood the concept of the target audience, you will understand why this is a problem: It is nearly impossible to adapt to a truly heterogeneous audience. Inevitably, what pleases some will alienate others, and vice versa. In many cases, rhetors face a two-audience dilemma; that is, the immediate audience to whom they speak is composed of one group, the American Legion, say, or the National Association for the Advancement of Colored People (NAACP), while the larger, mediated audience is highly diverse. In such circumstances, it is possible to be a resounding success with one audience and a disastrous failure with the other. In assessing such efforts, you will need to consider several questions:

1. Did the speaker know when he or she spoke that the speech would be transmitted via the mass media? Not all rhetors know that a second, large, heterogeneous audience will develop.[7]

---

[7]See, for example, Ron Dorfman, "George Wald: But for the Grace of the Boston Globe . . ." *Chicago Journalism Review* 2 (May 1969):4, for the story of how George Wald's address, "A Generation in Search of a Future," unexpectedly became available in print and on radio, and was made into a record. The speech is reprinted in K. K. Campbell, *Critiques of Contemporary Rhetoric* (Belmont, CA: Wadsworth, 1972), pp. 60–68. For an illustration of a critique that holds a speaker responsible for material excerpted in the media, see Robert L. Scott and Wayne Brockriede, "Hubert Humphrey Faces the Black Power Issue," *Speaker and Gavel* 4 (November 1966):11–17.

2. Is the rhetor a national leader who can reasonably be expected to speak to all of the people? For example, when the executive director of the NAACP speaks, she or he will be treated as speaking for many African Americans in the larger audience no matter what the ethnic background or ideology of the immediate audience. However, when we treat any woman as speaking for all women or any American Indian or Asian American or African American as speaking for all American Indians or Asian Americans or African Americans, it is time to re-examine our stereotypes and prejudices.

3. What discrepancies, if any, exist between the act as delivered and the act as transmitted via the mass media? Most rhetorical acts are transmitted only in excerpts, often as part of 99-second segments on the network news. Such snippets, chosen for their drama and pithiness, can give a most deceptive impression of the entire act, and critics need to assess the degree to which rhetors can be held responsible for what reporters pick up and pass on in newspapers, magazines, and radio and television newscasts and for the ways in which they frame their reports.

As these questions indicate, radio and television are often used to transmit rhetorical acts that occur in other settings—at conventions or rallies, for example. So, for instance, we watch President Reagan's Ambassador to the United Nations Jeane Kirkpatrick or Texas Governor Ann Richards speak to the national party conventions or we listen to Faye Wattleton, former head of the Planned Parenthood Federation of America, addressing supporters at a pro-choice rally. In such cases, the medium itself makes no special demands, other than limits of time. We expect to hear someone pound on a podium in a dramatic convention speech or shout at a rally when the audience is spread out over the mall in Washington, D.C. But rhetorical acts created for television are quite different, whether they are a speech by the president from the Oval Office, a debate between presidential candidates, a documentary, or an advertisement; additional constraints arise. Like radio, television is an intimate medium. We watch it in our living rooms and bedrooms; we look at close-up shots of people's faces most of the time; we witness domestic dramas on soap operas and in prime-time programming; and we hear the news from a "family" of local reporters who chat together informally. Accordingly, delivery that was effective at a convention or rally may be unpleasant on television— too loud, too strident, too formal, an irritating intrusion into the intimacy of our homes. In the 1980 debate between Carter and Reagan, commentators suggested that Reagan's success was linked to the greater suitability of his delivery and personality for the medium of television.[8] Similarly, in 1992, part of H. Ross Perot's success may have been his ability to express his ideas in memorable sound bites. Once again, evaluations of such rhetorical acts need to take account of the demands made by electronic, as well as print, media.

The visual component of televised rhetoric, whether of news or of political and product advertising, creates special challenges for consumers, voters, and critics. The visual dimension opens up new kinds of strategies, and some research suggests that the visual overwhelms the verbal. In addition, because ads and news stories pass by very quickly, we are exposed to them for only a short period, which makes it difficult to identify and interpret details; thus, it is easier for rhetors to exploit the possibilities of association and suggestion.[9]

Expectations and Requirements Created by the Occasion

In *On Rhetoric,* Aristotle described three types or genres of rhetoric: deliberative rhetoric dealing with future policy, which occurred in legislatures; forensic rhetoric dealing with criminal charges regarding past behavior, which occurred in the law courts; and ceremonial or epideictic (from *epideixis,* to show forth or display) rhetoric dealing with praise and blame, honor and dishonor, which occurred on special occasions. Epideictic rhetoric, tied to specific occasions, demands special evaluation because of the requirements and expectations created by these occasions.

Typical examples of epideictic rhetoric are inaugural addresses, Fourth of July speeches, commencement addresses, and eulogies. Such speeches appear on occasions that recur at regular intervals, and our experience with such rhetoric, and the traditions that have developed around them, create special constraints on rhetorical action. For each kind of occasional address, distinct expectations exist.

In general, however, epideictic rhetoric is closer to the nondiscursive than to the discursive end of the continua of rhetorical action (see Chapter 8). Its very name suggests its consummatory purpose; that is,

---

[8]*The Great Debates,* ed. Kraus, pp. 280–283.

[9]For analyses of political advertising, see K. H. Jamieson, *Packaging the Presidency* (New York: Oxford University Press, 1984) and *Dirty Politics* (New York: Oxford University Press, 1992). For a general introduction to the rhetoric of news, advertising, and politics see K. H. Jamieson and K. K. Campbell, *Interplay of Influence: News, Advertising, Politics, and the Mass Media,* 3d ed. (Belmont, CA: Wadsworth Publishing, 1992).

we are to celebrate or commemorate the occasion, and speakers are expected to display their artistic skills and be judged on their performance. The language of such rhetoric tends to be formal, poetic, and figurative. Structurally, it is likely to explore topically all aspects of a feeling or attitude. The occasions themselves suggest that supporting materials are likely to emphasize what is psychologically appealing and what reflects cultural values. Finally, such addresses are more likely to develop ritualistically than to provide logical arguments.

The eulogy (*eu* = well, *logos* = to speak; in short, to praise) is one kind of epideictic rhetoric. It appears on the occasion of death. The death of any person forces us to confront our own mortality, and it disrupts the human community of which the deceased was a part. The eulogy meets certain very basic human needs: It acknowledges death; it reunites the sundered community; it shifts the relationship between the living and the deceased and suggests that although dead in the flesh, the deceased lives on in spirit—in children, good deeds, or in principles—reassuring the living that a kind of immortality exists for all of us. The tone of the eulogy is personal (death is an intimate matter) and somber, and it frequently uses metaphors of rebirth to express the idea of immortality. If a eulogy is to be judged satisfactory, it must fulfill these functions in some way.

Eulogies fail when they do not meet our expectations. For example, eulogies cannot arouse controversy because controversy prevents the reunification of the community. As a result, when Senator Charles Percy bluntly advocated gun control and an end to the war in Vietnam in a eulogy to Senator Robert F. Kennedy, who died of gunshot wounds in 1968, he violated audience expectations and failed to perform the eulogistic function of unification. In short, the characteristics of the eulogy become bases for evaluating this particular kind of occasional rhetoric.

The presidential inaugural is another example of epideictic rhetoric, although the requirements for such a speech are less rigid and specific. Because it follows a long and divisive political campaign, we expect the newly elected president to reunify the nation. Because this is an occasion tied to fundamental national values (the speech is now given after the presidential oath of office has been administered), we expect the president to rehearse those values for us and make them come alive for us again. Because we fear the power of the executive, we expect presidents to be humble, to admit limitations, and to ask for the help of Congress, of the people, and of God in their efforts to govern. Finally, because this is the beginning of a new administration, we expect presidents to indicate the philosophy and tone of their administrations, to suggest in broad terms the foreign and domestic policies that are of primary importance. Presidential inaugural addresses vary greatly, but these expectations are criteria that can be used to evaluate how well a president meets audience expectations.[10]

They are also bases for distinguishing competent from outstanding inaugurals. Jimmy Carter, for example, did an outstanding job of unifying the country after what was not only a long and divisive campaign but also a period of national disgrace following Watergate in which we were governed by our first unelected president, Gerald Ford. Here is one report of the opening of Carter's address:

> The inaugural speech began with a moving gesture. "For myself and for our nation," said Carter, "I want to thank my predecessor for all he has done to heal our land." There was a swell of cheers; Ford blinked back tears and stood for a moment. "God bless you, sir," said Carter, "I'm proud of you." He extended his hand to Ford, who accepted it in a warm two-handed clasp—and the era of Jimmy Carter began.[11]

By contrast, he did only an adequate job of rehearsing basic values. He recalled most of our traditional values, but in a rather jumbled list of clichés. Carter was unable to breathe new life into old values so that they would still seem right for us. He asked for our help and that of Congress and God, but the request was not in a form that made us eager to cooperate. He told us nothing of his plans for the new administration. He indicated only his concerns for human rights and disarmament, and these were already well known from the campaign. In other words, if you look at Carter's inaugural in light of these expectations, you can begin to explain why his speech has not been memorable.

Functions and expectations are also a basis for recognizing outstanding rhetorical acts—ones that continue to express the kinds of feelings we have on such occasions. For example, use these criteria to compare Carter's inaugural to that of John Kennedy. In this case, you will discover a speech that not only met these expectations but met them in ways that were deeply moving, adapted to the occasion, and highly original.

---

[10]For extended discussion of inaugurals, see K. K. Campbell and K. H. Jamieson, *Deeds Done in Words: The Genres of Presidential Governance* (University of Chicago Press, 1990), pp. 14–51.

[11]"A New Spirit," *Newsweek,* January 31, 1977, p. 15.

SUMMARY

As an analyst or critic, your first task is one of descriptive analysis—
full and detailed understanding of the rhetorical act. Your second task
concerns the rhetorical problem: What obstacles did the rhetor face
and what resources were used to overcome them? Your third task is
evaluative. Four criteria can be used. You can assess the capacity of the
act to achieve its end (effects). You can evaluate the consistency between the picture presented in the discourse and that presented in
other works (truth). You can weigh the long-term consequences of
both the ideas advocated for society and the method of presentation
for the future of rhetorical action (ethics). You can judge the appeal
and force of the strategies or means used to achieve the ends (artistry
or aesthetics). Finally, you can refine your judgments by considering
the constraints created by the context (competition, surrounding
events, media of transmission) and by the occasion. The expectations
and requirements for some occasions provide special criteria for evaluation, as in the case of eulogies and inaugurals.

Models of critical analysis are suggested in the list of readings at the
end of this chapter.

▪   ▪   ▪

MATERIAL FOR ANALYSIS

On June 14, President Clinton announced his nomination of Ruth
Bader Ginsburg of the U.S. Court of Appeals for the District of Columbia to be an Associate Justice of the U.S. Supreme Court, replacing Justice Byron White. Clinton's announcement was a speech introducing
the nominee to the public and presenting the nomination as the ful-
fillment of a campaign promise to nominate someone with "the heart
and spirit, the talent and discipline, the knowledge, common sense,
and wisdom to translate the hopes of the American people as presented in the cases before it into an enduring body of constitutional
law." Clinton emphasized her years of service as a judge, "her pioneer-
ing work in behalf of the women of this country," and her ability "to
be a force for consensus building on the Supreme Court, just as she
has been on the Court of Appeals." He summarized her academic and
judicial background and her struggles to find an appropriate use for
her talents and training in the 1960s. Judge Ruth Bader Ginsburg's

speech accepting President Clinton's nomination to be a Justice of the Supreme Court also introduced her to the Senate and the public:[12]

1   Mr. President, I am grateful beyond measure for the confidence you have placed in me, and I will strive with all that I have to live up to your expectations in making this appointment.

2   I appreciate, too, the special caring of Senator Daniel Patrick Moynihan, the more so because I do not actually know the senator. I was born and brought up in New York, the state Senator Moynihan represents, and he was the very first person to call with good wishes when President Carter nominated me in 1980 to serve on the U.S. Court of Appeals for the District of Columbia Circuit. Senator Moynihan has offered the same encouragement on this occasion.

3   May I introduce at this happy moment three people very special to me: my husband Martin B. Ginsburg, my son-in-law George T. Spera, Jr., and my son, James Steven Ginsburg.

4   The announcement the president just made is significant, I believe, because it contributes to the end of the days when women, at least half the talent pool in our society, appear in high places only as one-at-a-time performers. Recall that when President Carter took office in 1976, no woman [had] ever served on the Supreme Court, and only one woman, Shirley Hufstedler of California, then served at the next federal court level, the United States Court[s] of Appeals.

5   Today Justice Sandra Day O'Connor graces the Supreme Court bench, and close to 25 women serve at the Federal Court of Appeals level, two as chief judges. I am confident that more will soon join them. That seems inevitable, given the change in law school enrollment.

6   My law school class in the late 1950s numbered over 500. That class included less than ten women. As the president said, not a law firm in the entire city of New York bid for my employment as a lawyer when I earned my degree. Today few law schools have female enrollment under 40 percent, and several have reached or passed the 50 percent mark. And thanks to Title VII, no entry doors are barred.

7   My daughter, Jane, reminded me a few hours ago in a good-luck call from Australia of a sign of the change we have had the good fortune to experience. In her high school yearbook on her

---

[12]Transcript, *New York Times*, June 15, 1993, p. A13.

graduation in 1973, the listing for Jane Ginsburg under "ambition" was "to see her mother appointed to the Supreme Court." The next line read, "If necessary, Jane will appoint her." Jane is so pleased, Mr. President, that you did it instead, and her brother James is, too.

8   I expect to be asked in some detail about my views of the work of a good judge on a High Court bench. This afternoon is not the moment for extended remarks on that subject, but I might state a few prime guides.

9   Chief Justice Rehnquist offered one I keep in the front of my mind: A judge is bound to decide each case fairly in a court with the relevant facts and the applicable law even when the decision is not, as he put it, what the home crowd wants.

10   Next, I know no better summary than the one Justice O'Connor recently provided, drawn from a paper by New York University Law School Professor Bert Neuborne. The remarks concern the enduring influence of Justice Oliver Wendell Holmes. They read, "When a modern constitutional judge is confronted with a hard case, Holmes is at her side with three gentle reminders: first, intellectual honesty about the available policy choices; second, disciplined self-restraint in respecting the majority's policy choice; and third, principled commitment to defense of individual autonomy even in the face of majority action." To that I can only say, "Amen."

11   I am indebted to so many for this extraordinary chance and challenge: to a revived women's movement in the 1970s that opened doors for people like me, to the civil rights movement of the 1960s from which the women's movement drew inspiration, to my teaching colleagues at Rutgers and Columbia and for 13 years my D.C. Circuit colleagues, who shaped and heightened my appreciation of the value of collegiality.

12   Most closely, I have been aided by my life partner, Martin D. Ginsburg, who has been since our teenage years my best friend and biggest booster; by my mother-in-law, Evelyn Ginsburg, the most supportive parent a person could have; and by a daughter and son with the tastes to appreciate that Daddy cooks ever so much better than Mommy and so phased me out of the kitchen at a relatively early age.

13   Finally, I know Hillary Rodham Clinton has encouraged and supported the president's decision to utilize the skills and talents of all the people of the United States. I did not, until today, know Mrs. Clinton, but I hasten to add that I am not the first member of my family to stand close to her. There is another I love dearly to whom the First Lady is already an old friend. My wonderful granddaughter Clara witnessed this super, unposed photograph taken last October when Mrs. Clinton visited the nursery school in New York and led the little ones in "The Toothbrush Song." The small person right in front is Clara.

14   I have a last thank you. It is to my mother, Celia Amster Bader, the bravest and strongest person I have known, who was taken from me much too soon. I pray that I may be all that she would have been had she lived in an age when women could aspire and achieve and daughters are cherished as much as sons. I look forward to stimulating weeks this summer and, if I am confirmed, to working at a neighboring court to the best of my ability for the advancement of the law in the service of society. Thank you.

Questions for Analysis

1. How does Bader Ginsburg's speech fulfill the audience's expectations for the occasion? What are those expectations? What are the different audiences for her speech? Are their expectations different?

2. How does Bader Ginsburg use the opportunity offered by the occasion to move beyond thanks to advance a cause?

3. Supreme Court nominations during this period were controversial and divisive, illustrated by the defeated nomination of Robert Bork and the controversy over the nomination of Clarence Thomas. What does Bader Ginsburg do to lessen controversy and to unify the audience?

4. One would expect a nomination acceptance speech to be personal. How does Bader Ginsburg use her personal experience in the speech?

EXERCISE

A Group Rhetorical Analysis

The class is divided into groups of four to six students, and each group is asked to do this exercise.

Select a rhetorical act for analysis. You might analyze

■ Television series (for example, whether or not *Murphy Brown* or *Roseanne* promotes feminist values; why *Funniest Home Videos* is such a hit) or just a single episode (you would need to make the episode available to class members, however)

■ A book (why *Rubyfruit Jungle* remains popular despite the controversial lifestyle it presents; what made *The Bridges of Madison County* such a commercial success)

■ A speech (why the speech of Marilyn Tucker Quayle, wife of then–Vice President Dan Quayle, at the 1992 Republican Convention produced such intense reactions)

■ A movie (why people "act out" at the *Rocky Horror Picture Show* and return to view it over and over; why *Mrs. Doubtfire* was so popular)

■ A presidential campaign debate or a debate on *Firing Line,* or news coverage of an event (such as the Hill–Thomas hearings)

There are four requirements:

1. You must turn in a prospectus at least two weeks before your oral presentation in which you indicate the act you have chosen, the general approach you will take (what issues you will consider, what questions you will raise), and the way in which you plan to divide your responsibilities (for example, Taylor will talk about political convention speeches—who has given them and how speakers are chosen; Leslie will identify what women have made convention addresses and give a thumbnail description of reactions; Lynn will provide a short biography of Marilyn Quayle to explain her ethos and authority; Lacey will describe the prior addresses and the kind of frame they created for her speech; Lynn will describe the varied responses; then all will discuss reasons why these intense reactions occurred). Turn in only one prospectus from each group; one page should be adequate. The instructor will return these with comments and suggestions.

2. The rhetorical act you analyze must be accessible to all class members (this is presumed to be the case for a regular television series or a major news event, but forewarning is needed to allow the class to pay special attention). If you are treating something that has been published, you need only tell where it can be found (you can probably arrange with the instructor to have copies made of an essay or speech). If you select a movie, be sure it is reasonably available for viewing before your presentation.

3. An oral presentation by the group to the rest of the class should take no more than 30 minutes, leaving time for questions and discussion by the class and the instructor.

4. You must turn in an essay summarizing your individual presentation; it should include a list of the sources you used in gathering information, analyzing the work, and developing an interpretation. The essay should not be identical to what you present orally as a member of the group, but it should describe your special contribution to the group analysis and the sources you used to develop it.

Use descriptive analysis in doing a close reading of the act itself. Use the rhetorical problem as a way of looking at the act strategically. Use the four evaluative criteria and special evaluations drawn from context, occasion, and medium of transmission to assess how and why and whether the rhetorical act achieves its ends and for whom.

SOURCES

Black, Edwin. *Rhetorical Criticism: A Study in Method.* 1965; Madison, University of Wisconsin Press, 1978, pp. 78–90. These pages include a speech and a critique based on the aesthetic criterion.

Campbell, Karlyn Kohrs. *Critiques of Contemporary Rhetoric.* Belmont, CA: Wadsworth, 1972; Campbell, Karlyn Kohrs, and Thomas R. Burkholder, 2d ed., Belmont, CA: Wadsworth, 1996. Each edition of this book contains a number of criticisms that illustrate principles developed in this chapter. The opening chapters also offer additional suggestions for critical analysis.

Hart, Roderick P. *Modern Rhetorical Criticism.* Glenview, IL: Scott Foresman/Little Brown Higher Education, 1990. This book provides more detailed instructions about criticism, including a number of critical profiles or précis of works by critics.

Leff, Michael C., and G. P. Mohrmann. "Lincoln at Cooper Union: A Rhetorical Analysis of the Text." *Quarterly Journal of Speech* 60 (October 1974):346–358. A close reading of the text reclassifies this famous speech and illuminates its purpose.

Ling, David. "A Pentadic Analysis of Senator Edward Kennedy's Address to the People of Massachusetts, July 25, 1969." *Central States Speech Journal* 21 (Summer 1970):81–86. A close textual reading of Kennedy's apologia for Chappaquiddick contrasts explicit statement and implicit argument.

Stelzner, Hermann G. "'War Message,' December 8, 1941: An Approach to Language." *Speech Monographs* 33 (November 1966):419–437. A close analysis of the style of F. D. R.'s declaration of war that illuminates aesthetic and strategic choices.

Windt, Theodore Otto, Jr. "The Diatribe: Last Resort for Protest." *Quarterly Journal of Speech* 58 (February 1972):1–14. This essay examines the effects of ideology on rhetorical form and compares the rhetoric of ancient cynics with that of such modern yippies as Abbie Hoffman and Jerry Rubin.

Zyskind, Harold. "A Rhetorical Analysis of the Gettysburg Address." *Journal of General Education* 4 (April 1950):202–212. This detailed generic analysis argues that Lincoln's speech is primarily deliberative rather than epideictic.

PART THREE

Resources for Rhetorical Action

CHAPTER 7

The Resources of Evidence

The other day my old classmate Allen and I were discussing who would be the next editor-in-chief of the influential magazine whose staff he had recently joined. I proposed Rosemary, the deputy editor: She had seniority, she was extremely able, she was practically doing the job already. Allen looked at me as though I had suggested sending out a spacecraft for the editor of *The Neptune Gazette*. Come on, he said patronizingly, you know they'd never give it to a woman. So who do you think it will be? I asked innocently. Well, he replied with a modest blush, actually, me.[1]

This introduction to a "Hers" column appeared in the *New York Times*. The author attracts our attention with a story, in this case, an example related to the subject she intends to discuss. Her use of the example illustrates one resource, supporting materials or evidence, that is available to rhetors to overcome their rhetorical problem.

After reading Chapters 3, 4, and 5, you may feel that the situation is a nearly hopeless one, that rhetors face obstacles so great that there is little they can do. That is not the case. There are many obstacles; there are also many resources for overcoming them. One of the most important is evidence. Along with the arguments used and the structure of the rhetorical act, these are resources that exist in our ability to use and respond to reasoning and data.

Writing long ago in *On Rhetoric*, Aristotle said, "There are two parts to a speech; for it is necessary [first] to state the subject and [then] to

---

[1]"Reflections on a True Meritocracy" by Katha Pollitt, a literary critic and author of a book of poems, *Antarctic Traveller* (Knopf), as it appeared in the *New York Times*, December 26, 1985, p. 14Y. © 1985 by The New York Times Company. Reprinted by permission.

demonstrate it" (3.13.1414a.30–1). His statement emphasizes the role of a central claim or thesis, arguments in its support, and data in persuasion. As Aristotle also noted, however, proof comes in different forms. He wrote about three modes of proof arising out of the discursive or rational linkages (*logos*), out of the demographics and the feelings, attitudes, or state of mind of the audience (*pathos*), and out of the audience's perceptions of the rhetor (*ethos*). Aristotle was also concerned with the resources of language, particularly of metaphor.

Aristotle's ideas are still valid. We cannot discuss evidence solely in logical or empirical terms. We must also consider its psychological impact on the audience—whether evidence makes ideas vivid, clear, and personally relevant or affects attitudes toward the rhetor.

In practical terms, every piece of evidence must be judged by two criteria: (1) What are its strengths and limitations as proof? and (2) What are its psychological powers? Ideally, good supporting materials show the truth (probative force) of a claim; they are clear, vivid, and concrete (salient and cogent); and they present the rhetor as competent and trustworthy.

EXAMPLES

The piece of evidence that opens this chapter is an example. An *example* is a case or an instance, real or hypothetical, detailed or undetailed, used to illustrate an idea or to prove that a particular kind of event has happened or could happen.

This story, a detailed example, also introduces the topic of the essay. The story is personal: One of the characters is the author; the second is a male, Allen, who not only finds sex discrimination acceptable but also stands ready to enjoy its benefits. The language is vivid, illustrated by the figurative analogy describing Allen's reaction to the author's suggestion that Rosemary was the best candidate, which is compared to proposing "sending out a spacecraft for the editor of *The Neptune Gazette.*" As proof, it simply shows us that this particular situation has happened once.

As you will have realized by now, the example is a weak form of evidence when judged logically or empirically. It merely shows that something happened once, and if the example is hypothetical or imaginary, it does not even do that. In order to illustrate the weakness of the example as proof, I tell my students the true story of a woman who was killed instantly while asleep in her bed by the fall of a large meteor. No matter how dramatically I tell the story or how detailed I make it, they are never frightened. From their personal experience, from the experience of others, and from news reports and astronomical data, they know that meteors rarely fall to the ground on our planet, especially in sizes that would be harmful, and that they rarely strike people or animals. The students' reaction is, "Okay, it happened once. The odds are it won't ever happen again, and the chances of its happening to me are infinitesimal."

Just like the story of the death from a falling meteor, the story of Rosemary and Allen by itself proves very little. As good critics, we ask, appropriately, Does this happen often? Is this a typical case? Is Rosemary and Allen's situation common enough so that we can draw conclusions from it? Without other evidence, without a different kind of evidence, such questions cannot be answered.

But Rosemary and Allen's story is a strong piece of evidence on psychological grounds. As human beings, we have trouble imagining hundreds or thousands or millions of anything—including males who benefit from sex discrimination. But we can imagine a specific conversation in which someone says something that shows that he assumes that just because he is a white male, he is obviously superior to any female or nonwhite male candidate. (Some of us may not have to imagine such conversations!) In other words, the rhetorical force of the example lies in its ability to prompt us to picture a scene, imagine ourselves in it, and identify with the people and events. The more detailed the example—and the more skillfully the details are chosen—the more we identify with the problem or situation and participate in it. It is this capacity to stimulate identification that makes examples such powerful pieces of evidence psychologically. They clarify through detail; they engage us by creating the bases for identification.

If you understand what an example can do at its best, you can also discriminate among examples that are more or less effective. In most cases, a real example of an actual event or person is better than a hypothetical or imaginary case. But real examples are not always available. For example, no terrorist as yet has acquired a nuclear device. If a rhetor is to describe such an event, it will be necessary to develop a hypothetical example, and events of this kind have already become the subjects of works of fiction. As proof, both logically and psychologically, a hypothetical example is strongest when it seems most plausible to the audience, when it has, in literary terms, the greatest verisimilitude; that is, it seems true to life; it appears realistic or likely based on our experience. For example, in the opening chapter of *Silent Spring*, "A Fable for Tomorrow," Rachel Carson dramatized the effects of pesticide pollution on a small pastoral town. A "strange blight" or "an evil spell" descended on it. Cows and sheep fell ill; children sickened and died.

Then the many birds for which the town was famous became silent. Carson encouraged readers to participate imaginatively in this ominous scene, and then added, "A grim specter has crept upon us almost unnoticed, and this imagined tragedy may easily become a stark reality we all shall know. What has already silenced the sounds of spring in countless towns in America? This book is an attempt to explain."[2] Subsequent chapters, which were full of statistics, chemical formulas, and experimental data, documented the verisimilitude of her fictional narrative, and the book went on to become one of the most important works of twentieth-century environmentalism. Another example is the depiction of a hypothetical scenario in Daniel Webster's reply to Hayne in Chapter 10. In other words, the details of the example should conform to what is known—imaginary cowgirls should behave like their real-life counterparts; imaginary nuclear accidents must take account of all the levels of protection in real-life nuclear plants, and so forth. Television films based on real-life events, such as the 1993 standoff between federal agents and Branch Davidians in Waco, Texas, or the 1981 wedding of Prince Charles and Lady Diana, capitalize on (some would say exploit) the feelings and excitement the original event aroused in order to attract large audiences.

Real examples too—indeed all examples—are judged by their plausibility, whether they seem likely, and their verisimilitude, whether they mimic what we experience and, hence, believe to be true or real. Although no example by itself can demonstrate its own representativeness, it should conform to common knowledge of what is likely to happen or likely to be true. In addition, our willingness to accept examples is heightened by the amount of detail that is provided. The details we know about Allen and Rosemary conform to what we know about those who hold most top-level positions in our society and the "glass ceiling" that many women face in attempting to climb the executive ladder. In addition, the details and the distinctive language help us to believe that there is a real Allen who is in this situation and feels just this way.

Plausibility is not just a function of the example itself; it is a function of the similarity between what happens in the example and the experiences of the audience. If an example is to create identification and invite participation by audience members, it must fit their experiences; otherwise you, as rhetor, must be prepared to show through other evidence that the case you provide is representative or relatively common. The example of Rosemary and Allen would be weak in this regard for many audiences.

---

[2]Rachel Carson, *Silent Spring*, 1962; 25th anniversary edition, Boston: Houghton Mifflin, 1987, p. 3.

In addition, you should note that a number of examples will strengthen an individual case so that, as a series, they suggest that each is typical or representative of a larger number of instances.

Examples also contribute to the ethos or credibility of the rhetor. They suggest that the rhetor is concerned with real people and events, and they imply that she or he has had firsthand experience with the situation. Very often, examples demonstrate the goodwill of the speaker and the expertise that comes from combining practical experience with theoretical knowledge.

In summary, then, the example is psychologically a vivid evocation that clarifies the meaning of an idea or problem. When details are given, and when the audience finds an example plausible because of detail or conformity to their experience, it becomes highly effective in creating identification and in involving the audience with the problem. Real examples are stronger than hypothetical ones. To be effective, a hypothetical case must establish its similarity to real-life situations. Examples are stronger when they are relatively detailed and when a series of them is used. Examples are weak as proof because they are single instances that may be atypical and unrepresentative. They are also weak if they are undetailed and if they contradict or lie outside the experiences of the audience.

AUTHORITY

Authority evidence is another way to bolster a claim. The contrast between a lay and an expert witness in a courtroom is a helpful way to define the special function of this kind of evidence. If you or I, as ordinary people or lay witnesses, testify in a court of law, we can testify only to what we have actually seen or heard or know from personal experience. (We give *testimony,* a form of the example.[3]) We are not allowed to draw conclusions and lawyers are not allowed to "lead" us, that is, to ask us to draw conclusions or interpret evidence. In contrast, the expert witness comes to court specifically to draw conclusions and interpret raw data. A ballistics expert draws on her experience and training to conclude that two bullets were shot from the same gun; a psychologist draws on her experience with the defendant and on her training to interpret the defendant's mental capacity. The functions of the expert witness are the same functions performed by

---

[3]For a detailed analysis of the many problems with this form of evidence, see Elizabeth F. Loftus, *Eyewitness Testimony* (Cambridge, MA: Harvard University Press, 1980).

authority evidence. For example, here is the next paragraph of the editorial quoted at the beginning of this chapter:

> This exchange made me think again about one of the more insidious arguments being made in the current onslaught against affirmative action: Advancing women and minorities on the basis of sex and race damages their self-esteem. According to Clarence M. Pendleton, Jr., chairman of the United States Commission on Civil Rights, those who benefit from social and legal pressures on their behalf know in their hearts that they are unworthy and suffer terribly because they fear, correctly, that they won't measure up. Worse, the women and minorities who would have won the golden prizes anyway—the college acceptance, the job, the promotion—are guilty by association: Everyone thinks they're tokens, even if they're not.

This is not more evidence for the same claim (that highly qualified women are overlooked for promotions) but for a different claim, of which the earlier conversation reminded the author. This new claim is that affirmative action has an evil side effect—it damages the self-esteem of those whom it benefits.

The authority for this argument is the chair of the U.S. Civil Rights Commission, an organization set up by Congress to investigate violations of and enforce the statutes protecting the civil rights of citizens. The chair is also known to be African American, in other words, someone with personal, firsthand knowledge of the psychological impact of such measures as well as in a position that gives him access to data about affirmative action programs and their effects. The damage, we are told, takes two forms. Some who benefit are unworthy, and they suffer because they know their inadequacies will be revealed. Some who benefit are worthy, but affirmative action makes others disparage them on the assumption that they did not earn their awards through merit.

In this case, the only information we have about Pendleton's expertise comes from his appointive position as chair of the Civil Rights Commission and from outside knowledge of his ethnicity. If you are a political junkie, you may recall that President Reagan wanted to eliminate the Civil Rights Commission, and when he could not, he named to it only those who opposed the affirmative action policies that he opposed. In other words, Pendleton was selected because of his beliefs about this very topic. In addition, we do not know whether Pendleton's opinion is based on the data gathered by the Civil Rights Commission or his personal views. In fact, we do not know what data underlie his conclusion.

In other words, although the power of authority evidence comes from the expertise and experience on which it is based, in some instances it may reflect a strongly held personal view that may or may not be based on an investigation of available data. As I detail how authority evidence works, many of its weaknesses become evident. We have no specific knowledge of Pendleton's training or expertise; we have only the authority suggested by the position he holds. We have no reason apart from his authority to believe that affirmative action psychologically harms those it benefits or even if the psychological harms he describes are greater than the economic or educational benefits of such programs. Nonetheless, that the chair of the Civil Rights Commission who is a member of a disadvantaged minority makes such a claim forces us to entertain it seriously.

Evidence from authority, like evidence from statistics, discussed next, can be misused. The commonest sort of misuse is to cite experts in one area as if they were experts in another. For example, I pay attention when Chris Evert assesses tennis strategies and the relative strengths of two tennis players. She not only was a winning professional tennis player, but she is also an articulate tennis analyst. When advertisers try to suggest that she speaks as an expert on consumer products, however, I am highly skeptical. Similarly, I doubt Robert Urich on the benefits of a particular brand of dog food; however, I would listen seriously to him on television acting because he has demonstrated his ability to perform successfully in this medium. (He starred in *Spenser, For Hire*, a detective series based on books by Robert B. Parker.) No one is an expert in all areas; the strength of authority evidence as proof is directly related to the authority's degree of expertise in the area in question.

Authoritative evidence is strongest (1) when we know the credentials of the authority—her or his training and experience; (2) when the relationship between the expertise of the authority and the subject is explicit; and (3) when we know details about the data used by the authority to make interpretations. Authority evidence is weakened when we do not know details about credentials, when the relationship of the authority to the subject is indirect or unclear, or when we do not know what data, principles, or experiences were used in drawing conclusions or making interpretations.

STATISTICS

To test the claim that Pendleton made, the author of the essay, Katha Pollitt, looked at the impact of such unfair advantages on white males, specifically, the impact on Allen.

We both attended Harvard-Radcliffe, for example, at a time when *the ratio of male to female students was fixed at 5 to 1.* Granted that *the pool of female applicants was smaller,* the fact remains it was harder for girls to get in. Everyone knew this, but Allen and his friends never saw themselves as having been rounded up to fill *an inflated male quota.* Nor did they see as tarnished victories their acceptance into the many all-male clubs and activities that flourished in those benighted years—the Signet Society, for instance, where literary Harvard men were served lunch by literary Radcliffe women employed as waitresses—or scorn to go off to Europe on postgraduate fellowships closed to female classmates.

A little later, she added:

At the Ivy League college where I taught last year, a delicious scandal came to light when an alumnus wrote an outraged letter to the campus newspaper alleging that his son had been passed over for admission in the rush to accept women and blacks. It turned out that *although the overall odds of acceptance were one in seven, for the children of alumni they were almost one in two.*

A *statistic* is a numerical or quantitative measure of scope or of frequency of occurrence. In the two paragraphs above, I italicized all the actual statistics or indications of relative numbers.

Rhetorically, statistics are measures of the size or extent of something and of its location in a population. Statistics also document certain recurring characteristics. In this case, all of the actual statistics are ratios: The ratio of five to one was a fixed quota on female students admitted to Harvard-Radcliffe; the overall odds of being accepted for admission at an unidentified Ivy League school were one in seven, although if you were the child of an alumnus the odds were considerably better at one in two.

Ratios are common measures of frequency of occurrence. For example, we are told that one in nine U.S. women will be diagnosed with breast cancer and that one in four U.S. women will be sexually assaulted during their lives. Ratios are particularly forceful when dealing with comparisons, another kind of evidence, discussed later in this chapter. In this case, we know that six out of every seven students (almost 86 percent) who apply to the anonymous Ivy League school will be rejected, but only one out of every two applicants (or only 50 percent) of those who are the children of alumni will be. We also know that when the author and Allen attended Harvard-Radcliffe, five male applicants were accepted for every female applicant, ensuring that only 16.6 percent of each new class would be women. Note that translating the ratios into percentages may help us to understand just what they mean.

Statistics are strong logically and empirically because they are careful measures of frequency. But as proof, they pose some problems. As the subtle cliché puts it, "Figures can't lie but liars can figure." In other words, numbers can be used to distort and misrepresent. At least two questions should be asked about every statistic: (1) What counts as an instance of what is being measured? and (2) How was the whole population sampled to obtain these data?

For another example, let us suppose that the state highway department reports speeding as the major cause in one-third of all fatal automobile accidents. It is not hard to determine what a fatal auto accident is, but it may be hard to decide just what speeding is. Is it exceeding the posted speed limit? If so, how do we know that was happening? Was someone clocking the speed? Is speeding traveling faster than is safe for the conditions? A fatal accident would seem to be proof that the driver exceeded the safe speed, but mechanical problems might cause such an accident even at low speeds. In addition, how do we decide what is the *major* cause? Suppose we know that someone was driving faster than the speed limit but was also legally drunk. Which is the major cause? If you ask such questions, you will realize that this statistic is a rough approximation of what state troopers believe is a major factor in serious auto accidents based on their reading of the signs (skid marks, damage, distance traveled after impact, Breathalyzer tests) and on extensive experience.

Other statistics are gathered through survey research, however, the kind of technique through which George Gallup, Louis Harris, Elmo Roper, and others question a random sample whose views are then taken to be representative of the views of all Americans "with a margin of error of plus or minus 5 percent" or some similar figure. A *sampling error* occurs when this smaller population—the group questioned—is unlike the larger population it is meant to represent. For example, in the 1948 election when pollsters predicted that Dewey would beat Truman, one major error seemed to come from sampling that included only people with telephones, people who were, at least in 1948, more affluent and more sympathetic to Republican candidates. A similar error might be made today if we sampled only those with cellular phones.

Many contemporary cigarette ads illustrate another kind of statistical distortion—the suggestion that a measurable difference makes a difference. Currently, brands of cigarettes are advertised as having only 1 or 4 or 7 milligrams of tar or nicotine, and the ads imply that it is healthier to smoke these brands. There is, however, no evidence of any medically significant advantage from smoking brands with lower levels of these ingredients as currently measured. Smoking any cigarette is bad for one's health. The undesirable effects of smoking may even arise, not from the amount of tar or nicotine, but from the products of combustion—carbon dioxide, nitrous oxide, sulfur dioxide, and the like. But the statistic makes it seem safer and better to smoke some brands than others, and if we fear the effects of smoking but cannot bring ourselves to stop, we may go along with the pretext that a numerical difference makes a medical difference.

The willingness to make such an assumption calls attention to a psychological asset of statistics: the appearance of objectivity and precision, which leads us to treat them as factual and true. Our "scientific," "technical" society reveres the empirical and "objective" so much that, as members of audiences, we are likely to be particularly impressed by statistical evidence.

This psychological strength is offset in part, however, by a psychological problem: Statistics are hard to understand and remember. An audience confronted with a series of statistics is likely to become confused and lost; special efforts must be made to translate large numbers remote from personal experience into more familiar terms. For example, ratios like those cited in Pollitt's essays simplify whole numbers by turning them into comparisons; the translation of those ratios into percentages is one way to make the ratios more intelligible.

Because of the problem of absorbing and recollecting a series of numbers, you may want to use visual aids when you present statistics. Statistical evidence often makes better sense to both readers and listeners if it is in the form of charts and graphs that depict quantitative relationships in visual terms. President Reagan, for example, was praised for using charts and graphs innovatively to illustrate his State of the Union addresses, speeches that are not particularly easy to present because they often discuss complex problems and solutions, the kinds of problems and solutions that most often involve statistical evidence. Independent 1992 presidential candidate H. Ross Perot used charts and graphs extensively in the infomercials in which he discussed the problems of the federal deficit; even with all the charts and graphs, his analysis was difficult for anyone other than economists to interpret and understand, in part because each chart and graph could be seen only for a few seconds. Without the charts and graphs, however, most of what Perot said would have been a mass of indigestible numbers.

Here is an example of a visual aid that tries to translate very large numbers into something meaningful.

FIREPOWER, THEN AND NOW[4]

One bomb represents the firepower unleashed in World War II, nonnuclear as well as the bombs dropped on Hiroshima and Nagasaki: 3 megatons.

Three bombs equal the firepower of the weapons on one U.S. Poseidon submarine: 9 megatons, enough to destroy more than 200 of the largest Soviet cities.

Eight bombs represent the firepower of the weapons on a new U.S. Trident submarine: 24 megatons, enough to destroy every major city in the Northern Hemisphere.

The 6,000 bombs below represent the 18,000 megatons of nuclear firepower shared by the United States and the then–Soviet Union.

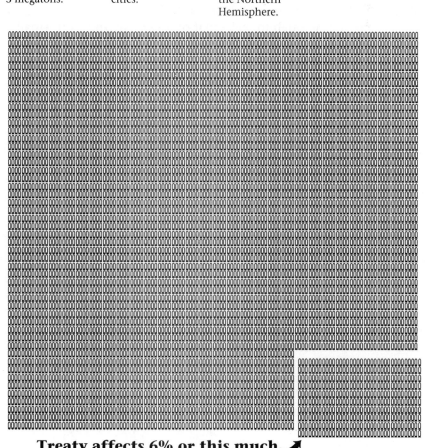

Treaty affects 6% or this much ⤴

[4][Mpls.] *Star Tribune*, September 19, 1987, p. 13A.

This pictograph (a chart representing numerical data pictorially) attempts to represent visually the meaning of some statistics. Note that in this case the numbers are transformed into visual entities in which size is represented by the space occupied by the bombs. This simplifies a mass of information in a form that lets us make comparisons easily. The size of each little bomb is defined experientially as the amount of firepower unleashed in World War II, including the atomic bombs dropped on Japanese cities. The significance of three bombs is defined in relation to armaments—the amount of firepower available on one Poseidon submarine—and the amount of damage that amount of firepower could do—destroy 200 of the largest cities in what was then the Soviet Union. Eight bombs represent the firepower on a single Trident submarine, which is enough to destroy every major city in the Northern Hemisphere. Note that "major" isn't defined—it's assumed that the scope is large enough to make that omission insignificant. Finally, we are told just how many of those little bombs are in the picture below and what that total represents in the firepower of the two major nuclear powers. One area of the chart gives a visual comparison to dramatize how small a part of the total arsenal is covered by the proposed intermediate-range nuclear missile treaty with the then–Soviet Union. In addition, that segment is translated into a percentage, another way to help us understand just how small a part it is. This is an excellent example of translating statistical evidence into a visual form that makes such huge numbers more intelligible.

You can also compensate for the weaknesses of statistical evidence by combining numbers with analogies, another kind of evidence, discussed next. For example, biological scientist Stephen Jay Gould claims that "Joe DiMaggio's 56-game hitting streak is the greatest accomplishment in the history of baseball, if not in modern sport." Gould explains that, despite the belief in "hot hands," or streaks, they just don't exist.[5] They can all be explained statistically: Better players have longer runs of success because they are better players, and less talented players have shorter runs. "There is one major exception, and absolutely only one—one sequence so many standard deviations above the expected distribution that it should not have occurred at all: Joe DiMaggio's 56-game hitting streak in 1941. . . . He beat the hardest taskmaster of all, a woman who makes Nolan Ryan's fastball look like a cantaloupe in slow motion—Lady Luck." At this point, Gould has used analogies to make the significance clearer. How hard is it to beat the odds? When

---

[5]See also Thomas Gilovich, *How We Know What Isn't So: The Fallibility of Human Reason in Everyday Life* (New York: The Free Press, 1991).

DiMaggio's streak is compared to Nolan Ryan's fastball, which has given that pitcher one of the winningest records in baseball, it makes Ryan's achievements appear to be nothing, as if his fastball had been so slow that it looked like a cantaloupe in slow motion, a pitch even the least talented of us probably could hit.

Gould explains that we have problems appreciating DiMaggio's feat "because we are so poorly equipped, whether by habits of culture or by our modes of cognition, to grasp the workings of random processes and patterning in nature." He argues that we cannot bear to accept the randomness of chance: "We believe in 'hot hands' because we must impart meaning to a pattern—and we like meanings that tell stories about heroism, valor, and excellence." He argues that DiMaggio's accomplishment was "a unique assault upon the otherwise unblemished record of Dame Probability." His feat combined extraordinary luck with great skill. Gould, a biologist, draws an analogy between DiMaggio's accomplishment and the biological entities that interest him:

> The history of a species, or any natural phenomenon that requires unbroken continuity in a world of trouble, works like a batting streak. All are games of a gambler playing with a limited stake against a house with infinite resources. The gambler must eventually go bust. His aim can only be to stick around as long as possible. . . . DiMaggio's hitting steak is the finest of legitimate legends because it embodies the essence of the battle that truly defines our lives. DiMaggio activated the greatest and most unattainable dream of all humanity, the hope and chimera of all sages and shamans: He cheated death, at least for a while.[6]

Several analogies are at work here. All attempts, Gould argues, to overcome the laws of probability, the power of chance, are like gambling. Thus, the efforts of species to survive are like a batting streak, and just as the gambler must lose eventually, and the batting streak must end, he implies that species die out. Hence, beating the laws of chance at the gaming table or in the batting box is like beating death—which you can do only for a little while. Notice that these analogies are considerably more powerful from a renowned biological scientist and a student of the statistical lore of baseball (and other sports). Note, too,

---

[6]Stephen Jay Gould, "The Streak of Streaks," *New York Review of Books,* August 18, 1988, pp. 8–12.

that the analogies also confer meaning on a pattern, ironically doing just what he has chided us humans for wanting to do!

Incidentally, sports fans are extremely reluctant to give up the belief in "hot hands" and "streaks," which is, in and of itself, a strong bit of evidence of the human need to perceive patterns and to make meaning out of random events, part of the psychological power of statistics.

In summary, statistics are a strong form of evidence that can convey how often something happens or the size and scope of a problem. To interpret statistics, you need to know how the raw data were gathered, how measurements were made, what counted as an instance of this event, how sampling was done, and what kinds of error might be involved.

Psychologically, statistics are strong because of the empirical and scientific bias of our society and our respect for objectivity, for "hard cold facts." However, despite this general attitude, statistics are a difficult form of proof to use effectively. Lists of numbers are hard to understand and remember. Speakers and writers must make special efforts to translate numerical measures into more familiar terms, into proportions and relationships that are within our personal experience. Often this is done through analogies, the last major form of evidence used in rhetorical acts.

ANALOGIES

Analogies are likenings or comparisons between things, processes, persons, or events. They appear in two varieties: literal analogies (usually simply called comparisons) and figurative analogies.

Literal Analogies

Literal analogies focus on the similarities between items that are obviously alike in some ways: two colleges, three hair styles, eight field hockey players, four rivers, and so on. Literal analogies are comparisons among items that are alike in detail and similar in explicit and obvious ways. The demands made on two professional tennis players are similar, for example, and you might compare their records of points on first serves and numbers of unforced errors in order to state that one is more skillful or talented than another. In the essay by Pollitt cited earlier, the author compares herself and Allen and compares the treatment of male and female applicants seeking entry into prestigious Ivy League schools.

Such comparisons serve the purposes of *evaluation* and *prediction*. One compares in order to evaluate just how serious and extensive discrimination was against women students by prestigious schools. One compares in order to judge which team or player is better or to predict which will be more successful in a future situation. It is risky, however, to predict a pitcher's success because her success also depends on the skill of her outfield and on the hitting power of her teammates. These complexities suggest the critical factors in the power of literal analogies as proof: the extent of relevant similarities and the presence of relevant differences. As a rule, the greater the number of relevant similarities between two cases, the better the basis for evaluation or prediction; the existence of relevant differences (differences directly related to the evaluation or prediction being made) lessens the strength and force of any claim. Baseball teams are just that—teams. The skill of a pitcher is only one element in a team's success, and the differences in talent and experience of other members of the teams being compared are significant for evaluating the performance and predicting the success of any one member.

Literal analogies enable us to go from what is known and tested and in operation to what is unknown, untested, and not yet working. In one high-crime neighborhood, for instance, traffic patterns are altered to prevent through traffic, and a crime control unit is set up to report suspicious events. The burglary rate drops 45 percent during the year after these changes are made. If we can replicate this success in other neighborhoods, people and property will be much safer. Careful analysis of such a project and determination of how similar—how analogous—any two neighborhoods really are should help us determine whether what worked in the one area will work in another.

Figurative Analogies

The process by which we go from what is known and familiar to what is unknown and unfamiliar is accentuated in the *figurative analogy,* a comparison of items that are unlike in obvious ways, that are apparently totally different if looked at with literal and practical eyes. The figurative analogy asserts a similarity that is metaphoric or that is a similarity in principle. For example, there are no obvious similarities between playing blackjack and batting a baseball except for their common relationship to the workings of chance, and there is no similarity between a baseball and a cantaloupe except their generally round shape. Despite Alvarez's protestations in Chapter 2, there are no obvious similarities between trying to stop a robbery or assault as it is happening and refuting the charges of sexual harassment against Clarence Thomas made by Anita Hill. No money was being stolen; no one was being physically assaulted; nothing that was occurring violated a law; yet Alvarez alleges that they share a common principle—inflicting an injustice.

The figurative analogy is one means by which a concept or problem can be made more vivid and dramatic. Through reading and other media, we have mental images of the psychological devastation that results from being mugged and robbed or of being beaten up by a gang. If we think of the hearings considering Hill's sexual harassment charges against nominee Thomas in those terms, we are more likely to empathize with Thomas and to accept his analogy, which compared the televised hearings on these charges to a "high-tech lynching."

Note, however, that Alvarez's comparisons and Thomas's figurative analogy were controversial and were harder to sustain before hostile listeners. African American women, for example, deeply resented Thomas's analogy, pointing out that it erased the pain African American women have experienced as a result of sexual harassment or assault. Those whose views are different from Alvarez's might argue that it would have been a crime to suppress these charges, and if they believed Hill, they might even argue that Alvarez was trying to exonerate the criminal who had done the assaulting. Such disagreements are a weakness of the figurative analogy—it may only reinforce the views of those who already agree. For them, it clarifies and enlivens, it makes a concept or problem vivid and dramatic, and it puts the abstract or unfamiliar into terms that are within our personal or imaginative experience.

In the essay cited earlier, Pollitt uses a figurative analogy to dramatically contrast the different standards used to judge white males with those used to judge minorities and women:

> It's a curious thing. As though we live in the realistic world of a Balzac novel as long as we're talking about white men competing with each other, a world in which we know perfectly well that Harvard C's beat A's from Brooklyn College, in which family connections and a good tennis serve never hurt, and sycophancy, back-stabbing, and organizational inertia carry the undeserving into top jobs every day of the week. Add women and blacks to the picture, though, and suddenly the scene shifts. Now we're in

Plato's Republic, where sternly impartial philosopher-kings award laurels to the deserving after nights of fasting and prayer. Or did, before affirmative action threw its spanner into the meritocratic works.

The author is charging that a double standard is being applied, but she does so with originality and indirection through allusions figuratively contrasting Balzac's novels and Plato's *Republic*. The allusions may limit the audience; the argument will be clear and forceful only to readers who know that the French author Balzac is thought to be the founder of literary realism; his novels depict ordinary, undistinguished lives with meticulous detail, and in the works forming *The Human Comedy,* he tried to create a complete social history of France. In such a world, when white men compete, one's alma mater, family name, and social advantages ("a good tennis serve"), along with skills for getting ahead and a tendency for organizations to stick to old patterns (perhaps the old-boy network?), make a difference, as we all know, according to the author.

When women and minorities enter the competition, however, Plato's idealism is substituted for Balzac's realism. Again, the power of the contrast is heightened by familiarity with the *Republic,* a dialogue in which an ideal state is described. Plato's utopia is a perfect meritocracy, meaning that position and status are determined entirely on the basis of merit. According to the author, whenever proposals are made to improve the competitive advantage of women, those who resist such proposals behave as if the world as it now existed was a perfect meritocracy. Note the metaphor comparing affirmative action to a spanner or monkey wrench (another figurative analogy) that, if thrown into working machinery, brings it to a grinding halt. The allusions dramatize and heighten the contrast, accenting the force of her claims of inconsistency, of a double standard.

The main weakness of the figurative analogy, however, is that, in logical and empirical terms, it gives no proof, makes no demonstration. But figurative analogies are not all equivalent in rhetorical force; some are stronger and more persuasive than others. As a rule, a figurative analogy is more powerful when it is more comprehensive, that is, when there are many points of similarity. Weaker figurative analogies rest on one or few similarities of principle, as illustrated by the comparison between a mugging and the hearing on Hill's charges against Thomas.

The strengths of the figurative analogy are, like the power of a metaphor or the force of a slogan, somewhat difficult to describe.

When the analogy is a fresh comparison that strikes the audience as highly apt, it has considerable persuasive force. The comparison of DiMaggio's hitting streak to the fate of species, for example, is disturbing and thought-provoking, especially from this source.

The figurative analogy derives its strength from its originality, its ability to make us see things from a new angle; from its aptness, its capacity to evoke an "aha" reaction; and from its brevity, its ability to crystallize a whole range of problems into a single phrase or image. That, too, is the power of the slogan, the brief phrase that expresses a position or idea in a vivid, unforgettable image. "Pro-choice" and "forced motherhood" struggle against the power of "right to life." "A woman's place is in the House—and Senate!" turns the stereotypic view of women on its head to express precisely the opposite point of view. This tactic of turning things around to express the opposite view is the best defense against a figurative analogy or slogan in argumentative terms.

Every advertiser seeks to find a vivid catchphrase to express the essence of its product or business, a phrase that captures the attention but cannot be parodied or ridiculed. Ads urging us to get "A Sony of Your Ony" or touting the good taste of the "Schweppervescence" of a brand of carbonated soft drinks illustrate the summarizing power of a clever slogan. At their best, figurative analogies have the same power.

SUMMARY

Knowing what you now know about the various forms of rhetorical evidence, what should you do to use evidence most effectively in your rhetoric? Combine the different forms of evidence so the limitations of one kind are compensated for by the strengths of another. Compensate for the impersonality of statistics with the vivid, concrete drama of an example; compensate for the lonely example with statistical measures showing frequency of occurrence; compensate for the complexity of data with analyses and interpretations of experts; predict specific cases, as you cannot with statistics, through detailed comparisons. Summarize an essential principle through the figurative analogy; contrast the generalizations of an expert with examples of testimony from people who have actually experienced the problem.

The functions of evidence are to prove, to make vivid, and to clarify. Each type of evidence has strengths and weaknesses, particular functions and limitations. Each enables you to do different things for an audience. Such data are the building blocks of rhetorical action. To fulfill their functions, they must be combined into larger units, into arguments and organizational patterns, which are the subjects of Chapters 8 and 9.

Summary Outline

I. Each form of evidence has particular strengths and weaknesses.

    A. An example is a case or instance, real or hypothetical, detailed or undetailed, used to illustrate an idea or prove that an event has happened or could happen.

        1. The example is weak logically and empirically because it demonstrates only that something could happen or occurred once.

        2. The example is strong psychologically because it is specific and concrete, because it puts ideas into human terms, and because it creates bases for identification.

        3. The testimony of laypersons is a form of the example.

    B. Authority evidence cites the interpretations and conclusions of experts.

        1. The strength of authority evidence as proof is directly related to the authority's degree of expertise on the subject.

        2. Psychologically, the force of authority evidence rests on the willingness of the audience to recognize the expert as an authority.

        3. Authority evidence is weakened when we do not know the expert's credentials, when we do not know how conclusions were drawn, and when the relationship between the subject and the expert is unclear.

    C. A statistic is a numerical or quantitative measure of frequency of occurrence, size, or scope.

        1. A statistic is strong as demonstration of typicality or extent.

        2. The strength of a statistic as proof depends on knowledge of how the data were collected or computed.

        3. Statistics are strong psychologically because of the empirical and scientific bias of our society.

        4. Statistics are weak psychologically because they are impersonal and hard to understand and remember.

    D. Analogies are literal or figurative comparisons.

        1. A literal analogy compares things that are obviously alike.

a. They are important as proof because comparisons are the bases for evaluations and predictions.

b. Their strength depends on the extent of relevant similarities and the absence of relevant differences.

c. They are strong psychologically because they compare what is known and familiar with what is unknown and unfamiliar.

d. They are vulnerable as proof because no two situations, processes, events, objects, or persons are ever identical.

2. A figurative analogy compares things that are not obviously alike and alleges a similarity of principle.

a. They are strong psychologically as vivid and dramatic comparisons of the familiar with the unfamiliar.

b. Their strength depends on the number and kinds of similarities of principle that can be shown.

c. Logically and empirically, they are not proof.

■ ■ ■

MATERIAL FOR ANALYSIS

This article appeared in *Mirabella* magazine in February 1991 on pages 97–98. It is based on an interview with Lisa Sliwa by the author Jan Hoffman, a *Village Voice* staff writer, who was studying criminal and family law at Yale Law School at the time. It's a somewhat unusual rhetorical act because the message of Lisa Sliwa is filtered through the author, whose comments weaken and strengthen Sliwa's message. What kind of a response does Sliwa seek from readers? What kind of a response does the author seek? Are they different?

The Sliwa Solution

1   "Women are an endangered species," pronounces Lisa Sliwa, the self-styled woman warrior who is the national director of the Guardian Angels. "I think it's wonderful that people are worried about dolphins and spotted owls. But the violence against women is so pervasive, so much a part of our culture now, that we're totally desensitized to it."

2   Lisa Sliwa is an extreme creature sprung from extreme times. We'll get to her castration remedy later.

3   It's been more than ten years since Sliwa started going on patrol with the Guardian Angels, those teenage boys with tough

chins and puffed-out chests who took to the New York City subways and streets to keep citizens safe from the bad guys. Now married to Angels founder Curtis Sliwa, she's 30 years old and still doing her two nights of street patrol in Manhattan's Hell's Kitchen, directing the Angels (a volunteer vigilante squad of 5,000 male teenagers nationwide), and lecturing on self-defense for women.

4   Sliwa has been concentrating most of her energy on speaking and organizing against the increasing violence toward women. "Five years ago we were doing most of our safety seminars for women in high-crime, inner city areas. When we were invited into the suburbs, it was mostly for curiosity—you know, I'm that model who can do karate. And now, I don't think I've met a woman—and we're talking from the Bronx to Beverly Hills—who has not been victimized in some way."

5   She sits on my couch, gesticulating fervently, a New Age Wonder Woman dressed in the Angels' signature shiny black police boots, black pants, white T-shirt, and rakish red beret, a dark honey-colored braid flung to the side, a chattering walkie-talkie at her hip. Slim, but sturdy and broad-shouldered, she dwarfs the place, looking at once faintly cartoonish and intimidating.

6   As she talks about the pervasiveness of crime, I nod. The statistics glare at us, unflinching, withering whatever remains of our fantasy that violence should be defined as something that happens to someone else. Every 18 seconds a woman is beaten. Three out of four women will be victims of at least one violent crime during their lifetimes. Every six minutes a woman is raped. A woman is ten times more likely to be raped than to die in a car crash.

7   "The harassment and abuse of women have skyrocketed. Remember wolf whistles?" Sliwa's tone is cut with acid, a bitter nostalgia. "Now they're yelling about doing the most disgusting things to every part of your body, parts you never heard of. I'm not talking about the old Chester the Molester type on the bus, who tries to rub against you. Now, it's a guy on a bicycle riding by a woman walking on the street, and he smacks her on the back, punches her in the breast, or slaps her face."

8   In response to the surge in crime, women are retreating, wary now. On the subway, we tuck necklaces under sweaters, grip our bags tightly under our arms. In New Haven, Connecticut, where I'm spending the year, it takes me scarcely ten minutes to walk to campus in the morning, but the trip back home in the evening lasts nearly an hour; after nightfall, the university urges us to hop its free shuttle bus, which lets us off in front of our doors and waits until we get inside. I hate the shuttle even as I use it faithfully, hate what it implies: that crime has bound our feet, forcing us back into tiny, centuries-old, hobbled-women steps.

9   A colleague tells me that recently, as an exercise, a professor asked her students to write down the routine precautions they take to prevent assault. Then she compared the lists by gender. The men's were fairly brief. But the women's were elaborate, detailing the safeguards we have come to regard as quotidian and necessary. We are so accustomed to parking under a streetlight, to taking out our keys long before we arrive at the door, that we've forgotten to get angry about it all anymore.

10   But not so for Wonder Woman! "Women are more courageous than men," she says. "Women have a stronger instinct to survive. . . . We have a right to be safe. If men are not going to protect us, we have to learn to do it ourselves. We should be taught self-defense in junior high." Insistent, clamorous, outraged, aggressive, she comes across as an antidote to fear.

11   She'll be the first to admit, though, that the self-defense moves she promotes so vigorously aren't in and of themselves always the answer. Several years ago, while working alone in an Angels office, Sliwa was attacked and badly beaten by three men. It wasn't until one assailant was straddling her, his pants down, that she shook off the pain and shock: She grabbed his genitals, bit his thigh, and bellowed. The men fled. Now, the twin pillars of her advice about self-protection are to remain clearheaded and bold. "They tell us not to fight back because you might get a rapist angry. And my response is, I have to worry about this guy's *feelings* because he's doing a number on me?"

12   The rules change if a weapon is involved: "You have to calm yourself down, because freaking out is feeding this guy's sense of power over you. Especially if he's coming down from drugs and needs money. You['ve] just got to do whatever you can to stay alive."

13   I ask her if she advises relying on a weapon. She wrinkles her nose. "I don't like Mace. It's one of those namby-pamby things they come out with for women. Do they advocate guys carrying Mace? Why do they consistently give us the second-rate weapons?" Sliwa herself does not carry a weapon, and does not advocate that women do, but "if you insist on carrying something," she says with a touch of exasperation, "get a very, very good dainty revolver. And learn how to shoot it. Blindfolded." She suggests wearing a whistle, but not to rely on it for protection. "They're great to alert people there's a crime in progress, but you can't expect that after a guy's getting physical and you blow a whistle, he'll stop."

14   "And if you're jogging and a gang jumps you, what do you do? Unless you have an AK-47, you're sunk. That's why penalties have to be multiplied for each assailant. If a rapist gets one year

for sexual assault but there were six guys, they should each get six years. The victim had been six times more intimidated, and that much less likely to remember faces."

15   She goes down her checklist of tips. The most blatant signal that a woman is vulnerable is when she is wearing headphones in public. "You can tell the rhythm of her walk is odd, that she's not in touch. And that's how victims get chosen." Businesswomen "are easy to mug," she adds, because they are trapped by straight skirts and high heels, encumbered by their briefcases and purses. She suggests that women wear flats and use pouches with keys and money at the waist.

16   Reluctant to sound like she's only telling women what *not* to do, she nevertheless cautions that getting drunk increases risk factors exponentially, because judgment becomes impaired. "And more than anything, you have to learn to trust your instincts. I've talked to so many women who said they had a feeling that something was going to happen but they rationalized their way out of that instinct, because we're brought up to be nice, liberal young ladies. The reality is you're dealing with a jungle, a victim/predator society."

17   And the rule of the jungle, she maintains, is that if a woman's greatest fear is of being raped and tortured, then a man's is of being castrated. And so she advocates gelding rapists, not for the sake of revenge, but as a significant disincentive for would-be rapists as well as their convicted brethren. "I have yet to find a rapist who's done it just once. Ask any top therapist, 'So, when would you let *your* daughter go out with this guy?'"

18   Of course, Sliwa allows, castration could be tried on an experimental, elective basis instead of prison, "because there are men who want to be free of this compulsion. And once they are, they can listen to classical music, do *The New York Times* crossword puzzle every Sunday, and they're not going to be climbing through your bedroom window."

19   She pauses, assessing what I suspect is a polite but quizzical expression on my face. "As soon as I mention castration, people have a heart attack"—she leans over, staring at me intently—"so why don't they react that way to rape?"

Questions for Analysis

1. Identify each type of evidence in the example, and consider the psychological and proof functions of each. How do they work together? What weaknesses do you detect?

2. The framework of the essay is a problem–solution analysis. The impact of Sliwa's proposal may be affected by the author, who intrudes herself into the flow of what Sliwa says. For example, she provides a forewarning that might make readers more resistant to the proposal. How might the problem–solution framework and the intrusions of the author affect a reader's response?

3. How is evidence used to influence you and to make the final solution less unthinkable? How does your gender affect your responses to this data?

4. Lisa Sliwa is an important element of the proof of the essay. How does her credibility affect the proposal she makes? Do the author's comments and comparisons add to or detract from her ethos?

5. What elements of the rhetorical problem apply? How do elements of the problem affect the need for and impact of the evidence?

6. What kinds of personal experience increase the chances that readers will participate in this act? What kinds might decrease participation?

EXERCISES

Adapting Evidence and Language

Prepare a speech designed to explain or to create understanding about something unfamiliar to the audience. Plan the speech carefully to run not more than five minutes. Ask "Are there any questions?" at each strategic point in the process.

The audience is expected to take notes and then to ask the speaker only two kinds of questions: (1) What do you mean? (a request for explanation, clarification, or definition) and (2) How do you know? (a request for data). No one should be allowed to argue with the speaker or to refute claims or challenge evidence; however, active audience participation is essential.

After completing the exercise, discuss problems of clarity (vocabulary, explanation) and audience needs for evidence that speakers did not recognize. Discuss the problems of delivery created when your presentation is interrupted by questions from the audience. Discuss why the speaker needs to solicit questions to make this exercise work. (Why won't you interrupt when you don't understand or want proof for an assertion? What communication norms are involved?) What factors seemed to make some speakers more effective than others in this assignment?

Using Audiovisual Aids

Prepare a speech on a subject that mandates the use of audiovisual aids, such as the styles of radio disc jockeys, methods of musical arrangement, a detailed statistical analysis, or an explanation of a form or map. Ideally, students should seek to use the full range of audiovisual aids: graphs, charts, audio- and videotapes, records, photos (shown on overhead projectors), slides, and films.

The importance of visual aids in presenting material is the special concern of those who belong to the Demonstrative Evidence Specialists Association, a trade group made up of businesses that provide graphic materials for lawyers and others.[7] The graphics they create range from charts that reduce a complex argument about damages into a simple bottom line that a jury can clearly understand to a-day-in-the-life-of videotapes of severely injured litigants that show the quality of their lives as a result of an accident. Obviously, graphics that can simplify a complex case can also oversimplify, but the need to tell a story in a culture that is now filled with visual images makes graphics an important tool in persuasion.

Those who study jury behavior, however, agree that fancy graphics cannot save a weak case. On the other hand, where both sides have strong cases, graphics might make the difference. To be admissible in court, graphics must conform to the rules of evidence, which are good rules for anyone using visual aids: They must be accurate, relevant, and not overly prejudicial, meaning that their emotional impact must not outweigh their value as proof.

Discuss the physical (delivery, lights, eye contact), mechanical, and temporal (how much more time they take) problems such aids create. What kinds of data do they make more accessible?

Here are some principles to follow in using visual aids.

1. The visual aid needs to be large enough to be easily seen by everyone.

2. Talk to the audience, not to the visual aid.

3. Your language should be as vividly descriptive as if there were no model, map, or diagram. Your visual aid should not substitute for vivid description.

4. Avoid blocking the audience's view of the visual aid.

---

[7]See Peter Applebome, "Showing Beats Telling in Many Lawsuits," *New York Times,* January 13, 1989, p. 22Y.

5. Make sure the visual aid has only enough detail to make your point; too much detail is distracting and may be confusing.

6. The visual aid should not talk down to the audience; it needs to provide information, not state the obvious.

7. Relationships among items on the visual aid should be clearly indicated.

8. The visual aid should be an integral part of the speech; don't use a visual aid just to have one.

9. Beware of spending time drawing diagrams on the blackboard; it's easy to get absorbed and lose track of time while boring the audience.

10. When you are finished with your visual aid, put it away; except in unusual circumstances, it will just be a continuing distraction.

CHAPTER 8

The Resources of Argument

No fact has any meaning by itself. To be significant, to have impact, evidence must become part of an argument, and arguments, in turn, must be combined into larger rhetorical wholes (the subject of Chapter 9). My concern in this chapter is with arguments, a key building block of rhetorical action. Just what is an argument?

Commonly, *argument* means a debate or a quarrel because arguments usually express differing viewpoints or disagreements. In a general sense, we can speak of the argument of a novel, referring to the principle or pattern of its development and the kind of experience it attempts to create. This usage reflects an understanding that arguments are structures, ways of organizing material. In this chapter, however, I use argument to refer to the process of giving reasons for or against some position. Thus, for rhetorical purposes, an argument is a claim or a conclusion backed by one or more reasons or justifications.

Based on that definition, here are some arguments: Capital punishment should be abolished because it is an ineffective deterrent against violent crime. Teenagers should receive sex education and contraceptive information because they are not yet equipped to be good parents. State lotteries should be abolished because they are a highly regressive and inefficient way to raise revenue. These are arguments because each makes a claim based on a justification or a reason.

These examples also illustrate the role of evidence in argument. One appropriate response to these arguments is, How do you know that capital punishment is an ineffective deterrent against rising murder rates? That teenagers are not equipped to be good parents? That lotteries are regressive and inefficient? And each question must be answered with evidence. Some arguments omit the evidence on which they are based, but all arguments are based on evidence. All imply that evidence exists and could be presented.

The most basic elements of an argument and their relationship can be illustrated this way:[1]

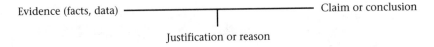

Evidence (facts, data) ——————————————— Claim or conclusion

Justification or reason

Because evidence was discussed in Chapter 7, I now turn to the other two elements.

CLAIMS

The shape or character of an argument is determined by the kind of claims it makes, the conclusion it draws. A *claim* or *conclusion* is an assertion. Some examples are: That is a dog. You are in good health. Smoking causes lung cancer. Affirmative action damages the self-esteem of those it is designed to help.

Every claim is an assertion, and every assertion is a claim that goes beyond the facts, beyond what can actually be proved. A claim involves a logical or inferential leap. Even when you make a claim as simple as "That is a dog," you jump to a conclusion based on a few surface characteristics that seem to indicate that this creature is a kind of canine. When we make such a claim, few of us have either the necessary data or the biological expertise to back up our statement by distinguishing canines from other mammals or domestic dogs from coyotes, dingoes, foxes, or wolves.

Even when the person who makes the claim is an expert who has lots of data, such a leap is present. During the summer of 1993, Reggie Lewis, a Boston Celtics basketball player, died while shooting baskets with a friend at the team's training center at Brandeis University.[2] Earlier, on April 29, during the opening game of the playoffs, Lewis had collapsed. After tests conducted by the team physician and a group of a dozen heart specialists, Lewis was found to have cardiomyopathy, a life-threatening condition that would have ended his athletic career. But a second team of physicians at another hospital disputed those findings and concluded that Lewis had a benign neurological condi-

---

[1]This is a much-simplified form of a model first developed by philosopher Stephen Toulmin.
[2]Lawrence K. Altman, "Autopsy Expected to Give Answers," *New York Times*, July 29, 1993, p. B7; Dave Anderson, "Lewis's Death on Celtics' Conscience," *New York Times*, July 29, 1993, p. B6.

tion known as neurocardiogenic syncope, a condition that causes fainting but rarely is fatal. In this case, each team of cardiologists made a leap from the data gathered by their tests to a conclusion about Lewis's health. Each conclusion was informed by empirical evidence drawn from echocardiograms, magnetic resonance imaging of the heart, monitoring of his heart rhythm while he ran a treadmill, and electrical stimulation of his heart to learn whether it was vulnerable to bursts of potentially fatal rhythms. Those test results were interpreted in light of the physicians' long training and years of medical practice establishing how to construe such test results.

Lewis's death was a dramatic and tragic reminder that the physicians' conclusions, like all argumentative claims, are inferential leaps that go beyond the available evidence. Obviously, none of these cardiologists wanted to put Lewis in mortal peril, and which conclusion to accept was a hard choice for the team and the player. Tragically, however, the inferential leap made by the group that Lewis and the Celtics chose to believe was wrong. Note, too, how belief, accepting one claim rather than another, follows self-interest: Lewis did not want to give up a satisfying and lucrative career in professional basketball, and the Celtics did not want to lose their 6'7" captain. The outcome, however, is dramatic evidence of the discrepancy between data (the test results) and the claim (that he did or did not have a life-threatening heart condition).

The special character of an argument is precisely this: that it makes a leap from data to a claim. That is why it is a fundamental building block in rhetorical action. That is also what gives an argument its force, and, as the example shows, it is what makes arguments risky and open to challenge.

REASONS

The leap made in an argument ordinarily is not a blind leap made in ignorance. As indicated in the diagram, we go from evidence or data to a claim via a justification or reason. A *reason* is an authorization or warrant for the leap made in an argument. In other words, reasons are grounds or bases for drawing conclusions. They are justifications for claims.

To illustrate this process, let us return to the example. In making tests, cardiologists gather all kinds of data about the heart—its muscle, its pumping efficiency and that of the vessels that feed it, its performance under stress, and so forth. When the results are in, they are measured against certain standards or norms established for identifying people who have different kinds of heartbeat variations and problems. By comparing the data from these tests with these standards, a cardiologist can decide whether someone has a life-threatening problem. Several reasoning processes are involved. It is assumed that (1) all reliable tests of heart activity were made; (2) they were made by competent cardiologists using accurate instruments; and (3) the results were compared to standard indicators of a potentially lethal or a relatively benign heart arrhythmia (variations in the rhythm of heartbeats) for persons of the patient's age and physical condition. Each of the following is a reason a cardiologist might use to support a conclusion about the health of an individual's heart: All essential tests were made; these tests were made and interpreted by experts; the results were compared to established standards for a given group of people with the characteristics of the individual being tested.

These reasons are related to medicine and cardiology; thus, such reasons are sometimes called field dependent because they belong to a particular field or area of expertise, and they rely on the authority of persons skilled in that field. (Recall that in Chapter 7 an *authority* was defined as a person thought competent to interpret data and to decide what conclusions could be drawn from it.) That reasons often arise out of the knowledge accumulated in a field of knowledge means that the reasons appropriate for one subject may not be appropriate for another.

ISSUES

An *issue* is a fundamental point in dispute, a question crucial in making a decision, choosing a stance, or selecting a course of action. Most issues fall roughly into these three types: questions of fact, of value, and of policy.[3] Issues distinguish kinds of arguments and reveal the resources of each.

Questions of Fact

A question of fact is a dispute about what evidence exists and how it should be interpreted. For example, several issues about capital punishment are really questions of fact: Does capital punishment deter

---

[3]Aristotle classified issues into four types: being (fact or conjecture), quantity (scope or definition), quality (value, mitigating circumstances), and procedure (including jurisdiction). See *On Rhetoric,* 1417b.21–28.

others from committing murder? (What evidence of deterrence exists? What is reliable evidence of deterrence? How can it be gathered?) Are a disproportionate number of poor nonwhites executed, and does the ethnicity of the victim affect such sentencing? (What proportion of capital crimes are committed by poor nonwhites? What kind of data exist about the socioeconomic status and race of executed persons? Do data show that those who kill whites rather than nonwhites are more likely to be executed?) Such disputes are not simple, as the conflicting evidence about deterrence demonstrates, but they reflect some fundamental agreements: that deterrence is an important goal; that penalties should be applied without class, ethnic, or other bias.

In other words, when you address a question of fact, the issues focus on the quality, accuracy, and adequacy of the evidence. As illustrated above, disputants agree on a common goal—deterrence—and proceed to examine the evidence to determine whether a specific policy, such as capital punishment, meets that goal. The dispute will focus on the amount and quality of evidence and its appropriate interpretation, and most of the warrants will be field dependent. Authoritative evidence will be particularly important because such evidence allows facts to be interpreted.

Questions of Value

A question of value, by contrast, is a dispute about goals, and it reflects a more fundamental disagreement. Some of the issues about capital punishment are questions of value: Should we avenge premeditated murder or obey absolutely the injunction against killing? What are the ethical implications of killing by the state? Is our goal to rehabilitate those who commit crimes or to protect society from murderers? Is our moral standard "better that ten guilty persons go free than that one innocent person dies"? Are there circumstances under which murder is justified (such as self-defense or the battered-woman syndrome)? Such issues reflect fundamental commitments, and no single rhetorical act is likely to change them.

Disagreements over values often define target audiences (those who share a fundamental value). They may serve as a measure of audience hostility, one facet of the rhetorical problem. Conflicts between the values held by individual members of the audience may be a resource for initiating rhetorical action. Such conflicts may be used to provoke individuals to reconsider their priorities and to seek ways to reestablish internal consistency within their value systems.

Values arise from our basic needs, from cultural norms, and from our peculiarities as individuals (see Chapter 3). All of these values are resources for argument because each value is a reason or justification. Such reasons are not field dependent; they depend on cultural norms and social mores. Reasons or justifications drawn from such values are sometimes called *motivational* because they are grounded in our motives as human beings, as members of a culture, or as unique individuals.[4]

When we are urged to act to ensure our survival—for example, when we are pressed to buy a year's supply of food to protect ourselves against the devastation of nuclear attack or economic depression—a motivational reason is at work. Such reasons are also present in many arguments that appeal to our need for esteem (vote for Texas Senator Kay Bailey Hutchinson or Texas Governor Ann Richards because she shares our values), for love (avoid dandruff and be attractive and desirable by using ABC shampoo), and for self-actualization (buy *How to Be a Success in Business*). When arguments appeal to basic needs, cultural values, or to personal achievement, motivational justifications are being used.

Questions of Policy

The issues in questions of policy are so universal that they are known as *stock issues* (they are commonplaces, always "in stock"). A *policy* is a course of action, a procedure that is systematically followed and applied. According to Aristotle, the central issue of what he called *deliberative rhetoric,* which treats questions of policy, is expediency, that is, "appropriateness to the purpose at hand" or the most efficient and effective means to an end. Stock issues arise from what a rhetor must do to make a good case for changing current policy, the means now in use. These issues can be stated as follows:

1. Is there a compelling need to change the current policy? To demonstrate this, show that:

   a. Someone is harmed or injured.

   b. The harm or injury is of sufficient scope to be of social concern.

   c. The harm or injury is a direct consequence of the policy presently in effect (what has been called *inherency*).

2. Is there an alternative policy? (More than one may need to be considered.)

---

[4]For a discussion of the complex interrelationship between our basic biological needs and their cultural modification through language, see Kenneth Burke, "Definition of Man," *Language as Symbolic Action* (Berkeley: University of California Press, 1966), pp. 3–24.

3. Is the alternative policy under consideration practical and beneficial?

a. Do we have the resources and expertise to put it into effect? Does it require what we consider an appropriate amount of resources?

b. Will the results of the policy improve the situation or is it likely to have side effects that would make it, on balance, undesirable?

Each of these elements combines questions of fact and questions of value.

A policy is a way of doing something. It is a systematic way of dealing with a particular kind of situation or event. Because we do not assume that change is good in itself, when you advocate policy changes, you assume an argumentative responsibility that is called *the burden of proof.* If you fulfill its requirements, however, as described next, then supporters of current policies are obligated to respond to your arguments and evidence.

First, you must show that someone is harmed (a question of fact and of value). A fact by itself does not demonstrate harm. The fact must be measured against a standard (or value) to show that what exists is harmful. Consider, for example, the startling fact that over 400,000 people in the United States die each year from the effects of smoking, a figure that dwarfs the 58,000+ Americans killed over several years in the Vietnam War. The deaths in the Vietnam War produced national concern and considerable social disruption. The deaths from smoking have been an accepted part of our culture for many years, and, until quite recently, little has been done to reduce those numbers. As these examples illustrate, a claim that some situation is harmful combines data with a justification drawn from a value.

But demonstrating harm is not enough. The harm must have a certain scope or magnitude. This measurement moves from injuries to individuals to harm affecting the well-being of society. A student did this well in a speech arguing that measles vaccinations should be required for all children. She transformed that topic from triviality to significance by citing evidence to show how many unvaccinated children would get measles, how many of those children would be permanently brain-damaged, and what the cost to society would be. Suddenly a rather unimportant childhood disease that had been quite remote from class members became a significant social problem with important financial implications for each of us.

As these examples suggest, scope or magnitude is usually demonstrated with statistics, but that is not always the case. A single innocent person who is executed through capital punishment is likely to raise serious questions, not only because of the importance of one human life, but also because that one instance is a sign that all the procedures designed to ensure justice were not sufficient to prevent its most serious miscarriage. Similarly, a single nuclear accident like that at Chernobyl, in which substantial amounts of radioactive materials were released into the air (something many thought could never happen), may be significant enough to call into question policies governing nuclear power plant construction and maintenance in the republics that used to form the Soviet Union. That single case may move other nations, including the United States, to provide monetary help to enable these republics to make a transition from closing these plants to developing alternative sources of energy.

But harm and scope are not enough by themselves. You must also demonstrate that these problems are the direct result of the present policy. In other words, you must prove that harm of this magnitude is intrinsic to, an inevitable part of, the current procedure. As an illustration, suppose that using your current method of study (the policy), you receive a D in nutrition. That grade, clearly harmful, does not automatically mean that you will conclude that your current method of study is at fault. Perhaps you were not adequately prepared for this kind of science course and are really proud that you passed it in spite of your handicap. Perhaps your teacher was unskilled at explaining ideas, inaccessible for conferences, and absentmindedly asked questions on the tests about material that wasn't covered in the text or lectures. Perhaps you were seriously ill during a major part of the semester, and any course you were able to pass was a victory over your health problems. Note that in these cases, the cause lies outside the policy. Change, if any, needs to occur somewhere else: in your preparation for the course, in the teacher's approach, in your health, but not in your mode of study.

This test is part of a question of policy because no policy is ever presumed to be perfect. All policies are carried out by imperfect humans who have bad days and who can create any number of problems for which the policy itself cannot be held responsible. As a result, in discussing the issue of whether a problem is intrinsic to a policy, you must show that the policy itself, not the persons who carry it out or some special set of circumstances, is generating the problem.

If you can demonstrate significant harm that is an inevitable part of the current policy, you must still show that an alternative course of action exists. In most cases this is easy—several alternatives will seem obvious. But the issue exists because if we are to change, there must be something to change to. Many students, for instance, do not consider changing the way they study because they are not aware of any alternative. Most students are not taught how to study or exposed to various approaches, and so they do not see any other way to do it. Conditions must exist that make change possible. After a certain number of heart attacks, for example, a person no longer has the opportunity to change lifestyle. Given a certain amount of damage, exercises to improve heart action and circulation are no longer possible. Those who mourn the effects of aging are often called up short by someone who says, "Consider the alternative!"

And if you demonstrate that an alternative exists, you still must show that it is practical. That is, you must show that the personnel, expertise, time, money, and materials are available to institute the new procedure. If these resources are not available or are difficult to obtain, or if the allocation required is too substantial to gain assent because of its impact on other areas of importance, the policy is not a realistic alternative. If the cost of the alternative policy is too high, we may decide to live with the current level of harm. For example, many students consider the cost involved in following a method of study that would produce an A average too high. They place higher priorities on time spent in recreation with friends or in extracurricular activities such as debate or athletics.

Finally, you must demonstrate that the alternative policy is, on balance, beneficial. This issue reflects a recognition that all policies, no matter how wonderful, have undesirable as well as desirable effects. If we change our procedure, we want to be assured that we shall come out ahead. For example, in the face of a large and increasing deficit, the president may propose measures to Congress, such as increased taxes on individuals and businesses, that will reduce the deficit but are likely to reduce economic growth, perhaps even induce a recession. Members of Congress will try to determine, to the extent they can, whether the benefits of reducing the deficit outweigh the evils of slower economic growth or recession (increased unemployment with its attendant social costs, for instance).

Each of these issues combines questions of fact and questions of value. Questions of harm and scope measure facts against values. Evaluation of the current policy depends on how clearly we can establish factually that it is responsible for the problem. That an alternative policy exists must be demonstrated before we can evaluate its practicality (what costs we are willing to bear combines facts and values) or benefits (evaluation of predicted effects). Policy questions are treated separately here not because they differ from questions of fact and value, but because certain demands must be met by any rhetor who advocates policy change. The values used to judge these questions may differ among persons or cultures, but these same issues are addressed whenever anyone evaluates policies.

INVENTION

The ancient Greek and Roman rhetoricians called the process of preparing for rhetorical action *invention* (from the Latin *invenire,* to come upon or find). The term reflects their understanding that, ordinarily, rhetors do not create original arguments from scratch, but rather discover appropriate arguments in their research, in the course of their training, in reports of research by others, in other speeches or essays, and in cultural ideas. These arguments are applied to new circumstances, and invention refers to the choice from among available argumentative options. Invention also reflects the creative role of the rhetor in selecting and adapting arguments and evidence in ways best suited to the occasion and audience, and in organizing these into an effective whole.

Skillful invention requires that you know yourself and the role you will play, that you know just what audience you are trying to reach, and that you are familiar with the available evidence and arguments and with the cultural history of your subject. Once again, an understanding of your specific rhetorical problem is essential to making wise choices in preparing your materials.

Some clues about the importance of arguments and evidence in rhetoric come from a body of research that is called *persuasive arguments theory.* This research has been done on decision-making in small groups, and the results suggest that arguments have more to do with attitude change than peer pressure, the influence of the attitudes of others on the positions taken by individuals.[5]

Persuasive arguments theory goes like this. It is estimated that there is a culturally given pool of arguments on an issue (what I have called the cultural history of the subject). In order to decide what position to take, individuals sample from this pool of arguments. Arguments vary

---

[5]See Eugene Burnstein and Amiram Vinokur, "Testing Two Classes of Theories about Group-Induced Shifts in Individual Choice," *Journal of Experimental Social Psychology* 9 (March 1973): 123–137; and "What a Person Thinks upon Learning He Has Chosen Differently from Others: Nice Evidence for the Persuasive-Arguments Explanation of Choice Shifts," *Journal of Experimental Social Psychology* 11 (September 1975):412–426. Also see Amiram Vinokur and Eugene Burnstein, "Effects of Partially Shared Persuasive Arguments on Group-Induced Shifts: A Group–Problem-Solving Approach," *Journal of Personality and Social Psychology* 29 (March 1974):305–315; and Amiram Vinokur, Yaacov Trope, and Eugene Burnstein, "A Decision-Making Analysis of Persuasive Argumentation and the Choice-Shift Effect," *Journal of Experimental Social Psychology* 11 (March 1975):127–148. A critique of this theory is found in Glenn S. Sanders and Robert S. Baron, "Is Social Comparison Irrelevant for Producing Choice Shifts?" *Journal of Experimental Social Psychology* 13 (July 1977):303–314.

in availability (the chance that they are known or will come to mind), direction (pro and con), and persuasiveness (impact on and salience for an individual). According to this research, people take positions on issues because of the balance of arguments; that is, they decide where they stand based on the number of pro or con arguments that have force for them that they know about or are exposed to. As a result, novel or unfamiliar arguments become especially important because such arguments may tip the balance and change an individual's attitude. This research also demonstrates the significance of cultural history as part of the rhetorical problem because, in these studies, attitude change was least likely to occur when all members of the group were familiar with the entire pool of arguments (that is, the entire cultural history of the subject was known to them).

One kind of evidence, citations from trusted and respected authorities, assumes special significance. When individuals encounter an unexpected position in a statement by a recognized authority, they tend to think up arguments that would explain why the authority would take such an unexpected position. These potentially novel arguments, constructed by members of the audience, can also shift the balance and change attitudes. For example, imagine that you are a committed conservative with high regard for former U.S. Ambassador to the United Nations Jeane Kirkpatrick. You discover, to your surprise, that she opposes U.S. air strikes against the Serbs in Bosnia. You then think up reasons that she might have for that position (perhaps it is difficult militarily to restrict involvement especially if spotters on the ground are needed to make this tactic effective, or if we act alone, we shall be blamed for whatever problems arise, and so on). The arguments you construct will be good reasons for you—sensible, salient, forceful. Such arguments are ideally adapted to their audience (you) and have a unique capacity to influence you.

This research suggests that evidence and arguments with which the audience is unfamiliar are particularly potent because they can prompt those exposed into rethinking a position and alter the balance of arguments to shift opinion. Audiences may construct highly potent novel arguments when confronted with an unexpected stance from a respected authority. The research underlines the rhetorical obstacles created by the cultural history of a subject; that is, attitude change is unlikely when the audience is familiar with the entire pool of arguments.

Some of the reasons that arguments are the building blocks of rhetorical action are now apparent. Arguments are essential units in rhetoric because they combine facts and values to advance claims that express our knowledge, understanding, and commitment. As such, they harness together the power of our knowledge and our values.

Arguments are building blocks because they address the fundamental issues of fact and value that are part of all choices. They focus on essentials, the grounds for belief and attitude. They are structures that make sense of the world. For all of these reasons, arguments are powerful rhetorical resources.

Another way of thinking about arguments comes from the theorizing and research of Richard Petty and John Cacioppo discussed earlier.[6] Their elaboration likelihood model (ELM) emphasizes self-persuasion, that is, the likelihood that audience members will be stimulated to participate in creating a message, to process or interpret it, to develop, clarify, or embellish it, and to consider its implications.

Note that from this perspective, a better, stronger argument is one that engages audience members, one that they collaborate in creating, translating it into their own words, attempting to clarify what seems ambiguous, and amplifying what the rhetor has voiced by contributing personal experiences, thinking up relevant questions, and the like. In other words, a good argument is one that the audience digests and makes its own.

Recall that according to their research as well as that of others, the single most important variable affecting one's desire or willingness to digest and amplify an argument is personal relevance, that is, the expectation that the issue addressed is vital or will have significant consequences for one's life. Put differently, personal relevance is the single greatest motivator prompting audience members to involve themselves in a message. That underscores the importance of adapting arguments to the audience and how essential it is to point out the relevance of issues for those you seek to reach and influence.

A number of other variables affect an audience member's propensity and willingness to elaborate. Some people are natural "noodlers" who love to play around with ideas; they are relatively easy to tempt into argumentative engagement. In addition, we are more willing to participate in messages that reflect our values and beliefs, our ways of looking at the world. Obviously, such messages speak to us in familiar language and offer justifications that we already accept as valid. The fields we choose or the professions we practice reflect such preferences: Engineers respect statistical proofs and practical applications; economists respond particularly to claims based on economic principles, and so on. For example, the essay "Jesus Was a Feminist" at the end of this chapter illustrates a rhetorical act with a somewhat controversial message addressed to those with strong religious beliefs. In this

---

[6]Richard E. Petty and John T. Cacioppo, *Communication and Persuasion: Central and Peripheral Routes to Attitude Change* (New York: Springer-Verlag, 1986).

case, the arguments are based on religious justifications, and personal salience arises out of a body of beliefs and a commitment to living one's life according to certain moral principles. By contrast, even those sympathetic to feminism but reared without much religious training or without strong religious beliefs are likely to be less responsive to this essay and less willing to participate actively in it.

As noted, ELM theory recognizes that persuasion does not occur solely on the basis of the quality of the evidence and the argument. The peripheral route we use for efficiency takes shortcuts that avoid the hard work involved in exploring the implications, arguments, and evidence. Instead of doing the work yourself, for example, you might turn to *Consumer Reports,* a magazine that sells no advertising; on that basis, you might ignore the details of their testing and the assumptions from which they worked and simply look for the bottom line, accepting whatever they say is the best brand of running shoes, which you then go out to buy. In this case, you have judged the source and used it as a peripheral cue on which to make a decision, a highly efficient way of making a choice. Arguments themselves may be peripheral cues; for example, we can be influenced by the sheer number of arguments offered—a peripheral cue—in effect concluding that because there are many reasons given, it must be the best choice.

The accumulated evidence of research on persuasion is quite consistent with the ELM view that there is a tradeoff between participating in messages—exploring and evaluating arguments and evidence—and relying on peripheral cues. In general, anything that reduces a person's ability and/or motivation to interpret, test, and amplify issue-relevant arguments also increases the likelihood that simple peripheral cues from the source, occasion, or context will influence the outcome.

Thus far, I have considered arguments as rational structures that make explicit claims backed by reasons and evidence. But arguments, even rational arguments, are often implicit, subtle, and fragmentary, especially when they appear in the statements of real human beings in contrast to neat diagrams in logic textbooks. The special kind of arguments found in rhetoric are called *enthymemes,* and they illustrate argumentative resources that lie outside the field of logic. They also emphasize the importance of audience participation in the process of persuasion.

Enthymemes

An enthymeme is a rhetorical argument. Ordinarily, it draws a conclusion that is probable rather than certain; it relies on reasons that are culturally or socially accepted; it often is deficient by strict logical standards; and its subject matter usually is concrete and specific rather than abstract. What distinguishes the enthymeme from other arguments, however, is that it is constructed out of the beliefs, attitudes, and values of the audience. An enthymeme is an argument jointly created by author and audience. It is an elaborated argument in the ELM sense, and it has force because audience members fill in details, add to the evidence from their experience, supply additional reasons, or draw the implications of claims for themselves. A rhetor can plan to try to prompt such processes, but an enthymeme can only be created if readers or listeners participate in it and amplify it.

The concept of the enthymeme comes from the work of Aristotle, but contemporary theorists also refer to the *interact* or the *transact* as the minimal unit of communication.[7] Transacts and interacts are concepts that emphasize that you cannot commit a rhetorical act alone. Rhetoric is a transaction (*trans* means across or over or through) or an interaction (*inter* means between or among). Each of us brings a store of experience, feelings, beliefs, values, and concepts to every encounter; these are the raw materials through which we participate in rhetorical action. Note that enthymemic processes are present in all parts of an argument; audience members can collaborate in creating evidence or data, reasons, or claims—or all three!

The actor Patrick Stewart, who played the captain on *Star Trek: The Next Generation,* has been featured in ads for automobiles. Presumably, like any other individual, he gives a kind of personal testimony applauding a car that he likes. His reaction is no more or less valid than that of any other individual; in fact, because we have no information about his knowledge of mechanics or cars, it is quite a weak endorsement. By contrast, Stewart is a skilled and talented actor, and if he were speaking about acting, he would be an expert to whom we should attend.

But there is a second argument, and its existence is the reason that Stewart is paid handsomely to make these commercials. Although he has played other roles, Stewart is virtually indistinguishable from the character he played in the television series. In the role of captain, he appears calm and authoritative; he is a capable leader, and the adventures through which he leads his crew are associated with the exploration of frontiers, high technology, and life in the future. The automaker assumes that audiences hear not Stewart but the captain of the

---

[7]B. Aubrey Fisher and Leonard Hawes, "An Interact System Model: Generating a Grounded Theory of Small Groups," *Quarterly Journal of Speech* 57 (December 1971): 444–453; C. David Mortenson, *Communication: The Study of Human Interaction* (New York: McGraw-Hill, 1972), especially pp. 14–21, 376–377.

Enterprise D giving them advice about the most advanced, even futuristic automotive technology. In this case, no claim is made about his expertise, but it is hoped that audiences will make the assumption just the same.

A commercial made for the George Bush presidential campaign of 1988 is a more dramatic and controversial example of these two levels of argument.[8] The ad was sponsored and aired by the National Security Political Action Committee and first appeared early in September. It opened with side-by-side pictures of Bush and Michael Dukakis, Bush's Democratic opponent. Dukakis appeared somewhat disheveled in a dark photo; Bush was smiling and well groomed in bright sunlight. As the pictures appeared, an announcer said, "Bush and Dukakis on crime." Then Bush's picture appeared as the announcer said, "Bush supports the death penalty for first-degree murderers." Then came a picture of Dukakis with these words: "Dukakis not only opposes the death penalty, he allowed first-degree murderers to have weekend passes from prison." At this point a close-up mug shot of William Horton appeared on the screen with the words, "One was Willie Horton, who murdered a boy in a robbery, stabbing him 19 times." A blurred black-and-white shot of Horton seemingly being arrested was shown with the words, "Despite a life sentence, Horton received ten weekend passes from prison." The words "KIDNAPPING," "STABBING," and "RAPING" in big white capital letters appeared as captions to Horton's mug shot as the announcer said, "Horton fled, kidnapping a young couple, stabbing the man and repeatedly raping his girlfriend." A photo of Dukakis then appeared, as the announcer said, "Weekend prison passes. Dukakis on crime."

There are, once again, two levels of argument. One is a rather simple and explicit argument. The claim: Vote for President Bush rather than his opponent Dukakis. The reason: Their contrasting stands on punishment of criminals. Bush supports the death penalty for first-degree murderers whereas Dukakis approved a weekend prison furlough for a lifer who committed violent crimes while out. The evidence: The sound of the announcer's words voicing Bush's position and the pictures of William Horton with the information about the crimes that he had committed to receive a life sentence and that he committed while on a prison furlough.

The second level of argument is subtle and implicit. The ad suggests that the Horton case is typical (it was not), and without identifying

---

[8]For a more detailed analysis of this ad, see K. H. Jamieson, *Dirty Politics* (Oxford University Press, 1992), pp. 12–42.

him as African American, the photos in the ad feed fears about rising crime (the fears are greater than the actual crime rate) and racist stereotypes that many whites have about crime by African American men. The ad helps to prompt the creation of that second argument visually through the contrasting photos of a sunny Bush and a shadowy Dukakis, the ugly, threatening mug shot of Horton, the large white letters that underscore the most inflammatory words that appear on the screen under Horton's photograph, and the bits of information that can easily be formed into a scenario worthy of becoming a script for a TV movie.

The subtle, second-level argument goes something like this: It would be dangerous to vote for Dukakis. Why? Because one African American criminal committed serious crimes while on a prison furlough. When spelled out in this way, the argument seems a little silly, but the subtle argument is powerful. Racial stereotypes prompt viewers to assume that Horton was typical (in fact, no other first-degree murderer of any ethnicity murdered or raped while on a furlough), and the Horton case triggers fears about violent crime that, as I noted, are greater than the actual crime rate, fears that often have racist overtones. The second level or nondiscursive argument not only illustrates how audiences construct the proofs by which they are persuaded, it shows us a case in which an argument is constructed out of pictures, associations, and stereotyping. The enthymeme, the process of rhetorical argument, involves processes in which we construct both discursive or logical and nondiscursive or nonlogical arguments out of visual and verbal materials.

In other words, rhetorical arguments come into being in the minds of members of the audience through direct and indirect means. In fact, all rhetorical action combines elements that are discursive (logical, formed out of propositions and evidence) and nondiscursive (nonlogical, formed by association, frequently visual and nonverbal). In order to understand the nature of argument, we have to step back to take a broader view of rhetorical action.

DIMENSIONS OF RHETORICAL ACTION

As I wrote in Chapter 1, rhetoric is the study of all the processes by which people are influenced. Some of these processes are logical; some are not. The dimensions of rhetorical action reveal the mixture of qualities that are found in it. Each of these dimensions is a continuum; that is, each dimension is formed by a pair of qualities related in such a way that one of them gradually becomes the other. The ends of each continuum represent extreme forms of the same quality or characteristic.

	Discursive (logical)	Nondiscursive (nonlogical)
Purpose	Instrumental (a tool)	Consummatory (expressive; for its own sake)
Argument	Justificatory (offers reasons)	Ritualistic (participatory, performative)
Structure	Logical (necessary links)	Associative (learned, from personal experience)
Language	Literal (describes world)	Figurative (describes internal state)
Evidence	Factual (verifiable)	Psychological (appeals to needs, drives, desires)

Each dimension focuses on the mixture of qualities involved in each facet of rhetorical action: purpose, argument, structure, language, or evidence.

Instrumental–Consummatory

Something that is *instrumental* functions as a tool; it is a means to an end. Something that is *consummatory* is its own reason for being—the purpose is the action itself; the end is the performance or enactment, "singing sweet songs to please oneself," as in singing in the shower. Most rhetoric is primarily instrumental because it seeks to achieve some goal outside itself: to share information or understanding, to change attitudes, or to induce action. But rhetorical action is also consummatory. For example, Ronald Reagan spoke at the 1992 Republican National Convention. That a former president, highly respected by most Americans, urged the reelection of President Bush was as important as, perhaps more important than, the specific reasons he offered for such a vote. Similarly, the boasts of victorious athletes during championship competitions are consummatory in celebrating their prowess. They are often instrumental, however, in spurring their opponents to new efforts, a reason that such boasting is discouraged by coaches. These are instances in which instrumental and consummatory purposes are mixed and interrelated.

Some rhetorical acts are primarily consummatory. If you were to attend a football or basketball game at the University of Kansas, you would see the Kansas fans rise and begin to murmur what sounds like a Gregorian chant while waving their arms slowly over their heads. They repeat, at an ever-increasing speed, the words "Rock Chalk. Jayhawk. K.U." Unless you are a member of the University of Kansas community, the words and gestures are meaningless.[9] But if you belong to the community, you chant and wave to reaffirm your membership in it. There is also an instrumental component. The chant expresses, indirectly, support for Jayhawk athletic teams, which represent the community on these occasions. Because morale affects play, the chant may increase the team's likelihood of winning.

Most rhetorical acts are a combination of these purposes, with the emphasis on instrumental ends. Consummatory purposes are often revealed in introductions and conclusions that express shared values and affirm membership in a community.

Justificatory–Ritualistic

An act that is *justificatory* gives reasons; it explains why something is true or good or desirable. *Ritual* refers to the prescribed form or order of an act (usually a ceremony), to the way it is performed. For this reason, ritualistic elements are often nonverbal or involve the sheer repetition of verbal elements, as in a chant. Ritual involves formal practices, customs, and procedures. Rituals do not justify or explain, they affirm and express. Some common ritualistic acts are pledging allegiance to the flag, standing to sing the national anthem, taking communion, or participating in the *Rocky Horror Picture Show*. Participating in a ritual requires behaviors such as standing, putting your hand over your heart, kneeling, throwing rice, eating, or drinking. Rituals are performed by members of a community; they are repeated over and over again; the form of their performance is very important. Many Roman Catholics, for example, were dismayed when the Latin liturgy was abandoned; many Protestants were unhappy when the King James version of the Bible was supplanted by translations using more

---

[9]They are also meaningless to many K.U. students who do not know that the waving arms symbolize waving wheat or that "rock chalk" refers to quarries in which skeletons of prehistoric animals were discovered by K.U. geologists, whose students originated the chant.

contemporary language. By contrast, justificatory acts imply an absence of shared belief, which requires the presentation of arguments and evidence. Note that the enthymeme illustrates the degree to which rhetorical action falls between these two extremes.

A vivid example of the use of ritual to make a rhetorical point occurred when women's peace groups in Israel kept a silent vigil every Friday to protest Israeli treatment of Palestinians in the West Bank and Gaza, especially those engaged in the uprising called the *Intifada*. Their action aroused intense responses, which ranged from physical attacks to shouted epithets. These women were accused of being traitors to the Jewish community, but their silent Sabbath vigil was a powerful accusation that many Israelis could not ignore. (See Chapter 11 for additional material on nonverbal rhetoric, which often uses rituals or violates them.)

Ritualistic arguments can also be made positively. For example, the conflict over school prayer is, in part, a conflict over the force of ritualistic appeal. Just how much pressure is put on a child when a teacher says, "Let us pray," and many of her schoolmates bow their heads?

Logical–Associative

Logical relationships are necessary relationships, such as effect to cause or cause to effect. Logical structures reflect such relationships; they express necessary or asserted connections. By contrast, *associative* relationships are learned through personal experience or based on cultural linkages or social truths. Associative relationships are based on personal experiences and subjective reactions, but, as illustrated by stereotyping, they can be shared by many individuals.

Associative structure is like juxtaposition—two things are placed in relation to each other, and because they are positioned that way, a relationship is inferred. Rorschach tests are associative, asking individuals to divulge what pops into their minds when they see giant ink blots. Thematic Apperception Tests (TATs), asking individuals to finish stories, are examples of associative structure. Commercials that show beautiful, young, sexy people in attractive locales drinking a soft drink are trying to create associations between the advertised brand and the qualities of the models who appear in the ad.

Logical structure is ordinarily explicit and overt. Claims are stated as propositions. The connections between ideas are made clear to us, and we can examine claims, evidence, and reasons, testing them against other evidence and the like. Associative structure is usually implicit and oblique. Relationships are suggested to us indirectly through juxtaposing ideas or events or pictures, and we test these connections against our personal experience and subjective response. As the ad for the Bush campaign illustrates, logical and associative links can be involved in the same rhetorical act. Note that the associations prompted by juxtapositions can act as substitutes for formal arguments.

The power of arguments based on personal relevance links these two concepts. Prior to the late 1960s, the argument that "if you're old enough to fight, you're old enough to vote" was dismissed as illogical. The qualities needed to fight are quite different from those needed to vote intelligently, so the implied literal analogy was rejected. During the Vietnam War, however, large numbers of men under the age of 21 were sent to fight in Vietnam, and the argument came to have greater force. Should those who would be asked to risk their lives have a right to choose those who would make that decision? Suddenly, the argument seemed analogous to "no taxation without representation," the view that no government should have the right to tax people who cannot vote to choose their representatives. Now the analogy was between choosing those who would have the power to take away either your property in taxes or your life in war. Note that the same basic argument can be seen as illogical or logical depending on which analogy is emphasized. That choice, of course, was deeply affected by personal relevance, and in 1971, the United States lowered the voting age to 18.

Many of the strategies discussed in Chapter 10 use the resources of language to make associative connections. Repetitions of sounds, words, and phrases create structures based on association. Relationships based on logic are only one kind of form that appears in rhetorical action. Other forms are based on relationships that emulate patterns in nature and in our experience: repetition, crescendo and decrescendo, and the like.[10]

Rhetorical action combines forms based on logic and on association. Both kinds of form prompt the creation of arguments in the minds of listeners. Television advertising is an excellent source of examples of the use of associative form to support claims.

Literal–Figurative

Literal language is prosaic and factual; it is intended to describe the world. *Figurative* language is poetic and metaphorical, and it reveals the person who uses it. Literal language deals with external reality; in

---

[10]Kenneth Burke, "Psychology and Form," *Counter-Statement* (Berkeley: University of California Press, 1968), pp. 29–44, discusses form as the psychology of the audience. Kinds of form and their appeal are discussed on pp. 124–149.

some cases, it can be tested empirically for accuracy. Figurative language reveals the experiences and feelings of the rhetor. One poet calls the moon "the north wind's cookie"; another calls it "a piece of angry candy rattling around in the box of the sky." These statements reveal the feelings of the authors but tell us little about the moon. As critics, we look for metaphors to discover how a rhetor perceives the world. For example, in his famous "I Have a Dream" speech in 1963, Martin Luther King, Jr., construed civil rights for Americans, including African Americans, as a promissory note and efforts to obtain them as analogous to attempting to cash a check and being told that there were insufficient funds. That metaphor captures the sense of legal obligation inherent in fundamental citizen rights and the profound injustice in being told by a bank that you have no right to the money on deposit there for you.

Rhetorical acts combine the literal language of factual statements with metaphors and other poetic devices. In her 1988 keynote address to the Democratic National Convention, Texas Governor Ann Richards used a figurative analogy to describe women's ability to perform well in situations usually associated with men, such as delivering keynote addresses: "After all, Ginger Rogers did everything that Fred Astaire did, she just did it backwards and in high heels." In a 1975 commencement address at Barnard College, playwright and author Lillian Hellman told a story to illustrate the problems that still existed despite some progress toward equal opportunity for women. The story involved a critic, George Brandes, and Henrik Ibsen, the Norwegian playwright who wrote the early feminist play *A Doll's House,* about a woman named Nora who leaves the safety of her marriage to seek her own life after she has discovered how little she was respected by her husband. As Hellman related the story,

> They were taking a walk on a wintry day in Oslo. They passed an open park with a great wind blowing through it. The park was empty except for a middle-aged woman sitting on a bench. Ibsen shook his head and said, "Poor lady." Brandes said, "I have always wanted to ask you. What happened to Nora?" Ibsen turned round, pointed back to the lady on the bench, and said, "That is Nora."[11]

Chapter 10 explores these and other dimensions of language and their role in rhetorical action.

---

[11]Lillian Hellman, "Commencement Address at Barnard College," *Women's Voices in Our Time: Statements by American Leaders,* ed. Victoria DeFrancisco and Marvin D. Jensen (Prospect Heights, IL: Waveland Press, 1994), p. 20.

Factual–Psychological

These qualities of evidence have already been explored in Chapter 7. The *factual* dimension of evidence can be verified to determine its accuracy or truthfulness. *Psychologically,* evidence appeals to our needs, drives, and desires. Evidence can be fictive or hypothetical, inducing us to imagine and speculate. Evidence can pander to our prejudices or reflect our opinions and beliefs, which may be wrong. Rhetorical evidence is both data about the world and our perception of the world in terms of ourselves, a process that transforms the "facts" of what exists into instruments for our use and into obstacles that frustrate us.

These continua express the discursive and nondiscursive dimensions of rhetorical action. Although the concept of argument emphasizes discursive or logical processes, rhetorical argumentation includes all kinds of cues that stimulate us to treat our associations as evidence, to construct reasons, and to draw conclusions. Many of these cues are nondiscursive. The characteristics of the enthymeme reflect the ways in which rhetorical action combines these dimensions. The section on nonverbal rhetoric in Chapter 11 is a resource for understanding nondiscursive dimensions of rhetorical action.

Additional material related to argument is found in Chapter 10 under strategies of proof.

SUMMARY

This chapter describes the resources of argument. They include:

1. Combining evidence (information, beliefs) and reasons (values, trust in authority) to draw conclusions

2. Addressing fundamental issues of fact and value (combined in issues of policy)

3. Structuring what is known and valued into ordered and meaningful units

4. Presenting novel perspectives or justifications that affect the balance of arguments on an issue

5. Using authority evidence to stimulate the construction of arguments

6. Selecting and adapting arguments for a particular audience

7. Stimulating the audience by using discursive and nondiscursive cues to participate in creating the proofs by which they are persuaded

The resources of argument, in turn, are combined into larger organizational units, which are the subject of the next chapter.

Summary Outline

I. Arguments are composed of claims, reasons, and evidence.

    A. A claim is an assertion that goes beyond what is known.

    B. A reason is a ground or justification for drawing a conclusion (the claim) from what is known (the data).

    C. Evidence consists of all forms of supporting materials.

II. Requirements for sound argumentation vary with the kind of issue.

    A. Questions of fact concern what data exist and how they are to be interpreted.

    B. Questions of value are disputes about goals.

    C. Questions of policy incorporate issues of fact and issues of value.

III. Invention is the process of selecting, ordering, and adapting arguments to the issue, audience, and rhetor.

    A. Rhetorical arguments or enthymemes call attention to the powerful role of the audience in creating the messages by which they are persuaded.

    B. Rhetorical invention selects, orders, and adapts in both discursive (logical) and nondiscursive (nonlogical) ways:

        1. Rhetorical purposes range from the instrumental to the consummatory.

        2. Rhetorical arguments range from the justificatory to the ritualistic.

        3. Rhetorical structures range from the logical to the associative.

        4. Rhetorical evidence ranges from the empirically verifiable to the psychologically appealing.

        5. Rhetorical language ranges from the literal to the figurative.

■ ■ ■

MATERIAL FOR ANALYSIS

The following essay appeared in the January 1971 issue of *Catholic World* on pages 177–183. The author, a faculty member of the religion department of Temple University in Philadelphia, has written a number of related works.[12] The form of the essay is discursively argumentative, setting out a thesis, defining terms, and setting forth the criteria by which the quality of the evidence and reasons, the proof, are to be judged. At the same time, it is targeted to a special kind of audience, one composed of people with deep religious beliefs who are strongly committed to living their lives in imitation of the model set by Jesus Christ. Because some of the strongest arguments against changing the status of women toward lives of greater opportunity and equality are often justified on the basis of scripture, particularly the epistles of St. Paul, the case that the author makes addresses an important facet of resistance to feminist efforts.

Jesus Was a Feminist

By Leonard J. Swidler

1   *Thesis: Jesus was a feminist.*

2   Definition of terms: By *Jesus* is meant the historical person who lived in Palestine two thousand years ago, whom Christians traditionally acknowledge as Lord and Savior, and whom they should "imitate" as much as possible. By a *feminist* is meant a person who is in favor of, and who promotes, the equality of women with men, a person who advocates and practices treating women primarily as human persons (as men are so treated) and willingly contravenes social customs in so acting.

3   To prove the thesis it must be demonstrated that, so far as we can tell, Jesus neither said nor did anything which would indicate that he advocated treating women as intrinsically inferior to men, but that on the contrary he said and did things which indicated that he thought of women as the equals of men, and that in the process he willingly violated pertinent social mores.

4   The negative portion of the argument can be documented quite simply by reading through the four Gospels. Nowhere does Jesus treat women as "inferior beings." In fact, Jesus clearly felt especially sent to the typical classes of "inferior beings," such as the poor, the lame, the sinner—and women—to call them all to the freedom and equality of the Kingdom of God. But there are two factors which raise this negative result exponentially in its

---

[12]Leonard J. Swidler, *Women in Judaism: The Status of Women in Formative Judaism* (Metuchen, NJ: Scarecrow Press, 1976); *Biblical Affirmations of Women* (Philadelphia: Westminster Press, 1979). With Arlene Swidler, he has edited *Women Priests: A Catholic Commentary on the Vatican Declaration* (New York: Paulist Press, 1977). © 1971 by *The Catholic World*. Reprinted by permission.

significance: the status of women in Palestine at the time of Jesus, and the nature of the Gospels. Both need to be recalled here in some detail, particularly the former.

The Status of Women in Palestine

5   The status of women in Palestine during the time of Jesus was very decidedly that of inferiors. Despite the fact that there were several heroines recorded in the Scriptures, according to most rabbinic customs of Jesus's time—and long after—women were not allowed to study the Scriptures (Torah). One first-century rabbi, Eliezer, put the point sharply: "Rather should the words of the Torah be burned than entrusted to a woman. . . . Whoever teaches his daughter the Torah is like one who teaches her lasciviousness."

6   In the vitally religious area of prayer, women were so little thought of as not to be given obligations of the same seriousness as men. For example, women, along with children and slaves, were not obliged to recite the *Shema,* the morning prayer, nor prayers at meals. In fact, the Talmud states, "Let a curse come upon the man who [must needs have] his wife or children say grace for him." Moreover, in the daily prayers of Jews there was a threefold thanksgiving: "Praised be God that he has not created me a gentile; praised be God that he has not created me a woman; praised be God that he has not created me an ignorant man." (It was obviously a version of this rabbinic prayer that Paul controverted in his letter to the Galatians: "There is neither Jew nor Greek, there is neither slave nor free, there is neither male nor female; for you are all one in Christ Jesus.")

7   Women were also grossly restricted in public prayer. It was (is) not even possible for them to be counted toward the number necessary for a quorum to form a congregation to worship communally—they were again classified with children and slaves, who similarly did not qualify (there is an interesting parallel to the current canon 93 of the *Codex Juris Canonici* [CIC], which groups married women, minors, and the insane). In the great temple at Jerusalem they were limited to one outer portion, the women's court, which was five steps below the court for the men. In the synagogues the women were also separated from the men, and of course were not allowed to read aloud or take any leading function. (The same is still true in most synagogues today—canon 1262 of the CIC also states that "in church the women should be separated from the men.")

8   Besides the disabilities women suffered in the areas of prayer and worship there were many others in the private and public forums of society. As one Scripture scholar, Peter Ketter, noted, "A rabbi regarded it as beneath his dignity, as indeed positively

disreputable, to speak to a woman in public. The 'Proverbs of the Fathers' contain the injunction: 'Speak not much with a woman.' Since a man's own wife is meant here, how much more does not this apply to the wife of another? The wise men say, 'Who speaks much with a woman draws down misfortune on himself, neglects the words of the law, and finally earns hell. . . .' If it were merely the too free intercourse of the sexes which was being warned against, this would signify nothing derogatory to woman. But since the rabbi may not speak even to his own wife, daughter, or sister in the street, then only male arrogance can be the motive." Intercourse with uneducated company is warned against in exactly the same terms. "One is not so much as to greet a woman." In addition, save in the rarest instances, women were not allowed to bear witness in a court of law. Some Jewish thinkers, as for example, Philo, a contemporary of Jesus, thought women ought not leave their households except to go to the synagogue (and that only at a time when most of the other people would be at home); girls ought not even cross the threshold that separated the male and female apartments of the household.

9   In general, the attitude toward women was epitomized in the institutions and customs surrounding marriage. For the most part the function of women was thought [of] rather exclusively in terms of childbearing and rearing; women were almost always under the tutelage of a man, either the father or husband, or if a widow, the dead husband's brother. Polygamy—in the sense of having several wives, but *not* in the sense of having several husbands—was legal among Jews at the time of Jesus, although probably not heavily practiced. Moreover, divorce of a wife was very easily obtained by the husband—he merely had to give her a writ of divorce; women in Palestine, on the other hand, were not allowed to divorce their husbands.

10   Rabbinic sayings about women also provide an insight into the attitude toward women: "It is well for those whose children are male, but ill for those whose children are female. . . . At the birth of a boy all are joyful, but at the birth of a girl all are sad. . . . When a boy comes into the world, peace comes into the world; when a girl comes, nothing comes. . . . Even the most virtuous of women is a witch. . . . Our teachers have said, Four qualities are evident in women: They are greedy at their food, eager to gossip, lazy, and jealous."

11   The condition of women in Palestinian Judaism was bleak.

The Nature of the Gospels

12   The Gospels, of course, are not the straight factual reports of eyewitnesses of the events in the life of Jesus of Nazareth as one might find in the columns of the *New York Times* or the pages of a

critical biography. Rather, they are four different faith statements reflecting at least four primitive Christian communities who believed that Jesus was the Messiah, the Lord and Savior of the world. They were composed from a variety of sources, written and oral, over a period of time and in response to certain needs felt in the communities and individuals at the time; consequently they are many-layered. Since the gospel writer–editors were not twentieth-century critical historians they were not particularly intent on recording *ipsissima verba Christi* [the exact words of Christ], nor were they concerned to winnow out all of their own cultural biases and assumptions. Indeed, it is doubtful they were particularly conscious of them.

13   This modern critical understanding of the Gospels, of course, does not impugn the historical character of the Gospels; it merely describes the type of historical documents they are so their historical significance can more accurately be evaluated. Its religious value lies in the fact that modern Christians are thereby helped to know much more precisely what Jesus meant by certain statements and actions as they are reported by the first Christian communities in the Gospels. With this new knowledge of the nature of the Gospels it is easier to make the vital distinction between the religious truth that is to be handed on and the time-conditioned categories and customs involved in expressing it.

14   When the fact that no negative attitudes by Jesus toward women are portrayed in the Gospels is set side by side with the recently discerned "communal faith-statement" understanding of the nature of the Gospels, the importance of the former is vastly enhanced. For whatever Jesus said or did comes to us only through the lens of the first Christians. If there were no very special religious significance in a particular concept or custom, we would expect that current concept or custom to be reflected by Jesus. The fact that the overwhelmingly negative attitude toward women in Palestine did not come through the primitive Christian communal lens by itself underscores the clearly great religious importance Jesus attached to his positive attitude—his feminist attitude—toward women: feminism, that is, personalism extended to women, is a constitutive part of the Gospel, the Good News, of Jesus.

Women and Resurrection from the Dead

15   One of the first things noticed in the gospels about Jesus's attitude toward women is that he taught them the Gospel; the meaning of Jesus's first appearance after his resurrection to any of his followers was to a woman (or women), who was then commissioned by him to bear witness of the risen Jesus to the Eleven (John 20:11ff.; Matt. 28:9f.; Mark 16:9ff.). In typical male Palestinian style, the Eleven refused to believe the woman since, according to Judaic law, women were not allowed to bear legal witness. As one learned in the Law, Jesus obviously was aware of this stricture. His first appearing to and commissioning women to bear witness to the most important event of his career could not have been anything but deliberate: It was clearly a dramatic linking of a very clear rejection of the second-class status of women with the center of His Gospel, His resurrection. The effort of Jesus to centrally connect these two points is so obvious that it is an overwhelming tribute to man's intellectual myopia not to have discerned it effectively in two thousand years.

16   The intimate connection of women with resurrection from the dead is not limited in the Gospels to that of Jesus. There are accounts of three other resurrections in the Gospels—all closely involving a woman. The most obvious connection of a woman with a resurrection account is that of the raising of a woman, Jairus's daughter (Matt. 9:18ff.; Mark 5:22ff.; Luke 8:41ff.). A second resurrection Jesus performed was that of the only son of the widow of Nain: "And when the Lord saw her, he had compassion on her and he said to her, 'Do not weep' " (cf. Luke 7:11ff.). The third resurrection Jesus performed was Lazarus's, at the request of his sisters Martha and Mary (cf. John 11). From the first it was Martha and Mary who sent for Jesus because of Lazarus's illness. But when Jesus finally came Lazarus was four days dead. Martha met Jesus and pleaded for his resurrection: "Lord, if you had been here, my brother would not have died. And even now I know that whatever you ask from God, God will give you." Later Mary came to Jesus and said much the same. "When Jesus saw her weeping, and the Jews who came with her also weeping, he was deeply moved in spirit and troubled; and he said, 'Where have you laid him?' They said to him, 'Lord, come and see.' Jesus wept." Then followed the raising from the dead. Thus, Jesus raised one woman from the dead, and raised two other persons largely because of women.

17   There are two further details that should be noted in these three resurrection stories. The first is that only in the case of Jairus's daughter did Jesus touch the corpse—which made him ritually unclean. In the cases of the two men Jesus did not touch them but merely said, "Young man, I say to you, arise," or, "Lazarus, come out." One must at least wonder why Jesus chose to violate the laws for ritual purity in order to help a woman but not a man. The second detail is in Jesus's conversation with Martha after she pleaded for the resurrection of Lazarus. Jesus declared himself to be the resurrection ("I am the resurrection and the life"), the only time he did so that is recorded in the Gospels. Jesus here again revealed the central event, the central message, in the Gospel—the resurrection, His resurrection, His being the resurrection—to a woman.

Women Disciples of Jesus

18 There are of course numerous occasions recorded in the Gospels, the Scriptures, and religious truths in general. When it is recalled that in Judaism it was considered improper and even "obscene" to teach women the Scriptures, this action of Jesus was an extraordinary, deliberate decision to break with a custom invidious to women. Moreover, women became disciples of Jesus not only in the sense of learning from Him but also in the sense of following Him in His travels and ministering to Him. A number of women, married and unmarried, were regular followers of Jesus. In Luke 8:1ff. several are mentioned by name in the same sentence with the Twelve: "He made his way through towns and villages preaching and proclaiming the Good News of the Kingdom of God. With him went the Twelve, as well as certain women . . . who provided for them out of their own resources" (cf. Mark 15:40f.). The Greek word translated here as "provided for" and in Mark as "ministered to" is *diekonoun,* the same basic word as "deacon"; indeed, apparently the tasks of the deacons in early Christianity were much the same as these women undertook. The significance of this phenomenon of women following Jesus about, learning from and ministering to Him, can be properly appreciated when it is recalled that not only were women not to read or study the Scriptures, but in the more observant settings they were not even to leave their households, whether as a daughter, a sole wife, or a member of a harem.

Women as Sex Objects

19 Within this context of women being disciples and ministers, Jesus quite deliberately broke another custom disadvantageous to women. There were situations where women were treated by others not at all as persons but as sex objects, and it could be expected that Jesus would do the same. The expectations were disappointed. One such occasion occurred when Jesus was invited to dinner at the house of a skeptical Pharisee (Luke 7:36ff.), and a woman of ill repute entered and washed Jesus's feet with her tears, wiped them with her hair, and anointed them. The Pharisee saw her solely as an evil sexual creature: "The Pharisee . . . said to himself, 'If this man were a prophet, he would know who this woman is who is touching him and what a bad name she has.'" But Jesus deliberately rejected this approach to the woman as a sex object. He rebuked the Pharisee and spoke solely of the woman's human, spiritual actions; He spoke of her love, her unlove, that is, her sins, of her being forgiven, and her faith. Jesus then addressed her (it was not "proper" to speak to women in public, especially "improper" women) as a human person: "Your sins are forgiven. . . . Your faith has saved you; go in peace."

20   A similar situation occurred when the scribes and Pharisees used a woman reduced entirely to a sex object to set a legal trap for Jesus. It is difficult to imagine a more callous use of a human person than the "adulterous" woman was put to by the enemies of Jesus [John 8:3–11]. First, she was surprised in the intimate act of sexual intercourse (quite possibly a trap was set up ahead of time by the suspicious husband) and then dragged before the scribes and Pharisees, and then by them before an even larger crowd that Jesus was instructing, "making her stand in full view of everybody." They told Jesus that she had been caught in the very act of committing adultery and that Moses had commanded that such women be stoned to death (Deut. 22:22ff.). "What have you to say?" The trap was partly that if Jesus said Yes to the stoning He would be violating the Roman law, which restricted capital punishment, and if He said No, He would appear to contravene Mosaic law. It could also partly have been to place Jesus's reputation for kindness toward, and championing the cause of, women in opposition to the law and the condemnation of sin. Jesus of course eluded their snares by refusing to become entangled in legalisms and abstractions. Rather, he dealt with both the accusers and the accused directly as spiritual, ethical, human persons. He spoke directly to the accusers in the context of their own personal ethical conduct: "If there is one of you who has not sinned, let him be the first to throw a stone at her." To the accused woman he likewise spoke directly with compassion but without approving her conduct: "'Woman, where [are] they [your accusers]? Has no one condemned you?' She said, 'No one, Lord.' And Jesus said, 'Neither do I condemn you; go, and do not sin again.'"

21   (One detail of this encounter provides the basis for a short excursus related to the status of women. The Pharisees stated that the woman had been caught in the act of adultery and according to the Law of Moses was therefore to be stoned to death. Since the type of execution mentioned was stoning, the woman must have been a "virgin betrothed," as referred to in Deut. 22:23ff. There provision is made for the stoning of *both* the man and the woman, although in the Gospel story only the woman is brought forward. However, the reason given for why the man ought to be stoned was not because he had violated the woman or God's law but "because he had violated the wife of his neighbor." It was the injury of the man by misusing his property—wife—that was the great evil.)

Jesus' Rejection of the Blood Taboo

22   All three of the synoptic Gospels insert into the middle of the account of raising Jairus's daughter from the dead the story of the curing of the woman who had an issue of blood for 12 years (Matt. 9:20ff.; Mark 5:25ff.; Luke 8:43ff.). Especially touching about this story is that the affected woman was so reluctant to project herself into public attention that she "said to herself, 'If I only touch his garment, I shall be made well.'" Her shyness was not because she came from the poor, lower classes, for Mark pointed out that over the 12 years she had been to many physicians—with no success—on whom she had spent all her money. It was probably because for 12 years, as a woman with a flow of blood, she was constantly ritually unclean (Lev. 15:19ff.), which not only made her incapable of participating in any cultic action and made her in some sense "displeasing to God," but also rendered anyone and anything she touched (or anyone who touched what she had touched!) similarly unclean. (Here is the basis for the Catholic Church not allowing women in the sanctuary during Mass—they might be menstruating and hence unclean.) The sense of degradation and contagion that her "womanly weakness" worked upon her over the 12 years doubtless was oppressive in the extreme. This would have been especially so when a religious teacher, a rabbi, was involved. But not only does Jesus's power heal her, in one of His many acts of compassion on the downtrodden and afflicted, including women, but Jesus also makes a great to-do about the event, calling extraordinary attention to the publicity-shy woman: "And Jesus, perceiving in himself that power had gone forth from him, immediately turned about in the crowd and said, 'Who touched my garments?' And his disciples said to him, 'You see the crowd pressing around you, and yet you say, "Who touched me?"' And he looked around to see who had done it. But the woman, knowing what had been done to her, came in fear and trembling and fell down before Him and told Him the whole truth. And He said to her, 'Daughter, your faith has made you well; go in peace, and be healed of your disease.'" It seems clear that Jesus wanted to call attention to the fact that He did not shrink from the ritual uncleanness incurred by being touched by the "unclean" woman (on several occasions Jesus rejected the notion of ritual uncleanness), and by immediate implication rejected the "uncleanness" of a woman who had a flow of blood, menstruous or continual. Jesus apparently placed a greater importance on the dramatic making of this point, both to the afflicted woman herself and the crowd, than He did on avoiding the temporary psychological discomfort of the embarrassed woman, which in light of Jesus's extraordinary concern to alleviate the pain of the afflicted, meant He placed a great weight on the teaching this lesson about the dignity of women.

Jesus and the Samaritan Woman

23   On another occasion Jesus again deliberately violated the then-common code concerning men's relationship to women. It is recorded in the story of the Samaritan woman at the well of Jacob

(John 4:5ff.). Jesus was waiting at the well outside the village while His disciples were getting food. A Samaritan woman approached the well to draw water. Normally a Jew would not address a Samaritan, as the woman pointed out: "Jews, in fact, do not associate with Samaritans." But also normally a man would not speak to a woman in public (doubly so in the case of a rabbi). However, Jesus startled the woman by initiating a conversation. The woman was aware that on both counts, her being a Samaritan and being a woman, Jesus's action was out of the ordinary, for she replied, "How is it that you, a Jew, ask a drink of me, a woman of Samaria?" As hated as the Samaritans were by the Jews, it is nevertheless clear that Jesus's speaking with a woman was considered a much more flagrant breach of conduct than His speaking with a Samaritan, for John related, "His disciples returned, and were surprised to find him speaking to a woman, though none of them asked, 'What do you want from her?' or, 'Why are you talking to her?'" However, Jesus's bridging of the gap of inequality between men and women continued further, for in the conversation with the woman He revealed himself in a straightforward fashion as the Messiah for the first time: "The woman said to him, 'I know that Messiah is coming.' . . . Jesus said to her, 'I who speak to you am he.'"

24   Just as when Jesus revealed Himself to Martha as "the resurrection" and to Mary as the "risen one" and bade her to bear witness to the apostles, Jesus here also revealed Himself in one of his key roles, as Messiah, to a woman—who immediately bore witness of the fact to her fellow villagers. (It is interesting to note that apparently the testimony of women carried greater weight among the Samaritans than among the Jews, for the villagers came out to see Jesus: "Many Samaritans of that town believed in Him on the strength of the woman's testimony. . . ." It would seem that John the Gospel writer deliberately highlighted this contrast in the way he wrote about this event, and also that he clearly wished to reinforce thereby Jesus's stress on the equal dignity of women.)

25   One other point should be noted in connection with this story. As the crowd of Samaritans was walking out to see Jesus, Jesus was speaking to His disciples about the fields being ready for the harvest and how He was sending them to reap what others had sown. He was clearly speaking of the souls of men, and most probably was referring directly to the approaching Samaritans. Such exegesis is standard. It is also rather standard to refer to others in general and only Jesus in particular as having been the sowers whose harvest the apostles were about to reap (e.g., in the Jerusalem Bible). But it would seem that the evangelist also meant specifically to include the Samaritan woman among those sowers, for immediately after he recorded Jesus's statement to the disciples about their reaping what others had sown, he added the above-

mentioned verse: "Many Samaritans of that town had believed in him on the strength of the woman's testimony. . . ."

Marriage and the Dignity of Woman

26   One of the most important stands of Jesus in relation to the dignity of women was His position on marriage. His unpopular attitude toward marriage (cf. Matt. 19:10: "The disciples said to him, 'If such is the case of a man with his wife, it is not expedient to marry.'") presupposed a feminist view of women; they had rights and responsibilities equal to men. It was quite possible in Jewish law for men to have more than one wife (this was probably not frequently the case in Jesus's time, but there are recorded instances, e.g., Herod, Josephus), though the reverse was not possible. Divorce, of course, also was a simple matter, to be initiated only by the man. In both situations women were basically chattels to be collected or dismissed as the man was able and wished to; the double moral standard was flagrantly apparent. Jesus rejected both by insisting on monogamy and the elimination of divorce; both the man and the woman were to have the same rights and responsibilities in their relationship toward each other (cf. Mark 10:2ff.; Matt. 19:3ff.). This stance of Jesus was one of the few that was rather thoroughly assimilated by the Christian Church (in fact, often in an overrigid way concerning divorce—but how to understand the ethical prescriptions of Jesus is another article), doubtless in part because it was reinforced by various sociological conditions and other historical accidents, such as the then-current strength in the Greek world of the Stoic philosophy. However, the notion of equal rights and responsibilities was not extended very far within the Christian marriage. The general role of women was *Kirche, Kinder, Küche*—and only a suppliant's role in the first.

The Intellectual Life for Women

27   However, Jesus clearly did not think of woman's role in such restricted terms; she was not to be limited to being *only* a housekeeper. Jesus quite directly rejected the stereotype that the proper place of all women is "in the home" during a visit to the house of Martha and Mary (Luke 10:38 ff.). Martha took the typical woman's role: "Martha was distracted with much serving." Mary, however, took the supposedly "male" role: She "sat at the Lord's feet and listened to his teaching." Martha apparently thought Mary was out of place in choosing the role of the "intellectual," for she complained to Jesus. But Jesus's response was a refusal to force all women into the stereotype; he treated Mary first of all as a person (whose highest faculty is the intellect, the spirit) who was allowed to set her own priorities, and in this instance had "chosen the better part." And Jesus applauded her: "It

is not to be taken from her." Again, when one recalls the Palestinian restriction on women studying the Scriptures or studying with
rabbis, that is, engaging in the intellectual life or acquiring any
"religious authority," it is difficult to imagine how Jesus could
possibly have been clearer in his insistence that women were
called to the intellectual, the spiritual life just as were men.

28   There is at least one other instance recorded in the Gospels
when Jesus uttered much the same message (Luke 11:27f.). One
day as Jesus was preaching a woman from the crowd apparently
was very deeply impressed and, perhaps imagining how happy she
would be to have such a son, raised her voice to pay Jesus a compliment. She did so by referring to His mother, and did so in a way
that was probably not untypical at that time and place. But her
image of a woman was sexually reductionist in the extreme (one
that largely persists to the present): female genitals and breasts.
"Blessed is the womb that bore you, and the breasts that you
sucked!" Although this was obviously meant as a compliment, and
although it was even uttered by a woman, Jesus clearly felt it necessary to reject this "baby-machine" image of women and insist
again on the personhood, the intellectual and moral faculties,
being primary for all: "But he said, 'Blessed rather are those who
hear the word of God and keep it!'" Looking at this text it is difficult to see how the primary point could be anything substantially
other than this. Luke and the tradition and Christian communities
he depended on must also have been quite clear about the sexual
significance of this event. Otherwise, why would he (and they)
have kept and included such a small event from all the years of
Jesus's public life? It was not retained *merely* because Jesus said
blessed are those who hear and keep God's word, but because that
was stressed by Jesus as being primary in comparison to a woman's
sexuality. Luke, however, seems to have had a discernment here
and elsewhere, concerning what Jesus was about in the question of
women's status that has not been shared by subsequent Christians
(nor apparently by many of *his* fellow Christians); for, in the explanation of this passage, Christians for two thousand years did
not see its plain meaning—doubtless because of unconscious pre-
suppositions about the status of women inculcated by their cultural milieu.

God as a Woman

29   In many ways Jesus strove to communicate the notion of
the equal dignity of women. In one sense that effort was capped
by his parable of the woman who found the lost coin (Luke
15:8ff.), for here Jesus projected God in the image of a woman!
Luke recorded that the despised tax collectors and sinners were
gathering around Jesus, and consequently the Pharisees and
scribes complained. Jesus, therefore, related three parables in a

row, all of which depicted God's being deeply concerned for that which was lost. The first story was of the shepherd who left the 99 sheep to seek the one lost—the shepherd is God. The third parable was of the prodigal son—the father is God. The second story was of the woman who sought the lost coin—the woman is God! Jesus did not shrink from the notion of God as feminine. In fact, it would appear that Jesus included this womanly image of God quite deliberately at this point, for the scribes and Pharisees were among those who most of all denigrated women—just as they did the "tax collectors and sinners."

30   There have been some instances in Christian history when the Holy Spirit has been associated with a feminine character, as, for example, in the Syrian *Didascalia,* where, in speaking of various offices in the Church, it states, "The Deaconess however should be honored by you as the image of the Holy Spirit." It would make an interesting investigation to see if these images of God presented here by Luke were ever used in a Trinitarian manner—thereby giving the Holy Spirit a feminine image. A negative result to the investigation would be as significant as a positive one, for this passage would seem to be particularly apt for a Trinitarian interpretation: The prodigal son's father is God the Father (this interpretation has in fact been quite common in Christian history); since Jesus elsewhere identified himself as the Good Shepherd, the shepherd seeking the lost sheep is Jesus, the Son (this standard interpretation is reflected in, among other things, the often-seen picture of Jesus carrying the lost sheep on his shoulders); the woman who sought the lost coin should "logically" be the Holy Spirit. If such an interpretation has existed, it surely has not been common. Should such lack of "logic" be attributed to the general cultural denigration of women or the abhorrence of pagan goddesses—although Christian abhorrence of pagan gods did not result in a Christian rejection of a male image of God?

Conclusion

31   From this evidence it should be clear that Jesus vigorously promoted the dignity and equality of women in the midst of a very male-dominated society: Jesus was a feminist, and a very radical one. Can his followers attempt to be anything less—*De Imitatione Christi?*

Questions for Analysis

1. What is the special role of authority evidence in this essay? How can the use of authority in the essay help you to understand its strengths and limitations?

2. Identify the warrants or justifications that the author uses to move from data to claims. What do they reveal about field-dependent reasons or warrants? How might these reasons have force for those who are not members of the target audience?

3. The essay appeared in a journal targeted to Roman Catholics. Is the essay less effective for Christians who are members of other denominations? Do comments about attitudes toward women in Judaism at the time of Jesus limit the essay's appeal for contemporary practicing Jews?

4. The author provides quite a bit of detail; however, are readers expected or required to provide additional details that would not be known to those outside the target audience? How much of this argumentation is enthymematic?

EXERCISES

The following are examples of persuasive strategies that have been identified as fallacies, that is, as appeals or tactics used by "propagandists" that invite audiences to behave in ways that are less than rational. In each case, consider the kinds of argument that each mimics and then discuss just how to distinguish between what would be considered a proper (logical or ethical) use of this tactic and what would not. For example, name-calling mimics the strategy of definition. When is a label descriptive and defining, and when does it become an instance of name-calling?

Name-Calling

Obviously, this is another name for labeling, in particular, pinning a label with strong negative connotations on a person or idea so those hearing the label will have an instant reaction of dislike or rejection.

Name-calling can be used against policies ("the Clinton health plan is socialism!"), practices ("those regulations are just a lot of red tape"), or beliefs ("condoning abortion is condoning murder"), as well as individuals, ethnic groups, or nations. Name-calling is at work when we hear a candidate called a "reactionary" or "a Washington insider." Some of the most effective epithets are those that are vague and do not denote anything specific, such as "Candidate X is a bleeding-heart liberal."

The persuader who uses name-calling doesn't want us to think, merely to react immediately and without thinking.

Glittering Generalities

This is name-calling in reverse, exploiting the positive connotations of words that evoke cherished values. Like name-calling, glittering generalities seek immediate acceptance and agreement. We believe in, fight for, and live by "worthy words" such as "the American dream," "liberty," "justice," "the American way," "the right to bear arms," and "free speech." These sound good because they remind us of important values, but they have no specific meaning as phrases—ask yourself, Just what is _____? as you try to understand their appeal.

When is a generalization not a glittering generality? How, if at all, is this related to arguments based on definition?

Transference—Guilt or Glory by Association

Using the process of association, transference invites us to accept or condemn a person or idea. In glory by association, persuaders try to transfer the positive feelings we have about something we love and respect to a product, group, or idea that is being advocated. Political candidates are mocked for wrapping themselves in God, motherhood, and the American flag. In 1994, some associated themselves with the vague phrase "traditional family values," hoping that our good feelings about families would rub off onto our feelings about them.

Guilt by association is this process in reverse, an effort to transfer our dislike or disapproval of one idea or group to some other idea or group that persuaders want us to reject or condemn. This is illustrated by linking an idea or group to some individual or group that the audience can be expected to dislike, such as attacking a program by saying that it's supported by the Ku Klux Klan or advocated by Rush Limbaugh.

If those who carry ideas affect their meaning, why is this a fallacy?

Begging the Question

The name of this strategy is somewhat misleading; it involves not asking a question but rather assuming that an issue or question that is yet to be proved has already been established. For instance, a persuader might say, "No thinking person could approve such a policy as this one," when the question to be discussed and argued is whether the policy is a good one.

In law, some matters are stipulated, that is, agreed on by both sides. In all argument, we make certain assumptions and presume that they are held in common. How do these differ from begging the question?

The False Dilemma

As a language, English tends to construe reality in sets of two extremes or polar opposites, as if there were only two alternatives available rather than many options. There usually are more than two extreme possibilities to consider, but our language tends to make us think in terms of good or bad, black or white, and the like. False dilemmas are at work in statements such as, "You're either for me or against me," "It's either free enterprise or socialism," or "America. Love it or leave it," implying that we must love and praise all things called American or we have to get out.

How does the false dilemma resemble or differ from a dialectical definition? (See the discussion of dialectical definitions in Chapter 10.)

Plain Folks Appeal

This is a device by which rhetors attempt to win our confidence and support by appearing to be just like us, "plain folks." This kind of appeal calls attention to efforts by those who are not like us (with different backgrounds and beliefs) to pretend to be like us. In addition, someone can be like us in background but not share our values or beliefs. Affiliations should be made of sterner, more specific stuff.

When do efforts at identification cross the boundary to become a plain folks appeal?

Argumentum Ad Populum

This is a Latin phrase meaning an "argument to the people" or telling the people just what they want to hear; as Socrates comments in one of Plato's dialogues, "it is not difficult to praise Athenians to Athenians." In the era of Nixon's presidency and as a result of the release of the Watergate tapes, this came to be called "stroking," a term that describes this process as one of caressing or petting audience members so that as they come to enjoy the praise, they come to like and approve of the person who does the praising and come to support his or her ideas.

We all like to hear good things about ourselves and the groups to which we belong, but our good qualities may have little or nothing to do with the issue at hand.

How is this similar to and different from creating the audience? How, if at all, does this differ from ingratiation?

Your discussion can be focused more specifically if you collect and discuss examples of these strategies from newspaper, radio, and television programming from current political campaigns or other disputes over policy, such as health care reform, mandatory sentencing, and the like.

CHAPTER 9

The Resources of Organization

Organization is a kind of argument. Through structuring materials, you can make ideas clearer and more appealing to others. Ideally, the pattern by which you develop your ideas should reflect a consistent point of view on a subject, clarify the relationships among concepts, and make a case effectively.

As noted earlier, Aristotle wrote, "There are two parts to a speech; for it is necessary [first] to state the subject and [then] to demonstrate it" (1414a.30–1). This is good advice for making an outline to develop your thesis, but, as Aristotle also recognized, you need to adapt your ideas to an audience. First I talk about the thesis and its development. Then I discuss introductions, conclusions, and other ways to adapt your presentation for an audience.

The key to organizing ideas rhetorically is a thesis. A good thesis statement:

1. Is a simple sentence (states one and only one idea). For example, "Heavy television viewing inclines children toward violence and stereotyping" is a problematic thesis, especially for a short essay or speech, because it involves two quite distinct claims that are related only indirectly. Either claim by itself would take a good bit of time to develop.

2. Is a declarative sentence (a statement, assertion, or claim such as "Mandatory sentencing for drug-related crimes should be abolished") or an imperative sentence (a command such as "Join the National Organization for Women!").

3. Limits your topic (narrows your subject). The standard for limiting has to be vague—what you can manage in the time or space you will have. This reinforces the first point, but note that even one of the two claims above about television might be too large for a short rhetorical act.

4. Suggests your purpose (implies the kinds of response you want)—understanding, belief, or action.

5. Is a capsule version of everything you will say or write. That is, it should sum up your purpose, and everything in the rhetorical act should be related to it.

Please note that you may never state your thesis quite as bluntly as it appears in your outline, but the central idea ought to be clear to your audience when you have finished.

OUTLINING

An outline is a visual representation of the relationships among ideas. Accordingly, it is a useful tool for testing the consistency of your approach and the strength of your case. To understand how this can be, consider this outline skeleton:[1]

I.
  A.
    1.
    2.
  B.
    1.
      a.
      b.
    2.

This outline form says many things. First, there is one central, all-inclusive idea, Roman numeral I. In a speech or essay, this would be the thesis. This central idea is divided into two relatively equal parts,

---

[1]Rhetorical acts inevitably violate ordinary outline form because they are unified by a single central idea, the thesis or specific purpose. In all of the illustrative outlines, Roman numeral I. indicates the thesis.

letters A and B. A and B are each divided into two parts, but the idea expressed at B1 requires fuller development, perhaps for more detailed explanation or proof. Overall, this format indicates which ideas are larger and which are smaller, which ideas are parts of other ideas, and which ideas will receive special emphasis.

In this outline, A and B are *main points*, A1 and A2 and B1 and B2 are *subpoints*, and B1a and B1b are *subsubpoints*. Notice, however, that there are three similar relationships in this outline form:

I.

    A.

      and

    B.

       A.   B.

        1.   1.

          or

        2.   2.

       B.

        1.

          a.

           and

          b.

In each case, a larger idea is subdivided into two parts. If the content of the outline reflects the form, these subdivisions should have three characteristics. They should be:

1. *Subordinate,* that is, they should be ideas of smaller scope than the claim they support or explain.

2. *Coordinate,* that is, the subdivisions should be of relatively equal scope and importance.

3. *Mutually exclusive,* that is, they should cover different aspects of the larger idea; their content should not overlap.

For example, here is the basic outline of a speech given by a student who was an advocate for the disabled:

I. The segregation of physically and/or mentally disabled children in U.S. schools must end.

    A. Integration teaches the very young to accept others' differences.

        1. Placing children together early in life decreases biases against the disabled.

        2. Among children who were exposed to minority populations during their school years, this acceptance lasted a lifetime.

B. Disabled and "normal" children learn from each other if educated together.

    1. Disabled children learn how to behave appropriately in a normal social setting where the majority is not disabled.

    2. "Normal" children learn that although some people in our society are different, they are still valuable.

    3. "Normal" children learn how to behave appropriately around the disabled and how to aid in caretaking.

C. Including disabled children in regular classrooms offers them a brighter future.

    1. Inclusion develops positive self-concepts.

    2. Inclusion develops higher-level cognitive skills.

    3. Inclusion in all schools would cause future decision makers to realize all that disabled people are capable of accomplishing.

Note that each main point is subordinate because each identifies a particular benefit of integration. Each point is roughly coordinate in covering bases for increased acceptance, mutual learning, and the beneficial effects on the disabled. There is a bit of overlap because the higher cognitive skills discussed under point C are presumably part of what disabled children learn from interaction with their nondisabled schoolmates, but that is normal in a rhetorical act of this type. The main points are not stated in parallel fashion, but the subpoints under C are laid out in that way.

Another student argued for the legalization of marijuana working from this outline:

I. Marijuana (hemp) should be legalized.

    A. Hemp is very beneficial for the environment.

        1. It reseeds itself in forests.

        2. Oil from hemp seeds has many commercial uses, particularly as a substitute for petroleum.

        3. Fibers in the stem can be used for textiles.

            a. Natural fibers are less damaging than synthetics to the environment.

            b. Hemp fibers are stronger than cotton fibers.

    B. Hemp has important medical uses.

        1. Extracts from its leaves can be used to aid cancer, multiple sclerosis, and AIDS patients as a painkiller and to stimulate appetite, e.g., following chemotherapy.

C. Hemp has important nutritional uses.

   1. After the oil is removed from the seeds, a substantial amount of protein remains.

       a. Hemp seeds have more protein than soybeans.

       b. Hemp seeds are more nutritious than alternatives for animal feed.

D. Marijuana is a far less dangerous drug than alcohol, which is legal.

   1. Alcohol is addictive, with high social costs in lost productivity and highway deaths.

   2. Alcohol is a health hazard.

       a. It destroys brain cells.

       b. It destroys liver cells, causing cirrhosis.

   3. The effects of marijuana are small.

       a. It lowers sperm count.

       b. Like other cigarettes, smoking it contributes to lung cancer.

       c. In some cases, heavy use causes memory loss.

Again, each point is subordinate; each sets forth a reason for legalization. The points are relatively coordinate in exploring environmental, medical, and nutritional benefits and in comparing the ill effects of a legal drug, alcohol, to those of marijuana. The fourth point shifts ground slightly. The earlier points talk about absolute benefits, whereas the last explores comparative benefits, which are actually comparative harms.

Main points such as these develop, divide, explain, and prove the thesis. Main points can explain just what the thesis means. Main points can try to demonstrate the truth of the thesis. The subdivisions of a thesis or of any point in an outline usually answer one of these questions: What do you mean? How do you know? How does it work? Why? In other words, there is a necessary relationship between a main point and its subdivisions. For example:

I. Capital punishment should not be legalized. (Why?)

(Because) A. It does not deter would-be murderers.

(How do you know?)

1. Comparisons of similar jurisdictions reveal that those with capital punishment have murder rates as high as those without.

2. Most murders are crimes of passion and lack the thought and planning that might make a deterrent effective.

In other words, an outline is (1) a way to plan how you will develop your ideas, (2) a way to lay them out so you can examine the relationships among them, and (3) a way to make relationships among ideas clear to your audience.

While some outlines need not be composed of sentences, it is essential that rhetorical outlines be sentence outlines. The reason is simple. The building blocks of rhetoric are arguments, and arguments exist only in sentences. A claim must be an assertion, a declarative sentence; and summaries of evidence and statements of justification (reasons or warrants) require expression in sentences. In short, you cannot make the sort of outline you need or use the outline to test the coherence of your ideas unless you use sentences.

Here is an outline that served as the basis for an excellent short speech:

I. Traumatic shock is a dangerous condition for which every injured person should be treated. (Thesis: The purpose is to alter perception of the condition known as shock and to create understanding in order to affect behavior.)

(Why? Because)

A. Traumatic shock is potentially fatal. (What do you mean?)

1. Shock is a substantial reduction in the vital functions of the body caused by a decrease in the volume of circulating blood. (defines and explains shock)

2. If shock is allowed to persist, the person will die. (details results of shock on an injured person)

(Why treat every person?)

B. Traumatic shock can result from almost any injury.

1. Common household accidents can produce shock.

2. Psychological factors may speed the onset of shock.

C. There are no reliable indications of the presence of shock.

1. The symptoms of shock can be misinterpreted or misunderstood.

2. A person can experience shock without showing any of the usual symptoms.

D. Treatment of shock is simple. (feasibility)

1. Keep the person in a prone position.

2. Keep the person warm but not overheated.

3. Try to reduce contributing psychological factors by reassurance.

This outline leaves out a number of things that happened in the actual presentation. But the outline is strong because it divides the topic and explains its dimensions, and the main points prove that the thesis is true (if A and B and C and D, then I must follow). In effect, the outline says you treat every injured person for shock because shock is life-threatening, it can result from any injury, you can't tell whether it is present, and it is relatively easy to treat.

FORMS OF ORGANIZATION

There are three basic ways to develop your thesis, central idea, or major claim: through time or sequence, by aspects or issues, and through analysis of the relations between causes and effects or problems and solutions. Each of these general patterns can be varied in several ways, and all three patterns may be used to develop parts of a single piece of rhetoric.

Through Time or Sequence

Chronological structure organizes an idea by its development through time or in a series of steps ordered in a sequence. This may involve division into historical periods or by phases or stages. Chronological organization argues that this topic, issue, or process is best understood in terms of how it develops or unfolds through time, or that you cannot achieve a goal without following a certain sequence. The most obvious form of chronological structure follows historical development. For example:

I. Contemporary feminism has gone through a series of ideological changes.

A. Until 1968, it was a relatively conservative, reformist movement.

B. From 1968 until 1977, it divided into conservative and radical factions.

C. Since the Houston Conference of 1977, the factions have unified into a less conservative but highly political coalition.

D. Following the Anita Hill–Clarence Thomas hearings in 1991, political activity escalated.

Chronological organization is also used to develop the steps or stages in a process. For example:

I. Follow a sequence in preparing for rhetorical action.
    A. Choose your subject.
    B. Research available materials.
    C. Select a thesis.
    D. Structure your ideas.
    E. Produce a first draft (orally from notes or in writing).
    F. Edit your work through rewriting or oral practice.

Organizational patterns that develop ideas historically or sequentially are common in rhetoric, but another, less common form of chronological organization is highly effective and impossible to outline. This occurs when ideas are shaped into a dramatic narrative, when a speaker or writer tells a story to make a point. An example of such a story is James Thurber's "The Little Girl and the Wolf," one of his *Fables for Our Times*. The story relies on cultural history in two ways. First, it adopts the form of the fable, a story with a moral, most familiar from Aesop's fables, and it assumes that we are already familiar with this form. Second, it assumes our familiarity with the plot of the fairy tale about Little Red Riding Hood, which it revises and parodies.

The Little Girl and the Wolf[2]
by James Thurber

One afternoon a big wolf waited in a dark forest for a little girl to come along carrying a basket of food to her grandmother. Finally a little girl did come along and she was carrying a basket of food.

---

[2]From *Fables for Our Time* (New York: Harper & Bros., 1940), p. 5. Published by Harper Collins. Copr. © 1940 James Thurber. Copr. © 1968 Helen Thurber. Reprinted by permission of Rosemary A. Thurber.

"Are you carrying that basket to your grandmother?" asked the wolf. The little girl said yes, she was. So the wolf asked her where her grandmother lived and the little girl told him and he disappeared into the wood.

When the little girl opened the door of her grandmother's house she saw that there was somebody in bed with a nightcap and nightgown on. She had approached no nearer than 25 feet from the bed when she saw that it was not her grandmother but the wolf, for even in a nightcap a wolf does not look any more like your grandmother than the Metro Goldwyn Mayer lion looks like Calvin Coolidge. So the little girl took an automatic out of her basket and shot the wolf dead.

Moral: It is not so easy to fool little girls nowadays as it used to be.

This revision is humorous because it pokes fun at the original story, but it also forces us to look anew at the old story and to consider the unstated moral that it implies. In the original story, Little Red Riding Hood is naive, incapable of defending herself against the evil in the world, and she, like her grandmother before her, is eaten by the wolf. Only when a hunter comes to their rescue can she and her grandmother be saved. Neither the story and the moral of either version can be reduced to outline form. They are nondiscursive or nonlogical structures, and they follow a different pattern of development. This pattern is followed by most stories, dramas, and jokes, and it looks something like this:

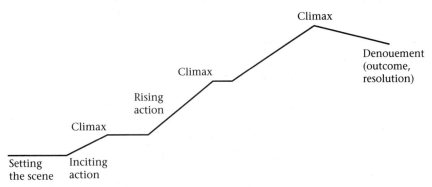

James Thurber's fable follows this pattern. The first paragraph sets the scene and alerts us that this is a retelling of a familiar fairy tale about a little girl, a wolf, and a grandmother; it introduces us to the wolf and the threat he implies, and we are reminded of who the main characters are in the familiar story. The inciting action is the appearance of the little girl. There is rising action as the wolf and she carry on a brief dialogue, which escalates the possible threat. A new pattern of rising action begins when the little girl arrives at her grandmother's house, sees that there is someone in her grandmother's bed, and recognizes that it is not her grandmother. The climax, the height of the conflict, occurs when she takes an automatic out of her basket and kills the wolf. The resolution or denouement is the moral, a comment that interprets the meaning of the story.

This story is a useful illustration for several reasons. First, as a fable, it is intended to teach and persuade. Second, it teaches and persuades in an entirely nondiscursive way. There are no arguments, and no data are presented. The story is wholly outside logical and empirical reality. If it teaches us and gains our assent, it does so because it is a revision that exploits our familiarity with the original story of Little Red Riding Hood. The humor arises out of our surprise at what happens in this version and in response to the highly original figurative analogy and a point made by the second meanings lurking in "little girls" and "wolves." It also works because it teaches by contrast, forcing us to think about the assumptions in the original story. How could we ever have believed that a little girl would mistake a wolf for her grandmother? Why did we assume that the little girl wouldn't have prepared herself to cope with the dangers of the dark forest?

Good stories have certain qualities. They follow certain patterns and develop through details that we can see or imagine, and the plot has universality or general application. (Fairy tales deal with the hopes and fears of all of us; fables such as those of Aesop comment on common human failings, made more palatable by being presented as the failings of animals, such as the stories of the fox and the grapes or the dog in the manger.) They usually develop one or more characters with whom we can identify, or they describe a situation in which we can imagine ourselves. They are organized around a conflict that increases in intensity so that we are drawn into the story and come to care about how it is resolved or "comes out." The rhetorical strength of many stories comes from their verisimilitude, that is, their formal resemblance to events and persons in our world of experience. In this case, the verisimilitude arises out of the story's resemblance to a familiar tale, out of a structure that follows the familiar form of the fable, and out of situations in which wolves wait to prey upon little girls.

A work that is structured as a dramatic narrative exploits the literary and poetic resources of language or the plot lines with which we are familiar. On the simplest level, such a story is an extended example, with all of the strengths and weaknesses of this kind of evidence. But dramatic narratives have compensating strengths. They can reach out to the audience to prompt identification and participation. They are easy to follow and pleasing and so invite involvement. In a dramatic narrative, we are invited to share the point of view of the narrator, to imagine ourselves in the experiences described. The rhetor's claim is expressed as a series of concrete experiences or dramatic encounters, and the conclusion is the meaning of the tale. If the story is well constructed, it is hard to reject such "claims." They become part of our experience, not simply an idea or an argument.

Narrative–dramatic development is less common than other forms of organization in rhetorical discourse, but when it appears, it illustrates these resources. The most famous examples are the parables of Jesus, stories he told to illustrate truths. "Toussaint L'Ouverture," a speech delivered many times by the abolitionist orator Wendell Phillips, is a rare instance of an entire speech organized in this way.[3] It is the story of the Haitian leader and revolutionary, and his life is intended to demonstrate that former slaves deserve full citizenship. The story itself is strong proof because a single contrary instance is enough to disprove a "biological law." If one person of African descent is clearly a human being of superior abilities, descendants of Africans as a group cannot be biologically inferior or incapable of all the rights and privileges of personhood and citizenship. But the story steps outside the usual antislavery–proslavery argumentation to involve us in the life and hopes and tragedy of one person. We share his experiences; we identify with him. Phillips's speech transcends the obstacles of cultural history and engages his listeners and readers in a more direct and participatory way.

There are other contemporary examples. Marilyn French's novel *The Women's Room*[4] is a powerful feminist work dramatically describing the emptiness of women's traditional roles and the discrimination against women in education and employment, including discrimination in the courts against those who have been sexually assaulted. Rita Mae Brown wrote a delightful, funny novel about growing up lesbian, *Rubyfruit Jungle,* that was designed to debunk stereotypes about gay women and that has proved remarkably appealing and enduring. Movie director Oliver Stone's film *J.F.K.* was his way of arguing the controversial position that there was a conspiracy behind the assassination of President Kennedy. In each of these cases, a dramatic narrative transcends the obstacles created by cultural history, diminishes hostility toward a controversial group or idea, or reaches across the chasm of cultural differences to create identification between rhetor and audience.

---

[3]*American Speeches,* ed. W. M. Parrish and Marie Hochmuth (New York: Longmans, Green, and Co., 1954), pp. 311–332.
[4]New York: Summit Books, 1977.

You should choose some form of chronological structure—historical or sequential or narrative–dramatic development—if you wish to emphasize development over time or in steps or stages. It is a good choice if the audience knows little of your subject, because this pattern is ideally suited to provide background and to develop relationships among events. This structure is also easily adapted to hold the attention of the audience because it emphasizes progress through time, completion of a process, or movement toward a climax.

Through Facets or Aspects

Topical structure develops a subject in terms of aspects or facets or dimensions. Sometimes the divisions are integral parts of the subject, such as the executive, judicial, and legislative branches of the U.S. government. Frequently, however, the topics are familiar perspectives we take on many subjects—the economic, legal, and social implications of, say, affirmative action programs in the automobile industry, or of discontinuing federally funded programs to create jobs for inner-city youth, or of congressional efforts to end Medicaid funding for abortion. In other words, the earlier outline about legalizing marijuana is a rather typical example of a topical outline. Note that the student considers marijuana/hemp in terms of environmental, medical, and food benefits. Similarly, in the outline on integrating disabled students into regular classrooms, the argument develops by topics of accepting differences, learning from each other, and improving the future of the disabled.

Topical organization is ideally suited for selecting some parts of a subject for discussion or emphasis. For example, a contemporary feminist wants to talk about the forms of social control that limit the options open to women. Because there are many forms of social control, she must narrow her focus and select only some forms for discussion. Her outline might look like this:

I. U.S. women suffer from overt and covert social controls.

   A. The laws control women overtly.

      1. Marriage laws have been the most oppressive controls.

      2. So-called protective labor legislation has limited access to jobs, promotions, and higher wages, with effects that persist.

      3. The Supreme Court has refused to extend Fourteenth Amendment protections to women.

B. Socialization controls women covertly.

    1. A female child is reared to believe that she is limited.

    2. Education discourages women from many fields of endeavor.

    3. Popular culture reinforces stereotypes and gender-related limitations.[5]

In this case, topical organization structures main points A and B in relation to the thesis as well as A1 and 2 and 3 and B1 and 2 and 3. Under A, the rhetor selects three kinds of laws for attention. Under B, she discusses three elements of socialization: child-rearing, education, and popular culture.

Topical organization can explore natural divisions of a subject (fiction and nonfiction, regular and cable television, print and electronic media, for example). It can explore selected parts of a subject (soap operas and situation comedies as examples of kinds of television programming). Or it can apply familiar perspectives to a subject (the legal, economic, psychological, social, and medical aspects of state-run lotteries or mandatory sentences or nuclear power).

Because there usually is no necessary relationship between the points in a topical structure, this kind of organization can also be put to nondiscursive use. In such a case, the work develops associatively, in a manner analogous to the structure of the lyric poem, and becomes an exploration of the aspects of an attitude or feeling. Such organization is uncommon in rhetorical acts, but it can be highly effective.[6] When topical organization is used well, it divides a subject into parts that seem appropriate to the audience, parts that reflect a clear appraisal by the rhetor of what is important, what is typical. In addition, these parts should be arranged into some sort of hierarchy so we move from one point to another with a sense of progression. The outline on legalizing marijuana, for example, could be rearranged into a crescendo or climax pattern moving from smaller benefits to larger ones.

The outline on the social control of women works differently. The development and proof of point A, that women are overtly discriminated against in law, prepares us for point B, that they are subtly controlled through socialization. If we assent to point A, we are far more

---

[5]See Jo Freeman, "The Building of the Gilded Cage," *The Second Wave: A Magazine of the New Feminism* 1 (Spring 1971):7–9, 33–39.
[6]Karlyn Kohrs Campbell, "Stanton's 'The Solitude of Self': A Rationale for Feminism," *Quarterly Journal of Speech* 66 (1980):304–312.

likely to assent to point B; the relationship between the two ideas is *a fortiori:* If the first is true (overt discrimination by law), it is much more likely that the second is true (covert discrimination in socialization).

Topical structure is an ideal pattern for narrowing a broad subject to a manageable size. It is also a method of emphasis by which you can indicate what parts of a subject are most important.

Cause–Effect, Problem–Solution

So-called *logical structures* assert that ideas or situations stand in some necessary relationship to each other. This pattern expresses processes of cause and effect or defines a problem and its solution. As you might guess, logical organization is often used to develop questions of policy. The relationship between questions of policy and logical structure is illustrated by most television commercials (commercials ask you to change policy by buying a new product or by switching brands or to resist the appeals of competing products). Many ads are little problem–solution dramas. For example, a man in a commercial is shown anxiously discussing the lack of interest his girlfriend is showing. His friend suggests the solution of a toothpaste for sparkling teeth and sweet breath. We then see the man with his sexy girlfriend in a scene that leaves no doubt that his romantic problems are over. In other words, if you have a problem being attractive to someone, solve it by brushing with Brand X toothpaste.

Here is an example of a problem–solution outline:

I. A state lottery can provide essential funding for education.

   A. The need for new buildings, additional teachers, and special education programs makes major state expenditures indispensable.

   B. Providing the needed funds requires raising property taxes or offering a lottery.

   1. Polls indicate that voters will not support school bond issues based on property taxes for education.

   2. Polls indicate that voters support state-run lotteries.

   C. Therefore, if educational needs are to be met, a state-run lottery must be instituted.

In this case, the thesis implies a goal (providing the resources needed to offer high-quality education to all children) and indicates that there are two alternative courses of action to raise the funds to reach it. Point A states the problem or need, and B indicates that two alternatives are available to raise the needed revenues. Point B1 eliminates one alternative, and point B2 indicates popular support for the proposal (which requires statutory action), leaving the alternative advocated in the thesis.

Many speeches combine topical and logical structure, as in this detailed outline for a speech.

"The State as Bookie"

I. State-run lotteries should be abolished.

   A. Lotteries are not a painless and effective way to raise revenues.

   1. In 1990, lotteries in 33 states generated $7 billion in state revenues based on $20 billion in gross sales, but were only 2 percent of state revenues in states with games (U.S. Census Bureau, *Consumers Research,* January 1990:13), and many states with lotteries have had to raise state taxes subsequently.

   2. Lotteries are an inefficient way to raise revenues: Traditional taxes cost a penny or two per dollar to collect; lotteries cost up to 75¢ per dollar because of administration, promotion, and vendor fees along with prizes (Flaherty, *Progressive,* March 1986:31).

   B. Lotteries have been sold to the public as funding to improve education, but revenues just replace other sources of school funding.

   1. In California, the lottery was established on the promise that 34¢ of every dollar would go to education; since then, however, lottery revenue has simply replaced other school funding.

   a. California schools chief Bill Honig describes further damage to education funding: "The public is now reluctant to pass education bond issues because they think we're floating in lottery money" (*Fortune,* March 25, 1991:113).

   2. Governor Lawton Chiles of Florida called that state's lottery "a giant hoax" and promised that if he were elected, the funds would be used as intended—to improve schools (*ibid.*).

   C. Legalized gambling is the most regressive form of taxation that can be devised.

   1. Daniel Suits, a Michigan St.U. economics professor, says the lottery is 2½ to 3 times as regressive as sales taxes; the Federal

Commission on the Review of National Policy Toward Gambling reached a similar conclusion in 1976 (*Progressive,* March 1986:32).

2. According to Duke University economists Charles Clotfelter and Philip Cook, 20 percent of lottery players account for 65 percent of lottery wagers, with poor African Americans and Latinos doing most of the gambling; a CA study found that 10 percent of the players, who were disproportionately poor, purchased more than 50 percent of the tickets; in the Chicago area, spending per capita on lottery tickets in a recent year was $76 in affluent communities, but $221 in neighborhoods with the lowest incomes and the highest dependence on public aid (*Washington Post,* October 11, 1992:B4).

3. A 1988 study of Michigan lottery records by the *Ann Arbor News* cautioned that lotteries offer a particularly raw deal for the poor: Although Michigan lottery dollars were disproportionately provided by inner-city residents, a greater share of the profits was channeled to wealthier school districts outside the city (*Consumers Research,* January 1990:15).

D. Legal games do not drive out illegal gambling or eliminate crime.

1. It is estimated that gross revenues for illegal numbers gambling increased 25 percent from 1982 to 1988 because it offers gamblers a better deal than the state-run version.

    a. According to Robert Blakey in the *Journal of Social Issues,* illegal games frequently offer better odds, a higher payout, cheaper tickets, and faster drawings than state-run lotteries; in addition, illegal numbers games have runners who will come to your door to collect tickets and pay back winnings (cited in *Consumers Research,* January 1990:14).

2. In the rush to promote gaming, states risk corruption and infiltration by organized crime.

    a. A NJ lottery commission chair pleaded guilty to falsifying evidence in a state investigation of charges that he sought private business from companies with state lottery contracts (*Progressive,* March 1986:33).

    b. PA was plunged into scandal when a $1 million drawing was found to be fixed (*ibid.*).

    c. Three Ohio lottery directors resigned following allegations of kickback schemes (*ibid.*).

E. Lotteries are not harmless; "dreams" and "fun" come at high costs.

    1. Lotteries foster irresponsible thinking about money: "They promote a desire for instant gratification and feed on people . . . [who] think money will solve all of their problems," says Valerie Lorenz, a gambling addiction therapist (*Washington Post,* October 11, 1991:B1).

        a. States do not just offer an opportunity to gamble; they promote these games aggressively in order to increase revenue; if they don't, sales decline.

            (1) To succeed, such advertising promotes the lottery as a better investment than saving or education or hard work.

                (a) For example, the storyboard for "Misspent Youth," a Connecticut TV lottery ad, reads as follows (*The New Republic,* March 4, 1991:14):

                Opening: older man sitting in boat, afloat in a calm, mountain lake . . . Golden Pond *ambience—loons, birds.*

                Man: (reflective) "When I was younger, I suppose I could have done more to plan my future. But I didn't. I guess I could have put some money aside. But I didn't. Or I could have made some smart investments. But I didn't. . . . Heck, I could have bought a CT Lotto ticket, won a jackpot worth millions, and gotten a nice big check every year for twenty years. (Smiling broadly) And I did! I won! . . . I won millions—me!"

                A voice-over spells out the sell: "Play LOTTO. You only have to win once. Jackpot prize paid out in twenty installments. Overall chance of winning is 1 in 30."

                (b) Syndicated columnist George Will describes aggressive government marketing of gambling as "giving a legitimizing imprimatur to the pursuit of wealth without work" (*Newsweek,* May 8, 1989:78).

                (c) Gambling by those who can least afford it is increased because many people have an exaggerated and inaccurate perception of the likelihood of winning.

                    (i) Curt Suplee (*Harper's*) calculated that a person was 7 times more likely to be hit by lightning than to win $1 million in an instant-lottery game (cited in *New Yorker,* December 19, 1988: 27); according to *Fortune* (March 26, 1991:109), your chances of winning a big jackpot (at about 13 million to 1) are far less than of being killed by lightning (400,000 to 1).

(ii) The larger the jackpot, the smaller the odds of winning it, yet statistical analysis of lotto sales confirms that sales per capita are driven by the size of the jackpot and are insensitive to the objective probability of winning.

> **[a]** A survey by Duke economists Clotfelter and Cook showed that only 12 percent of radio and TV ads reveal the true odds, and when the size of the jackpot is revealed, it is rarely mentioned that the money is usually paid out over 20 years, cutting the money won in half.

2. There is evidence that lotteries increase compulsive gambling.

a. A California Senate's study cited research that lotteries can increase compulsive gambling by as much as 10 percent (*Progressive,* March 1986:32).

> **(1)** The distribution of alcohol consumption is similar to that among lottery players: most adults abstain (33 percent) or drink moderately (57 percent); the remaining 10 percent average about ten drinks per day and account for half of total alcohol consumption, suggesting they are similar addictions (Charles T. Clotfelter and Philip J. Cook, *Selling Hope: State Lotteries in America* (Cambridge: Harvard University Press, 1989, p. 94).
>
> **(2)** Compulsive gambling, with its social effects, has increased in states with longer experience with lotteries.

The thesis of this outline is a policy statement urging abolition of state lotteries. Points A and B state arguments made in their favor, which are then attacked. Point C appeals to an unstated value, fairness in taxation, to point to undesirable qualities of lotteries. Point D is like A and B in stating and attacking pro arguments; point E argues that lotteries erode fundamental civic values. In other words, the main points are formed around what the rhetor believes are the major arguments for and against state lotteries. Note also that the full sentences in the outline enable you to read the outline and get a rather complete sense of what a speech or essay developed from it might say and that it includes references to the evidence to be used. In a sense, such an outline becomes the notes from which you could write a first draft of an essay or begin to practice your speech. Note, however, that the outline has not been adapted to create an introduction or conclusion, nor has it been shaped for a particular target audience.

Cause–effect structure is a variation of problem–solution structure. Note that causal arguments are asserted or attacked in the above outline on state lotteries. Cause–effect structure ordinarily focuses on the first stock issue of a question of policy, the need for a change. Emphasis is placed on effects (the scope of the harm) and their cause (intrinsic to the current policy). For example:

I. High rates of minority unemployment are caused, in part, by a lack of skills.

    A. Education in urban ghettoes and in the rural South does not provide basic reading and arithmetic skills.

    B. Few vocational training programs are available.

    C. Minorities are denied access to union apprenticeship programs.

    D. Federal programs do not teach marketable skills.

Once again, this outline combines topical and logical structure. The thesis asserts a cause–effect relationship, but the main points are a topical list of the major causes of the problem—lack of skills.

As these examples illustrate, logical structure is ideal for treating questions of policy. It allows you to meet the requirements for defending a change of policy, and it can be used to explore causal relationships. In all cases, logical structure reflects necessary relationships between ideas or events.

There are, then, three basic forms of organization for development of your thesis. These, in turn, can be subdivided, and each type of structure has certain strengths or advantages.

I. The forms of organization available are the following:

    A. Material can be organized chronologically.

        1. It can be developed by historical periods.

        2. It can be presented as steps in a sequence or stages in a process.

        3. It can be dramatized in a story.

    B. Material can be organized topically.

       1. It can divide a subject into its natural parts.

       2. It can examine a subject in terms of a variety of familiar perspectives.

    C. Material can be organized logically.

       1. It can divide material into cause(s) and effect(s).

       2. It can examine a problem and its solution.

II. Each form of organization has certain advantages.

    A. Chronological structure emphasizes development over time.

       1. It is ideal for providing information and background.

       2. It takes advantage of the appeal of progression through time or of a process that moves toward a climax.

       3. A narrative is a special form of this.

    B. Topical structure selects and emphasizes.

       1. It allows you to narrow a broad subject.

       2. It allows you to indicate what is more important.

    C. Logical structure develops necessary relationships.

       1. It allows you to defend changes in policy.

       2. It is ideally suited to affix responsibility.

Each form of organization is a kind of argument. Each structure offers a particular kind of perspective on a subject. You can combine these different forms in a piece of rhetoric, but in each case, you should choose the kind of structure best suited to the kind of argument you are trying to make.

ADAPTING STRUCTURE TO THE AUDIENCE

In the early part of this century, U.S. philosopher John Dewey published a book entitled *How We Think*.[7] The book laid out the stages in reflective thinking, the processes by which we recognize problems and then go about solving them. These stages included:

---

[7]Boston: D. C. Heath, 1910.

1. Perceiving a felt difficulty or recognizing that a problem exists.
2. Analyzing the problem, including attempts at definition.
3. Exploring possible solutions and evaluating them.
4. Selecting the best solution.
5. Discovering how to implement the selected course of action.

Dewey's analysis reflects the stock issues of a question of policy, especially in stages 2, 3, and 4. But the first and last steps are additions, and they are clues to one kind of structural adaptation that needs to be made in presenting material to an audience. Step 1 is introductory; it establishes the facts and values that suggest that we ought to be concerned about something, that we ought to find out what sort of problem this is and whether and how it can be solved. Step 5 goes beyond the stock issues to ask how we can go about setting in motion the change we have decided would be a good one. It concerns concrete action; for example, how do we go about getting H. Ross Perot on the ballot in our state now that we have decided that the solution to our political woes is this third-party candidate?

Dewey's book was probably the stimulus for the motivated sequence that Alan H. Monroe developed.[8] This structural form illustrates the adaptation of logical organization for presentation to an audience. The steps in the *motivated sequence* are as follows:

1. Attention: Call attention to the problem; in Dewey's terms, make the difficulty felt.

2. Need: Demonstrate that a need exists (develop the first issue of a question of policy to prove that harm of significant scope arises out of current practice).

3. Satisfaction: Show the audience that the need can be met (that there is a practical and beneficial alternative policy).

4. Visualization: Describe vividly and concretely what will happen if the problem is or is not solved (picture good or bad consequences).

5. Action: Call for immediate action from the audience; show them how to bring about the solution.

---

[8]*Principles and Types of Speech,* 2d ed. (Glenview, IL: Scott, Foresman, 1939). Both were probably influenced by Francis Bacon's *Advancement of Learning,* in which he developed the concepts underlying faculty psychology and in which he wrote that "the duty and office of rhetoric is to apply reason to the imagination for the better moving of the will."

As you examine this sequence, you will see that steps 2 and 3 develop the stock issues of a policy question. In other words, the motivated sequence is a form of logical organization that is appropriate only for advocating a course of action. However, steps 1, 4, and 5 are structural elements designed to adapt materials for presentation to an audience. Step 1 precedes the thesis in order to involve the audience in the subject. Step 4 is designed to increase the motivation of the audience by vividly depicting what their world will be like with or without the proposed policy. For example, in ads for exercise machines or diet aids, "before" and "after" photographs are juxtaposed to perform this function. Step 5 presumes that the audience needs specific instructions on how to bring about a solution—where to go, what to do, whom to write or call, and so on. It is designed to bring the proposed policy or course of action closer to reality. In sales, it becomes the closing. Steps 4 and 5 also require additions to the outline forms described previously. They require special sections that make your ideas vivid and concrete and that give the audience assistance in implementing policy change. The motivated sequence is an excellent pattern to follow in adapting logical organization for presentation to an audience, but all rhetorical action requires similar adaptations. At a minimum, it is necessary to begin with an introduction and to end with a conclusion.

Introductions

The basic functions of an introduction are to gain attention, to create accurate expectations in the audience for what follows, and to suggest the relationship between the subject and the audience. These functions are good general touchstones for anyone preparing for rhetorical action. But the introduction also serves a vital purpose in overcoming the rhetorical obstacles that you face on any given occasion. For this reason, the introduction is the first attempt to cope with these difficulties. The choices a rhetor makes should be guided by the answers to these questions:

1. What is the relationship between the rhetor and the audience? Do they share many experiences and values, or is the rhetor seen as an alien or outsider?

2. What is the attitude of the audience toward the subject and purpose? Will the audience perceive the subject as overworked and complex or as fresh, vital, and intelligible? Is the reaction to the purpose likely to be hostile and indifferent or sympathetic and interested?

3. What is the rhetor's relationship to the subject? Is she or he an expert or an interested amateur?

As these questions indicate, introductions should be adapted to the attitude of the audience toward your subject and purpose, to the relationship between you and your audience, and to the relationship between you and your subject. It is in light of these considerations that you need to gain attention, create accurate expectations, and develop connections between the subject and the audience.

Kenneth Burke wrote, "Only those voices from without are effective which can speak in the language of a voice within."[9] His statement emphasizes the importance of identification between a rhetor and audience and recalls the role that the rhetor plays as a context for the message. One of the most important functions of an introduction, therefore, is to create common bonds between speaker and audience, that is, to overcome the perception that the rhetor is different, not like the members of the audience. Very often, personal experience is used to create connections and to establish common grounds. For example, here is part of an introduction Maryland Senator Barbara Mikulski used in a speech on "The American Family" in the summer of 1988 in Atlanta, Georgia. Notice how she moves from introducing herself in ways that make her distinctive to identifying herself with the subject and reaching out to a broad general audience:

> Fellow Americans. My name is Barbara Mikulski. I come from Baltimore, Maryland. I love the Orioles, Chesapeake Bay crabs, and I love my family.
>
> I grew up in a large family and still live in the old neighborhood. I know my neighbors. I've got two sisters and I'm Aunt Barb to six nieces and nephews.
>
> So I know a lot about the family. I know the American dream begins with the family.
>
> It's nurtured around the kitchen table, at the family barbecue, Thanksgiving dinner, and Sunday church. It grows on the family farm, thrives at the neighborhood block party, builds new strength at the suburban PTA meeting.

This part of the introduction indicates that Senator Mikulski thought the first and major obstacle she faced would be the perception

---

[9]Kenneth Burke, *A Rhetoric of Motives* (1950; reprint ed., Berkeley: University of California Press, 1969), p. 39.

of the audience that she was not like them and that, because she was unmarried and childless, she couldn't talk about this topic. If she was going to say anything about the American family that they were going to hear, she had to create a relationship between them and her and establish that she had the personal experience and values that made her an appropriate speaker on this subject. The introduction acknowledges differences, but it aims at creating identification, a combination of shared values and personal experiences.

But she had more work to do before she could begin to develop her point of view. After pointing out that some families have to cope with terrible problems, she said:

> But family life should be more than just coping and making ends meet; more than just pinching pennies and dipping into the nest egg. If there is anything that concerns the American family today it is this—our government hasn't caught up with the new facts of American family life. Families have changed, so why can't Washington?
>
> New fact: Mom's working. Nearly 65 percent of all mothers are working. Part-time. Full time. All the time. Keeping the family together. Making ends meet. Making America more prosperous.
>
> Working mothers need affordable day care and the pay they deserve. Too often they can't get either.

This part of the introduction is an attempt to make a transition from shared views toward a more controversial area. She starts with problems and economic struggles, which often push women into the workforce, then states a fact that shocks the audience into recognizing the extent of changes, and then links that change first to women's hard work and then to shared values—keeping the family together, making enough to pay the bills, and, in the process, producing goods and services that are part of the nation's well-being. Then, and only then, does she move to the more controversial claims, for affordable day care and the pay they deserve (note that she doesn't say equal pay or comparable worth—her stand is ambiguous). These moves begin to alter perception of the problem and to lessen audience resistance to her proposals.

Introductions may be composed of almost any of the resources available to a rhetor—examples, analogies, statistics, quotations from authority, a literary reference, personal experience, explanation, description, and so forth. What an introduction needs to do in a given case depends on the specific obstacles you face. You always need to gain attention, create appropriate expectations, and seek to involve the audience with your subject. But how you accomplish these depends on the audience's attitude toward your subject and purpose, your relationship to the audience, and the nature of your expertise on the subject.

Conclusions

A good conclusion (1) summarizes the major ideas that lead to the claim that is your thesis and (2) fixes the specific purpose in the audience's mind. In addition, the conclusion ought to be both an ending and a climax. It should be an ending in the sense that it provides a sense of closure, a feeling of completion. Rhetorical action should end, not just stop or peter out. A conclusion can be an ending in the simplest and most obvious way—as a summary that recalls the processes by which rhetor and audience drew a conclusion. Unless the act is unusually short or the structure is very simple, a review of the arguments is highly desirable and probably necessary. If you doubt this advice, listen closely to some television commercials and note the amount of repetition that occurs even in these relatively short bits of rhetoric.

Ideally, the conclusion ought also to be the climax or emotional high point, and the material in the conclusion should epitomize (typify, embody) the thesis. Such a conclusion might include a story that captures the essence of what you are saying. It might present a metaphor or analogy that represents the idea. Obviously, a literary allusion or quotation, a citation from an authority, or other kinds of resources might be used as well. Here is an example from a speech by Katherine Davalos Ortega, then treasurer of the United States, at the West Point Savings Bond Kickoff on April 21, 1988:

> But through all the years and all the changes, one thing has not changed. That is the idea behind bonds—the notion that patriotism and profit are teammates, that because we cooperate in selling bonds, our country will be able to better compete in a world where the economic race is to the swift. At the ancient Olympic games, kings ran side by side with soldiers—the only prize a modest wreath of olives. Yet the name of the victor would be inscribed with the immortals.
>
> Today you put your name on the passport to America's future. And in doing so, you make our common journey uncommonly

successful. Because you enter the competitive ranks, we all run faster. Because of this room full of winners, America wins. Thank you very much.

Ortega appeals to the long history of savings bonds and, using alliteration, links patriotism to personal profit. She uses an athletic metaphor—teammates, running a race—and reinvigorates it through an allusion to the early Olympic games, echoing the words of the Bible ("the race is not to the swift"—Ecclesiastes 9:11). At this point she mixes her metaphors, referring to the bonds as a "passport" related to our national "journey," after which she returns to her original metaphor. She praises the audience for running the race, calling all of them winners, and reaffirming that their willingness to participate contributes to U.S. success. This is not an eloquent conclusion—the metaphor is too familiar, and its power is weakened by the metaphoric mixture. The Olympics allusion is undeveloped, which lessens its force. But overall, she summarizes her main point, makes the idea more vivid through imagery, and praises the audience, all of which contribute to her goal.

On January 19, 1988, JoAnn Zimmerman, then lieutenant governor of Iowa and a nurse, spoke to the Iowa Nurses Association on their Legislative Day.[10] She began by defining *political*, then told detailed stories about Florence Nightingale's many political activities. This is how she ended her speech:

> Florence Nightingale understood how to make things happen. Unfortunately our nursing history stresses her origination of modern nursing practice and education and gives little space to the tremendous amount of time and energy she spent "politicking!"
>
> I give you this story of modern nursing for you to understand the importance of influencing the political world. Please understand the political world is also the work world, your place of practice.
>
> Clara Barton also learned to use the political process in gaining funds for her work.
>
> Mary Breckenridge, the founder of the frontier nursing service, Wendover, Kentucky, also understood the importance of gaining the support of a political network.

---

[10] Text courtesy of Lieutenant Governor JoAnn Zimmerman's office.

In 1935, the Maternity Center Association and the Lobenstein Midwifery Clinic applied to the State of New York to consolidate under the name of Maternity Center Association.

Early private registries eventually turned to the public sector to validate our profession in a codified registry—a legal certification.

Many of our predecessors have understood the art [and] practice [of] influence. We, too, must unify, choose some major priorities upon which we can agree, and move to solidify our position as a profession. Our bickering and divisions will destroy our ability to apply political pressure. As our numbers shrink in the nursing shortage, we *must,* must understand this is the time to move forward as a profession! It is imperative that we become involved in the political process, attend the local caucus, or vote in the primary, and develop resolutions to shape the political party platforms! We can have our say and make it count!

Based on the text of the speech, an important part of the rhetorical problem as Zimmerman saw it was persuading nurses in the association to become politically involved and to convince them that their involvement could have an effect. These are important elements of the problem of control. In addition, it appears that she believed many nurses might see such activity as inappropriate for them. Accordingly, she turned to an important role model, the originator of nursing as a profession, to demonstrate the importance of political activity from the very beginning. In the conclusion, she refers to other role models—Clara Barton, founder of the American Red Cross, and Mary Breckenridge, a role model for nurses on the frontier. These examples are intended to reinforce the need for and the efficacy of political action for her audience. Notice that the supporting material in the speech, the detailed examples from the life of Florence Nightingale, and the undeveloped examples in the conclusion are adapted to this particular audience and will have special force for them. These are women that nurses would like to emulate professionally. Zimmerman is arguing that they should be imitated in other ways—by engaging in political activity. Note that this purpose is consistent with the speaker, who is herself an example of a nurse who has become active in politics, and with the occasion, a day on which the nurses focus on issues related to legislation, that is, political issues.

Finally, here is the conclusion to the speech that Elizabeth Cady Stanton made at the first woman's rights convention at Seneca Falls, New York, in 1848. The speech was long and complex, setting forth arguments to respond to all of the major justifications offered for women's special and limited place. At the end, wishing to rouse her listeners to action, she said:

> "Voices" were the visitors and advisers of Joan of Arc. Do not "voices" come to us daily from the haunts of poverty, sorrow, degradation, and despair, already too long unheeded? Now is the time for the women of this country, if they would save our free institutions, to defend the right, to buckle on the armor that can best resist the keenest weapons of the enemy—contempt and ridicule. The same religious enthusiasm that nerved Joan of Arc in her work nerves us to ours. In every generation God calls some men and women for the utterance of truth, a heroic action, and our work today is the fulfilling of what has long since been fore-told by the Prophet—Joel 2:28: "And it shall come to pass after-ward, that I will pour out my spirit upon all flesh, and your sons and your daughters shall prophesy." We do not expect our path will be strewn with the flowers of popular applause, but over the thorns of bigotry and prejudice will be our way, and our banners will beat the dark storm clouds of opposition from those who have entrenched themselves behind the bulwarks of custom and authority, and who have fortified their position by every means, holy and unholy. But we will steadfastly abide the result. Un-moved we will bear it aloft. Undaunted we will unfurl it to the gale, for we know that the storm cannot rend from it a shred, that the electric flash will but more clearly show to us the glori-ous words inscribed upon it, "Equality of Rights."[11]

At the time of this speech, women were not allowed to speak in public, and when they married, they ceased to exist in law—they could not sue, bear witness, or own property, including their own earnings, and had no guardianship rights in their children. Cady Stanton knows that it will be very difficult for women to pay the costs in ridicule or to face the intense hostility of most men and women to their cause. She seeks to raise their morale, to give them courage to pursue this cause. She does so in the high style of nineteenth-century U.S. public address, but her appeal is powerful, particularly to an au-dience with deep religious commitments. Joan of Arc is a model of a woman who stepped out of her traditional place in order to pursue a

---

[11]Elizabeth Cady Stanton, "Speech at the Seneca Falls Convention, 1848," *Man Cannot Speak for Her: Vol. 2: Key Texts of the Early Feminists*, ed. K. K. Campbell (Westport, CT: Greenwood Publishing, 1989), pp. 69–70.

moral cause; the words of the prophet Joel foresee a time when women will speak for moral causes. She also ends with an appeal to the nation's fundamental values. Thus, in the face of what she knows will be great obstacles, she energizes her audience with religious and patriotic appeals that may enable them to withstand fierce resistance.

These examples illustrate the basic functions that conclusions should perform. They are competent, real illustrations of experienced public speakers trying to end their rhetorical acts effectively.

ADAPTING YOUR OUTLINE TO THE AUDIENCE

If you were to follow the form of your outline in presenting your ideas to the audience, your rhetorical action would be presented *deductively,* starting from a general conclusion and moving to illustrations and applications of it. In fact, all outlines are deductive in starting from a thesis and moving to its divisions. But such a pattern may not be the ideal way to present your ideas under all circumstances. For example, if an audience is hostile to your purpose, or if the subject is controversial, announcing your thesis (forewarning) might stir up resentment and prevent the audience from hearing or considering your ideas. In such a case you might want to present your ideas inductively.

Deductive Structure

The advantages of presenting your ideas in deductive order, as in your outline, are that (1) such a structure avoids ambiguity and possible misinterpretation, and (2) such a procedure is perceived as honest and straightforward. The disadvantages are that hostility may be created or increased by a blunt statement of the thesis and by a failure to acknowledge opposing viewpoints or arguments. The problems of hostility can be handled to some extent through the introduction. The clarity of this pattern is a very strong advantage. As you will note in the later section on two-sided structure, it is possible to incorporate a deductive approach into a two-sided presentation of the pro and con arguments on an issue. In all cases, however, your choice of the pattern in which you present your materials should be a conscious one that you make after having considered carefully the obstacles that you face and the strengths and weaknesses of alternative modes of presentation.

Inductive Structure

Logically, *induction* is a process of going from specifics to a general conclusion. In fact, in traveling from data or evidence to a claim, induction involves the inferential leap described in Chapter 8. You will probably follow such a pattern of thinking in the preparation of your speech or essay. But it would be strange indeed if you were to operate inductively while you were speaking to or writing for an audience. That would mean that you were drawing your conclusions and deciding on your thesis at the same moment you were presenting them to the audience. As a thoughtful rhetor, you will have reached conclusions before you present your ideas to an audience. However, an inductive structure is an attempt to recreate for the audience the process by which you arrived at your conclusions. Obviously, you cannot replicate that process exactly. But you might shorten and streamline the process you went through while giving the listener or reader a sense of how you came to draw the conclusions you are advocating.[12] The inductive format has several advantages. It is likely to increase audience involvement, as they will participate more directly in the processes by which conclusions are drawn. This form of presentation also minimizes hostility. The audience has fewer opportunities to disagree, fewer chances to dispute the positions taken by the author. But there are disadvantages. Inductive presentation takes more time or space for development. Also, unless the audience participates very actively—listens acutely or reads intently—they may miss the point, fail to draw the conclusion, and misunderstand your purpose.

Two-Sided or Refutative Structure

As described, an outline is a brief or series of arguments developing reasons for taking one position rather than another. But many subjects of rhetorical action are controversial issues with arguments on both sides that need to be considered and examined. When speaking about such an issue, you might wish to use *refutative structure* by exploring the opposing arguments as part of the process of explaining why you have decided to advocate another position. In effect, you look at the pool of available arguments in order to show that the weight of the evidence and of available arguments falls on one side or the other. A two-sided presentation also can present you as a mediator

---

[12]An exceptionally fine example of this is Virginia Woolf's *A Room of One's Own* (1929; reprint ed., New York: Harbinger, 1957).

who has examined more extreme positions and who seeks to find a compromise between them. Kansas Senator Nancy Landon Kassebaum often takes this approach in examining controversial foreign policy issues.[13]

Two-sided or refutative structure is also more appropriate for certain audiences. A two-sided presentation allows you to incorporate refutation into your presentation. That is essential under several conditions: (1) when you know that the audience is familiar with opposing arguments or will be exposed to competing persuaders; (2) when a one-sided presentation may motivate the audience to seek out opposing views; (3) when a one-sided view of an issue may need to be corrected; and (4) when your opposition is also a significant part of your audience.

In the first situation, opposing arguments are already in the minds of the audience or they soon will be. As a result, it is essential that you respond to questions they have in their minds or prepare them for the arguments they will hear from competing persuaders. When arguments already exist in the minds of audience members, you ignore them at your peril, as they are competing with you whether you know it or not (note how this is done in the outline attacking state lotteries). When the audience will eventually be exposed to opposing arguments, you can inoculate them by suggesting weaknesses in the arguments, which will make the audience less susceptible to the appeals of competing persuaders. Without such inoculation, the arguments of opponents may become the novel arguments that shift the balance and alter opinion.

As indicated in Chapter 3, there are three conditions in which audiences seek information that challenges their beliefs or values: when audience members have generally higher levels of education, when the information is very useful, and when the audience members' past history of exposure leads them to believe they have heard a biased or one-sided presentation. Thus, two-sided presentations are desirable with knowledgeable audiences—a slanted or one-sided presentation can create a desire on the part of the audience for competing information. That is particularly true when the position you take is extreme or unusual. If you claim that ingesting almonds cures AIDS but don't acknowledge contradictory views, you may drive your audience to seek out competing medical studies. If you claim that there is no evidence that smoking is dangerous to health or that the amount of cholesterol

---

[13]See Lisa R. Ashner, "Nancy Landon Kassebaum: Speaker and Senator." Honors thesis, University of Kansas, 1984.

in foods we eat has no effect on heart condition, you are likely to send your audience off to competing persuaders to look at the opposing evidence. At a minimum, you will need to qualify your claims. At best, you will acknowledge opposing arguments.

There are also situations in which only one side of an issue has been raised, for example, only our side of international issues, such as our trading disputes with Japan. If a good trading agreement is to be made, Americans (and Japanese) will need to familiarize themselves with the issues as seen from the other side of the disagreement. In 1983, speaking to the Third Annual Conference on International Affairs at the University of Kansas, Sen. Kassebaum attempted to address this problem.[14] First, she briefly enumerated the arguments from the U.S. perspective. Then she said:

> This litany infuriates many Americans and not without reason. But, as is so often the case, there is another side to the story which leaves one wondering if the glass is half full or half empty.
>
> William Cline, of the Institute for International Economics, noted recently that "there is little systematic, empirical evidence that Japan protects its market substantially more than the United States does its own." A recent report from the House Ways and Means Committee states, "Japan is generally an open trading nation, although some very tough residual attitudes of protectionism remain."
>
> In thinking about what infuriates us about Japan we also must not forget that Japan is a valued ally of the United States. After Canada, Japan is our largest export market. One-tenth of all U.S. exports go to Japan. We shipped $21.8 billion worth of goods to Japan in 1981 including $6.7 billion in agricultural produce or 15 percent of our total farm exports. Indeed, Japan is our largest foreign buyer of U.S. agricultural produce taking from us almost all of their soybean needs and more than half of their wheat and feed grain requirements.
>
> Imports from Japan, moreover, have expanded the range of products available to the American consumer. Would life be the same without Honda motorcycles, Toyota cars, Sony Walkman stereos, or Nikon cameras? Indeed, the popular video games

---

[14]"U.S. and Japan—A Troubled Partnership," Third Annual Conference on International Affairs, University of Kansas, 1983. Text courtesy of Senator Nancy Landon Kassebaum's office.

Space Invaders, Donkey Kong, and even Pac Man come from Japan.

In short, we continue to have a relationship of mutual benefit. But legitimate questions remain. . . .

Here is a case in which audience members are likely to be familiar with only one side of the issue. Kassebaum briefly suggests another perspective, relying heavily on authority evidence from U.S. sources: statistics about Japan as an important buyer of U.S. goods (with an emphasis on the agricultural goods so important to many Kansans), with examples to remind U.S. listeners of the benefits that accrue to them from Japanese imports. She is trying to correct an imbalance in knowledge and concerns that she believes must be redressed before policy changes are made or new trading relationships are negotiated.

Finally, in some situations those holding opposing views are part of your target audience. One of the finest examples of two-sided or refutative structure is an essay on the birth of the "Black Power" slogan written by Dr. Martin Luther King, Jr.[15] King's opposition included more militant civil rights activists who were using the slogan and a more militant approach to civil rights protest. But those same people were part of his primary audience, because he sought to reconcile these competing groups and to unify the effort for civil rights. However successful his efforts at persuasion might have been, he would have failed if he had not demonstrated to his opponents that he understood their position and respected it. As a result, the essay is both a persuasive statement for a nonviolent approach and a moving statement of why the slogan and a more militant approach became attractive to civil rights workers. The essay is so balanced that it is an excellent source of information about the motivation of more militant civil rights groups. Despite his fair treatment of the opposition, King makes a powerful case for his own point of view. But a two-sided presentation was ideally suited to the conditions in which he found himself: competing with those whom he needed to persuade. When your opposition is also your audience, you must not only make a two-sided presentation, but you must also present opposing arguments fairly and sympathetically.

---

[15]"Black Power," the second chapter of King's book, *Where Do We Go from Here: Chaos or Community?* (New York: Harper and Row, 1967). It is reprinted in Robert L. Scott and Wayne Brockriede, *The Rhetoric of Black Power* (New York: Harper and Row, 1969), pp. 25–64.

SUMMARY

Summary Outline

I. An outline enables you
   A. To see the relationships among ideas
   B. To test the consistency of your development of the thesis

II. Specific ways of developing your thesis are
   A. Chronological organization based on time, sequence, or narrative
   B. Topical organization, selecting particular facets or aspects of a subject
   C. Logical organization, focusing on cause–effect and problem–solution relationships

III. Methods of adapting materials for presentation to the audience include
   A. The motivated sequence, adapted to advocate changes in policy
   B. The introduction, adapted to obstacles arising from
      1. The relationship between rhetor and audience
      2. The relationships between audience and subject
      3. The relationship between rhetor and subject
   C. The conclusion, adapted
      1. To recall the process of argumentation
      2. To create a sense of closure
      3. To provide an emotional climax
   D. Deductive presentation, adapted
      1. To avoid ambiguity and misinterpretation
      2. To make a case straightforwardly
   E. Inductive presentation, adapted
      1. To minimize hostility
      2. To increase audience participation
   F. Two-sided presentation, adapted
      1. To refute or to inoculate against competing persuasion
      2. To present a fair and balanced view
      3. To show respect and understanding when the opposition is also the target audience

■ ■ ■

MATERIAL FOR ANALYSIS

What follows is a speech made by Rose Elizabeth Bird, Chief Justice of the Supreme Court of California from 1977 to 1986, at the first annual community forum on breast cancer, Los Angeles, California, May 31, 1980. Bird was appointed Chief Justice by Governor Edmund G. "Jerry" Brown, Jr., but she lost an election for a subsequent 12-year term.[16] As she notes in this speech, she faced serious health problems while on the court and during the election.

In this speech, Bird does not speak as a legal scholar or judicial expert but as a woman who has had breast cancer treatment and as a person who has faced the terrors of cancer. The speech is testimony, and it unfolds primarily as an extended narrative of her experience.

Remarks on Breast Cancer

1   It is a pleasure to be with you today at this first annual community forum on breast cancer. In inviting me to speak, Dr. Plotkin and Dr. Frileck asked that I talk about my own personal experience with cancer. That request gave me a moment of pause.

2   Although I have discussed the matter privately with many women who were facing the same thing, this marks the first time that I have delivered a public address on the subject. I would note that I do so as an individual—as a woman who has had cancer and a mastectomy and who also happens to be the Chief Justice of California.

3   As a basically private person, it is with some reticence that I undertake this "oral history." But if my remarks prove helpful to others facing this disease, then my participation will have been worthwhile. I would only ask that you hear me through. My message is essentially a positive one, though its words may at times convey the fear and pain that are part of coming to terms with having cancer.

4   Let me begin with some facts. My right breast was removed in 1976 using modified radical surgery techniques. It is almost

---

[16]Those opposing Bird and two other justices who were up for continuation argued that the Bird Court had defied the will of the people on the death penalty by permitting no executions after California reinstated the death penalty via a ballot initiative in 1978. See Tom Wicker, "A Naked Power Grab," *New York Times* (September 14, 1986):E25, for an editorial in her support.

impossible to put into words the shock and terror you feel when you learn you have this dreaded disease. Your emotions run the gamut from disbelief to fear to feelings of great loss. Disbelief, because cancer is always something that happens to the next person, not to you. Fear, because everyone living in this society has been conditioned to believe that a diagnosis of cancer is equivalent to a death warrant. It is not true, but that is the popular conception. Accepting our own mortality is difficult under any circumstances. But in a society which finds euphemisms for the very word "death" and which encourages its people to pursue youth with a vengeance, it is doubly difficult. We come to the task ill-equipped, and our society does little to help prepare us.

5   No one in my family had ever had cancer, as far as I was able to learn. I was in my late thirties and had never in my life had a major illness of any sort. The only operation I had ever had was a tonsillectomy, which was done routinely when I was a child in the doctor's office. I simply could not and would not believe that at my age and with my health I could possibly have cancer. But it was a fact I had to face. My doctor was encouraging after my mastectomy and indicated there was little chance of reoccurrence.

6   I dealt with the situation by denying that possibility. I went through the operation, forced myself back to work in less than two weeks, and promptly attempted to forget all about it. I chose to deny rather than to deal with the myriad conflicting emotions that one needs to face and understand. I threw myself into my work.

7   Despite my efforts, it proved impossible to totally blot out what had happened. Whenever you have had a disease that may reoccur you become very sensitized to the messages that your body sends to your mind. Whether it is a cold or a simple ache or pain, you experience the fear that this might signal a reoccurrence of some sort. And that fear brings with it the larger fear that the disease will inevitably cause your death. It is essential to face these fears and come to terms with them, for you will know no peace until you do. Fortunately, there is a very positive side to this confrontation—I learned to listen to my body and what it was saying to me, but this self-knowledge did not come quickly or easily.

8   After my operation I submerged myself in my work and became the picture of the traditional workaholic. I suppose I fell prey to the "macho man" complex in which I wanted to prove to myself and those around me that my illness was just a minor happenstance and did not really affect my life. However, about seven months after I became Chief Justice, I noticed a very small nodule on the muscle above where my breast was removed. It was at this juncture that I was forced to confront all the frightening possibilities that I had been unwilling to face before.

9   My surgeon removed the nodule in his office and told me that he would let me know the pathologist's findings. He called me a few days later during the Los Angeles calendar of the court and told me what I had dreaded and had hoped never to hear: It was cancerous. It was a reoccurrence. He said we had to talk about what the next steps should be. He would see me that following Monday when I returned to the Bay Area.

10   I cannot begin to explain what a devastating blow that news was to me. However, I was in the midst of a very heavy calendar of cases and as a result had little time to ponder the situation. Besides, I did not want to worry my family or my staff so I kept the news to myself.

11   Upon my return that next Monday, I kept my appointment with my doctor. Unfortunately, he could not keep his with me. The nurse greeted me with tears in her eyes. She was very sorry, but my doctor would not be able to see me because he was unable to leave his home. For the first time I learned that he, too, had cancer. His was of the pancreas, and they did not expect him to live very long. He died about three weeks later; and I was never able to see him again.

12   This shock was one that sent me reeling. How was it possible that my surgeon, who had seen me through so much, was himself a victim of cancer? How could this have happened? How could I cope; whom should I see; what should I do? If the medical establishment was unable to save my doctor, whom could they save? It was a terrifying revelation; and it made me very skeptical about whether doctors really could treat this disease and about how advanced the state of the art really was.

13   As a direct result of these two circumstances, I went through a type of catharsis. I began to read as much of the literature as I could. I felt I needed to know as much as the doctors did. For the first time since my mastectomy, I forced myself to face the statistics on breast cancer and the mortality rates. And for the very first time in my life, I had to seriously consider the possibility that I might have only a few years left to live.

14   As I observed earlier, this society does not prepare us very well for that eventuality. During most of our lives, we deny, defy, or attempt to ignore the fact of death. We place our old people in homes or hospitals beyond our line of sight so that we need not face their suffering—out of sight, out of mind, as the old saying goes. We would worship instead at the fountain of youth. We sand our skin, lift our chins, and dye our hair or replace it. We fool ourselves by creating an illusion, instead of marking proudly the milestone that each gray hair and wrinkle signify.

15   When you face the fact of your own mortality, you must also face the facts about what you have done with your life. In a peculiar way, death can teach you what life is all about. It is a painful lesson and a difficult journey, but I am personally grateful that I was made to travel this path at a relatively early age. For I have learned much about myself, much about what I want out of life, and much about how precious life and people are. It is our relationships with others, especially those whom we love, that give the fullest meaning to life. I don't think I ever really knew that, emotionally or intellectually, until my second bout with cancer.

16   After my second operation, I set about trying to modify my behavior so that I might live a healthier, more normal life. I changed my diet to one that largely consists of fresh fruits and vegetables with little or no meat. There are some in the field who believe that stress may suppress the immune system, so I tried to deal more effectively with the stresses in my life. However, my personal experience with cancer was not at an end.

17   A few months after a particularly nasty and personalized political campaign in the fall of 1978, I had my second reoccurrence. As a result of my previous self-evaluation, I found myself in much better shape to handle this last blow. I suppose the greatest problems for a person suffering from a disease like cancer are the feelings of helplessness and loss of control, as well as the gnawing sense of inevitability. You hope and pray for remission, but each reoccurrence reinforces the fear that death, and a painful one at that, may be unavoidable. I believe it is important to maintain a positive frame of mind about cancer, but I would be less than honest were I to tell you that it is always possible to do so.

18   Thankfully, there are today many hopeful signs in the treatment of cancer. It does not mean an automatic death sentence. But it is a disease for which there is presently no complete cure. That is a reality which each person who contracts cancer must acknowledge. That fact also presents special problems for the doctors who treat cancer patients. With many other diseases, there are proven cures, tried and tested plans of treatment, courses of action that bring respite and relief. With cancer, there is only trial and error, remission and reoccurrence, expectation and frustration.

19   If I might be so bold, I would like to leave a few thoughts with the doctors who may be attending this forum. Cancer is a difficult disease for the patient to deal with for some of the same reasons that it must be frustrating for the doctor. The patient must come to terms with the fear of death in a society that denies death's existence. The patient must deal with a disease that makes

him or her feel helpless, since the conventional courses of treatment give the patient absolutely no role to play. All too often, the
patient becomes a passive object for the interplay of surgery, radia-
tion, and chemotherapy. The surgeon's knife, the nuclear medicine machine, and the vial of toxic chemicals become the actors in
this drama, and the patient is simply written out of the script.
There is perhaps no feeling more helpless than that. It's your life,
but you no longer have any control over it. I think that is a princi-
pal reason why patients find cancer so very difficult to deal with.

20   The doctor also has a diminished role to play for he has no
cure. He is no longer the traditional giver of life, the healer that he
is accustomed to being. He will be challenged more often by frus-
trated and frightened patients. His knowledge and even his authority will be questioned, and he, too, will feel that he has lost a
measure of control over his professional life.

21   Understandably, many doctors feel threatened by these
encounters with uncertainty and react by adhering even more
firmly to the conventional methods of treatment, almost as
though they were articles of religious faith. This sort of intransigence on the part of many in the medical profession compounds
the problem of dealing with cancer both for the patient and for
the doctor. For example, many doctors refuse to consider the possibility that diet may be a factor that should be part of an overall
treatment program. Or, they dismiss the idea by saying that if diet
does make a difference, it was the diet you were fed as a youngster
that counts. But if we know that the incidence of cancer is much
higher among people living in affluent areas where the ingestion
of animal protein and fat is high, what is wrong with experiment-
ing with diet as part of a therapy program? At the very least, if
patients are allowed to play some part in their treatment through
regulating their diet, they feel less helpless. They become less like
objects to be acted upon and more like individuals who can take
responsibility along with their doctors in dealing with a disease for
which neither of them has the answer.

22   Another area where the patient may be able to participate
is the control of stress. Many degenerative diseases are considered
to be stress-related since stress may play a part in suppressing our
immune systems. Although it has not been scientifically shown,
why not allow and encourage patients to come to terms with
stress in their own environment? Why not work cooperatively
with psychologists in this area? If it accomplishes nothing else, it
permits patients to deal constructively with many of the emotions
they experience as a result of facing a serious disease. Further, it
cannot hurt anyone to review his or her lifestyle and to try to lead

a less stressful existence. Again, the patient is given an active role in what has been a very passive treatment process. Encourage your patients to try meditation, biofeedback, and other methods of coping with stress.

23   From my own experience, I can tell you that such things are helpful. During the two reoccurrences that I have had, I have been in the public spotlight. Anyone who has been in public life during times of societal transition can tell you that at best it amounts to cruel and unusual punishment. If you do not come to terms with the spotlight's constant focus upon you and the unrelenting criticism that comes with that public glare, it would be impossible to remain in the position.

24   If I had not come to terms with the possibility of my own death and my mortality, if I had not been able to accept the fact that I had cancer and to face the fears that cancer creates, I would have been devastated by many of my everyday experiences. Let me provide you with a couple of examples. About one week after my third operation was discussed in the press, one of my most vocal critics began to make public speeches about the importance of getting rid of the "cancer" at the top of the court. That, of course, was a euphemism for getting rid of me. I was surprised at the venom that such a statement revealed, but I was able to keep some perspective and even my sense of humor about it precisely because I had come to terms with my disease.

25   On numerous occasions, my secretary has received perhaps five phone calls a day from the press. The callers would indicate that they had been informed by some reliable source that I was seriously ill and that my death was imminent. I later learned that the systematic nature of these calls was due to the fact that the rumors were being deliberately spread to the press for political advantage. As you might imagine, it can be very disconcerting, to say the least, to be bombarded by callers asking how soon you are going to die. One might almost think that someone intended that I give the suggestion serious consideration. In fact, as recently as two weeks ago, a major California newspaper printed an article referring to rumors about my impending death and speculating on who might be my successor. If I had not already come to terms with the reality of my disease, I would not have been able to see the gallows humor in all of this. But thankfully I can observe along with Mark Twain that the reports of my death are greatly exaggerated.

26   If I may leave the doctors here today with one suggestion, it is this: Let your patients have a role in the treatment of their disease. Don't shut them out, don't resent their questions, don't

close your mind to alternatives. Remember that it is the patients' lives that are at stake here, and they should have some say about what happens. Be concerned not only about the quantity of their lives but also about the quality. Let the patients make the ultimate decisions along with you. Don't let them become pawns to be moved about at will; don't let them become helpless objects to be acted upon. Instead, let them become partners with you. Let them take some responsibility for their own lives. Their dignity as individuals and your dignity as physicians depend upon it.

27   For those of you who are facing this disease and for those of you who may one day face it, let me say to you what Franklin Roosevelt said at a difficult time in our nation's history: "The only thing we have to fear is fear itself." Have courage, face the facts, and you will find that when you have faced your fears and stood your ground there occurs a kind of liberation. It is not an easy journey. It can be quite painful and lonely. But it is a journey that must be made.

28   I want you to know that it is not a hopeless situation. It is neither too painful nor too fearful to face. Most importantly, it is an opportunity to find out about life. And isn't that really why each of us has been placed here?

29   Thank you and good luck.

Questions for Analysis

1. A single example based on one's personal experience generally is a very weak form of proof. What are the ways in which that experience is made powerful for the audience, both in a psychological and in a logical sense?

2. What is the structure of this speech? What holds it together?

3. In what ways are the supporting materials suited to the purpose or the purpose shaped to fit the available evidence?

4. How are the speaker's persona, her language, and the evidence she offers related to each other? How do they interact?

5. How would you evaluate the effect of Bird as a public figure, the Chief Justice of California, giving this speech? What kinds of risks is she taking?

6. Bird makes some medical suggestions in the conclusion. How does she avoid crossing the line into areas that lie outside her experience and expertise?

EXERCISE

Two-Sided Presentations

Prepare a speech or write an essay organized to present two sides of a controversial topic. Select one of these obstacles as your focus:

1. Inoculating the audience against the arguments of competing persuaders or refuting the major arguments of the opposition.

2. Moderating the views of extremists; for example, urging extreme conservatives to moderate their demands on politicians, urging abortion foes to permit abortions in cases of rape, incest, or where there is a threat to the mother's life, or urging pro-choice advocates to limit their appeals to the first trimester, and the like.

3. Presenting arguments from another perspective to an audience likely to be familiar with only one side of an argument, such as describing minority or women's points of view to majority/male audiences.

4. Acknowledging the justice of arguments on both sides while taking a point of view; for example, acknowledging the problems of censorship while arguing that the linkage of sex and violence in pornography is more significant, or acknowledging the evils of pornography while arguing that the evils of censorship are more significant.

Focus attention on the strengths and weaknesses of this form of organization and attempt to locate the particular rhetorical situations in which it is likely to be most effective.

CHAPTER 10

The Resources of Language: Style and Strategy

The language of a rhetorical act may be casual (It just blew my mind . . .) or formal (Fourscore and seven years ago, . . .), vague (Play it loud!) or precise (Only 2 calories in an 8 oz. glass), figurative (Using a different fat-free slice on this Reuben would be like using steak sauce on salmon) or literal (Compare Teletire's cut prices on these performance radial tires). But whatever its style and whatever strategies are used, language is a powerful and significant resource.

However else it may be defined, rhetoric is the art of using symbols. All the resources of rhetorical action have their foundation in language. Given its importance, the student of rhetoric needs to understand the characteristics of language that allow it to play such a special role in rhetorical action.

THE CHARACTERISTICS OF LANGUAGE

In its ordinary sense, *language* refers to verbal symbol systems such as Sindebele or Hmong. However, language also includes other symbol systems based on space, movement, sound, pitch, time, color, and so on. In their most developed forms, such symbol systems are dance, music, sculpture, painting, architecture, and the like. Through symbol systems, we order our experiences and assign them meaning. Instead of being bombarded by billions of distinct stimuli, with language we can make sense of the chaos so that we can perceive and respond to a world of recognizable objects and events.

There are three primary characteristics of language: naming, abstracting, and negation.

Naming

The first characteristic of language is *naming*—the process by which we notice, recognize, and label certain elements or qualities in ourselves and in our world. Names permit us to identify and isolate significant events. For this reason, the vocabulary of an individual or a community is a rough index of what is or has been important to that person or group, a relationship reflected in the verbal ability sections of college entrance examinations.

Naming is a process of ordering the world and of focusing our attention. A name does not label one single thing but a category of relatively similar objects or events. As labels that refer to categories, names permit us to ignore the differences among objects and events and to lump them together into groups to which we can respond similarly. For example, if I identify an object as a "chair," I respond to it as a humanly created object with arms or a back, intended for a category of actions labeled "sitting," and I ignore the unique characteristics of this particular chair. If this process of labeling and responding is to work well, however, there must be standards to determine when a particular object, person, or event may be included in a particular category, that is, when it may properly be labeled with a particular name. Such standards are set by definitions.

A *definition* specifies the essential qualities that something must have to be labeled in a particular way in a given linguistic community. Definitions, collected in dictionaries, give the denotative meanings of words. But people do not learn meanings from dictionaries. They learn meanings in situations by having experiences with words and with the persons, events, and objects to which words are applied. In these real, concrete situations, people not only learn denotative meanings, but they also learn to associate the feelings they experience in these situations with the words. Such meanings, called *connotations* (*con* = together with, *notate* = to mark or note), refer to the associations a word calls up.

For example, some years ago while reading a William Faulkner novel, I came across the word *vicegeral*. I looked it up in the dictionary with some irritation (Why don't I know that word? Why does Faulkner use such unusual words in his novels?) and discovered that it is defined as "acting as an agent." I expected that once I had learned it, it would reappear, but it did not. After several years had passed, I went to a performance of the play *Hadrian VII* and heard actor Hume Cronyn make a speech that referred to the pope as acting in a vicegeral capacity. For me, *vicegeral* not only means to act as an agent, it also means one of the unusual and sometimes irritating words in a Faulkner novel, the kind of role played by a pope, a word used in the play *Hadrian VII*, and a good example to use in this book explaining how connotative meanings develop. If you remember the word, one part of your connotative meaning will be related to reading about it in this book.

Semanticists (students of meaning) say that meaning is in people, not in things or even in words. The connotative meanings associated with all symbols illustrate this idea. They also show that names are not just factual or descriptive. Words are labels for our experiences, so names are valuative as well as descriptive. Meanings include subjective qualities such as associations and connotations.

Names are valuative at the most basic levels because they are signs of interest and relevance. For example, if you already knew the meaning of vicegeral, your knowledge would indicate past experience with the word. Like me, you may have encountered it in a novel or a play, or you may be a student of the papacy, or you may even have run across it in the dictionary. But I doubt that the term produces strong reactions, because it is unlikely to be a word that you associate with intense or disturbing experiences.

Contrast *vicegeral* with *masturbation*. The latter term is, for many, associated with disquieting sexual feelings and taboos. In a class on the psychology of sex at the University of Kansas students asked their professor not to use that word because it was so upsetting. The students decided they preferred *self-pleasuring*. Denotatively, *masturbation* and *self-pleasuring* are identical, but connotatively they are not. *Masturbation* calls up many highly charged associations, but *self-pleasuring,* a less familiar term, is unlikely to have been used to label forbidden feelings and behaviors. As a result, hearing and using it are less disturbing. In 1994, for example, then U.S. Surgeon-General Joycelyn Elders was pressured to resign in part because she publicly acknowledged masturbation as an alternative sexual outlet that avoids the dangers of AIDS. Many news media reports of these events shied away from using the disturbing word, usually substituting *self-pleasuring* for it.

When we speak of *loaded language,* we are referring to words that provoke strong feelings; the person who hears or reads them has vivid, intense associations because of emotion-laden experiences with them. No term understood by a person is simply neutral or factual. It is always bound up with experiences and will always contain evaluations resulting from feelings associated with those experiences. In some cases, however, the response is so strong that it interferes with communication. For many people, it is not possible to talk calmly about abortion or rape or condoms or homosexuality or AIDS. Think, for example, about euphemisms that we use in order to talk about such subjects as death, money, and sexual intercourse, among others. Euphemistic terms are one strategy we use to avoid such intense reactions.

Connotations change. For example, at the beginning of the 1960s *Negro* had positive connotations as a term of respect and *black* was a term of disrespect. In the course of that decade, protestors changed those connotations so that Negro was associated, negatively, with persons who sought approval from whites and who were ashamed of their culture, their past, and their physical characteristics. By contrast, *Black,* now capitalized, became associated with racial pride. *African American* is now the preferred term (formerly, but no longer, hyphenated) because it has become associated with ethnic history and ethnic pride.

Naming, the first dimension of language, enables us to order, call attention to, focus, define, and evaluate. Names have denotative meanings, found in dictionaries, that define the accepted conditions for their use. Names have connotative meanings that reflect our experiences and associations with terms and their use. The connotations of terms can change for us as individuals and for us as members of a culture as our experiences with terms change.

Abstracting

The second characteristic of language is *abstracting,* which is a process of leaving out details. The most basic kind of abstracting occurs with names. As titles for categories, names leave out all the distracting details. You call what you sit in a desk, ignoring its color, the gum underneath the seat, the initials carved in its surface or inscribed in ink, and the differences between it and the desks your professors have in their offices. The most basic element in abstracting is omission—leaving out or ignoring details in order to treat different objects in similar ways.

Abstracting moves us farther and farther from concrete, specific details. In fact, we can go on and on leaving out more and more details. The word *abstract* is defined as "not concrete or specific, without reference to a specific instance, theoretical, not easily understood, abstruse." That definition alerts you to problems in communication that arise from abstracting. As we move farther from concrete detail, an idea or concept becomes more and more difficult to grasp and the chances of misunderstanding increase. However, abstracting is also a major linguistic resource.

Symbols are abstractions that permit us to talk about an absent world. We write books about the remote past, most of whose details have vanished; we read books and talk about places we have never seen; we argue about a future that is outside our experience; we explore concepts we can never see or touch. Here is an example of abstracting as a process of including more and more experience but omitting more and more detail.

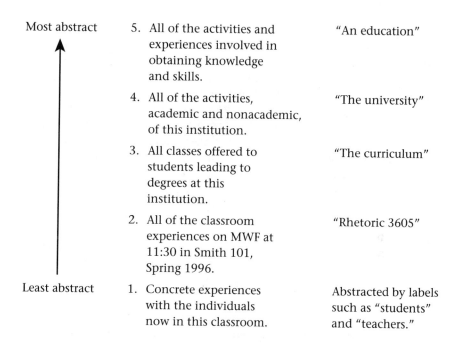

Most abstract

5. All of the activities and experiences involved in obtaining knowledge and skills.   "An education"

4. All of the activities, academic and nonacademic, of this institution.   "The university"

3. All classes offered to students leading to degrees at this institution.   "The curriculum"

2. All of the classroom experiences on MWF at 11:30 in Smith 101, Spring 1996.   "Rhetoric 3605"

Least abstract

1. Concrete experiences with the individuals now in this classroom.   Abstracted by labels such as "students" and "teachers."

Even at the most concrete level in the here and now, abstraction occurs. It occurs as we label our experiences, as, for example, when we ignore individual differences and label people as "students" and "teachers." As we move up each level, we include greater amounts of experience as we omit more details. Level 2 lumps together many hours of varied activity under a single label. Level 3 lumps together all the courses offered to students and orders them into one giant pattern. And so on.

The advantages of abstracting are evident; they enable us to combine, for thinking and talking, ever-larger areas of experience while ignoring varied and complex detail. As we move up the ladder of abstraction, it becomes more difficult to understand these abstractions—they are farther from our personal experience. It also becomes easier to ignore significant differences—to forget that students differ in background, age, social skills, verbal ability, maturity, and so on, and to treat them as stereotypes. Abstraction allows us to manipulate great hunks of the world verbally; it tempts us to forget that these chunks are made up of highly varied concrete events, objects, and individuals. The capacity of language to abstract permits us to talk about the absent, the past, and the future, and it allows us to conceptualize ideas, such as love, truth, beauty, and rhetoric, that lie far beyond our concrete experience.

Abstracting is a powerful source of identification and has great potential to prompt participation. Politicians exploit this potential by speaking in less concrete, more general terms hoping that listeners will interpret such language in different ways, enabling them to appeal to diverse groups. Many of us may believe that change is needed and respond to a politician who says that, as many voters did to Bill Clinton's statements in 1992, only to discover later that the politician's idea of change and the listeners' ideas of change are very different. Is anyone opposed to "family values," for example? But what does the person espousing them really mean by that phrase? Reducing or eliminating abortion? Opposing sex education in schools? Providing family leave to parents of newborn or newly adopted children? Providing tax writeoffs for childcare services? All of these might be part of whatever someone might mean by that phrase.

Negating

Negating is a third characteristic of language. Definitions are based on negating because when we say what something is, we are also saying what it is not. The rhetorical power of negation is reflected in the Judeo-Christian cultural heritage. As the Ten Commandments state, "Thou shalt not . . ." But negation is very tricky, because such prohibitions imply their opposites. Whenever you say to a child "Don't . . ." and describe some proscribed action, you are, at the same time, suggesting an enticing possibility! Thus, even positive commands imply their opposite, suggesting the option not to do whatever it is that we are being told to do.

Negation is also involved in abstracting. To abstract is to omit (negate) details and ignore (negate) differences. In fact, the ability to use symbols at all requires an understanding of negation. Whatever a name is, it is not what it stands for. "Cat" is a bit of black ink or a few sound waves, not this furry creature that meows and purrs, bites and scratches, grooms by licking, and adores its catnip toy.

Negation underlies all comparisons and contrasts, including those involved in literal and figurative analogies. As discussed in Chapter 7, literal analogies allow us to evaluate and to predict. But comparisons are also involved in definitions.

A *dialectical definition* defines by contrast. For example, if you wish to define capitalism, you might compare it to socialism and conclude that what is distinctive about it is the private ownership of the means of production. Such a definition uses socialism as a perspective through which to look at capitalism; it ignores similarities and emphasizes differences. We can also compare capitalism and democracy. In this case, the focus shifts to assumptions made about individuals. Capitalism presumes that some will have more economic power (capital) while democracy affirms the right of each individual, regardless of economic or other differences, to an equal voice in how he or she is governed. If we compare capitalism and feudalism, the focus shifts to the reciprocal obligations of liege lord and vassal and the absence of such mutual obligations between capitalist/employer and laborer/employee. Comparisons between capitalism and communism might emphasize the difference between production controlled by the market and production determined by state planning. In each case negation, in the form of contrast, directs our attention and shapes the definition that results. Dialectical definitions are effective ways to define highly abstract terms.

Negation is also the basis for the figurative analogy and for metaphorical language generally. The moon is not "the north wind's cookie" or "a piece of angry candy" or "a ghostly galleon tossed upon cloudy seas" as it has been described by poets. We can understand and use such metaphors precisely because we recognize that they are not literally true. This form of the negative extends the range of our symbols to include comparisons between anything and anything. In addition, the negative allows us to use irony (to say one thing but mean something else), develop satire, and speak in a sarcastic tone.

These, then, are three fundamental characteristics of language: the capacities to name, to abstract, and to negate. From them come all the powers of language to influence our perceptions and our attitudes. And from them arise the specific resources of style and strategy.

STYLE

Style is what is distinctive about the language of a rhetorical act, and all rhetorical action, willy-nilly, has a style. The style of an act can vary. It can be more or less formal, more or less precise, more or less literal, and more or less redundant, for example.

Formality

Whenever we speak or write, we make certain assumptions about what kind of language is appropriate to the situation at hand. Basically, this amounts to deciding how formal or informal to be. Rhetorical style ranges from the formality of a presidential address or a scholarly article on the one hand to the informality of a newspaper article or a conversation with a friend on the other. Generally speaking, as style becomes more informal it becomes more conversational or colloquial.

Informality may be a way of identifying with those to whom you appeal or from whom you seek support. Barbara Christmas, a 1992 candidate seeking to represent Georgia's First District in Congress, spoke like the people from whom she sought support. She presented herself to voters as follows: "Remember, ah'm just a country girl from Tattnall County. . . . No way ah'm against gun controls. . . . Ah grew up with a gun rack in the pickup truck. . . . Ah'm no ultraliberal feminist. Ah'm a traditional—but progressive—woman." Christmas received support from the National Organization for Women, but she also is the daughter of a retired warden of the Reidville state penitentiary, and she commented, "Y'see, that way I built this incredible Good Ol' Boy network of my own? . . . A network of law-enforcement people, state troopers, sheriffs, lawmakers? They all know I'm all right." In other words, the language she used reflected real links to the community she wanted to represent, but her accent and her colloquial style were also reminders of them.[1]

The factors influencing the degree of formality are those already discussed as parts of the rhetorical problem: the audience, the subject and purpose, and the rhetor. Whatever is serious and important will be presented in a more formal style. The more authoritative the rhetor is or wishes to appear, the more formal the style. The relationship between rhetor and audience also affects formality. Formal prose creates distance between rhetor and audience while informality minimizes distance.

The differences between formal and informal prose are chiefly matters of grammar, sentence structure, and vocabulary. Formal prose is strictly grammatical and uses complex sentence structure and a lofty or technical vocabulary. Informal prose is less strictly grammatical and uses short, simple sentences and ordinary, familiar words. Informal style may include sentence fragments and some colloquialisms or slang.

How formal or informal should you be? Obviously the answer depends on your subject and purpose, the role you will play, and your relationship to your audience. Most public rhetorical action observes

---

[1]Frances X. Clines, "Showing the Good Ol' Boys How to Play Their Own Game," *New York Times*, September 25, 1992, p. A18. Christmas did not win the election.

conventional niceties of grammar, is modestly complex in sentence structure, and avoids excessive use of colloquialisms (words or phrases found more frequently in conversation than in writing). That is, it is relatively formal, although the rhetor must determine just where on the continuum from highly formal to informal a particular rhetorical occasion should be placed.

Precision

Language can be highly precise, specific, and verifiable, or it can be ambiguous and vague. Precise language expresses ideas clearly and distinctly. It is exact and sometimes technical. Ambiguous language is open to more than one interpretation, and vague language is inexplicit and indefinite. For the most part, good style aims for precision and avoids ambiguity.

Precise language indicates that a rhetorical act is emphasizing empirical evidence and logical proof. Only clearly stated arguments can be evaluated logically; only exact statements are capable of verification. Precision in language indicates purpose and reflects the rhetor's assumptions about the audience. More complex, technical subjects require the use of formal, technical vocabulary. In addition, precision reflects the expertise of the speaker or writer.

Some apparently precise terms, however, can be highly ambiguous. Many advertisements illustrate how technical words can confuse and mislead. For instance, a brand of skin care lotion advertises itself as "oxygen therapy," although all skin is constantly exposed to oxygen in the air, and no externally applied product can introduce oxygen into skin cells. Similar instances can be drawn from military jargon. "Collateral damage" in the Gulf War, for example, referred to Iraqi civilians killed unintentionally by missiles or bombs that missed their primary targets. In such a case, apparently precise terms turn out to be vague, even deceptive.

The persuasive advantages of vagueness are illustrated in many advertisements. Commercials tell us that a brand of heating and air conditioning is an "Rx prescription for home comfort," that we should "Just do it," that a particular makeup "acts like skin care," or that "X is more than a mouthwash." These are pseudoclaims, statements that sound like conclusions but assert nothing. What is a prescription for home comfort? What should we "just do"? What does it mean to "act like skin care" (like washing one's skin? like putting on lotion?)? More *what* than a mouthwash?[2] In these cases, imprecise statements are used as cues to suggest arguments to or evoke memories in viewers, and if the ads are successful, viewers participate to embellish these statements to create arguments—enthymemes—in their minds.

Some imprecision in language is inevitable. No word (except some proper nouns) refers to only one thing. The abstraction of language makes ambiguity inevitable. We need some vague terms such as middle-aged to refer to conditions that have no definite boundaries. We require the ambiguity of euphemism (substituting an inoffensive term, such as passed away or self-pleasuring, for ones considered offensively explicit) to deal with some highly controversial, emotionally charged subjects. We need figurative language to make concepts vivid and to enlarge the bases for comparison.

Stylistic precision is good for complex subjects and for exact proof. Precision implies that the rhetor is expert. The ambiguities of abstraction, euphemism, and figurative language are important resources for persuasion, but at the same time they open wide vistas for confusing, misleading, and deceiving audiences.[3]

Literalness

The style of a rhetorical act can vary in its use of figurative or metaphorical language. Figurative language grasps and defines the intangible qualities of experience. Such language can be used to explain or illustrate a difficult concept. Although it may not be verifiable, it involves another kind of precision—the vividness of immediate sensory experience. In a parody of the clichés mouthed to college graduates, Tom Lehrer wrote a song that told them, "Soon you'll be sliding down the razor blade of life." Such an image is painfully vivid.

Figurative language holds our attention. An ad headline says, "Rekindle your love affair with New York. Our new guide will provide a few sparks." If you've enjoyed New York City in the past, the metaphor may be enough to induce you to read the smaller print and, per-

---

[2]For almost 100 years, ads for Listerine claimed that the product prevented colds and sore throats. It does not. In 1977 the court upheld the Federal Trade Commission requirement that the next $10 million of Listerine's regular advertising include the corrective statement, "Listerine will not prevent colds or sore throats or lessen their severity" (*Warner-Lambert Co.* v. *FTC*, 562 F.2d 762 [1977]).

[3]See M. Lee Williams, "The Effect of Deliberate Vagueness on Receiver Recall and Agreement," *Central States Speech Journal* 31 (Spring 1980):30–41, for empirical evidence about the advantages and disadvantages of precision and vagueness.

haps, seek out the guide to help you to savor it even more. Like the figurative analogy, the metaphor connects what is known and familiar with what is unknown and unfamiliar.

Metaphors reflect attitudes. If life is a dance, it follows a pattern and is influenced by individual artistry. If life is a chess game, it is a competitive struggle of wits. If life is a crap game, it is ruled by chance. If "life is a banquet and most poor suckers are starving to death," as Patrick Dennis's Auntie Mame claimed, then it's time to dig in and eat up!

Metaphors evaluate. Sensory images express our values. Bad books are dry. A conservative refers to "hemophiliac" liberals bleeding for every cause; liberals, on the other hand, sometimes call conservatives heartless.

There is an ongoing tension between literal and figurative language in rhetorical action. Literal language is more precise and exact but is often less vivid and engaging. Literal language is part of accurate description and an effort to produce careful proof. Metaphorical language enlivens ideas and arouses participation. Rhetoric is made effective by both.

Redundancy

Style varies in its use of repetition or restatement. Advice to writers usually suggests that they aim for economy of language, avoiding wordiness and circumlocution. The amount of repetition needed depends on the complexity of the subject and argument and on the knowledge of the audience.

Oral style, whether in live public speeches or in radio and television commercials, differs from written style. Most commercials repeat their claims at least three times and usually many more. Highly creative ads restate their central ideas in several amusing ways, frequently in oral, visual, and nonverbal terms. All repeat the product's name many times over. Engaging ditties and the attractive faces and graceful or humorous actions of skilled actors help to relieve the monotony.

Oral style must be more redundant. Because you can reread material and pause to think between paragraphs, a writer need not repeat and restate, at least not as often. But listeners do not have such options. Accordingly, successful speaking requires internal summaries, transitions connecting ideas, repetition of the major steps in the argument, and the like. Such redundancy increases both comprehension and impact for listeners. Used in print, such devices become irritating under all but the most unusual circumstances.

No other quality so consistently distinguishes oral and written style. Both oral and written rhetoric range along the other dimensions. Both can be highly formal or informal. Both reflect the possibilities of precision and ambiguity, although formulations demanding the most precision appear in writing. Both exploit the possibilities of figurative language and require literal expression for careful proof. Because oral style is often related to informality, it is likely to be more personal, with greater use of personal pronouns. But the impersonality and formality of presidential addresses indicate that such qualities are not an inevitable part of oral discourse.

Evaluating Style

Good style is clear, vivid, appropriate, and consistent.

Clarity   To say that style has clarity is to say that it is immediately intelligible to the audience. There is no delay in understanding it; no translation is required. The vocabulary is familiar to the audience, the syntax meets the norms of listeners and readers, and the discourse develops according to a pattern that can be followed easily. The speech at the end of Chapter 9 is a good example of clarity of style. Obviously, if you write or speak on a technical subject, all of your language will not be immediately clear to most audiences, who will not be experts. The standard simply requires that unfamiliar terms and concepts be defined and illustrated so they can be understood by nonexperts or by members of the audience you are addressing. No rhetorical act can achieve its goals if it leaves the audience puzzled, confused, or at sea.

Vividness   Good style is vivid. It comes alive. It makes us see and hear and imagine and feel. It creates virtual experience. Vividness is essential to catch and hold the attention of the audience, a prerequisite to successful rhetorical action. It also speaks to the psychological dimension of proof—we must give assent, not just recognize facts. Vivid style depicts, dramatizes, personifies, and describes. It employs the resources of language to focus and emphasize, to make ideas memorable. Vivid style fills our eyes, noses, ears, and mouths with associations and enriches the connotations of words and ideas with sights, smells, sounds, tastes, and memories.

Appropriateness   Like all other elements of rhetorical action, style is contingent on the audience, subject and purpose, occasion, and rhetor. Your style should reflect the formality of the occasion and the seriousness of your purpose. It should be suitable for the complexity of the subject, and it should be adapted to the expertise and attitudes of the audience and to them as members of a linguistic community. Your style must be appropriate to you—to your expertise on the subject, to your relationship to the audience, and to the persona you present in this situation.

These statements reflect general admonitions to apply your analysis of the rhetorical problem to stylistic choices. The material for analysis sections at the end of most chapters provide models for rhetorical analysis; and the choices made by these specific speakers and writers should be used to refine these comments.

Consistency Good style is consistent. All elements fit together so that your discourse is a unified whole. Your language should reflect your tone, your persona, your purpose, and your relationship to the audience. Style may vary, but avoid contradictions among the elements of your rhetoric or major shifts in your perspective.

The importance of consistency should focus special attention on introductory statements. Opening lines establish tone and create expectations. As a result, stylistic choices made at the outset become important commitments for the statements that follow.

Strategies are one route by which speakers and writers achieve some of their stylistic goals.

STRATEGIES

A *strategy* is a plan of action, a maneuver designed to overcome the obstacles in a particular rhetorical situation. Strategies are part of rhetorical invention. They are discovered or found in your materials as you prepare for rhetorical action, and they are part of the creativity of your role as a rhetor. Strategies are used to cope with controversial and complex issues, with hostile and skeptical audiences, and with difficulties in establishing your credibility and expertise as a source.

Many of the resources already discussed can and should be used strategically. Evidence should be selected and presented strategically to speak to the audience, to refute competing persuaders, and to present your subject and perspective clearly. Each organizational pattern is a strategic way of unfolding a position. The arguments you select should be chosen strategically for the response you seek and the audience you want to reach. Introductions and conclusions are particularly important as strategic responses to the rhetorical problem. In the speeches and essays you analyze, consider how speakers and writers have used opening and closing statements to respond to the obstacles in a particular situation.

Despite the strategic character of most rhetorical choices, specific strategies are usually devices that exploit the capacities of language. Although their purposes overlap, strategies are designed to assist in proof, to make ideas vivid, and to create connotations. All strategies require participation by the audience and illustrate how rhetorical action is jointly constructed by rhetor and audience.

Strategies of Proof

Strategies of proof resemble or mimic logical arguments. Through the identification and participation of the audience, they invite the audience to provide material that will justify a claim or conclusion.

Rhetorical Question   A *rhetorical question* is a question to which no answer is expected or to which only one answer can be given. It is an idea put in the form of a question for greater effect. It is a question whose answer is known by the audience. Presidential campaigns often include rhetorical questions. In 1952, Dwight D. Eisenhower said, "The Democrats say you never had it so good. Do you want it any better?" That's a particularly effective rhetorical question because few people would answer no. But it was a highly strategic choice for Ike in this campaign. It allowed the audience to supply the defects of the Democrats so that the heroic leader of the allied forces in Europe in World War II did not have to stoop to making nasty charges. In 1980, Ronald Reagan asked, "Can anyone look at the record of this administration and say, 'Well done'? Can anyone compare the state of our economy when the Carter administration took office with where we are today and say, 'Keep up the good work'? Can anyone look at our reduced standing in the world today and say, 'Let's have four more years of this'?"[4] Once again, the questions need no answer. Note that they also presented Reagan as merely reminding us of what we all knew (the questions worked as enthymemes) rather than as making charges against a sitting president, and that the questions direct our

---

[4]"Acceptance Speech," *New York Times,* July 18, 1980, p. A8.

attention to economic and foreign policy issues, areas in which the Carter administration was particularly vulnerable because of high inflation and the Americans held hostage by the Iranians.

A Fortiori   *A fortiori* means "to the stronger." As an organizational strategy, it connects two claims so that if we accept the first, it becomes more likely we will accept the second. For example, if it can be shown that a politician betrayed a close friend who trusted him, it becomes more plausible that he would betray his constituents. Early in the contemporary women's movement, political scientist Jo Freeman wrote an essay designed to show the subtle forces at work that limit women's achievement by teaching women not to take risks or deviate from traditional patterns. She structured her essay following *a fortiori* principles. The opening sections of the essay document the history of discrimination against women in law, followed by sections that document the effects of socialization on women's ambition. If it can be shown that women are discriminated against overtly in law, it becomes much more plausible that they are discriminated against covertly in socialization. Again, the strategy aims at proof. Where arguments are in an *a fortiori* relationship, the claim in the second is made more likely by proof of the first.

Enumeration   A bill of particulars is specified, or a list of examples is provided. If this is done well, we are swamped with a mass of details, and each particular or example gains force from all those that have preceded it. In the essay referred to above, feminist Jo Freeman used enumeration as part of her proof to show the effects of socialization on women as reported in studies in the 1950s:

> To understand how most women are socialized we must first understand how they see themselves. . . . [one study] showed that women strongly felt themselves to be such things as uncertain, anxious, nervous, hasty, careless, fearful, dull, childish, helpless, sorry, timid, clumsy, stupid, silly, and domestic. On a more positive side women felt they were understanding, tender, sympathetic, pure, generous, affectionate, loving, moral, kind, grateful, and patient.[5]

---

[5]"The Building of the Gilded Cage," in Karlyn Kohrs Campbell, *Critiques of Contemporary Rhetoric* (Belmont, CA: Wadsworth, 1972), p. 165. The study cited was that by Edward M. Bennett and Larry R. Cohen, "Men and Women: Personality Patterns and Contrasts," *Genetic Psychology Monographs* 59 (1959):101–155.

This long list of adjectives functions strategically to overwhelm us with evidence of the negative attitudes women have had toward themselves. Note, however, that the list works only if you see these self-descriptions negatively. If these are qualities you believe desirable in a "true woman," then the strategy will fail. Note that the lists in the sermon found at the end of this chapter are examples of enumeration, and Fred Craddock's efforts to make those lists come alive should alert you to potential problems arising out of the use of lists.

Refutation   Answering and rebutting the arguments of the opposition is one of the commonest but most important strategies. In an organizational pattern that examines pro and con arguments, it can work strategically to answer questions in the minds of the audience and to inoculate them against competing persuaders. One form of refutation, however, deserves special mention. *Debunking* refutes opposing positions by making fun of exaggerated claims. Debunking is a process of deflating pretense, of shrinking opposing arguments to their "proper" size. It is often done through names that serve as labels. For example, a public speaking text addresses the problems of using slang and jargon, and the authors write:

> The observations about the use of slang apply also to the use of the special terminology and jargon of, let us say, sports commentators, the entertainment world as represented in the publication *Variety,* and such cults as the libbers and the discotheque enthusiasts.[6]

Feminists are being debunked as "libbers" and as extremists and fanatics (a cult). That it is feminists who are being debunked is most evident if we rewrite the paragraph to make the style consistent: "the special terminology and jargon of, let us say, sports jockeys, show biz gossip, and such cults as the libbers and disco freaks." Now each group is treated with equal informality, and all are debunked by unflattering labels.

Once again, note that the strategy depends on the beholder. The strategy is most evident to feminists who resent such chummy labels and is least evident to those who share the authors' views. Note that the list of examples also functions as enumeration.

---

[6]Donald C. Bryant and Karl R. Wallace, *Fundamentals of Public Speaking,* 5th ed. (Englewood Cliffs, NJ: Prentice-Hall, 1976), pp. 320–321.

Definition   Those with experience in debate quickly learn that definitions are strategic. Definitions are critical elements in determining just what must be proved in order to establish a claim. The dialectical definitions discussed earlier are also examples of strategic definitions. Definitions explain highly abstract terms, and they are often used in an attempt to change the perceptions of the audience. Bernice Sandler, for example, used this strategy in a 1991 speech at Illinois State University in Normal to explain the meaning of an unfamiliar and technical sociological term.

> At a very early age, boys learn to use girls as what the sociologists call a "negative reference group." In other words, the boys define themselves by comparing themselves favorably to girls, the lesser group, the females. After all, what is the worst thing you can call a little boy? A sissy—which means he is acting like a girl. By teasing girls a boy begins to feel good about himself—he is better than they are, and teasing them makes him feel like a "real boy." Moreover, by putting down girls and females he can get closer to his buddies. They can all put down the girls, and feel better and bigger than the girls. Harassment, and even sexual assault, can be, for many men, the way in which they show other men how "manly" they really are. We see this in its extreme in the case of gang rape, where psychologists have noted that the men are not raping for sexual reasons but are really raping for each other. This is how they show their friends how strong, how virile, how manly, how wonderful they really are.[7]

Sandler's statement combines a number of strategies. It defines by enumerating the various activities that illustrate the meaning of the phrase "negative reference group." The illustrations are arranged in a *climax construction* that works from the least to the most harmful manifestation, from teasing girls to gang-raping them. The phrase, its definition, and the illustrations are all part of an effort to demonstrate the harmful effects of sexism in our society and to make us more willing to intervene to prevent the earliest indications of such attitudes among boys. Note that the final sentence uses the terms strong, virile, manly, and wonderful in a sarcastic way.

---

[7]Bernice Sandler, "Men and Women Getting Along: These Are the Times That Try Men's Souls," in *Contemporary American Speeches*, 7th ed., ed. Richard L. Johannesen, R. R. Allen, and Wil A. Linkugel (Dubuque, IA: Kendall/Hunt, 1992), pp. 228–229.

Other strategies aid the rhetor in making arguments and substantiating claims, but these are the most important. These examples should illustrate the nature of these strategies and that strategies appear in combination and depend on the participation of the audience.

Strategies to Animate and Vivify

Nearly all strategies catch and hold attention and, in that sense, make ideas more vivid. But some strategies have this as their chief function. They are intended to make people and events come alive before our eyes, to create virtual experience by allowing us to see and hear and feel what the rhetor is talking about.

Description   Providing the detail that makes a scene or person come alive before our eyes is the function of description. It creates the sensation that you are there watching events as they occur. An editorial by physician Mark DePaolis describes in detail a videotape of the procedures involved in liposuction, with narration, to warn readers about this method of removing fat from thighs or abdomen. According to his report of the videotape, after areas of the patient's body are marked for removal,

> a sharp metal tube like a curtain rod is inserted under the skin, and "the powerful suction machine is turned on." . . . Suffice it to say that the tube is moved back and forth in "a piston-like motion" to suck up the fat. . . . Meanwhile, the patient's skin, which has evidently grown accustomed to those fat deposits, is putting up a valiant fight to keep them. This requires several burly assistants to keep the patient on the table while the surgeon works. . . . In the next hideous scene, as the narrator puts it, "fat can be seen moving through the transparent tube. . . . No more than 2,000 ccs are removed at any one time," the doctor says finally, showing us what looks like an extremely heavy two-liter soda bottle. . . . The tube is removed, the incision is sewn shut, and several miles of gauze is wrapped around the patient. This is to hide the fact that her thighs now look like gallons of ice cream with one scoop taken out. . . .
>
> After seeing this tape, "liposuction" has moved to the top of my "don't do" list, underlined and with several added stars.[8]

---

[8]Mark DePaolis, "A Power-Tool Approach to Weight Loss," [Mpls.] *Star Tribune,* July 16, 1993, p. 19A.

Note that the description incorporates figurative analogies ("like a curtain rod"; "piston-like"; "like gallons of ice cream with one scoop taken out") and emotive language that reflects his reaction ("suffice it to say"; "hideous"). He also personifies the skin over the fatty deposits, which he describes as "putting up a valiant fight" not to have the fat removed, a struggle intensified by describing the assistants who are holding the patient down as "burly." He translates the statistic 2,000 ccs by explaining that that amount would fill a two-liter bottle of soda. These details help to create virtual reality and, he hopes, deter us from considering this procedure.

Dr. Helen Broinowski Caldicott, a founder of the group Physicians for Social Responsibility, was a nuclear freeze activist, whose work for a freeze culminated rhetorically with "This Beautiful Planet," the annual Phi Beta Kappa oration, delivered during Commencement Week of 1981 to an audience of 700 in Sanders Theatre at Harvard University. *Harvard Magazine* called the speech "powerful" and "chilling" (July–August 1981:50, 52, 53). Based on a series of articles published in the *New England Journal of Medicine,* she described the horrors of nuclear war in vivid detail, as adapted to a Cambridge, Massachusetts, audience:

> A 20-megaton bomb is equal to 20 million tons of TNT. That is four times the collective size of all bombs dropped during the Second World War. It is a small sun. It explodes with the heat of the sun. It will do this to Boston: It will carve out a crater about half a mile to a mile wide and 300 feet deep. . . . Every human being within a radius of six miles from the hypocenter will be vaporized. . . . Concrete and steel will burn. Out to a radius of 20 miles, most people will be dead. . . . If you happen to glance at the blast from 35–40 miles away, the flash would instantly burn the retina and blind you. It will create a firestorm of 15,000 to 30,000 square miles . . . creating a holocaust fanned by hurricane winds, so if you were in a fallout shelter, you would be pressure-cooked and asphyxiated as the fire used all the oxygen.[9]

Dr. Caldicott uses descriptive language to make statistics vivid and real. The literal analogy to the bombs dropped in World War II helps us to grasp the existential size of a 20-megaton bomb. The figurative analogy to a small sun gives a sense of its brightness, which is heightened by her description of what would happen should a person be

---

[9]"This Beautiful Planet," Phi Beta Kappa Oration. In *Speak Out,* ed. Herbert Vetter. Boston: Beacon Press, 1992:85–93.

unfortunate enough to look at the blast even from a distance of over 30 miles away. It is plausible that there would be a firestorm, like that seen during powerful forest fires, that would cover many square miles. Its power and devastation are heightened by comparing the winds to those in a hurricane, and the lack of safety in a fallout shelter is made vivid by the analogy to what happens to food in a pressure cooker and the reminder of how much oxygen such a fire would consume. Here description serves primarily to dramatize the size and impact of a catastrophic event.

Another function of description is shown in an earlier event. A great deal of controversy was aroused when the Walker Report labeled the behavior of Chicago police officers at the 1968 Democratic National Convention as a "police riot." Most Americans view police officers as helpful protectors and believe that if they misbehave, they must have been provoked. In combatting such attitudes, the Walker Report used eyewitness accounts such as this one to describe the kinds of confrontations that occurred between Chicago police and antiwar demonstrators:

A federal legal official relates an experience of Tuesday evening.

I then walked one block north where I met a group of 12–15 policemen. I showed them my identification and they permitted me to walk with them. The police walked one block west. Numerous people were watching us from their windows and balconies. The police yelled profanities at them, taunting them to come down where the police would beat them up. The police stopped a number of people on the street demanding identification. They verbally abused each pedestrian and pushed one or two without hurting them. We walked back to Clark Street and began to walk north, where the police stopped a number of people who appeared to be protesters and ordered them out of the area in a very abusive way. One protester who was walking in the opposite direction was kneed in the groin by a policeman who was walking toward him. The boy fell to the ground and swore at the policeman, who picked him up and threw him to the ground. We continued to walk toward the command post. A derelict, who appeared to be very intoxicated, walked up to the policeman and mumbled something that was incoherent. The policeman pulled from his belt a tin container and sprayed its contents into the eyes of the derelict, who stumbled around and fell on his face.[10]

---

[10]Daniel Walker, "A Summary of the Walker Report," in *Counterpoint: Dialogue for the 70s,* ed. Conn McAuliffe (Philadelphia: J. B. Lippincott, 1970), p. 153.

This instance illustrates the convergence of evidence and strategy. The cited material is testimony (an eyewitness account) that provides a series of examples of police behavior. Because the eyewitness is described as "a federal legal official," his observations shift toward authority evidence rather than mere testimony: He may be competent to judge what is improper behavior, and his status gives his report greater credibility. But it is the descriptive details that give this evidence its force. The police "yell," "taunt," "abuse," and "push." As described, the attack on the "boy" is wholly unprovoked, and because it is an attack on a *boy,* it is doubly offensive (note that the police officer's ability to pick him up and throw him to the ground lends credence to this label). The description gives us the sense of walking down the street with this group and watching what occurs. We come to see the events as the observer does and to judge them, unfavorably, with him. Such descriptions are particularly effective ways to induce readers to participate in creating the proofs by which they are persuaded. Note that these are the verbal counterparts of the visual images from Somalia, Bosnia, and Rwanda that have horrified Americans and energized efforts to aid the suffering.

Depiction is an intensified form of description. To represent in picture or sculpture or to portray in detail is what *depiction* literally means. It is a particularly vivid form of description, and it usually involves dramatization, presenting material as a story, a drama of characters in conflict. If successful, it should create virtual experience. Woman suffragist Anna Howard Shaw used detailed examples in refuting arguments of antisuffragists. In a speech delivered in New York in 1915, for instance, she responded to the argument that if women voted, it would cause conflict and destroy happy homes. In her words:

> Then they will tell you all the trouble that happens in the home. A gentleman told me that in California,—and while he was talking I had a wonderful thing pass through my mind, because he said he and his wife had lived together for 20 years and never had a difference of opinion in the whole 20 years, and he was afraid if women began to vote that his wife would vote differently from him and then that beautiful harmony which they had had for 20 years would be broken, and all the time he was talking I could not help wondering which was the idiot,—because I knew that no intelligent human beings could live together for 20 years and not have differences in opinion. All the time he was talking I looked at that splendid type of manhood and thought, how would a man feel being tagged up by a little woman for 20 years saying, "me too, me too." I would not want

to live in a house with a human being for twenty hours who agreed with everything I said. The stagnation of a frog pond would be hilarious compared to that. . . . Now it may be that the kind of men . . . that the antisuffragists live with is that kind, but they are not the kind we live with and we could not do it. Great big overgrown babies! Cannot be disputed without having a row! While we do not believe that men are saints, by any means, we do believe that the average American man is a fairly good sort of fellow.[11]

The overall strategy is refutation of the argument that voting will cause friction between spouses. To do so, she tells the story in some detail of a particular man who raised this objection so that her listeners can assess the objection in a particular case. This depiction is rather unusual, because it also includes a description of what goes on in Shaw's mind as she listens to what he says, through which she invites us to join her in treating this objection as absurd, and she dramatizes that absurdity by imagining the wife going around after the husband saying, "me too, me too." The comments following the story are important because the depiction of this man is an effort to isolate him, to present him as a special case, quite unlike other men who can tolerate differences of opinion without starting a row. Isolating this man as unusual allows Shaw to help to create the audience of male agents of change that she must persuade in order to obtain the ballot for women. Consider how pleasing it must be for men to see themselves as she describes them and how effective this must have been in creating a role that her male auditors would have been happy to play, a role that would make them more likely to support suffrage. She not only refutes but also debunks fears about political conflicts between spouses as unrealistic, which is more effective as the story she tells is real, not hypothetical. Note, too, that strategies often come in groups. Depiction here includes refutation, a figurative analogy, and an effort to create the audience—to invite them to see themselves in ways that are helpful to her purpose. The example also is a vivid case of Shaw's ability to use humor that debunked her opposition while making them laugh. Finally, this example is from a stenographic record of a stump speech, and the informal style and the small grammatical errors reflect its extemporaneous delivery and its orality.

---

[11]Anna Howard Shaw, "The Fundamental Principle of a Republic," in *Man Cannot Speak for Her: Key Texts of the Early Feminists,* ed. K. K. Campbell (Westport, CT: Greenwood Press, 1989), 2:451.

The most famous example of depiction in rhetorical literature occurs in a speech by Senator Daniel Webster of Massachusetts given in reply to Senator Robert Y. Hayne of South Carolina in 1830. The crux of the debate was the issue of slavery and the power of the federal government to regulate it. Hayne advocated state nullification, that is, that states should have the right to nullify acts of the federal government, and Webster argued that this doctrine must inevitably lead to war. But Webster chose to make his case not through logical argument but through depicting what must happen if a state should nullify a federal law. He uses the tariff law and nullification by South Carolina as his example:

> We will take the existing case of the tariff law. South Carolina is said to have made up her opinion upon it. . . . She will, we must suppose, pass a law of her legislature, declaring the several acts of Congress, usually called the tariff laws, null and void, so far as they respect South Carolina, or the citizens thereof. So far, all is a paper transaction, and easy enough.

(At this point, Webster has set the scene for his depiction.)

> But the collector at Charleston is collecting the duties imposed by these tariff laws. He, therefore, must be stopped. The collector will seize the goods if the tariff duties are not paid. The State authorities will undertake their rescue, the marshal, with his posse, will come to the collector's aid, and here the contest begins.

(The depiction includes a drama, and Webster prepares us for conflict.)

> The militia of the State will be called out to sustain the nullifying act. They will march, Sir, under a very gallant leader; for I believe the honorable member [Hayne] himself commands the militia of that part of the State. He will raise the nullifying act on his standard, and spread it out as his banner! It will have a preamble, setting forth, that the tariff laws are palpable, deliberate, and dangerous violations of the Constitution! He will proceed, with his banner flying, to the custom-house in Charleston,
>
> > All the while,
> > Sonorous metal blowing martial sounds.

Arrived at the custom-house, he will tell the collector that he must collect no more duties under any of the tariff laws. . . . But, Sir, the collector would not, probably, desist, at his bidding. He would show him the law of Congress, the treasury instruction, and his own oath of office. He would say, he should perform his duty, come what might.

Here would ensue a pause; for they say that a certain stillness precedes the tempest. The trumpeter would hold his breath awhile, and before all this military array should fall on the custom-house, collector, clerks, and all, it is very probable some of those composing it would request of their gallant commander-in-chief to be informed a little upon the point of law; for they have, doubtless, a just respect for his opinions as a lawyer, as well as for his bravery as a soldier. . . . They would inquire, whether it was not somewhat dangerous to resist a law of the United States. What would be the nature of their offense, they would wish to learn, if they, by military force and array, resisted the execution in Carolina of a law of the United States, and it should turn out, after all, that the law was constitutional? He would answer, of course, Treason. No lawyer could give any other answer. . . . How, then, they would ask, do you propose to defend us? We are not afraid of bullets, but treason has a way of taking people off that we do not much relish. How do you propose to defend us? "Look at my floating banner," he would reply; "see there the nullifying law!" Is it your opinion, gallant commander, they would then say, that, if we should be indicted for treason, that same floating banner of yours would make a good plea in bar? "South Carolina is a sovereign State," he would reply. That is true; but would the judge admit our plea? "These tariff laws," he would repeat, "are unconstitutional, palpably, deliberately, dangerously." That may all be so; but if the tribunal should not happen to be of that opinion, shall we swing for it? . . .

Mr. President, the honorable gentleman would be in dilemma, like that of another great general. He would have a knot before him which he could not untie. He must cut it with his sword. He must say to his followers, "Defend yourselves with your bayonets"; and this is war,—civil war.[12]

This excerpt from Webster's speech is justly famous as an outstanding example of the depiction of a hypothetical encounter, and like many

---

[12]Daniel Webster, "Reply to Hayne," in *Famous Speeches in American History,* ed. Glenn R. Capp (Indianapolis: Bobbs-Merrill, 1963), pp. 57–58.

strategies, it combines animation and demonstration. As proof, it spells out the consequences of Hayne's position, but the proof depends on the plausibility of the scene for the listener. It is highly effective refutation that shows that, contrary to Hayne, state nullification means civil war. The humor of the depiction serves to debunk Hayne's position, to reduce it to absurdity. Webster also uses an allusion to the story of Alexander the Great cutting the Gordian knot as a figurative analogy to illustrate that Hayne's position must end in violence. Webster's depiction is structured as a drama. He sets the scene, presents characters, sets forth the conflict, presents the dialogue between Hayne and his militia, and even provides the theatrical spectacle of banners and trumpets. The conflict within the doctrine, dramatized in the dialogue, escalates to a climax, which is followed by a denouement that draws his conclusion: "This is war,—civil war."

The detail Webster provides is worth noting. The marshall and his posse, supporting the federal customs collector, confront Hayne and the state militia. The acts of the collector are detailed. The dialogue between Hayne and the militiamen spells out the internal contradiction in Hayne's position.

Webster might easily have chosen to set forth these consequences in a logical argument, but depicting this scene animated his claim, a process that was essential if civil war was to be averted. He attempted to create virtual experience, to allow his audience to imagine a scene in all its detail so they would perceive, in human terms, the results of Hayne's position.

Personification and Visualization   Closely allied to description and depiction are the strategies of personification and visualization. Personification represents an object or an abstract idea as if it were a human being or had human capacities. Advertisers personify products as characters or cartoon figures, such as the Energizer bunny or "scrubbing bubbles." The longevity of a battery or the power and gentleness of a cleaning agent cannot be seen or experienced directly. The strategy of personification attempts to overcome this problem. Visualization puts an idea into visual form. A long-running series of commercials showed someone drinking a glass of iced tea and then falling backward into a swimming pool. The ad visualized what you might experience if you drank a glass of cold, refreshing iced tea.

Enactment   When there is *enactment* the speaker or writer is proof of the claim that she or he is making. Enactment is both proof and a way to present evidence vividly. For example, Rep. Barbara Jordan gave the keynote address at the Democratic National Convention in 1976. In her speech she said, "And I feel that, notwithstanding the past, my presence here is one additional piece of evidence that the American dream need not forever be deferred."[13] That she, an African American woman, had achieved the stature to be asked to give the address was proof that minorities and women can reach the highest levels of achievement in the United States. A similar move was made by Geraldine Ferraro in her nomination acceptance address in 1988 and in Ruth Bader Ginsburg's speech at the end of Chapter 6. Enactment is powerful evidence because members of the audience see and hear the evidence for themselves, directly. The references to the mob in Angelina Grimké Weld's 1838 speech, quoted later in this chapter, are another example. This form of proof is particularly vivid—it is alive in front of and around the audience!

Other Animating Strategies   Alliteration, assonance, rhyme, and rhythm are some of the ways of arranging words so that ideas and phrases become more vivid and memorable. *Alliteration* is the repetition of initial consonants, a strategy advertisements and speeches use effectively. In a speech urging adoption of his budget on August 3, 1993, President Clinton spoke of opponents of his plan as "guardians of gridlock." Columnist William Safire, a former White House speechwriter well known for using alliteration, commented, "I would have added an alliterative advance adjective 'grim' to convey a full nattering-nabob-of-negativism flavor," noting that current speechwriters are more restrained."[14]

Assonance is the repetition of a vowel sound, and it produces a kind of rhyme. In his inaugural address, for example, John F. Kennedy spoke of "the steady spread of the deadly atom." The repetition made the phrase memorable, and the creeping vowel seemed to mirror the creeping danger. Actual rhymes occur less frequently in both oral and written rhetoric. Interesting contemporary examples appear in the speeches of Jesse Jackson, who said to Alabama State legislators:

> If our people can learn to play together on the ball field and die together on the battlefield, then we can teach them the value of turning to each other to improve their economic and social conditions, rather than turning on each other in racial and economic hostility. Right here in the legislature, we must elevate

---

[13]*New York Times,* July 15, 1976, p. A26.
[14]*New York Times,* August 5, 1993, p. A15. Safire was the author of the line "nattering nabobs of negativism," which was used in a 1969 speech by then–Vice President Spiro Agnew to characterize those who opposed the Vietnam War.

people from the battleground, find a common ground, and then move to a higher ground.[15]

Such rhymes not only make ideas vivid, but they also work to change the attitudes of the reader. Michael Kinsley, a political commentator, wrote, "that Bob Dole rushes to accuse Democrats of 'appealing to religious bigotry' suggests that there is more cheap political advantage to be gained from kissing Christians than dissing them."[16] Note that such rhymes appear in popular rap songs and in raps used in advertisements, suggesting their power to engage us and be memorable.

Parallelism is a strategy that creates rhythm in prose. It can also enhance the precision of language and create an impression that the rhetor thinks in a very orderly fashion. Perhaps the most famous example is the repeated "I have a dream . . ." in Dr. Martin Luther King, Jr.'s, famous speech of that name. Like King's speech, it may take the form of a series of sentences or paragraphs, all of which begin with the same phrase. For example, in his inaugural address, John F. Kennedy addressed his statements, "To those old allies, . . . To those new states, . . . To those peoples in the huts, . . . To our sister republics . . ." He began each of his statements addressed to adversaries with the phrase, "Let both sides . . ." Such parallelism creates patterns that are easy for listeners to follow, and such patterns help fix ideas in our minds. They are particularly well suited to oral rhetoric.

Parallelism can also create contrast and emphasis. *Antithesis* is a kind of parallelism that contrasts one idea with another. Two examples in contemporary speeches have proved particularly memorable. In 1960 John F. Kennedy said, "Ask not what your country can do for you: Ask what you can do for your country." In 1964 Barry Goldwater accepted the Republican nomination for the presidency and said, "I would remind you that extremism in the defense of liberty is no vice! And let me remind you also that moderation in the pursuit of justice is no virtue!" Republican strategist William Kristol rang a change on this in 1994 when he said of health care reform, "We should make clear now that there will be no deal. 'Obstructionism,' when it comes to protecting our health care system, is no vice."[17] As these examples illustrate, rhetoric builds on prior rhetoric,

---

[15]"From Battleground to Common Ground to Higher Ground," by the Rev. Jesse L. Jackson before a joint session of the Alabama State Legislature, Montgomery, May 24, 1983. News release from PUSH.

[16]*New York Times,* July 5, 1994, p. A15.

[17]*New York Times,* July 3, 1994, p. E3.

and the memorable antithesis remains a resource. Antitheses juxtapose two ideas, and the contrast not only defines the speaker's position more clearly, it animates it with emphasis.

Climax constructions are also a form of parallelism. In a *climax construction*, repetition builds to a high point of excitement or tension, a climax. For example, consider the climax created in Angelina Grimké Weld's 1838 speech in Pennsylvania Hall, Philadelphia, delivered to abolitionists who could hear the yells of a mob that surrounded the building as stones were being thrown through the windows:

> What is a mob? What would the breaking of every window be? What would the leveling of this hall be? Any evidence that we are wrong, or that slavery is a good and wholesome institution? What if the mob should now burst in upon us, break up our meeting and commit violence upon our persons—would this be anything compared to what the slaves endure? No, no: and we do not remember them "as bound with them," if we shrink in the time of peril, or feel unwilling to sacrifice ourselves, if need be, for their sake. (*Great noise.*) I thank the Lord that there is yet life left enough to feel the truth, even though it rages at it—that conscience is not so completely seared as to be unmoved by the truth of the living God.

Many strategies are at work here, of which a climax construction is only one, but one of great importance. The speaker begins by asking a question that suggests that a mob is a trifling thing, relatively unimportant, but the questions that follow steadily raise the cost of remaining in the hall and fearlessly demonstrating a commitment to antislavery. The questions refer to real possibilities—stones had already been thrown through the windows, and that night the hall would be burned to the ground by their opponents. Surely every person there felt the threat and longed to escape. Yet the speaker argues that even that would not prove anything about their cause. Her next question raises the possibility that the worst will happen, that the mob will breach the doors and beat or kill them, but even that becomes nothing when compared to what the slaves whom they seek to free must suffer. She answers her rhetorical question and appeals to the strong religious values of the abolitionists by quoting from the Bible (Hebrews 13:3) a verse that reaffirms the identification of Christians with those who are oppressed. Finally, she reinterprets the threat of mob violence as evidence of their success, that their efforts have pricked the consciences of slavery advocates. Hence, the very threat that should drive them away becomes proof of the rightness and success of their cause. The biblical material is, of course, allusion; a rhetorical question is part of the climax construction, and the series of questions develop the climax through parallelism. Finally, of course, the actions of the mob function as enactment, as the immediate and experienced proof of what she is saying.

In his speech to the 1978 midterm Democratic convention, Senator Edward Kennedy argued that Democrats "are the heirs of a great tradition in American public life." He supported that statement and then used it to call for passage of national health insurance based on this climax construction:

Our party took up the cause of jobs for the unemployed in the Great Depression. Our party took up the cause of civil rights for black and brown Americans and the cause of equal rights for women in America and the people of the District of Columbia. And in that same tradition of leadership it is time for the Democratic Party to take up the cause of health.

Notice how the strategy seems to make this outcome inevitable. If audience members accept the great traditions of the past, they must commit themselves to this policy, which is an extension of it.

Finally, recall that parallelism also appears in patterns of organization. Ideally, main points in an essay or speech will be stated in parallel form so that major ideas will stand out for the reader or listener.

Once again, these are only some of the strategies that can be used to make ideas vivid. Sources cited at the end of the chapter will lead you to more extended discussions of such devices.

Strategies to Change Connotations

The strategies described in this section are directed at our attitudes. They are attempts to change associations so that we will become more positive or negative toward an idea or position. Successful rhetorical action changes verbal behavior. Our speech reflects our perceptions, understandings, and attitudes, and if these change, our speech will change. But the reverse is also true: If we change the way we talk, changes in perception and attitude will follow.

The preceding statement is highly controversial, although the protest movements of Blacks and Chicanos illustrate the power of a name change to mobilize a social movement.[18] The argument is at the heart of disputes over whether the pronoun "he" or the word "man" can function generically to include both men and women. Feminists present examples to show that they cannot, as in "Man, being a mammal, breast-feeds his young." Or "All men are mortal; Sophie is a man; therefore, Sophie is mortal." They also argue that shifts in words, such as the use of chair or chairperson, and in pronouns, "s/he" or "he and she," raise consciousness about the sexism of our society.[19] In all these cases, all the parties involved behave as if the words we use are very, very important.

Labeling   The commonest strategy used to alter attitudes is labeling, and it is often related to debunking. A label is a name or epithet chosen to characterize a person or thing. For example, one conservative, referring to Ronald Reagan's choice of George Bush as a running mate, said that Reagan sounded like Winston Churchill but behaved like Neville Chamberlain. Former British prime minister Winston Churchill is recalled as a great leader who rallied Britons during World War II with his stirring words. Conversely, because of the Munich agreement in which he attempted to prevent a war by appeasing Adolf Hitler, former British Prime Minister Chamberlain has become a symbol of compromise and betrayal. By associating Reagan's choice of Bush with Chamberlain's compromise at Munich, we are asked to view it unfavorably. In this case, the labels are also historical allusions. As the example illustrates, labels work by creating associations.

At the beginning of the early woman's rights movement of the nineteenth century, women activists were told that if they spoke in public, they would be "unsexed," that is, they would lose their femininity. In the 1960s, at the beginning of the contemporary women's movement, women activists were called lesbians or dykes, once again implying that women who sought to improve their status were not feminine. These are powerful attacks because success for women has been defined as attracting a male and marrying, which presumably places a high value on traditional femininity. Even those contemporary advertisements that show women in settings outside the home continue to

---

[18]See Karlyn Kohrs Campbell, "The Rhetoric of Radical Black Nationalism," *Central States Speech Journal* 22 (Fall 1971):151–160; Richard J. Jensen and John C. Hammerback, "Radical Nationalism among Chicanos: The Rhetoric of José Angel Gutierrez," *Western Journal of Speech Communication* 44 (Summer 1980):191–202.

[19]See, for example, Wendy Martyna, "Beyond the 'He/Man' Approach: The Case for Nonsexist Language," *Signs: Journal of Women in Culture and Society* 5 (Spring 1980):482–493.

reinforce the beauty myth, present women as sex objects, and show women primarily in the role of mother, all of which reinforce traditional concepts of femininity.[20] Accordingly, being attacked as unfeminine is a strong deterrent to feminist identification and activism.

Slogans   Labels expanded become slogans. They are highly effective because they condense into a single phrase or sentence a whole world of beliefs and feelings. This power to sum up is illustrated in phrases such as "the American dream," "the personal is political," "black is beautiful," and "rugged individualism." Phrases like these are powerful unifiers because, although individuals have their own ideas of just what they mean, the level of abstraction is such that disputes over meaning are avoided.[21] Because of their broad appeal, they are especially attractive to advertisers and politicians who seek to reach the widest possible audiences. An effective slogan draws together a whole world of ideas in a short, cleverly expressed phrase or sentence. Advertisers seek such catchphrases: "The un-cola." "Just do it." "Everything you always wanted in a beer. And less." Every political campaign manager tries to find such a slogan because, in a short, memorable phrase, it can sum up many associations and evoke strong reactions.

Metaphors   Many labels and slogans are also metaphors. Figurative language not only makes ideas vivid, but it also changes our attitudes toward them, and it clarifies meaning. A particularly famous example comes from the speech Booker T. Washington made at the Atlanta Exposition in 1895. Washington, an African American, tried to allay the hostility of whites while urging them to support the economic and educational development of his people. The metaphor he used illustrates how metaphors can clarify, vivify, and change connotations. He said, "In all things that are purely social we can be as separate as the fingers, yet one as the hand in all things essential to mutual progress."[22]

In his famous "I Have a Dream" speech of 1964, Dr. Martin Luther King, Jr., translated the issues of civil rights into terms every listener could understand. He said, "In a sense we have come to our nation's

---

[20]M. A. Masse and K. Rosenblum, "Male and Female Created They Them: The Depiction of Gender in the Advertising of Traditional Women's and Men's Magazines," *Women's Studies International Forum* 11 (1988):127–144.

[21]Murray Edelman, *The Symbolic Uses of Politics* (Chicago: Markham, 1971), pp. 6–11, discusses the powerful role of condensation symbols in political rhetoric.

[22]Booker T. Washington, "Atlanta Exposition Address," in *Famous Speeches in American History,* ed. Glenn Capp (New York: Bobbs-Merrill, 1963), 115.

Capitol to cash a check. When the architects of our republic wrote the magnificent words of the Constitution and the Declaration of Independence, they were signing a promissory note to which every American was to fall heir. . . . Instead of honoring this sacred obligation, America has given the Negro people a bad check, a check which has come back marked 'insufficient funds.' But we refuse to believe that the bank of justice is bankrupt."[23] The idea of civil rights is abstract, and many statements about it were known and familiar (cultural history). The imagery King used made the abstract concrete and familiar to all his hearers, yet the metaphor was original, making his appeal fresh and vivid.

Allusion   Closely related to metaphors are allusions to items from our shared cultural knowledge, such as references to history, the Bible, Greek and Roman mythology, Shakespeare's plays or other works of literature, or to elements of popular culture such as television programs, films, comic books, or national advertising. James N. Rowe used allusions to describe the conditions of prisoners of war in Vietnam:

> It is not the *Hogan's Heroes* concept that many people have, because in South Vietnam and in North Vietnam, we found that an American prisoner of war is not a military prisoner, he is a political prisoner. . . . The American prisoners find themselves being manipulated and being made more pliable by Communists using principles that we have read about in Koestler's *Darkness at Noon,* perhaps in *1984.*[24]

In this case, Rowe is struggling with the cultural history of a subject that has been distorted by a television program that portrayed prison camp life in World War II in humorous terms. Rather than merely describing conditions, Rowe uses allusions to two powerful novels of tor-

---

[23]"I Have A Dream. . . ." in *Selected Speeches from American History,* ed. Robert T. Oliver and Eugene E. White (Boston: Allyn and Bacon, 1966), pp. 291–292.

[24]James N. Rowe, "An American Prisoner of War in South Vietnam," in *Contemporary American Speeches,* 7th ed., ed. Richard L. Johannesen, R. R. Allen, and Wilmer Linkugel (Dubuque, IA: Kendall Hunt, 1992), p. 48. Arthur Koestler wrote *Darkness at Noon,* a grim novel about the moral struggles of an idealistic revolutionary who is persuaded to confess to crimes against the state that he did not commit. George Orwell wrote *1984,* a satirical novel set in a totalitarian state of the future in which propaganda replaces information and historical records are destroyed, making the search for truth impossible. Thought and love are punished; there is no privacy because "Big Brother" is always watching.

ture and oppression as a kind of shorthand to suggest the grim conditions prisoners faced.

Biblical materials are also a common source of allusion. Such materials are frequently used to demonstrate that God is on our side or that we are doing God's will. In defending U.S. involvement in Vietnam, for example, Richard Nixon said, "Let historians not record that when America was the most powerful nation in the world we passed on the other side of the road and allowed the last hopes for peace and freedom of millions of people on this earth to be suffocated by the forces of totalitarianism."[25] The allusion is to the story of the good Samaritan, and it was intended to convince us that in Vietnam we were behaving as good neighbors.

Allusions can be used to perform acts that would not be acceptable to an audience if they were done directly and explicitly. Most audiences, for example, do not take kindly to being threatened. Yet, in what is surely one of the most controversial of all Fourth of July addresses, in 1852 the African American abolitionist orator Frederick Douglass used the story of Samson in Judges 16:23–30 to threaten the audience:

> The Fourth of July is yours, not mine. You may rejoice, I must mourn. To drag a man in fetters into the grand illuminated temple of liberty, and call upon him to join you in joyous anthems, were inhuman mockery and sacrilegious irony. Do you mean, citizens, to mock me by asking me to speak today? If so, there is a parallel to your conduct. And let me warn you that it is dangerous to copy the example of a nation whose crimes, towering up to heaven, were thrown down by the breath of the Almighty, burying that nation in irrevocable ruin![26]

If you know the story of Samson (stripped of his prodigious strength by the cutting of his hair, captured by the Philistines, blinded, taken to Gaza, brought to the temple for sport on the feast day of their god Dagon, praying for strength, pulling down the temple, and killing more Philistines in death than he had in life), there are powerful parallels between it and the situation of Frederick Douglass on July 5, 1852 (He spoke on this date as a protest.). If you do not know the

---

[25]Speech delivered November 3, 1969, *Congressional Record*, Vol. 115, Part 24, pp. 32784–32786.

[26]*The Frederick Douglass Papers, Series One: Speeches, Debates, Interviews, Volume 2: 1847–54*, ed. John W. Blassingame (New Haven, CT: Yale University Press, 1982), pp. 359–388. Cited material, p. 368.

story, you may not recognize the allusion, much less feel its impact. Allusions work only if the audience recognizes them and can fill in the necessary details. Biblical allusions are powerful if they are familiar, because our culture is Judeo-Christian, and many persons accept the Bible as the word of God. For contemporary readers, that is only half the problem. To appreciate the parallels one must know biographical facts about Douglass (an escaped former slave speaking in Rochester, New York, at a time when slavery was still a fact in much of the country). These problems illustrate the limitations of allusions, which, like the enthymeme, depend for their impact on knowledge in the minds of the audience.

Identification   Finally, the strategy of identification uses language to create positive associations between the rhetor and the audience; it suggests shared experience or common viewpoints. For example, Robert F. Kennedy, in the introduction to his Law Day Address at the University of Georgia on May 6, 1961, both created identification and made fun of the strategy itself:

> For the first time since becoming Attorney General, over three months ago, I am making something approaching a formal speech, and I am proud that it is in Georgia. Two months ago I had the very great honor to present to the President Donald Eugene McGregor of Brunswick, Georgia. Donald McGregor came to Washington to receive the Young American Medal for Bravery. . . . And, as the President said, Donald McGregor is a fine young American—one of a long line of Georgians who have, by their courage, set an outstanding example for their fellow Americans.
>
> They have told me that when you speak in Georgia you should try to tie yourself to Georgia and the South, and even better, claim some Georgia kinfolk. There are a lot of Kennedys in Georgia. But as far as I can tell, I have no relatives here and no direct ties to Georgia, except one. This state gave my brother the biggest percentage majority of any state in the union, and in this last election that was even better than kinfolk.[27]

The first paragraph creates identification in a traditional and serious way. The speaker praises someone who is also admired by his audi-

---

[27]Glenn R. Capp, ed., *The Great Society: A Sourcebook of Speeches* (Belmont, CA: Dickenson, 1967), p. 75.

ence, and he praises qualities admired by them. He does honor to his audience by identifying this brave young man as one of a long line of Georgians with similar qualities. The second paragraph creates identification indirectly by honestly acknowledging differences: The speaker has no family ties with Georgians or Southerners. The statement that Georgia gave strong support to his brother in the last election, however, suggests that the speaker and the audience have strong ties of party, ideology, and policy.

Speakers and writers traditionally identify ties of kinship, shared beliefs, and common experience as ways to create bonds between themselves and the audience. When Joan Konner, Dean of the Columbia University School of Journalism, delivered a speech at the New Jersey Press Women's Association in Paterson in 1990, she began this way:

> Good afternoon. Thank you for inviting me. I am pleased to have the chance to address the New Jersey Press Women's Association for several reasons. One, I grew up in New Jersey. Paterson is my home town. My children and my grandchildren still live here. My first job was in New Jersey in the Bergen *Record,* where I enjoyed one of the best jobs in this business.[28]

Note the list of items used to underscore her links to New Jersey and to Paterson in particular.

Similarly, when Philippine President Corazon Aquino addressed a joint session of the U.S. Congress on September 18, 1986, she began by making a personal connection to the audience. She said, "Mr. Speaker, Senator [Strom] Thurmond, distinguished Members of Congress, three years ago I left America in grief to bury my husband, Ninoy Aquino. I thought I had left it also to lay to rest his restless dream of Philippine freedom. Today, I have returned as the president of a free people." She was able to personalize and dramatize the remarkable, peaceful revolution through which the Philippines returned to a democratic system.

Aquino reinforced her links to the U.S. audience through repeated allusions to President Abraham Lincoln's second inaugural address, which was delivered close to the end of the Civil War when it was clear that the Union would prevail. She needed to persuade members of Congress and President Reagan that she would seek to reconcile the

---

[28]Joan Konner, "Women in the Marketplace: Have Women in Journalism Made a Difference?" *Vital Speeches of the Day,* September 15, 1990, p. 726.

supporters of defeated President Ferdinand Marcos and that she would take a tough stand to resist the military efforts of communist guerrillas who still resisted her presidency. Responding to the first concern, she said, "As I came to power peacefully, so shall I keep it. That is my contract with my people and with God. He had willed that the blood drawn with the lash shall not, in my country, be paid by blood drawn by the sword but by the tearful joy of reconciliation." She appropriated Lincoln's words to make a powerful promise not to exact revenge from Marcos's supporters.

Later in the speech, she again used Lincoln to defend her willingness to seek a peaceful resolution to the guerrilla conflict that threatened her newly elected democratic government:

> I will not stand by and allow an insurgent leadership to spurn our offer of peace and kill our young soldiers, and threaten our new freedom.
>
> Yet, I must explore the path of peace to the utmost, for at its end, whatever disappointment I meet there, is the moral basis for laying down the olive branch of peace and taking up the sword of war. Still, should it come to that, I will not waver from the course laid down by your great liberator:
>
> "With malice toward none, with charity for all, with firmness in the right as God gives us to see the right, let us finish the work we are in, to bind up the nation's wounds, to care for him who shall have borne the battle, and for his widow and for his orphans, to do all which may achieve and cherish a just and lasting peace among ourselves and with all nations."
>
> Like Lincoln, I understand that force may be necessary before mercy. Like Lincoln, I don't relish it. Yet I will do whatever it takes to defend the integrity and freedom of my country.[29]

The strategy of appealing to shared values is now directed to a new purpose. By linking Lincoln to a policy that seeks mercy and reconciliation first, rather than a military struggle, Aquino effectively preempts objections that she is not taking a hard enough line against the guerrillas. Thus, what began as a strategy to create identification becomes a strategy through which she can refute those who oppose her policy.

---

[29]Corazon Aquino's speech was published in *Democracy by the Ways of Democracy: Speeches of President Corazon C. Aquino: Official Visit to the United States of America, September 15–24, 1986*. Manila: Philippine Information Agency, National Printing Office, 1986. It is also found in the *Congressional Record* H 7073–7075.

What Aquino does might be described as a strategy of appealing to cultural values, an appeal through which she seeks to change the audience's feelings about her. In her second statement, Alvarez also does this when she refers to herself as just a "John Q. Public" and "a real American," associating herself with ordinary citizens who do the right thing and with patriotic values embodied in "real" Americans. These strategic moves broaden the concept of connotation to show its similarities to the processes of identification with an audience, which, in turn, is related to developing the rhetor's ethos.

These, then, are strategies that serve primarily to alter attitudes toward people, objects, events, or ideas. The most basic is the label, which designates in a valuative way to color our perception or response. The label works by association, connecting the qualities associated with a category with the person, thing, or idea labeled. Closely related to the label is the slogan, which sums up a whole series of feelings and experiences in a cleverly put and memorable statement. Allusions to items in popular culture, literature, the Bible, or history also serve to change the emotional valence. Allusions may compare or contrast or they may serve to designate. Allusions may be used subtly to make an argument, as in the threat made by Frederick Douglass. Metaphorical language serves both to make ideas vivid and memorable and to alter an audience's emotional response to an idea. Finally, language that creates identification between rhetor and audience works to alter the audience's attitude toward the rhetor and the rhetor's purpose.

These are some of the strategies available for rhetorical action. Strategies are techniques that use language to prove, vivify, and alter attitudes. Each of these functions is a central element in rhetoric. Strategies provide important resources by which to overcome the obstacles of the rhetorical problem.

SUMMARY

The fundamental capacities of language, to name, abstract, and negate, enable us to perform these and other symbolic actions. Style is an encompassing term that describes the possibilities that exist in word choice and grammar. Style can vary in formality, precision, literalness, and redundancy. Good style is clear, vivid, appropriate, and consistent. The resources of style are increased by strategies that contribute to proof, animate, and change connotations.

Summary Outline

I. Language (here, verbal symbol systems) has three characteristics.

   A. Naming is the process of noticing, identifying, and labeling elements in ourselves and our world.

   1. Names have denotative meanings (definitions).

   2. Names have connotative meanings that reflect our experiences and feelings.

   B. Abstracting allows us to omit details.

   1. Naming involves abstraction.

   2. We can omit more and more details, referring to ever-larger wholes.

   C. Negating reflects the relationship between words and things.

   1. Whatever a word is, it is not what it signifies.

   2. Naming requires us to ignore differences.

   3. Abstracting requires us to omit details.

   4. Figurative language rests on negation.

II. Stylistic choices are rhetorical choices.

   A. As style becomes more informal, it becomes more conversational.

   B. Precision reflects an emphasis on empirical evidence and logical proof, but ambiguity can be persuasive.

   C. Figurative language grasps and depicts intangible qualities of experience.

   D. The level of redundancy should reflect the subject's complexity and the audience's knowledge.

III. Good style is clear, vivid, and appropriate.

   A. Good style is immediately intelligible.

   B. Good style creates virtual experience.

   C. Good style fits the subject, occasion, purpose, and rhetor.

IV. Strategies are linguistic resources for overcoming rhetorical obstacles.

   A. Some strategies resemble logical arguments.

   B. Some strategies create virtual experience.

   C. Some strategies change connotations and alter attitudes.

▪ ▪ ▪

MATERIAL FOR ANALYSIS

Frederick B. Craddock is a professor of homiletics (preaching) and New Testament at the Candler School of Theology of Emory University in Atlanta, Georgia, which is one of the official seminaries of the United Methodist Church.[30] The sermon is Tape No. 50 in a 1987 tape series, "Preaching Today," gathered by the editors of *Christianity Today* and made available in seminary libraries as models of "good" preaching. This sermon is filed under "Thanksgiving" and follows the text of Romans 16:1–16. You will appreciate the sermon more if you consult that text before reading it.

"When the Roll Is Called Down Here"

by Fred Craddock

1   I hope you will not feel guilty if your heart was not all aflutter during the reading of the text. It's not very interesting. It's a list of names, a list of strange names. I always tell my students in preaching class, "When you're preaching from biblical texts, avoid the lists. They're deadly. Don't preach from the lists." It seems that Paul is calling the roll. That's a strange thing in itself. I have never worshipped in a church in which anyone got up and called the roll. It could be very dull. Well, it could . . . it could be interesting in a way.

2   Calling the roll sometimes is not all that bad. Last December I was summoned to Superior Court, DeKalb County, Georgia, to serve on the jury. On Monday morning at nine o'clock, 240 of us formed the pool out of which the juries for civil and criminal cases would be chosen. The deputy clerk of the Superior Court stood and called the roll. Two hundred forty names. She did not have them in alphabetical order. You had to listen. And while I was listening, I began to *listen.* There were two Bill Johnsons. One was black and one was white, and they were both Bill Johnson. There was a man named Clark, a Mr. Clark, who answered when the clerk read "Mrs. Clark." He said, "Here."

And she looked up and said, "Mrs. Clark."

And he said, "Here."

---

[30]Craddock is the author of many books. Of particular interest is *Preaching* (Nashville, TN: Abingdon Press, 1986). I am indebted to Todd J. Rasmuson for this text.

And she said, "Mrs. Clark."

And he stood up and said, "Well, I thought the letter was for me, and I opened it."

And she said, "We summoned Mrs. Clark."

And he said, "Well, I'm here. Can't I do it? She doesn't have any interest in this sort of thing."

And the clerk said, "Mr. Clark, how do you know? She doesn't even know she's been summoned."

3   This roll call *was* pretty good. There was a man there whose name I wrote down phonetically because I couldn't spell it. His name was Zerfel Lashenstein. I remember it because they went over it five or six times, mispronouncing it. He insisted it be pronounced correctly and finally stood in a huff and said, "I see no reason why I should serve on a jury in a court that can't pronounce my name."

The woman next to me said, "Lie-shen-stein. I wonder if he's a Jew?"

I said, "Well, I don't know. Could be. Does it matter?"

And she said, "I am German. My name is Zellar."

And I said, "Well, it doesn't matter. That was 40 years ago." And she said, "He and I could be seated next to each other in a jury."

I said, "Well, you were probably just a child when all that happened years ago."

And she said, "I was 10 years old. I visited Grandmother. She lived about four miles from Buchenwald. I smelled the odor."

4   You know, a person could get interested in Paul's calling the roll. Even if it's no more than to say, "I wonder how Paul knew all those people since he had never been to the church?" I wonder if back then you could buy mailing lists? After all, he wants to raise money in Rome for his Spanish mission, and he is politically wise.

5   He says, "Tell this one hello and that one hello." Some scholars think this doesn't even belong in Romans. He's never been to Rome. But I could get interested in the roll call because it gives a kind of sociological profile of the membership of the church.

6   Now, I don't expect you to remember, but in the list there is a husband and wife, Aquila and Priscilla. There's a man and his mother, Rufus and his mother. There is a brother and sister, Nereus and his sister. There are brothers, Andronicus and Junias. There are sisters, Tryphaena and Tryphosa. There is an old man, Epaenetus. Isn't that an interesting profile of the church? There is a single

woman, Mary. There's a single man, Herodian. Not a lot of nuclear family there at all, except as Christ has called them together. It's an interesting list, sort of. Not very.

7   But for Paul it's not a list. Don't call it a list. He's packing his stuff. He's in the home of Gaius in Corinth, who is host to Paul and host to the church in Corinth. Paul is getting ready to go west to Italy and Spain. He's about to move to a new parish, one far away. He is now about 59 years old, I would guess. He feels he has one more good ministry in him. Most churches don't want a person 59 years old, but those churches had no choice, because Paul started his own. He wants to have one other ministry because he got a late start. He was probably about 35 when he started. He doesn't have much to pack: his coat and his books and a few other things. And while he is throwing things away to trim down the load for packing and moving, he comes across some notes and some correspondence, and he sits down among the boxes and begins to remember. Don't call it a list.

8   You've done it yourself. When my wife and I finished our service at the student church when in seminary, our last Sunday there they gave us a gift. It was a quilt some of the women of the church had made, and they stitched into the top of the quilt the names of all the church members. And every time we move and we come across that quilt, we spread it out on the bed and we start remembering. We remember something about everyone—there's Chester, who voted against and persuaded the others to vote against my raise. There's Mary and John, who put new tires on our car. There's Loy, very quiet, never said anything. There is his wife, Marie. There is this marvelous woman, Loyce, lived with that man who drank and became violent, and yet she was always faithful and pleasant. And he was dying of cancer when we went—my first funeral there, you remember. This is the way we go over the quilt. Don't call it a list.

9   Paul said, "Don't call it a list. Aquila and Priscilla, they risked their necks for me. Andronicus and Junias, we were in jail together. Phew! They're great Christians. There's Mary. Mary worked hard. She was there when everybody else quit. She's the one who always said, 'Now, Paul, you go on home; I'll put things up. I'll put the hymnals away, and I'll pick up all the papers and straighten the chairs. You go on home; you're tired.' 'Well, Mary, you're tired too.' 'Yes, Paul, but you've got to ride a donkey across Asia tomorrow. You go on. I'll pick up here.' Mary worked hard.

10   "Epaenetus, the first person converted under my preaching, and I didn't sleep a wink that night, saying, 'Thank God. Finally somebody heard.' The first one to respond to the gospel. What a marvelous day that was! Tryphaena and Tryphosa,

obviously twins. You hear it, don't you, in the names? Tryphaena and Tryphosa. They always sat on this side, and they both wore blue every Sunday. I never knew them apart, really. One of them had a mole on her cheek, but I didn't know if it was Tryphaena or Tryphosa. I never did get them straight. And Rufus. Tell Rufus hello, and tell his mother hello, because she's my mother, too."

11   Isn't that something? Some woman earned from this apostle the title "Mother." Can't you see her, this woman able to be mother to Paul? Probably stayed in their home. She was a rather large woman. Always had an apron, a lot of things stuffed in the pocket of the apron. Hair pulled back in a bun. Fixed a good breakfast. Paul said, "I'm sorry. I can't stay. I have to be on my way."

"Sit down and eat your breakfast. I don't care if you are an apostle, you've got to eat."

Tell my mother hello—this is not a list.

12   I remember when they brought the famous list to Atlanta. The workers set it up in the public place, block after block to form a long wall of names. Vietnam names. Some of us looked at it as if it were a list of names. Others went over closer. Some walked slowly down the column. There was a woman who went up and put her finger on a name, and she held a child up and put the child's hand on a name. There was a woman there who kissed the wall at a name. There were flowers lying beneath the wall. Don't call it a list. It's not a list.

13   In fact these names in Romans 16 are for Paul extremely special, because even though he says, "Say hello to," what he really is saying is good-bye. Oh, he's going to Rome, he says. But before he goes to Rome, he has to go to Jerusalem. He's going with the offering, and he's going into a nest of hostility. And so at the end of Chapter 15, he says to these people, "Pray with me. Agonize with me, that I won't be killed in Jerusalem, that the saints will accept the money in Jerusalem, that I'll get to come back and be with you. Please pray." These are not just names.

14   Do you have a piece of paper? Well, use your worship bulletin. Would you write in the margin somewhere or at the bottom these words: "I thank my God for all my remembrance of you." And write a name. You choose the name. You remember the name. Write another name, and another name, and another name.

15   Before I married and was serving a little mission in the Appalachians, I moved in my service down to a place on Watts Bar Lake, between Chattanooga and Knoxville—a little village. It was the custom in that church at Easter to have a baptismal service. My church immerses, and this baptismal service was held in Watts

Bar Lake on Easter evening at sundown. Out on a sandbar, I, with the candidates for baptism, moved into the water, and then they moved across to the shore, where the little congregation was gathered singing around the fire and cooking supper. They had constructed little booths for changing clothes, with blankets hanging, and as the candidates moved from the water, they went in and changed clothes and went to the fire in the center. And finally, last of all I went over and changed clothes and went to the fire.

16   Once we were all around the fire, this is the ritual of that tradition: Glenn Hickey, always Glenn, introduced the new people, gave their names, where they lived, and their work. Then the rest of us formed a circle around them while they stayed warm at the fire. The ritual was each person in the circle gave her or his name and said this: "My name is _____, and if you ever need somebody to do washing and ironing." "My name is _____, and if you ever need anybody to chop wood." "My name is _____, if you ever need anybody to baby-sit." "My name is _____, if you ever need anybody to repair your house for you." "My name is _____, if you ever need anybody to sit with the sick." "My name is _____, if you ever need a car to go to town." And around the circle. Then we ate, and then we had a square dance. And at a time they knew—I didn't know—Percy Miller, with thumbs in his bibbed overalls, would stand up and say, "It's time to go." Everybody left, and he lingered behind and with his big shoe kicked sand over the dying fire.

17   At my first experience of that, he saw me standing there still. He looked at me and said, "Craddock, folks don't ever get any closer than this." In that little community, they have a name for that. I've heard it in other communities too. In that community, their name for that is *church*. They call that church.

18   Have you written any names? Do you have a name or two? Keep the list. *Keep* the list, because to you it's not a list. In fact, the next time you move, keep that. Even if you have to leave your car and your library and your furniture and your typewriter and everything else, take that with you. In fact, when your ministry has ended, and you leave the earth, take it with you.

19   I know, I know, I know. When you get to the gate St. Peter's going to say, "Now, look, you went into the world with nothing, you gotta come out of it with nothing. Now what have you got?"

And you say, "Well, it's just some names."

"Well, let me see it."

"Well, now, this is just some names of folk I worked with and folk who helped me."

"Well, let me see it."

"Well, this is just a group of people that if it weren't for them, I'd have never made it."

He says, "I want to see it." And he smiles and says, "I know all of them. In fact, on my way here to the gate I passed a group. They were painting a red, big sign to hang over the street, and it said, 'Welcome Home.'"

Questions for Analysis

1. What does the introduction tell you about the sort of rhetorical problem that Craddock faces in deciding to preach on this text?

2. There is a refrain that runs through the sermon, "Don't call it a list." How does Craddock change the meaning of "list" as the sermon proceeds? How does this process illustrate the meaning of "connotation"?

3. Stories or narratives are the primary supporting material in the sermon. How would you describe those stories? Are they personal, biblical, contemporary, real, or hypothetical? Which and how many characters speak in them? How do they illustrate concepts developed by Walter R. Fisher?[31] In what sense are these "good" stories?

4. How does Craddock invite or prompt participation from his listeners?

5. How does the sermon influence your view of Craddock's ethos?

6. What is the specific purpose of this sermon? What belief, attitude, or action is being urged?

7. How would you evaluate extended examples as a means to reinforce beliefs already held by an audience?

8. Think about the organization of this sermon. What holds it together or unifies it? Why is it difficult to fit the sermon into one of the traditional forms of organization?

9. Compare this sermon to Elizabeth Cady Stanton's "The Solitude of Self."[32] What is a lyric structure? To what kinds of purposes is it particularly suited?

---

[31]See *Human Communication as Narration: Toward a Philosophy of Reason, Value, and Action* (Columbia: University of South Carolina Press), 1987.

[32]Elizabeth Cady Stanton, "The Solitude of Self," in *Man Cannot Speak for Her,* ed. Karlyn Kohrs Campbell (Westport, CT: Greenwood Press, 1989), vol. 2, pp. 371–385. The speech is analyzed in volume 1, pp. 133–144, and in the *Quarterly Journal of Speech* 66 (October 1980):304–312.

SOURCES

Frank, Francine Wattman, and Paula A. Treichler. *Language, Gender, and Professional Writing: Theoretical Approaches and Guidelines for Nonsexist Usage.* New York: Commission on the Status of Women in the Profession, Modern Language Association, 1989.

Langer, Susanne K. *Philosophy in a New Key,* 3d ed. Cambridge, MA: Harvard University Press, 1942. Basic reading for those who wish to understand the dimensions and capacities of language.

Osborn, Michael. "Rhetorical Depiction." *Form, Genre, and the Study of Political Discourse.* Ed. Herbert W. Simons and Aram A. Aghazarian. Columbia: University of South Carolina Press, 1986. 79–107.

Strunk, William, Jr., with revisions by E. B. White. *The Elements of Style,* 3d ed. New York: Macmillan, 1979. Elementary rules of composition, usage, and style are provided by this clear and readable work.

CHAPTER 11

Nonverbal Elements in Rhetoric

Anyone who has played charades knows that words are more effective than gestures for expressing complex and abstract ideas. The ideas in this or any other book could not be presented nonverbally unless the gestures were part of a symbol system like American Sign Language, the language of deaf Americans. All oral rhetoric is accompanied by nonverbal elements, however, such as a drawl, a frown, a stare, a handshake, or a bow, and even written rhetoric has some nonverbal dimensions, such as margins, type face and size, illustrations (or the lack of them), and typos, for example.

This chapter is not an extended analysis of all nonverbal communication, but sources that will allow you to pursue these ideas are provided at the end of the chapter. The focus of this chapter is the role of nonverbal elements in oral rhetoric and the strengths and limitations of nonverbal rhetoric generally. I address these questions: (1) How do nonverbal elements affect the meaning of and response to oral rhetoric? (2) What can be communicated nonverbally? (3) What are the strengths and limitations of nonverbal rhetorical acts?

Nonverbal communication includes the human actions that accompany speech, nonverbal acts *perceived* as communicative, and nonverbal acts intended to be rhetorical. The problem of rhetorical intention, discussed in Chapter 1, recurs here. Some nonverbal elements are random, idiosyncratic, and unintentional. Others are part of established symbolic patterns shared by a pair of friends, a family, an organization, or a culture.[1] Random, unintentional, idiosyncratic behavior may be

---

[1]See C. David Mortenson, *Communication: The Study of Human Interaction* (New York: McGraw-Hill, 1972), pp. 211–217, for a discussion of the problems of analyzing and interpreting nonverbal behavior. See also Gary Cronkhite, "Perception and Meaning," *Handbook of Rhetorical and Communication Theory*, ed. Carroll Arnold and John

taken as communicative, as when a squinting attempt to see something on the blackboard, occasioned by forgetting my glasses, was interpreted as a frown of disapproval by someone whose teaching I was observing. As critics and analysts, the potential influence of such behaviors has to be considered. Rhetorical action, however, can only encompass intentional behaviors that can reasonably be expected to communicate conventional meanings to others.

NONVERBAL ADJUNCTS TO SPEECH

No oral communication takes place in a vacuum. In any act of oral communication, there are senders and receivers (rhetors and audiences are both), and they must be in some physical relationship to each other (from face-to-face to back-to-back), at some distance, in some posture (sitting, standing, leaning, kneeling, slouching). These relationships are studied in the area of nonverbal communication called *proxemics.* Every oral message is accompanied by body movements ranging from obvious gestures to tiny facial movements and general muscle tension. These behaviors are studied in *kinesics.* Every oral message includes vocal modifiers (volume, rate, pitch, quality) and noises of the vocal tract that carry meaning but aren't thought of as language (such as mm-hmm, tsk-tsk, coughs, laughing). These are studied in *paralinguistics.* People who participate in rhetorical acts have bodies of different sizes and degrees of attractiveness, with more or less hair; they are clothed in different ways and adorned by a variety of objects (earrings, watches, pipes, briefcases). Their interactions occur in environments (in halls, on streets) and on certain kinds of occasions (a birthday party, a political convention, a class meeting). All of these are nonverbal elements that inevitably accompany spoken language.

Much of nonverbal behavior is learned just as language is learned. Accordingly, it varies from culture to culture. Britons curtsy to show respect to a monarch; Japanese bow. What Americans see as an OK sign, Greeks see as a vulgar sexual invitation. Important cultural differences in the use of distance, time, voice, and gestures can create misunderstanding and generate resentment.[2] One reason for studying

Waite Bowers (Boston: Allyn and Bacon, 1984), pp. 51–229, esp. 100–111. See also Robert Gifford, "Mapping Nonverbal Behavior on the Interpersonal Circle," *Journal of Personality and Social Psychology* 61 (1991):279–288.

[2]See, for example, Robert L. Saitz and Edward J. Cervenka, *Columbian and North American Gestures: A Contrastive Inventory* (Bogota: Centro Colombo Americano, 1962); P. Ekman, W. V. Friesen, and J. Bear, "The International Language of Gestures," *Psychology Today* 18 (1984):64–69.

nonverbal behavior is to improve our ability to communicate with people from other cultures.

Problems can also be created nonverbally between people of different subcultures or ethnic backgrounds. For example, some studies show that patterns of eye contact between African Americans and between Euro-Americans in the United States differ. For some African Americans, looking another person directly in the eye is considered rude—a putdown or a confrontation—and avoiding eye contact is a way of communicating recognition of authority.[3] Because norms among most Euro-Americans differ from these, requiring direct eye contact to indicate attention and interest, problems arise for these African Americans in interactions with Euro-Americans, particularly when the latter are in positions of authority as teachers or employers.

Researchers do not agree about the origins of nonverbal acts. Some presume them to be caused biologically. Others argue that "the observed 'sex differences,' 'race differences,' and 'class differences' in nonverbal behavior may be traced to differences in power; and that these are learned differences which serve to strengthen the system of power and privilege that exists."[4] No one denies that observed behaviors differ; but there are at least two explanations of them.

Whatever their origin, nonverbal behaviors communicate power and reflect patterns of dominance and status in a culture. For example, a pair of experiments carried out by a team of Princeton investigators illustrates how nonverbal cues can reinforce racist stereotypes.[5] In the first experiment, white male subjects believed they were interviewing applicants for a team position in a group decision-making experiment. African American and white male "applicants," actually confederates, were trained to act in a standard way, and their performances were rehearsed until all applicants appeared equally qualified. But the white interviewers behaved differently toward the African American applicants. They placed their chairs at a significantly greater distance from them, they made more errors of grammar, usage, and pronunciation,

---

[3]Albert Scheflen, *Body Language and the Social Order* (Englewood Cliffs, NJ: Prentice-Hall, 1972), pp. 95–96; Kenneth R. Johnson, "Black Kinesics—Some Nonverbal Communication Patterns in Black Culture," *Florida FL Reporter,* Spring/Fall 1971, p. 18; M. LaFrance and C. Mayo, "Racial Differences in Gaze Behavior During Conversations: Two Systematic Observational Studies," *Journal of Personality and Social Psychology* 33 (1976):547–552. This also appears to be true for some American Indians as well.

[4]Nancy M. Henley, *Body Politics: Power, Sex, and Nonverbal Communication* (Englewood Cliffs, NJ: Prentice-Hall, 1977), p. 2.

[5]Carl O. Wood, Mark P. Zanna, and Joel Cooper, "The Nonverbal Mediation of Self-Fulfilling Prophecies in Interracial Interaction," *Journal of Experimental Social Psychology* 10 (1974):109–120.

they showed less immediacy (a measure combining eye contact, forward lean, and shoulder angle), and they ended the interviews significantly sooner.

The second experiment tested the effects of such nonverbal differences on applicants. In this case, the interviewers were trained confederates and the applicants were naive subjects, white males who believed they were being interviewed as part of a training program and who were given a monetary incentive to compete for the job. Interviewers were trained to exhibit either immediate or nonimmediate behaviors to applicants, that is, to vary proximity, speech errors, and interview length. The applicants responded in kind, reciprocating the degree of immediacy of the interviewer. Judges who observed the applicants without knowing about the experiment rated those receiving nonimmediate behaviors as performing less well generally and as having less composure during the interview. The subjects also rated less immediate interviewers as less competent and friendly. These experiments illustrate several principles of nonverbal communication. Nonverbal cues are read very quickly and accurately.[6] They are reciprocated to alter the transaction that occurs, and they are taken as reliable signs of ethos. In this case, they also functioned as a self-fulfilling prophecy (behavior that guarantees a predetermined result). In other cases, they can be shown to influence decision making.[7]

The person who tries to overcome such problems faces large obstacles. As Henley notes, for example, you cannot teach women to violate norms of femininity in assertiveness classes and then expect that all will be well. A woman who does not conform to the submissive female stereotype may be ignored, her action may be misinterpreted as a sexual invitation, and/or she may be punished physically

---

[6]See, for example, Robert Rosenthal et al., "Body Talk and Tone of Voice: The Language Without Words," *Psychology Today* 8 (September 1974):64–68. Even when exposures were reduced to only one-twenty-fourth of a second, observers correctly identified the emotions being portrayed on film by an actress two-thirds of the time. See also G. Kirouac and F. Y. Dore, "Accuracy and Latency of Judgment of Facial Expressions of Emotions," *Perceptual and Motor Skills,* 57 (1983):683–686.

[7]A study by S. Forsythe, M. F. Drake, and C. E. Cox, "Influence of Applicant's Dress on Interviewer's Selection Decisions," *Journal of Applied Psychology* 70 (1985):374–378, suggests that sex-role stereotypes may be limiting employment opportunities for women. J. M. Puckett, R. E. Petty, J. T. Cacioppo, and D. L. Fischer found that socially attractive authors were rated as more persuasive than unattractive authors when the arguments of the essay were strong. When the arguments were weak, however, attractive authors were criticized more and rated as less persuasive than unattractive authors, further evidence of the strong relationship between attractiveness and persuasion. See "The Relative Impact of Age and Attractiveness Stereotypes on Persuasion," *Journal of Gerontology* 38 (1983):340–343.

(nonverbally) or labeled as a deviant, a bitch, or a lesbian. Or her expression of dominance may be accepted.[8] It is possible to change nonverbal behavior, but the results may not be those desired. Once again, the receiver will play a significant role in determining the kind of transaction that takes place.

Nonverbal elements always accompany oral communication. Like language, these behaviors are learned. Differences between cultures and subcultures make misunderstanding easy, and nonverbal behaviors influence the relationships between sexes, classes, and ethnic groups.

NONVERBAL MEANING

Just what can we communicate nonverbally, and how significant are such messages in the total pattern of meaning? Most researchers agree that the nonverbal channels carry more social meaning than the verbal channels.[9] This means that we communicate attitudes and feelings nonverbally. Specifically, we communicate likes and dislikes, dominance and status, and responsiveness.[10]

Evaluations

We communicate our evaluations, our attitudes, our likes and dislikes (good–bad, pleasant–unpleasant, beautiful–ugly) primarily through signs of immediacy. We move closer, lean forward, take a face-to-face position, touch, look at, maintain eye contact with, and speak to persons we like; we move away from, lean back, turn away from, avoid, and look away from persons we do not like. Members of an audience will use such nonverbal gestures as data from which to infer the speaker's feelings at a given moment and to make judgments about

---

[8]See Henley, *Body Politics*, pp. 196–205, for a discussion of body politics and women's liberation.

[9]In "Attributions of Personality Based on Physical Appearance, Speech, and Handwriting," *Journal of Personality and Social Psychology* 50 (1986):792–799, R. M. Warner and D. B. Sugarman found that judges can consistently identify the emotion expressed and can also estimate its strength in content-free speech (a recording device that eliminates verbal content but preserves vocal cues); however, the exact vocal cues that convey individual emotions have not been identified.

[10]The framework for this analysis is drawn from Albert Mehrabian's *Silent Messages*, 2d ed. (Belmont, CA: Wadsworth, 1981).

character. For example, persuaders perceived as attractive are more successful and are rated higher on credibility scales.[11] Audience members will also draw conclusions from stylistic signs of immediacy, a point at which nonverbal and verbal communication converge.

Your language can reflect immediacy and involvement or nonimmediacy and distance. The rhetor who talks about "those people" or addresses the audience as "you" or "you people" is distancing herself or himself from the people being discussed, as Ross Perot discovered in 1992 when he referred to an audience of African Americans as "you people" and found that his distancing was treated as evidence of lack of sympathy for their concerns. "These people" lessens the distance, and "we" becomes evidence of close identification. Errors of grammar and pronunciation suggest distance and reflect a subject that distresses the speaker or is not of great interest. Stylistic choices that connect speaker and statement are evidence of commitment, as in "I think" versus "it is thought" or "researchers think." The active voice (I finished it) is more immediate than the passive (It is finished). Such stylistic markers are cues that the audience will use to infer your feelings and attitudes and your involvement and commitment. They are indicators of tone.

Power

We communicate power, dominance, and status nonverbally. The dynamics of such communication are described by Henley: "The humiliation of being a subordinate is often felt most sharply and painfully when one is ignored or interrupted while speaking, towered over or forced to move by another's bodily presence, or cowed unknowingly into dropping the eyes, the head, the shoulders."[12] As children, as students, as employees, we have all had such experiences. Our social power is expressed through nonverbal behaviors expressing strength, size, and weight.

Erving Goffman used these concepts as the basis for studying gender differences in magazine, newspaper, and television advertisements and found that marketing and advertising specialists have taken advantage nonverbally of the common stereotypes of gender differences. In these advertisements, males were found to be larger than females in relative size; females are shown physically lowering them-

---

[11]K. Debevac, T. J. Madden, and J. B. Kernan, "Physical Attractiveness, Message Evaluation, Compliance: A Structural Examination," *Psychological Reports* 58 (1986):503–508.
[12]Henley, *Body Politics*, p. 3.

selves or in lower positions in relation to males, portrayals that he called the "ritualization of subordination." Females are portrayed as outlining and touching objects more often (the feminine touch), as engaging in "licensed withdrawal," that is, removed "psychologically from the social situation at large, leaving them unoriented in it and to it, and presumably, therefore, dependent on the protectiveness and goodwill of others," illustrated by daydreaming during an interaction.[13] These nonverbal stereotypes reinforce traditional concepts of gender as they are used to make persuasive appeals.

In general, those who show submission speak softly, occupy less space (stand and sit in tense positions with arms close to the body), keep their distance, lower their eyes, hesitate to intrude upon another's space, bow their heads, cringe, and cuddle. Persons expressing dominance and status speak more loudly, occupy more space (stand with hands on hips and elbows turned outward, sit in relaxed and sprawling positions, and gesture widely), take the initiative in increasing intimacy, look into the eyes, violate territory with aplomb, raise their chins, stand erect (often on platforms), and put their hands on or their arms around others.

Audiences use nonverbal evidence to make inferences about the speaker's confidence, commitment, and expertise. Your knowledge of the subject will be tested against nonverbal cues that you provide.

Dynamism

We communicate activity and responsiveness nonverbally. We do so through evidences of life and vitality and through the rate of our activity. We react, adapt, shift position. By contrast, passivity, lack of movement, and rigidity reflect a lack of vitality. Dynamism is expressed in the sheer amount of interaction that occurs and in changing facial expressions, vocal variety, and gestures.

These three factors—evaluation, power, and dynamism—interact and overlap. Evidences of liking may also indicate status, and nonverbal dynamism reflects dominance. Those of higher status feel more comfortable increasing immediacy, and nonverbal signs of immediacy are also cues of dynamism and responsiveness. These three factors are closely related to the elements of ethos discussed earlier in Chapter 5. Immediacy seems to be the counterpart of trustworthiness, power is related to competence and expertise, and responsiveness, activity, and

---

[13]Erving Goffman, "Gender Advertisements, *Studies in the Anthropology of Visual Communication* 3 (1976):69–154. Cited material is on p. 127.

dynamism seem to be identical both as factors of ethos and as dimensions of nonverbal communication. In other words, overcoming the obstacles you face as a rhetor, at least in oral communication, is directly related to nonverbal behavior.

Responses to Nonverbal Cues

Nonverbal behavior expresses emotions. The importance of such communication is magnified in this culture in at least two ways. First, we have a tradition of restraint about expressing feelings, but we believe that such feelings will out, if not overtly in speech then covertly in actions. Thus, we look for signs of feelings in nonverbal cues and take them as good evidence of attitude and character. Second, we learn nonverbal behaviors unsystematically and indirectly. Until relatively recently, they were studied primarily by actors. Accordingly, we believe nonverbal cues are produced spontaneously so that it would be difficult to lie nonverbally, although in some research deceptions tested in this way cannot be perceived accurately.[14] Nonetheless, we trust these cues, and when inconsistencies appear, we are likely to believe the nonverbal rather than the verbal message.

The nonverbal adjuncts to verbal messages can be contradictory or inconsistent. The simplest examples are sarcastic and ironic statements. The assistant who does much of the work of her boss for one-third of his pay says, "Yes, my boss is a fantastic administrator," and she leaves no doubt about her contradictory attitude. Sarcasm and irony illustrate that we use nonverbal cues to interpret the meanings of messages, to decide between alternative possibilities.[15] As speakers, we use nonverbal cues to indicate what we mean, and nonverbal elements greatly extend the meanings of words. For example, Elaine May

---

[14]Charles F. Bond, Jr., Adnan Omar, Adrian Mahmoud, and Richard Neal Bonser, "Lie Detection Across Cultures" *Journal of Nonverbal Behavior* 14 (Fall 1990):189–197; B. M. DePaulo, J. I. Stone, and G. D. Lassiter, "Deceiving and Detecting Deceit," in *The Self and Social Life,* ed. B. R. Schlenker (New York: McGraw-Hill, 1985), pp. 323–370; Paul Ekman, "Lying and Nonverbal Behavior: Theoretical Issues and New Findings," *Journal of Nonverbal Behavior* 12 (Fall 1988):163–175. See also Paul Ekman, *Telling Lies: Clues to Deceit in the Marketplace, Politics and Marriage* (New York: W. W. Norton, 1991).

[15]Henley cites an interesting example: "When Richard Nixon sent transcripts, rather than tapes, of presidential conversations to the House Judiciary Committee investigating the question of his possible impeachment (April, 1974), members quite rightly complained that transcripts could not convey the full or correct meaning of an utterance, having no voice inflection, stress, or other such nuances, and demanded the tapes. This exchange is a landmark in recognizing the legitimacy of paralinguistic communication, those characteristics of speech that affect its interpretation but are not part of the usually recognized language" (*Body Politics,* note, p. 7).

and Mike Nichols recorded a dialogue in the 1960s using only the words "George" and "Martha" that some radio stations considered too erotic to broadcast.

Nonverbal messages produce intense responses in receivers. This is not surprising since the bulk of what is communicated involves attitudes and feelings. The fury generated by long-haired, bearded young men in the 1960s, some of which persists, is just one example of this kind of reaction. But such responses are mirrored in our dislike of tense and nervous people, in our anger at persons who violate our territory, "barging in without knocking," and in our rebellion at unwanted backslapping and fondling. You can be sure that your audience will not only pick up nonverbal cues, it will react to them, trust them, and use them as a major source of information about your feelings, attitudes, and ethos.

Nonverbal cues call up memories of experiences that have strong emotional valences. Smells, for example, remind us of mother's homemade bread, of Christmas trees, of ripe tomatoes and fresh fruit, or of a person who wears a particular scent. They also remind us of unpleasant experiences—the smell of formaldehyde may recall unpleasant lab dissections or a delighted moment of discovery, and certain body odors are quite repellent to most of us. Merchandisers manipulate such memories by spraying Christmas trees with evergreen scent, by placing fans over freshly baked bread that blow the smell out into the street to tempt us, and by spraying new car scent onto automobiles in show rooms. These efforts are intentionally rhetorical, but they persuade us in ways that we usually are not fully aware of.

NONVERBAL RHETORIC

Some rhetorical action is wholly nonverbal. For example, consider this button:[16]

---

[16]Used by permission.

When I showed it to a class of freshmen students, they interpreted it variously. All recognized the sign $\bigcirc$, now common on traffic markers, that something is prohibited. But just what was prohibited was unclear. One person said, "No more hangups." Another said, "Don't keep me hanging." Only one person was certain. She recognized the button as one distributed by the National Abortion Rights Action League and translated it as "No more illegal, unsafe abortions."

The button illustrates some of the problems involved in nonverbal rhetoric. Because such acts are highly abstract, they are very ambiguous. The ordinary audience member is free to interpret them in many different ways, some of which may be quite different from what was intended. For that reason, nonverbal rhetoric works best with "true believers," those who already agree. An ideal audience for the button is a member of N.A.R.A.L. who recalls the higher rates of maternal death and sterility that resulted from illegal abortions performed under unsanitary conditions and with improper instruments, such as a coat hanger. In other words, nonverbal rhetoric works best as ritual, as a reaffirmation of belief. The important role of gestures and actions in rituals reflects this fact.

Nonverbal rhetoric is simple, an expression of feeling. It provides no explanations or justifications. There are no qualifiers to modify the claim. It is usually intense, even simplistic. As a result, reactions to such rhetorical acts are also intense. Under such circumstances, there is no opportunity to explain just what is intended, to provide evidence and reasons to justify the claim reflected in the gesture, to discuss what kinds of changes are needed. There is just a dramatic assertion.

However, nonverbal rhetoric has compensatory strengths. Most examples are like slogans, vivid symbols that summarize a whole realm of intense associations and thus call up emotional responses in those who see them. They are rallying cries that unify and raise the morale of like-minded groups. Like their weaknesses, their strengths come from their high level of abstraction and their emotional power.

Some time ago, one of my students made a speech against abortion and used as visual aids pictures from a pamphlet called "Life or Death" distributed by the Kansas Right to Life Organization. The pictures were large, colored photographs of aborted fetuses. They were dramatic evidence of the human features that appear during the early weeks of life and of the physical effects of various abortion procedures. But the response of the class was overwhelmingly negative. They said things like, "After I saw those pictures, I just didn't want to think about it." "I was insulted." "Those just aren't appropriate for any speech." Only one person was positive: a student who, like the speaker, took a strong antiabortion stand.

The pictures are nonverbal rhetoric. They illustrate once again that nonverbal channels communicate emotional material and that, for those who do not share your views, the channels can easily become overloaded. In that case, the response will be intensely negative. For this reason, nonverbal rhetoric has to be used with great care whether in isolation or in conjunction with a speech. Be aware of its ambiguity and the intensity of its message and of the potential responses, and remember that it is most effective for those who already share the views that it espouses. Think about the legal principle that the emotional impact of a visual aid should not outweigh its function as proof.

Verbal and nonverbal rhetoric interact in powerful ways. For example, as a nonverbal element, the setting for a rhetorical event can add significantly to its meaning and impact. On Easter Sunday, 1939, Marian Anderson sang to an integrated crowd of 75,000 at the Lincoln Memorial. She began by singing, "My country 'tis of thee, Sweet land of liberty, To thee we sing," not "Of thee I sing," the usual lyric. As historian Scott A. Sandage comments, "The change made the national hymn subtly political, painting 'land of liberty' as more aspiration than description."[17] Anderson's concert there was the culmination of a struggle to find a place for her to sing after the Daughters of the American Revolution (DAR) barred her from their tax-exempt Constitution Hall, and the District of Columbia Board of Education refused her the use of a high school auditorium. After Eleanor Roosevelt publicly resigned from the DAR, she was permitted to sing at the Lincoln Memorial. Sandage writes that the "Lincoln Memorial may be the best example of . . . a 'memory site': a place where we struggle over tensions between our experience of the past (memory) and our organization of it (history)" (p. 137).

Why is the Lincoln Memorial such a significant setting? It is a memorial to one of our most revered presidents. Yet President Lincoln can be remembered either as the savior of the Union, a unifying symbol, or as the great emancipator who freed the slaves, which links him to ongoing civil rights agitation. The monument itself is located on the Potomac River opposite Robert E. Lee's former Virginia home, which helped to make it symbolize sectional reunion originally. As early as the Memorial's 1922 dedication, it became contested ground, when former President Taft's speech of dedication omitted any mention of slavery, whereas Robert Russa Moton, who had succeeded Booker T. Washington as head of Tuskegee Institute, praised Lincoln

---

[17]"A Marble House Divided: The Lincoln Memorial, the Civil Rights Movement, and the Politics of Memory, 1939–1963," *The Journal of American History* (June 1993):135–167. Cited material on 136. Subsequent citations are in parentheses in the text.

for giving freedom to a race. Events like the Anderson concert emphasized Lincoln's role as the great emancipator and called attention to the gap between espoused principles and their application to African Americans. Sandage writes:

> Conceived in a quest for white consensus, Lincoln's temple has subsequently been defined through interracial conflict and transformed into a "moral high ground" from which to exhort America to finish what Lincoln called "the great task remaining before us." In this way, the memorial is a powerfully confrontational site. Protestors presented themselves as orderly, patriotic citizens. They made the past a resource and made Lincoln a signifier of the dissonance between America's professed and achieved values. (p. 160)

To watch and hear Dr. Martin Luther King, Jr.'s, 1963 "I Have a Dream" speech at the Lincoln Memorial as part of the March on Washington is to see and feel the rhetorical power of the Memorial as a setting for civil rights protest. Sandage's work calls attention to the possibilities created by the site and by Lincoln's complex legacy and to the process by which civil rights protest activities from 1939 to 1963 exploited the possibilities of that location to make the Memorial a powerful element in their appeals. As his analysis indicates, verbal and nonverbal rhetoric interact to alter meaning, including the meaning of sacred national monuments.

SUMMARY

No oral communication takes place in a vacuum. It is always accompanied by nonverbal elements that affect its meaning. Nonverbal behaviors are learned; they differ between cultures; and they are an important source of misunderstanding. The origins of nonverbal behaviors may be biological or social, but they reflect patterns of dominance within a culture.

Nonverbal channels communicate attitudes and feelings, specifically evaluations, power, and dynamism. We tend to trust nonverbal cues as reliable indicators of both momentary feelings and general character. Hence, they strongly affect audience perceptions of the ethos of the speaker.

The strengths and limitations of nonverbal rhetoric reflect the general qualities of all forms of nonverbal communication. Such acts are abstract and ambiguous and are open to varied interpretations. They communicate highly emotional messages that produce intense responses. They are most effective for a target audience that shares the beliefs and values expressed in the rhetoric. Nonverbal rhetorical acts can symbolize large amounts of experience, but they cannot explain, justify, or qualify. Great care should be taken in using them as visual aids in speeches. Unless the audience shares your point of view, a boomerang effect of intense disapproval may occur.

■ ■ ■

MATERIAL FOR ANALYSIS

The power of nonverbal communication is illustrated by the power of cherished symbols. On the Fourth of July, 1986, the Statue of Liberty was the focus of a celebration. Pictures of it were everywhere in New York City, and there were even souvenir green foam-rubber hats that allowed tourists and celebrants to transform their heads into liberty's crown. Writing in the *New York Times,* July 17, 1986, critic Paul Goldberger explored the transformative power of this symbol in a commentary entitled "The Statue of Liberty: Transcending the Trivial."[18]

> The events of Liberty Weekend focused more attention on a single object than almost any single object can possibly bear, and that object came through it with every bit of its dignity intact.
>
> What is it about the Statue of Liberty that has made it transcend the trivial so remarkably? Almost any other object would have crumbled into cliché because of the intensity of the spotlight that has been shined on the Statue of Liberty, but the statue now, after all of this attention, seems as strong and as fresh as ever. It stood above all attempts to reduce it to a kind of visual slogan.
>
> Part of the reason, of course, is not the statue itself, but what it symbolizes—the idea of freedom, though it has been trivialized by man [sic], in and of itself transcends all slogans and easy, glib symbolism. But that does not really explain why the Statue of Liberty could hold such power over us as we saw it again and again, for hour after hour, day after day.

---

[18] © 1986 by The New York Times Company. Reprinted by permission.

Neither is it explained by Frédéric Auguste Bartholdi's talent as a sculptor, which was considerable, though hardly on a scale to command the highest position in European art. One does not look at a Bartholdi and forget Rodin. . . .

Is it the simple idea of monumental sculpture, then—the very notion of an immense statue, so much bigger than life, that is unusual enough that it continues to seem fresh to the eye, even after a hundred years? . . .

It is really not any one of these things, but all of them, in exquisite balance, that contributed to the success of the Statue of Liberty as a work of art. The statue *is* a powerful symbol of an essential value in our society; it is not the only such symbol, but it is the most intensely personal one, and the only one of its kind. But it is also a fine piece of sculpture, gracefully proportioned, and existing in tandem with a perhaps even finer piece of architecture [its base]. And its scale makes it a very special kind of monumental work.

In the end, though, there is another factor, perhaps the most important of all. The Statue of Liberty was not placed where it stands by accident. It is not in the middle of Nebraska or even in the middle of Brooklyn. It is out in the harbor, on an island, where it faces out to the sea, and it performs a gesture of welcoming.

By so doing, it enters into an essential relationship with the city, and this is the real key to its brilliance as a symbol. The Statue of Liberty actually turns the harbor into a door; it makes the place where the sea becomes New York Bay an entry, not just a body of water, and it makes the city itself, not to mention the nation that lies to the west, seem more tangible, more understandable, more coherent as a place.

Goldberger describes the Statue of Liberty as transforming the city where it is found, that its location allows it to impose a special meaning on that space. The statue itself is a nonverbal symbol. How do the words of Emma Lazarus's poem, "The New Colossus," found on its base, affect its nonverbal meaning? Is Goldberger wrong to ignore them as part of its meaning?

As you can imagine, nonverbal rhetorical acts create particularly difficult ethical and constitutional issues. The following essay raises such questions for discussion around an issue that had deep emotional meaning for many Americans. It was written in the midst of controversy over a Supreme Court decision that found burning the flag a form of speech protected under the Constitution. It was written by Hendrik Hertzberg and appeared in *The New Republic*.

Flagellation[19]

Many a bum show has been saved by the flag.
—George M. Cohan

1   Amid the current hysteria an important ontological point has been overlooked: You can't burn the flag. It can't be done. *A* flag, yes. *The* flag, no. *The* flag, the American flag, is an abstraction—a certain arrangement of stars, stripes, and colors—that exists (a) in the realm of Platonic ideals and (b) in the minds and hearts of people. To say this is not to denigrate the flag; on the contrary, it is to place the flag where it belongs, in a higher realm of existence than the material. *A* flag, any particular flag, is merely a copy. You can no more destroy *the* flag by burning *a* flag than you can destroy the Constitution by burning a copy of the Constitution.

2   The flag, as long as it exists in human hearts, is fireproof. The Constitution, however, is more vulnerable. It can be desecrated quite effectively—by amending it in ways foreign to its spirit and hostile to its purposes. Members of Congress rushed to do just that in the wake of *Texas* v. *Johnson*. George Bush, in the first truly sickening act of demagoguery of his young presidency, has now put the impetus of his support behind them.

3   Have you read the actual Texas statute the Supreme Court ruled on? It makes it "a Class A misdemeanor" for anyone to "deface, damage, or otherwise physically mistreat [a state or national flag] in a way that the actor knows will seriously offend one or more persons likely to observe or discover his action." What's surprising is not that this bit of legislative flotsam was struck down, but that four of the nine justices deemed it consistent with the First Amendment.

4   All the opinions in this case are notable for their passion. The dissenters' passion is reserved mostly for the flag, the majority's mostly for the Constitution. The dissenters venerate the symbol; the majority venerates the thing symbolized. Both have emotion on their sides, but the majority has logic, too.

5   Chief Justice Rehnquist devotes many pages to explicating the special meaning of the flag. His dissent is studded with verse:

---

[19]Hendrik Hertzberg, "Flagellation," (TRB from Washington) *The New Republic*, July 17 & 24, 1989, p. 4. © 1989 by The New Republic. Reprinted by permission.

four lines of Emerson's "Concord Hymn," the opening stanza of
"The Star-Spangled Banner," two full pages of "Barbara Fritchie."
He succeeds beautifully in making the point that the flag is a powerful symbol of a particular set of sentiments or ideas. Or, as Justice Stevens puts it, in a transcendently absurd passage I can't resist quoting:

> The message conveyed by some flags—the swastika, for ex-
> ample—may survive long after it has outlived its usefulness as
> a symbol of regimented unity in a particular nation.
>   So it is with the American flag.

6   What the justice means is . . . well, never mind. But Rehnquist and Stevens want to have it both ways. The flag conveys a
message that nothing else conveys, but burning a flag (in Rehnquist's words) "conveyed nothing that could not have been conveyed and was not conveyed just as forcefully in a dozen different
ways." These assertions, Justice Brennan remarks in a footnote, "sit
uneasily" next to each other. If flying the flag is symbolic speech,
so is burning one; and speech, in this country, is supposed to be
free.

7   Rehnquist argues that we outlaw "conduct that is regarded
as evil and profoundly offensive to the majority of people—
whether it be murder, embezzlement, pollution, or flag burning."
We don't, however, outlaw murder, embezzlement, and pollution
because they're offensive. We outlaw them because they inflict
palpable harm on actual people. Flag burning merely offends, and
it offends by what it says.

8   When the decision came down, I allowed myself to hope it
would be the occasion for nothing worse than a harmless festival
of hokum calculated to bring pleasure to the shades of [H. L.]
Mencken and Sinclair Lewis. And that's how it was, the first day.

9   The inimitable Bob Dole rushed a wild, all-caps statement up
to the Senate press gallery. It began this way:

> MAYBE THOSE WHO SIT IN IVORY TOWERS AGREE WITH
> THE SUPREME COURT. MAYBE. AS THE MAN WHO BURNED
> THE FLAG, MILLIONS OF PEOPLE HATE AMERICA. HATE
> THE FLAG. IF THEY DO, THEY OUGHT TO LEAVE THE
> COUNTRY. IF THEY DO NOT LIKE AMERICA, THAT'S FINE.
> GO FIND SOMETHING YOU DO LIKE. IF THEY DON'T LIKE
> OUR FLAG, GO FIND ONE YOU DO LIKE.

10   That was a paragraph to savor, especially the way the ante-
cedents chased each other like enraged bees. Meanwhile, over on
the House side, one rascal after another was having his say. The

fifteenth to rise was Douglas Applegate, Democrat of Ohio, who, after proclaiming that it would be all right with the Court for his colleagues to rip down "the flag right here in this Chamber" and "defecate on it," shouted, "Are there no limitations? Are they going to allow fornication in Times Square at high noon?" As if on cue, up got Donald E. "Buz" Lukens, Republican (and underage girl fancier) of Ohio. "Mr. Speaker, what does it say to the world that Americans can now legally burn the flag? . . ."

11   The show got ugly the next day, when the texts of proposed amendments started filling the hoppers—amendments like this one, offered by 17 members of the House:

> SECTION 1. The misuse or desecration of the symbol, emblem, seal, or flag of the United States is not protected speech under the First Amendment to the Constitution of the United States.
>
> SECTION 2. The Congress shall have power to enforce this article by appropriate legislation.

12   And so on. An America capable of writing this sort of tripe into its Constitution would be a country at once less serious and less funny than the country we thought we were living in. And less free, too.

13   President Bush's role in all this is unusually contemptible. His first reaction was to say that while he regards flag burning as "dead wrong," he could understand why the Court decided as it did. That was the reasonable, moderate fellow one stupidly keeps hoping is the "real Bush." After a day's reflection—and lunch with Lee Atwater—Bush decided that "the importance of this issue compels me to call for a constitutional amendment."

14   If Bush has his way, the Bill of Rights will be amended for the first time in American history—and for what? Because of what danger? Flag burning is extremely rare and, though offensive, essentially harmless. It has no "importance." It is not even an "issue," since no one, apart from a few isolated political cultists, is in favor of it. So what's going on?

15   The mystery vanishes when one recalls Bush's use last fall of the Pledge of Allegiance "issue." Now, if he has his way, the same cynical manipulation of patriotic symbols, as perfected by political consultants, is to be enshrined in the Constitution. Negative campaigning is to be raised to the level of a civic sacrament. The desecration of the flag, which is not a problem, is to be made the pretext for the desecration of what the flag represents. For George Bush, nice guy, the defilement of the Bill of Rights itself is just another tactic for narrow partisan gain. And it's hard to see, at this point, who's going to stop him.

Questions for Analysis

1. What's the difference between the Statue of Liberty and the flag as nonverbal symbols? Why is there a difference between defacing the Statue of Liberty and burning a flag?

2. Why do actions that destroy a flag produce the intense reactions described by Hertzberg? What are some of the experiences that give the flag such a powerful meaning?

3. In what sense is burning a flag (or otherwise damaging it) political speech? What are the arguments for protecting such speech? What arguments were used by the Supreme Court Justices in their opinions in *Texas v. Johnson?*

4. How are making and wearing green plastic hats in the shape of Statue of Liberty's crown and burning the flag similar and different? Do the hats offend? If flag burning were to be made illegal, why not outlaw green plastic hats in the shape of the statue's crown?

5. How are the flag and the Bill of Rights related? Read Carolyn Marvin, "Theorizing the Flagbody: Symbolic Dimensions of the Flag Desecration Debate," *Critical Studies in Mass Communication* 8 (June 1991):119–138, as a way to help you formulate issues embedded in this question.

SOURCES

Articles in the *Journal of Nonverbal Behavior* are an excellent source of research findings in this area.

Many texts treat nonverbal communication generally. Among them are *Nonverbal Communication: Studies and Applications,* 3d ed., by Mark L. Hickson III and Don W. Stacks, Madison, WI: William C. Brown & Benchmark, 1993; *Nonverbal Communication,* 2d ed., by Loretta A. Malandro, Larry Barker, and Deborah Ann Barker, New York: Random House, 1989; *Nonverbal Behavior in Interpersonal Relations,* 2d ed., by Virginia P. Richmond, James C. McCroskey, and Steven K. Payne, Englewood Cliffs, NJ: Prentice-Hall, 1991.

Bate, Barbara, and Anita Taylor, ed. *Women Communicating: Studies of Women's Talk.* Norwood, NJ: Ablex, 1988.

Goffman, Erving. *Gender Advertisements.* 1976; New York: Harper & Row, Harper Torchbooks, 1979. As the title indicates, this book focuses on the gender relationships in advertisements.

Henley, Nancy M. *Body Politics: Power, Sex, and Nonverbal Communication.* Englewood Cliffs, NJ: Prentice-Hall, 1977. An excellent survey of research on nonverbal expressions of power.

Langer, Susanne K. *Feeling and Form: A Theory of Art.* New York: Charles Scribners Sons, 1953. A beautifully written work that focuses on the nondiscursive elements in art forms, including music and architecture.

Mayo, Clara, and Nancy Henley, eds. *Gender and Nonverbal Behavior.* New York: Springer-Verlag. 1981. An anthology of essays on this topic.

Sharp, Gene. *The Politics of Nonviolent Action: Power and Struggle.* Boston: Extending Horizons Books, 1973. This work explores the rhetorical dynamics of marches, vigils, parades, sit-ins, boycotts, and the like.

Sontag, Susan. *On Photography.* New York: Farrar, Straus and Giroux, 1977. A provocative book on the cultural meanings of photographs.

Wolfgang, Aaron, ed. *Nonverbal Behavior: Perspectives, Applications, Intercultural Insights.* Lewiston, NY: C. J. Hogrefe, 1984. An anthology that explores dimensions of nonverbal communication, including gender and culture.

Wood, Julia. *Gendered Lives: Communication, Gender, and Culture.* Belmont, CA: Wadsworth, 1994.

APPENDIX

Your Rhetorical Act

Early in most practical courses, students and teachers face a dilemma. On the one hand, students need to begin applying their developing skills in order to understand problems concretely and to discover ways to handle specific situations. On the other hand, students do not yet know many of the concepts they need to cope with difficulties, and teachers have not had time to present them. Clearly acknowledging this dilemma, this appendix is included to provide practical advice on preparing your first classroom exercise.

At the end of the appendix, there is a strategy report and a list of assignments your instructor may wish to use for your first exercise. The strategy report is designed to make you aware of your choices and their implications and to develop your skills as a critic. Each of the exercises presumes that your first speech or essay will be directed toward the most limited and manageable rhetorical purposes: to alter perception and/or to explain, the most fundamental grounds out of which to attempt to influence others. The suggestions in the rest of the appendix, however, are appropriate for preparing any kind of rhetorical effort.

The prospect of initiating rhetorical action is frightening, even for the most skilled practitioners. In fact, one survey reported that Americans fear speaking before a group more than they fear snakes, heights, disease, or even death.[1] Those of us who lecture regularly never overcome the fear of seeming trivial or boring, of saying something foolish, of forgetting important material. These are normal and appropriate fears. Anyone can misread an audience, presenting material the audience already knows and, hence, produce a humdrum act. Anyone

---

[1] "The Only Thing We Have to Fear Is Speaking Before a Group," 1988, *Psychology Today.* Reprinted, [Mpls.] *Star Tribune,* March 19, 1991.

can forget important material, be ill prepared, or make a silly or foolish statement. The material in this appendix is designed to provide you with the best possible insurance against such experiences when you speak or write for an audience. I divide my suggestions into four areas: picking a topic, researching a subject, organizing your material, and preparing for the final presentation.

PICKING A TOPIC

Much of the fear you feel in a rhetorical situation arises from a sense that the situation is not under your control. Admittedly, unforeseen things can happen, but they are much less likely if you choose an appropriate topic. The most basic advice to the rhetor is: Speak and write from your own knowledge and experience! If you do, you will prepare with greater ease and confidence because you are working from familiarity. You will have general knowledge against which you can test information from other sources. Your own experiences will provide a stock of examples that will make the subject more personal and vivid for the audience. If you share values and experiences with members of your audience, your relationship to the topic will make it easier to connect them to the topic. In addition, your research will be easier as you will probably have access to firsthand information from people who work with or experience the topic directly every day. Here are some general questions that will help you find suitable topics for speeches or essays:

1. Where did you grow up? Each of you has special knowledge and experiences from growing up on a farm, in the inner city, on army bases, in a mining town, in the mountains, or in the desert. These experiences can be the starting point for a speech or essay. In the past, students who have grown up on farms have spoken on support prices, insecticides, fertilizers, and beef imports; students from cities have written about redlining, street repair, and variations in police protection in areas of the city. In no case was the personal experience and knowledge of the student sufficient, but in each case the research was easier, and familiarity with the subject increased the rhetor's confidence.

2. What are your parents' occupations? As the child of a plumber, a lawyer, an assembly-line worker, or the owner of a hardware store, you have special firsthand experience and access to a source of firsthand

information. For example, in the past, students have used this experience to explain how plumbers are licensed and why they command such high pay, the feasibility of converting factories from oil to coal (a parent sold such machinery), medical malpractice, carpal tunnel syndrome, awards from juries (the child of a lawyer), and the nature of capital gains taxes (the child of an accountant). Once again, your experience can be the starting point for your rhetorical act, and you will write and speak from special knowledge and familiarity.

3. What jobs have you done? Even temporary or part-time work teaches you a lot. For instance, a grocery clerk discussed the arguments for and against automated check-out equipment; a student who had worked as a building inspector wrote about city laws governing apartments and how to make complaints to compel landlords to meet the requirements of the building code; a student who had worked as the manager of a fast-food restaurant discussed the pros and cons of franchises.

4. What are your hobbies and interests? In past classes, a member of the track team talked about why some shoes increase your speed and last longer; a collector of stamps argued for their value as an investment; a student who had raced cars claimed that 55 mph is the safest maximum speed limit; an auto buff spoke about why changing the oil regularly is the single most important maintenance task a car owner can perform.

5. Have you family or friends with special problems, distinctions, or unusual characteristics? Many rhetorical acts spring from tragedy. An alcoholic father prompted a speech on organizations that help the families of alcoholics; a schizophrenic sister prompted a speech on megavitamin therapy—what it is and how it works; the suicide of a friend's brother prompted an essay on suicide among college students; an epileptic brother occasioned a speech on misconceptions about epilepsy; a father's death from a shot of penicillin inspired an essay on the dangers of allergies.

Success and honor can also be the source of topics: The daughter of a mother who patented a new chemical process talked about how patents are acquired; a basketball player used the career of Lynette Woodard, the star of Kansas Women's basketball, who scored more points than any male or female college basketball player, to write about the limited opportunities for extraordinary women athletes; a scholarship student in ballet demonstrated and explained the basic movements of ballet as part of a speech to increase appreciation of ballet performances.

6. Have you had unusual experiences? The survivor of a severe automobile accident wrote vividly of seat belt safety; a girl who was threatened by a drunken boy with a loaded gun argued for gun control; a foreign exchange student spoke about currency problems.

These are only a few examples of the many instances in which students have drawn on their special experiences.

Speaking or writing from your own experience has additional benefits. In most cases, you will be deeply involved in your topic and your sincerity will be catching—the audience will care too. When you draw on personal experience, your audience will find you knowledgeable and credible, worthy of being believed. Your rhetorical act will not seem a mere exercise for a class; rather, the audience experiences you telling them something you know about firsthand, that you care about, and they will consider what you write or say seriously and with respect. You will be on the way to a successful presentation.

If you have considered these questions carefully, you will recognize some weak approaches. Don't write from research you did for last semester's term paper unless you can personalize the topic for yourself and your audience. A similar warning goes for a rhetorical act drawn from articles in newspapers or magazines. Don't pick a topic just because you read about it in a magazine in the dentist's waiting room. Again, pick a subject that is close to you as a person, one with which you have had firsthand experience.

Firsthand experience and personal knowledge alone, however, are not sufficient. You must test your experience and broaden your knowledge with information drawn from other sources.

RESEARCHING A SUBJECT

If you wish to be an effective speaker or writer, you must make the library a helpful friend. It is the primary resource for testing personal experience, refining understanding of the subject, and collecting concrete material that will explain and prove your claims and make your subject vivid.

Begin with a general survey of libraries at your school and at other schools nearby along with convenient public libraries. Find out where things are and what procedures you must follow to take out materials. Locate the computerized card catalog in each and learn how to use it;

locate the reference room and write down the hours when reference librarians are there to help you. Find out what computerized resources exist in your library and how to use them. Find the periodicals room and the reserve room. Find out where there is a government documents depository, and learn where microfilms are kept. Find out how to request materials through interlibrary loan. Does a computer printout show which periodicals the library holds and where they are? Does the computerized card catalog indicate if someone has the book you want? If it is on reserve? Are there special libraries for certain kinds of materials, such as artistic works or archives? Many libraries provide tours; most have brochures identifying materials and listing hours. In other words, "case the joint" carefully before mounting an assault to find specific materials.

What will you need to know and how can you find it? Obviously, your needs and problems will differ for each effort, but you can follow some general procedures. First, because personal experiences are ordinarily narrow and limited, you will need general background on a particular subject and an understanding of terms and concepts. Begin in the reference room. Here you will find general sources of information and indexes that will lead you to more detailed information.

General Sources

Three basic general sources can help you: encyclopedias, dictionaries, and almanacs and statistical yearbooks. The least specialized and most general sources are large encyclopedias such as the *Encyclopedia Britannica* or the *Encyclopedia Americana*. These will give you general and historical information on people, places, concepts, and events. The articles are written by experts, and each ends with a list of books and articles that will provide additional information. You may also find it helpful to look up your topic or related subjects in a slightly more specialized but still encyclopedic reference such as the *Encyclopedia of Philosophy,* the *Encyclopedia of Social Work,* or the *American Negro Reference Book.* Once again, these will give you background plus a list of more detailed sources.

You are familiar with general dictionaries such as *Webster's International Dictionary* and the *Oxford English Dictionary* and their more compact and abridged versions. In them you can check the meanings of terms, the history of changes in meanings, and the etymology or the linguistic origin of meanings. As with encyclopedias, specialized dictionaries may be helpful. For example, the *Dictionary of the Social Sciences* explains terms peculiar to or with special meanings in the social sciences; the *Oxford Classical Dictionary* focuses on figures from ancient Greece and Rome and on concepts needed to study classical literature and philosophy. There are similar dictionaries for medicine, law, sociology, psychiatry, and the like. Some of these may be available on CD-ROM.

If you seek more recent information, particularly quantitative information, as background for your research, turn to almanacs and statistical yearbooks. These books contain information, usually for a single year, and are compiled by a variety of agencies usually named in the titles—the *CBS News Almanac,* the *New York Times Almanac,* the *Reader's Digest Almanac,* the *World Almanac,* and the *Information Please Almanac,* among others. These sources are usually current within a few months of the events you may be researching. Similarly, the *Statistical Abstract of the United States* provides quantitative information of all sorts for a single year (often with comparisons to other recent years).

Specific Sources

When you have gathered this general background and statistical information, you will need more detailed information and specialized analyses. In general, material in books is likely to be more comprehensive, based on more research, and drawing on a variety of sources. Because book publication takes time, such material is not as contemporary as that found in current newspapers and periodicals. Reading books on your subject will give you general background and a familiarity with research already done; on the other hand, if you have a "hot" or emerging topic, there may be no books on it, or such material may be out of date.

The most efficient way to search for contemporary material is through computerized databases. In exploring the library, you may have learned something about the available and useful sources for doing research via computers and some basic information about gaining access to those databases. To illustrate the kind of searching you can do via computer, I shall follow a hypothetical student who is preparing a speech about a topic of recent concern, sick building syndrome, through this kind of search.

Each computerized library has an online system that includes a catalog of most of the books and periodicals in the library's collections as well as many indexes of periodicals and newspapers. If your personal computer is equipped with a modem and appropriate software, you may be able to gain access to the online system of the library you intend to use before you actually go there. Most universities make available telephone numbers that connect your computer to the online system.

Another useful computer system is the CD-ROM (Compact Disk, Read-Only Memory), which uses optical disks produced and read by means of a laser. The CD-ROM is a powerful research tool in retrieving information relevant to your speech topic. *Periodical Abstracts Ondisc* and *Newspaper Abstracts Ondisc,* for example, are two CD-ROM products. The *Periodical Abstracts Ondisc* includes indexing and brief abstracts of articles published from 1986 to 1994 in over 1300 general-interest, scholarly, and trade periodicals covering current events, as well as the arts, science, health, business, and consumer-related topics. The *Newspaper Abstracts Ondisc* includes indexing and brief abstracts of eight major national newspapers, including the *New York Times, The Wall Street Journal,* the *Chicago Tribune,* and the *Los Angeles Times* from 1985 to 1994.

In order to obtain relevant information from a CD-ROM, you insert an appropriate compact disc into the CD drive of the computer you are using. If you are looking for relevant newspaper articles, for example, you should use the *Newspaper Abstract Ondisc.* If you were preparing a speech on a local topic for a local Minnesota audience, you might want to use the Minneapolis *Star Tribune* on CD-ROM for your research. Obtaining data is easy; you just follow the instructions and make choices as they appear on the screen. In most libraries, you have to find an appropriate workstation depending on which CD-ROM product you need.

If you were to use the regular online catalog, once in the system you would be given a series of choices. Here is what you might see:

```
Screen 1=========================================================
MNCAT—U of Minnesota Introduction

MNCAT     U of MN Library Catalog
          Press ENTER to go directly to the Catalog
MNNEW     New Titles in MNCAT
INFO      U of MN Libraries Information
GOPHER    U of MN Libraries Gopher
INDEXES   Indexes and Abstracts
LOCAL     Twin-Cities & Regional Library Catalogs
BIGTEN    "Big Ten" University Library Catalogs
OTHER     RLIN/Eureka, WorldCat and Other Library Catalogs
==========================================================
```

From that list, if you type "indexes," the next screen looks like this:

```
Screen 2=============================================================
Terminal: L4ASCH33       LUMINA - University of Minnesota Libraries

INDEXES AND ABSTRACTS
Type the number shown at left to select a category ===> 7
and press Enter

1 Multidisciplinary Databases
2 Agriculture, Biology, and Ecology
3 Arts and Humanities
4 Engineering, Math, and Physical Sciences
5 Health Sciences
6 Social Sciences
7 List of ALL available databases
====================================================================
```

If you press 7 and the ENTER key, this is what you will see:

```
Screen 3=============================================================
LUMINA - University of Minnesota Libraries ALL DATABASES
(page 1 of 4)
Type the code shown at left to select a database ===> acad    and
press Enter

ACAD      Academic Index (journals and magazines, some full-text),
              1985-date
AGRI      AGRICOLA (agricultural sciences), 1970-date
ANTH      Anthropological Literature, 1984-date
ASTI      Applied Science and Technology Index, 1983-date
AFIR      ArticleFirst (current index to over 9,000 journals),
              1990-date
AHCI      Arts and Humanities Citation Index, 1980-date
ARTI      Art Index, 1984-date
AVERY     Avery Index to Architectural Periodicals, 1977-date
====================================================================
```

This is only the beginning. If you continue, usually by pressing ENTER, you will see more databases.

If you select ACAD, you will see this screen, which describes the database:

```
Screen 4========================================================
Database Description
-=Academic Index=-

Years of Coverage:  1985 to date
     Updates:  Monthly
     Last Updated:  08/05/94
     Subject Areas:  Academic Index offers a single source for
broad coverage of journals and other periodicals heavily used for
undergraduate research. More than 1000 periodicals are included,
covering education, history, arts, sociology, psychology,
literature, political science, religion, anthropology, geography,
and computers, in addition to Asian, Middle Eastern, Eastern
European, African and Latin American studies. (c) Information
Access Company, a division of Ziff Communications Company
=================================================================
```

The next step is to type in the subject word or phrase you are interested in; in this case, type "SU=sick building syndrome" and press EN-TER. The next screen will look like this, telling you that there are 69 articles in this database:

```
Screen 5========================================================
Search ALL Document/Results
Database - ACAD-
Search Term                              Documents

1     SICK BUILDING SYNDROME                   69

Enter your next search, or command.

SC-Scan Result  QD-Quick Display  LT-Limit Search  RE-Revise
H-Help  BR-Browse Terms  C-Change DB  MC-More Commands  O-Off/Quit
=================================================================
```

If you type QD and press ENTER, the system will give you abstracts of these items. For example:

```
Screen 6=============================================================
Document Display Database - ACAD-
Search 1: SICK BUILDING SYNDROME      69 Documents
FULL-TEXT IS AVAILABLE. Type FT to display.


Document: 1
Accession No.: 16013844. 9407.
   Author: Lang-Susan-S.
   Source: Human-Ecology-Forum. volume 22, issue n1, Wntr, 1994,
         p4(1).
         (940100).
   Title: Sick building syndrome linked to fibers. (includes
         related article).
   Descriptors: Sick-building-syndrome: Causes-of.
        Fibers: Health-aspects.

To see full display, enter number(s). For more documents,
  press Enter.
Document ->
S-Search  P-Previous  N-Next  FT-View Full Text  T-Tag  H-Help
BR-Browse Terms  C-Change db  MC-More Commands  O-Off/Quit
=====================================================================
```

If you now type FT and press ENTER, you will be able to see the article in full:

```
Screen 7 (Full Text)=============================================
Document Display Database - ACAD

Search 1: SICK BUILDING SYNDROME      69 Documents
 Document: 1
Accession No.: 16013844. 9407.
 Copyright: COPYRIGHT New York State College of Human Ecology 1994.


Full Text:
(1 OF 16) Sick building syndrome (SBS) sometimes may be caused by
synthetic fibers floating in the air from ceiling tiles,
insulation, and ventilation systems and is unrelated to smoking or
many other indoor air pollutants, according to studies by Alan
Hedge, associate professor of design and environmental analysis.
(2 OF 16) While implicating man-made mineral fibers (MMMF) as the
cause of SBS, the studies also dispel the view that cigarette smoke
substantially affects a building's indoor air quality and that poor
indoor air quality alone causes SBS.
(3 OF 16) "Although people assume that sick building syndrome is
related to gaseous air pollutants, many studies, including ours,
```

have been unable to find the link," Hedge says. "When we look at MMMF, however, which are currently often not measured in buildings, we find much higher reports of SBS where the MMMF are high. And when we install filters that collect the fibers, the number of reports dramatically declines."

(4 OF 16) Hedge also found that women and other workers with higher levels of job stress were at double the risk for reporting SBS symptoms. Job dissatisfaction and VDT use were also linked to higher rates of SBS.

(5 OF 16) These findings come from a series of studies by Hedge and research support specialist William Erickson and statistician Gail Rubin, both at Cornell.

(6 OF 16) SBS is a collection of workplace symptoms, including eye, nose, throat, and skin irritation, headache, lethargy, and respiratory and skin problems. MMMF, which may be suspended in air until they settle in dust, are present in ceiling tiles and thermal and acoustic insulation, duct linings of ventilation systems, and other building construction materials.

(7 OF 16) Hedge has also found that smoking policies have no significant effect on standard indoor air quality measures or on reports of SBS symptoms; that the amount of outdoor air used in air-conditioned buildings has no effect on SBS, indicating that air quality may be unrelated to SBS; that the more MMMF found in settled office dust, the higher the number of SBS symptoms that were reported among workers in the office; and that when filters that could remove most airborne particles were installed, reports of SBS and absenteeism declined.

(8 OF 16) "Chances are SBS is triggered by a range of factors, just like most other illnesses," Hedge concludes. "People who report SBS symptoms are being exposed to real irritants, but in many cases they are evidently not from gases in the air. Rather, air can be filthy with fibers and particulates that now are not being measured or considered."

(9 OF 16) Analysis of SBS Reports.

(10 OF 16) Hedge and his colleagues analyzed reports of SBS in 27 office buildings with more than 4,000 workers in nine eastern states. They report the following findings.

(11 OF 16) * No relationship was found between significant indicators of indoor air quality, such as carbon monoxide or dioxide, formaldehyde, temperature, and relative humidity, and reports of SBS.

(12 OF 16) * Smoking policies had no significant effect on standard indoor air quality measures or on reports of SBS symptoms.

(13 OF 16) * Although air-conditioned buildings have more SBS reports than naturally ventilated buildings, the amount of outdoor air used in air-conditioned buildings has no effect on SBS.

```
(14 OF 16) * The more MMMF found in settled office dust, the higher
the number of SBS symptoms reported among workers in the offices.
(15 OF 16) * When a filtration system that could remove most
airborne particles was installed on one floor of an office
building, concern with indoor air quality and SBS declined as did
sickness absences, while self-reported productivity significantly
increased.
(16 OF 16) "These findings strongly suggest that MMMF may be a
major player in SBS," Hedge concludes.
======================================================================
```

After reading the full text, you can resume scanning the 69 documents, looking at the abstracts to decide if you want to read the full text of others, when available.

Now let us suppose that you want to search to find out if there are relevant newspaper articles. If so, you choose:

Database: Indexes—NEWAB [i.e., Newspaper Abstracts]
    Search: "sick building syndrome"

Then you see:

```
Screen 1========================================================

DATABASE: NewsAbs
SEARCH: su:sick building syndrome        FOUND 117 Records

____NO.__TITLE_____SOURCE_____YEAR
 1 The greening of home construction: Builde  Washington Post 1994
 2 Pipe break soaks part of Suffolk courthouse Boston Globe    1994
 3 Storm over Plum Grove School subsiding     Chicago Tribune 1994
 4 2nd study on school: It's safe             Chicago Tribune 1994
 5 Plum Grove's 1st day comes with new worry  Chicago Tribune 1994
 6 'Sick building' symptoms hit more workers  Boston Globe    1994
 7 School's 'health' at issue still           Chicago Tribune 1994
 8 Study says Rolling Meadows school isn't's  Chicago Tribune 1994
 9 Everyone awaits Plum Grove health report   Chicago Tribune 1994
10 Bad air forces courts to close             Boston Globe    1994
 . . .

======================================================================
```

After looking at this selection, you decide to look at the first article:

```
Screen 2==============================================================

DATABASE: NewsAbs
SEARCH: su:sick building syndrome
Record 1 of 117_____

  NEWSABS NO: 03197791
    AUTHOR: Mariano, Ann
    TITLE: The greening of home construction: Builders and
      architects are working to make houses more environmentally
      sound
    SOURCE: Washington Post
SEC,PG:COL: E, 1:1
    DATE: Oct 15, 1994
    ABSTRACT: Experts on environmental hazards say more people are
      checking for possible pollutants, either before or after
      buying homes; often they find them.
  ~ ~ ~ ~ ~ ~ ~ ~ ~ ~ ~ ~ ~ ~ ~ ~ ~ ~ ~ ~ ~ ~ ~ ~ ~ ~ ~ ~ ~ ~ ~
  ARTICLE TYPE: News
  ARTICLE LENG: Long (18+ col inches)
  SPECIAL FEAT: Photograph
  DESCRIPTORS: Sick building syndrome; Pollution; Construction
  AVAILABILITY: UMIACH; 60208.00
  JOURNAL CODE: WP
  JOURNAL ISSN: 0190-8286
==================================================================
```

This should give you enough information to decide whether you want to look at the entire article.

Obviously, these are extensive sources of recent information. You will need to learn the meanings of the different commands in the system that you use, however, and because it is organized by subject, you will need to make a list of related topics, subjects, or key words, suggested by your general background research, under which you might find information. For example, in this case, you might search "indoor air pollution" to obtain more information. Remember that every filing system, including computerized library catalogs and indexes, reflects a way of looking at reality. Because your perceptions and those of the catalogers may differ, a list of subjects will be more helpful than just one subject in finding what you need. A list of such topics will help you find all relevant information on your topic in the card catalog organized by subject.

If you want to stick to print sources, the *Readers' Guide to Periodical Literature* indexes general-subscription magazines from 1900 to the present. (The first page lists the periodicals that are included.) Because articles are indexed by subject, come armed with a list of possible headings. Note that you will need to use this source if you are looking for information published before the 1980s.

Another large and helpful index is that of the *Congressional Record.* The *Congressional Record* is a record of debate in Congress and contains all articles and items that are inserted into it by members of Congress. As a result, it covers many topics and contains much useful information.

Some newspapers, including the *New York Times, The Wall Street Journal,* and the *Washington Post,* also have print indexes. Check to see which newspaper indexes your library holds. If you seek information from an unindexed newspaper, you will need to have a rough idea of the dates on which material appears or face a long process of searching.

In addition to the computerized indexes discussed above, you might try the *Humanities Index* and the *Social Sciences Index,* which list articles published in scholarly journals.

There are also print indexes to special kinds of information. For example, the *Book Review Digest* and the *Index to Book Reviews in the Humanities* will guide you to what reviewers have said about books you may be using as sources, and the *Dramatic Criticism Index* cites reviews of plays. Again, check to see which are available via computer, and which can be searched only in the reference room.

As a rhetor, you need to cite opinions of authors and researchers. You will also need to know the qualifications and experience of persons you quote as authorities. Among the special references that can help you are the *Directory of American Scholars, American Men and Women of Science,* and *Who's Who in America.* Sources such as these will help you judge the authority and credibility of a source and will indicate to the audience how much weight should be given to a person's statement.

As you expand your knowledge of library resources, you will find that you are expanding your abilities as a rhetor.

Taking Notes

Like all researchers, rhetors need to learn to take notes so citations are accurate and complete and so they can return to a source easily if need be. The ideal way to take notes is on note cards because they are easily filed and rearranged and can be used easily in speaking or writing. If you plan to take small amounts of information from many sources, 3″ × 5″ cards are suitable; however, in most cases 4″ × 6″ or 5″ × 7″ cards will be more convenient because there is more space on which to write or type. The smaller cards are best for keeping track of sources to compile a bibliography.

The only reasonable alternative to note cards is a notebook in which you record all your notes on a subject together. This is less convenient because you cannot discard or reorganize material as easily. If you use a notebook, be sure to leave spaces in the margins for classifications by subject so you can find the notes you need. You must recopy your data onto cards to use the information in a speech.

Whether you are speaking or writing, your notes need to contain all necessary information about the source. Some of this material may be omitted in speaking, but in writing, it must all be shown in footnotes or the bibliography. This is a good time to acquire a style manual, such as those listed at the end of this appendix, which will teach you a system that you will be able to use throughout your academic career. A style manual will also help you with rules for writing. If you learn the proper form to use on note cards, you will find it easy to write correct footnotes for papers and articles.

ORGANIZING YOUR MATERIAL

Chapter 9 discusses organization in detail. You may wish to consult that chapter when you have finished reading this material. What follows are some preliminary and general considerations to use in limiting your topic and in planning the structure of your rhetorical act.

Narrowing or Limiting Your Topic

Most rhetorical acts are relatively brief, a five- to seven-minute speech or a 1500-word essay. Our culture is fast-paced; even most presidential addresses can be fitted into a half-hour for transmission by television or radio. Because of school schedules, speeches and essays for classes have to be fairly short. Your first concern, then, is to narrow your topic. Three questions will help you do this: (1) What parts of this topic are most significant and interesting for this audience? (2) What parts of this topic are most important, most serious, or have the broadest implications? and (3) What aspect of the topic is most easily explained, or what aspect can be discussed most fully in the time or space allotted?

The first question focuses your attention on the audience. What aspects of the topic will be new to them? What parts of the topic touch their lives or are directly related to their immediate circumstances? As an example, imagine that you want to talk about energy problems. Most college students do not pay utility bills directly, and many do not own cars, so the price of gas may be remote. Few live in houses heated by solar energy; in most cases, few will have the necessary expertise to compare coal and gas as sources of energy. If there is no nuclear plant in the area and none proposed, even the dangers of nuclear power may not be particularly relevant.

Assume, however, that student activity fees have been raised because of the increased costs of heating and cooling the student union, and that fees for board and room in dormitories have been raised for the same reason. Some research leads to the discovery that these buildings waste energy because of the way they were built. Perhaps your topic should be narrowed to the relationship between architecture and construction and energy consumption. Recognize that you are trying to alter the perceptions of this particular audience, and that your first concern should be to approach the topic so that its significance for them is apparent.

The second question is designed to fit your subject to the particular circumstances of the audience. Consider here what any audience should know about this subject. On the basis of your research, you may decide that the problems of nuclear energy are the most pressing despite their remoteness from the immediate concerns of the audience. If so, you need to think carefully about how you can make this facet of the energy question interesting and significant for the audience. You might decide to begin with the nuclear plants built more than 20 years ago that are now obsolete and that no one knows how to protect, make safe, or dismantle. Such dangers can be made concrete and personal for a community and for individuals. Members of the audience can identify with dangers to people like themselves and to communities similar to their own.

Whatever facet of the subject you choose, this second question will help you explain to the audience why you have chosen it. If you decide to discuss the relationship between building construction and fossil fuel consumption, you may need to explain briefly why you are not discussing nuclear power but instead have selected what may appear to be a less important part of the subject of energy. (Obviously, the need for energy in general and for nuclear energy in particular would be lessened if consumption dropped. You might argue that that makes the question of construction a very important one.)

The third question, what aspect of the topic can be most easily explained or fully discussed in the time or space allotted, is designed to call the rhetor's attention to clarity and intelligibility. In Chapters 3 through 5, which examine the rhetorical problem, I discuss the problems created by the complexity of some topics and purposes. The decision you make on this question is intended to simplify as much as possible so the audience will understand what you are discussing.

For example, the problems of energy are many, and each is complex. The problems of nuclear power alone cannot be discussed in five minutes or in 1,500 words. In order to make sense of the subject, you might decide to limit your discussion entirely to the problem of what to do with existing nuclear plants that are out of date. This choice ignores a great deal—whether there is sufficient uranium, whether nuclear wastes can be disposed of, whether the products of breeder reactors can be kept from terrorists, whether alternative energy sources exist, and so on. But it focuses on a concrete problem that already exists: By the year 2000, there will be more than 100 inactive atomic plants, and hundreds of smaller nuclear installations, such as nuclear medicine facilities and navy ship reactors, will have ceased to operate. All of them will stay radioactive for hundreds or even thousands of years, and they remain a serious threat.

A rhetorical act on this subject may serve as a case study of the problems of nuclear power, as a concrete way for you to explore the kinds of problems that exist in the use of atomic energy. It's important, it's concrete, and it is sufficiently limited to be fully explained and explored in a relatively short rhetorical act. In other words, the third question should bend your energies toward finding a facet of the subject that you can cover thoroughly and clearly in the time or space allotted.

In sum, narrowing the topic should take into consideration the ways in which the subject is significant for the audience, the most important facets of the topic, and which aspects of the subject can be treated fully and carefully in a limited time or space.

Choosing a Thesis

Narrowing your topic leads naturally into the most important decision you make about organization: the selection of a thesis. Ordinarily, the general purpose of a rhetorical act is determined by the occasion or the assignment. For example, editorials, feature stories, and general news stories have rather clearly defined general purposes, but the writer must choose how she or he will translate the general purpose into a specific purpose. Occasions for speeches also usually define a general purpose—commencement speakers are expected to praise the new graduating class and talk about their future; sermons are intended to reinforce belief; reports are expected to provide information and create understanding. And again, in each case, the rhetor must decide just how he or she will translate the general purpose into a specific thesis.

Deciding on a thesis or central idea is difficult, and you should expect to find it troublesome. First, it represents a commitment that is hard to make—"I want the audience to know and understand precisely this: 'Storage facilities for nuclear wastes cannot be guaranteed safe for longer than 20 years.'" When you choose such a thesis, you make a claim to knowledge; in effect you say, "I have researched this topic, and I stake my credibility and authority on the accuracy of my research." In addition, you eliminate material and limit yourself drastically. In this case, all research that does not bear directly on storage of nuclear wastes must be discarded. So the choice of a thesis is an extreme decision that specifies the precise claim you want to make and represents a drastic limitation of the topic. The thesis should be a simple declarative sentence that answers the question, "Just what do I want the audience to know or understand (or believe or do) when I finish?"

Here are some examples of good theses:

Building a solar home or converting a home to solar energy is a practical solution to the energy crunch for individuals.

Note that the topic is narrowed in two ways: to solving the energy problem for individuals (not industry, for example) and to solar energy. It is a good thesis because it focuses on practicality. As the audience for this rhetorical act, we would expect to hear about costs of building and conversion, availability of materials, ease of construction, knowledge needed for maintenance, climatic conditions needed, and so forth. The thesis is also good because the claim of the rhetor is explicit and clear, and we know how to judge whether the claim is adequately supported.

Nuclear breeder reactors are unsafe.

This is a larger and more difficult claim that is aimed at a speech to formulate belief. It is good, however, because it narrows the topic to breeder reactors and because it narrows the perspective to questions of safety. As an audience, we would expect such a rhetorical act to focus on the problems of disposing of plutonium wastes and of preventing nuclear material suitable for explosive devices from falling into unauthorized hands.

55 mph is the maximum safe speed limit.

This is a good thesis because the claim is specific—the fastest safe speed limit is 55 mph. Note that it ignores questions of energy altogether and focuses only on questions of safety. We would, as an audience, expect to hear about reaction times, stopping distances at various speeds, statistics on auto deaths, and the relation of auto deaths to speed. Note again that the thesis is clear, explicit, and limiting.

Here are some poor thesis statements:

The deregulation of natural gas.

This is poor because it isn't a sentence and doesn't make a claim. It isn't clear what we are to know or understand about deregulation. That makes it a poor thesis, although it does a good job of narrowing the subject to natural gas and to questions about the relationship between price, availability, and government controls. Contrast this statement with a more explicit version:

The deregulation of natural gas will increase both the supply and the price.

The following is a very poor statement that reflects a common error:

How a nuclear plant runs.

It is not a sentence and does not state a purpose or a goal. One may rightly ask, Why should I know or care about how a nuclear plant runs? The thesis ought to give an answer. Contrast this statement with a more explicit one:

A nuclear power plant has a major impact on the environment.

This claim cannot be substantiated without explaining how a plant runs, but it also says, Here's why you should know how it runs. Recall that you, as rhetor, must always concern yourself with relevance and significance. Just as you may ask about classes and lecture materials, Why should I learn that? your audience will always ask, Why should I know? Why should I care? What difference does it make to me? Your thesis should be a statement that gives an answer.

People should drive more carefully.

This statement is a sentence, and it has a purpose. But it's hard to imagine how anyone could disagree. It's also hard to see how it could be developed or argued. No matter how careful drivers are, they could still drive more carefully. This seems to put the statement beyond argument. Just what is meant by "more carefully"? That very general phrase, open to many interpretations, ought to be translated into more concrete terms: not driving while on medication, while ill, while drunk, or in a car with poor brakes. A speech or essay on a particular kind of carelessness would come to grips with an issue that should challenge you and the audience.

People drive too fast.

This statement is a sentence, and it has a purpose. Its problems arise from its very general nature. The rhetor who uses this thesis will be all right if she or he narrows and specifies in the speech or essay just what benefits are to be derived from slower driving, although "too fast" is rather vague. Contrast it with a more specific statement:

You can save lives and money by obeying the 55 mph speed limit.

The following sentence is a problem because it contains two theses and implies two different rhetorical acts:

We must build nuclear power plants and convert industries to coal.

Each claim is adequate separately, but the rhetorical act that combines them will be somewhat at odds with itself. Each claim could be stated more clearly. "There is no economically feasible alternative to nuclear power," for example, is a clearer statement of the first claim. It is still very general, and it implies that the speaker will prove that natural gas, oil, solar energy, geothermal energy, and coal will all be proved inadequate. Actually, the only economically feasible alternative to nuclear energy that has been proposed, at least in the short run, is coal, so the best statement would be:

Our supplies of coal are inadequate to meet our energy needs.

That statement explains why the two theses were combined. If coal is not adequate to meet our needs, then nuclear plants will have to be built (unless we reduce consumption greatly). However, the rhetor in this case should consider whether all of this can be treated in a single rhetorical act, given the constraints of space or time.

A good thesis statement should

- State a specific claim
- Express a single unified purpose
- Indicate significance and relevance

You will have conquered many of the problems of organizing your material when you have decided on a thesis and stated it clearly. As is evident from the examples I have given, clearly stated theses imply the internal organization of the speech or essay. The structure of your rhetorical act is the development of your thesis. The main points of the rhetorical act should be statements (sentences making claims) that prove and explain the thesis. These main points should answer the questions Why? or How do I know? For example, the thesis "The deregulation of natural gas will increase both the supply and the price" implies a two-part development:

A. It will increase the supplies available across state lines.
B. It will raise the interstate price to the level of the intrastate price.

The statement "Nuclear breeder reactors are unsafe" implies that the main points will give reasons why such power plants are unsafe.

A. There are no safe methods for storing plutonium wastes.
B. There is no way to prevent the theft of plutonium.

Note that these reasons will need to be developed, in turn, by statements that show how the rhetor knows these things to be true or highly probable.

The specific purpose of making people believe that "55 mph is the maximum safe speed limit" suggests a development with main points like these:

A. Under ideal conditions, a car traveling at 55 mph requires a distance of more than seven car lengths to stop.

B. Road and weather conditions limit visibility and maneuverability.

C. Reaction times of drivers are increased by age, medications, and the consumption of alcohol.

D. The substantial decline in auto accidents deaths since the speed limit has been lowered demonstrates the greater safety of lower speeds.

For your initial exercise, you should do only two additional things to organize your material: Indicate how you will develop these main points, and plan an introduction and conclusion. For example, if you were to take as a thesis the statement "The 55 mph speed limit on our highways saves lives and money," your outline might look like this:

A. The 55 mph speed limit is better suited to actual driving conditions.

  1. Under ideal conditions, an alert, healthy driver needs about seven car lengths to stop a car going 55 mph.

    a. This distance includes reaction time (thinking distance) and braking distance.

    b. Small increases in speed make a difference because the distance needed to stop and the force of impact increase geometrically.

  2. Many drivers aren't in ideal condition.

    a. We have an aging population that will see and hear less well and react less quickly.

    b. Medicines and alcohol are even bigger problems.

      (1) Over-the-counter remedies affect driving ability.

      (2) Many commonly used prescription drugs are a serious threat to safe driving.

(3) Even relatively small amounts of alcohol impair driving ability.

3. Road and weather conditions are often less than ideal.

   a.   Many sections of our best highways are in poor condition.

   b.   More limited visibility at night has always required lower speed limits.

   c.   Rain, ice, and sleet are serious driving hazards, especially on limited-access roads.

4. Many cars are poorly maintained.

B. The 55 mph speed limit also saves lives.

   1. Since its enactment, for the first time in our history, there has been a dramatic drop in the number of highway fatalities.

   2. This drop is caused by lower speeds as well as less travel.

C. The 55 mph speed limit also saves money and energy.

   1. Most cars burn fuel with maximum efficiency at about 50 mph.

   2. Efficient gas use by all Americans saves energy.

Now two things need to be added: an introduction and a conclusion. The introduction should get the attention of the audience and indicate the significance of the topic for us. If you chose this topic because of a tragic or near-tragic personal experience, that story might be the ideal way to begin. A student who made a speech on this topic came to class scratched and bruised. He told of the miraculous survival of himself and his companions in an accident in which the driver had avoided a head-on collision only by taking to the ditch and hitting a tree. He told the story of the accident, reported that they had been traveling between 60 and 65, and said that he, personally, was now convinced that speed kills. He talked about his attitude and the attitudes of other people he knew about the 55 mph limit. He said his purpose was to defend that limit, not just because it saved energy, but because it saved lives. That was a superb introduction. It was vivid, personal, and attention-getting. It located accurately the attitudes of the audience. It showed his personal commitment to the topic and purpose. It prepared us for what followed; we knew what to expect. In other words, a good introduction

■ Gets the audience's attention

■ Creates accurate expectations about what will follow

■ Suggests the relationship of the topic to the audience

In this case, the introduction also showed the relationship between the rhetor and the subject, a highly desirable characteristic of introductions.

The conclusion of a rhetorical act is good if it is such that the act ends rather than stops. Ideally, a conclusion should do two things: (1) Summarize the major ideas that lead to the claim embodied in the thesis and (2) fix the specific purpose in the audience's mind. What is most important is that you plan carefully just how you will end. In the case of the student who had the near-tragic accident, the speaker said something like this: "I've shown you that if you are healthy and alert, if your car is in good mechanical condition, and if you're driving 55 mph, it will take you 218 feet from the time you see a problem until you can stop. If you're tired, if you've had a drink or have taken an antihistamine, if your tires are worn or your brake fluid is down, if it is dusk or raining, it will take you longer. When you drive over 55, you are not only breaking the law and wasting gas, you may be driving too fast to avoid an accident. And I've got the cuts and bruises to prove it."

That conclusion is simple and effective. It recalls most of the major ideas of the speech so that it summarizes, but it does so in concrete terms that will be relevant and intelligible to each member of the audience. That helps to make each idea memorable. In addition, the speaker uses himself as a vivid visual reminder of the dangers of fast driving. The conclusion illustrates another useful technique for concluding—the explicit reference to an anecdote or example that was used in the introduction. This creates the effect of "completing a circle" and hence a very strong impression of completeness.

PREPARING YOUR PRESENTATION

The quality of your final oral or written presentation depends on your skills as a critic and on your willingness to practice or rewrite. You can develop and refine your critical skills through preparing the strategy report described at the end of the appendix. A strategy report is a written analysis of the choices you made in preparing your rhetorical act, in light of the obstacles you faced and your purpose. In addition, if the act is oral, you must practice it aloud, standing, and, at the same time, try to imagine yourself as a member of the audience. If your act is written, you must learn to polish and refine your efforts through rewriting, a process made much easier if you use a word processor.

At this point, you have an outline that states the specific purpose, lists the main points, and cites the evidence you will use to explain and prove your assertions. You have made some rough notes for what you will say in the introduction and conclusion. You now need to move from the outline toward the composition of a complete and finished rhetorical act. Your first concern should be clarity. Focus your attention on two areas: the clarity of the relationships among ideas and the clarity of each piece of evidence you will present.

The clarity of the relationships among the main ideas depends on the soundness of the argument's structure and on the kinds of transitions or bridges made between ideas. If you have done your outline carefully and have made certain that your main points answer the questions Why? and How do I know? the relationships among the main points should be clear. There is a relatively simple test you can apply to determine the adequacy of your argument. If your main points are A, B, C, and D, then, if the argument is sound, it should be the case that:

> If A is true, if B is true, if C is true, and if D is true, then it should necessarily and inevitably follow that the claim you make in your specific purpose is true.

If you apply this test to the outline about 55 mph speed limits, you will notice the fit between the main points and the specific purpose. However, the material under A1 will need some explanation to show how these figures were arrived at. In main point A3, the rhetor is saying that ideal driving conditions rarely exist. After you eliminate stretches of limited-access superhighways, the places with the best visibility, fewest traffic problems, and best surface, driving hazards are likely to increase. That needs to be clear as the argument is presented. Point A2 is really saying that even young and healthy persons can have slowed reactions from cold medicine or a couple of beers, and this fact needs to be emphasized. Also, the audience may wonder about enforcement—are people really driving more slowly? If you think about the whole argument, you will realize that the rhetor is admitting that there may be places and persons and times for which it's safe to drive faster than 55 mph; but he or she is saying that 55 mph is the maximum realistic speed limit, and a speed limit should be set not for ideal but for real and normal driving conditions. The rhetorical act should emphasize that point if it is to be really effective. Note that such a survey of the outline helps to clarify for the rhetor just what the purpose is, what should be emphasized, and what qualifications may need to be made—for example, the recognition that it might be safe to drive faster under some conditions. In spite of such qualifications, you can make a strong and forceful argument, and by qualifying your claim you may avoid resistance from members of the audience who recognize exceptions.

Transitions are statements you make to ensure that the audience understands and recognizes the relationships among ideas. Although some members of your audience will listen or read actively, testing your arguments and trying to understand, others will listen or read relatively passively and will not see relationships unless you make them explicit. Here are some examples of transitions that might be used in the rhetorical act on 55 mph speed limits:

> A good speed limit is geared to averages—normal reaction time, normal mechanical conditions, normal conditions of visibility and road surfaces. As a result, I'll begin by talking about optimums—ideal reaction time, ideal mechanical conditions, ideal visibility and road conditions. But I'll also talk about the use of common medications and alcohol and about the conditions of roads and the problems of weather.

That statement creates connections and also previews what will happen in the speech. This sort of transition usually connects the attention-getting introduction to the body of the rhetorical act (the section that develops the specific purpose). It clarifies by creating expectations: Here is what I shall do and here is the general relationship among all these ideas.

The next transition explains two parts of one subpoint: the distance it takes to stop a car at a particular speed.

> Two elements are involved in stopping a car: thinking distance and braking distance. The first refers to the distance you will travel during your reaction time. The second refers to the distance you travel after you've stepped on the brakes. It is a measure of the distance it takes for your car to stop mechanically. Let's consider reaction times first.

This transition clarifies by reminding the audience that there are two parts and allows the speaker to talk about each separately while creating in the audience an awareness of their relationship.

The next transition is really an explanation of how you and the highway department arrived at certain conclusions:

> To understand how far you travel at different speeds, the State Highway Department talks in feet per second. The math works like this: There are 5,280 feet in a mile. At speed 60, you travel one mile per minute, or 5,280 divided by 60, or 88 feet per second.

The transition clarifies by explaining, but it also shows the relationships among speed, reaction time, and the distance it takes to stop.

Here's another kind of transition and explanation, one on the deregulation of natural gas:

> I've shown you how and why federal deregulation will increase the supplies of natural gas across state lines. What I've told you should make it pretty obvious that increased supplies depend on and are a result of higher prices for interstate gas shipments. In fact, deregulation will raise interstate prices to the intrastate level and will probably raise the prices for both in a few years.

This is a transition between two main points to indicate their relationship to each other. In addition, the transition is a preview of what the rhetor intends to do under the second main point. It clarifies by showing the relationship between these two parts of the argument.

Practicing aloud and editing/rewriting are the processes by which rhetors prepare oral and written rhetorical acts, respectively. Both are essential to produce a good final product. Practicing aloud serves two purposes. First, it creates a physical memory of what you intend to say that will help you speak smoothly. It prevents your oral presentation before the audience from being frightening because it is the first time you make your speech. Part of the fear associated with speaking is the fear each of us has about doing things that are new and different and in which we feel unskilled. You can diminish that by oral practice. Stand up as you intend to before the audience, hold your notes as you intend to, and speak your speech as you plan to do it on the actual occasion. If there are tongue twisters, you'll find them and be able to overcome them or make changes. If there's complicated material that's hard to explain, you'll discover it and have time for extra practice. Moreover, by the time you give your speech, it won't be the first time—it will be the ninth or tenth—and the material will feel familiar when you begin once again to present your speech. Second, it is the means for refining and reorganizing. For example, you practice your five-minute speech aloud and it runs 15 minutes, or what was supposed to run 1,500 words actually runs 3,000. Clearly, you haven't narrowed the topic enough, and you need to do some cutting. Or, as you listen to yourself or read what you've written, you realize that to be clear you have to add something—and you figure out how to add it and how to make the idea clearer. Please note, however, that none of these benefits occurs unless you read your work with the critical eye of a stranger or practice aloud exactly as if you were presenting the speech to your audience and listen to yourself critically. You must pretend to be your own audience, listening to the speech or reading the essay as someone unfamiliar with the subject. Such listening and reading enables you to catch problems and make needed changes. (Of course, you can also snag a cooperative roommate or friend and ask that person to respond candidly about questions and problems that arise in reading or listening to what you say. But such a person is only a poor substitute for developing your abilities as your own best listener or editor.)

Your speech should be presented from notes, not from a manuscript on which you have written out, word by word, what you intend to say. Presenting a speech from a manuscript is a difficult skill, as illustrated by actor and former President Reagan's more skillful and President Bush's less skillful delivery. Do not add to your problems by attempting this in the initial exercise. Tailor your notes to your personal needs. In my case, I memorize the introduction and write only one or two words from it on a card. You may need a chain of terms to create associations to help you remember all the elements of the story you want to tell and the order you want to follow.

After these terms, write a phrase or word that will suggest the transition into the thesis or specific purpose, and then write out the purpose in full. Next write a word or phrase suggesting the transition into the first main point and write this main point out in full. You should depart from outline or key term form only for evidence that should be written out in full so you can cite it accurately and completely, along with its source. Here is an example of the notes for the speech on the 55 mph speed limit:

(intro.)   alive today bec lucky
             Friday nite, returning from KC, hwy 10,
             60–65 mph, car passing, head-on collision

	couldn't stop, into ditch, hit tree injuries—minor bec of seat belts I now believe speed kills
(trans.)	attitudes of others; possible change in national policy
(thesis)	The 55 mph speed limit saves lives and money.
(trans.)	ideal vs. real: reaction time, mechanical condition of car, road and weather conditions A. 55 mph better for actual driving conditions 1. Under ideal conditions, ideal driver needs 7 car lengths to stop going 55 mph. a. Combines reaction time (thinking distance) and braking distance.
(evidence)	At 55 mph, travel 80.66 ft. per second, so takes 218 ft. to stop from time see problem. Ks. Driving Handbook, p. 42.
(trans.)	what difference if lower only 5-15 mph? b. Small increases in speed make big difference.
(evidence)	Distance needed to stop and force of impact increase geometrically; if double speed, 4 times distance to stop. Ks. Driving Handbook, p. 42.
(trans.)	but drivers, roads, and cars aren't in ideal condition 2. Many drivers aren't in ideal shape. a. aging population b. over-the-counter remedies, e.g. Dristan or
(evidence)	Sinutabs. Ks. Driving Handbook, p. 46. c. warnings about drowsiness on prescription drugs, e.g. tranquilizers, pain remedies, antihistamines. d. alcohol
(evidence)	Driving is impaired by as little as 1 drink of whiskey or 2 beers. Ks. Driving Handbook, p. 46.
(trans.)	boast of our fine roads, but many problems, and these compounded by weather
(evidence)	3. Many sections of best highways in poor condition, e.g., Interstate 80. NYTimes, 6/18/94 4. Weather conditions: ice and sleet obvious; also rain esp. on limited-access highways.
(evidence)	hydroplaning: when so much water on highway tires can't "wipe" the road so car starts to run on film of water.

Starts at 35 mph, by 55 car traveling entirely on water and out of control. Ks. Driving Handbook, p. 45.

(trans.)   can be more realistic and save money and energy and lives

B. 55 mph saves lives

1. For first time in history, sudden and dramatic drop in number of highway fatalities.

(evidence)   Motor Trend, August 1994, p. 37.

2. Drop came from a combination of less travel and less speed.

(evidence) Study of 31 turnpikes showed that traffic was down 18% but fatalities were down 60%. Motor T, p. 38.

C. 55 mph also saves $ and energy.

1. Most cars burn fuel with maximum efficiency at about 50 mph, so get most for gas $.

2. Efficient gas use by all Americans would save energy—travel farther on energy $

(concl.)   if healthy and alert

if car well maintained

if drive 55, need 7 car lengths to stop
    BUT

if tired, had a drink, or taken an antihistamine

if tires worn or brake fluid down

if dusk, night, raining

—takes longer

when drive over 55, breaking law, wasting gas

may also be driving too fast to prevent accident

I have cuts and bruises to prove it.

As you practice, add whatever notes you need for changes or additions. Be sure that what you have written on the cards is easily legible. Hold your notes slightly above waist level and use them every time you practice. Do not try to avoid looking at them (you will lose your place, fail to shift the cards as you progress, and have to search desperately if you need to consult them). Practice looking at them regularly, and plan to consult each card, moving the top card to the bottom as you finish the ideas it covers. Stand up firmly, speak aloud, try to imagine the audience in front of you. Practice until you can present the whole speech smoothly and easily. When your moment arrives, you will be well prepared to make a competent presentation.

DELIVERING YOUR SPEECH

Concerns about delivery are closely related to communication apprehension or stage fright. Fears about speaking are normal and appropriate. We fear what is unfamiliar and unknown, and most people who come to a rhetoric class have not had extensive experience speaking publicly or reading their work aloud to others. We fear the consequences of committing ourselves. Initiating rhetorical action requires that you do just that. By speaking or reading aloud, you say, "I have made a decision, I know, I believe, and I am ready to urge you to do likewise." Most of us are somewhat reluctant to set ourselves up as authorities, to take the responsibility of giving advice. As a result, speaking creates apprehension.

Speaking involves a social risk, and we fear isolation from and rejection by others. In most speaking situations, the audience clusters together in comfortable anonymity while the speaker stands alone. Nonverbally, it feels as if it's you against them. Because rhetorical action asks for and requires the participation of others, every speaker risks rejection. In face-to-face situations, the evidence is immediate and unavoidable. Audience members send hundreds of nonverbal messages registering their responses. It is disheartening to speak to listeners who show visual disregard while you are speaking—by reading a newspaper or falling asleep. Under such conditions and faced by such possibilities, some fear is appropriate. All good speakers, even those with much experience, feel some apprehension. On every occasion, a speaker takes responsibility for a commitment, is partially isolated from the audience, and chances a rebuff. Apprehension is a recognition of what is involved in acting as a rhetor.

However, such fears diminish greatly with practice, and most speakers become relatively comfortable after two or three experiences. In addition, if you have prepared carefully and practiced aloud so that you are in command of your material, your fears will be manageable after a few sentences. Human beings are symbol-using creatures, and despite our fears, we take pleasure in communicating with others, in expressing our ideas and feelings. You will enjoy the experience even more if you consider the following bits of advice.

Preparing the Scene

Insofar as it is possible, take control of the scene. If you are speaking, arrive early and case the joint. If possible, move chairs so that you lessen your isolation from the audience. This will make you more comfortable and create an environment in which participation by the audience is easier. If the audience is scattered over a large area, ask them to move forward so that they are closer together. Unless the occasion is extremely formal, be sure that lights are arranged so that you can see the audience. Stage lighting separates you from the audience and turns you into a performer or entertainer, a role that can limit your rhetorical efforts.

In general, avoid the use of a lectern and stand in front of tables or desks. A lectern shuts off much of your nonverbal communication and reduces your immediacy. Both lessen ease of audience participation. Use a lectern or table if you will feel more comfortable behind one or if you are in a situation in which you must use a manuscript, but do everything you can to minimize the barrier between you and the audience. Try standing next to the lectern. In this way you will be able to rest one hand on the lectern, and yet you won't be as severely "fenced off" from the audience.

Check to ensure that all materials you need are present and working. Test the microphone and look for a blackboard or a place to put visual aids. If any machines are to be used, be sure that they are there and working. Nothing destroys your efforts more quickly than a tape recorder that won't work or a beautiful visual aid that keeps collapsing.

If there are problems that can't be solved, acknowledge them to the audience in good humor. Try to make them your confederates in struggling to cope with a cold room, a noisy radiator, a defective mike, or whatever. Your role as rhetor requires you to take charge of the scene and to be responsive to what goes on in it.

Presenting Materials

Audiovisual aids such as charts, maps, pictures, and taped or filmed materials create special problems. Use them only when they contribute something essential to your presentation, and prepare them carefully. Visual aids are essential when you are presenting large amounts of statistical material or when ideas and relationships are difficult to explain verbally—for example, locations on maps.

Obviously, visual aids are a useful persuasive tool. As you prepare such aids, follow these general guidelines:

1. Be sure that they are large enough to be seen easily by all members of the audience (check sight lines).

2. Prepare them for easy display. Maps should be on a stiff backing so they can be stood up. Flip charts should be used with your own stand. Printing should be done in thick dark lettering.

3. Keep them simple so the audience can look at them and understand them, but be sure to explain them verbally in your speech.

4. Look at the audience, not at the visual aid. Keep your face toward the audience and talk to them. Remember, you are speaking to the audience, not to the chart or blackboard. Note: An overhead projector is preferable to a blackboard because it permits you to point out things on the visual display without turning your back to the audience.

5. Use them only when they contribute directly to your speech. Any visual aid is a competing, potentially distracting message. Unless an aid contributes to your entire speech, remove the distraction when you have finished using it. Do not pass items out while you are speaking.

Similar principles should be followed in the use of tape and film. Be sure that taped material is loud enough to be heard easily. Have the tape set up and ready to play. Use only the amount of taped or filmed material essential to make your point. Be prepared for mechanical problems!

Notes are one element in your own visual appearance. They are perfectly acceptable in all speaking situations, but some kinds of notes are preferable. Because your aim is immediacy, freedom of movement, and ease of use, print or type your notes so they are easily read on 3″ × 5″ or 4″ × 6″ cards. These can be held easily so you can stand anywhere, and one hand remains free for gestures. Because they are stiff, note cards can never betray your nervousness by rattling. Use your notes as you practice aloud (as you practice you will learn where items are on the cards). When you speak, refer to them regularly so that you do not lose your place or have to struggle to find a quotation.

Presenting Yourself

Dress   Dress with due consideration for the occasion, the role you will play, your purpose, and the expectations of the audience. Clothing is a major source of messages for the audience, and it can detract and distract. Follow these simple rules:

1. Dress for comfort and ease of movement. Avoid tight, stiff clothing, high heels that wobble, or climbing shoes that squeak.

2. Dress to avoid distraction. Avoid bright, busy, loud patterns that attract attention away from your message. Eliminate any item that can rattle, such as coins, keys, or bracelets.

3. Dress in an outfit that is harmonious. Minimize the time the audience will spend noticing your clothes.

Posture and Gesture   Before you begin to speak, walk slowly to the front of the room and position yourself comfortably. Do not begin to speak until you are standing firmly on both feet. You will create anticipation for what follows, and you will take charge of the scene. Avoid standing on one foot, rocking back and forth, and slouching. Arrange your hair so that it does not fall into your face, and avoid repetitive motions flicking it back. All of these distract from your message and suggest discomfort and lack of involvement. Feel free to move about, but move with purpose and for emphasis.

Hold your notes at chest level in one hand for easy reading and gesturing. Do not clasp your hands in front of you or behind you, fold your arms, or play with your notes. Avoid pointless or repetitious gestures. Aim for movement that will in no way distract from what you are saying.

Your eyes are a major source of contact with the audience. To establish your involvement and to hold attention, you will be most effective with most U.S. audiences if you look at them directly. Be sure to include everyone. For the audience, your gaze is a primary indicator of immediacy. And, of course, you can't respond to messages from the audience unless you are looking at them.

Voice   The ideal speaking voice is easy to hear and pleasing to listen to. Good delivery involves vocal variety and patterns of pause and emphasis that increase our understanding of what is said. The most common vocal problem among novice speakers is speaking too fast for clear articulation or comprehension. Writing "slow down" on each note card is a useful reminder, and practicing at slower rates helps to change habits. However, audiences may respond to rapid speech as dynamic, and most native speakers will be able to decode all but the most hurried speech.

These suggestions for delivery are grounded in the principles of nonverbal communication. As a rhetor, your goal is participation by the audience. Initiating joint action requires dynamism on your part. Your eyes, face, arms, and body should communicate your interest and involvement. Participation is made easier by indicators of immediacy such as lessening the distance between you and the audience and maintaining eye contact. As the initiator, you must establish your authority and competence. Gestures, posture, and physical relaxation all bespeak your competence. If rhetorical action is your goal, you must seek it both verbally and nonverbally. And remember that, while these hints may be helpful, preparing your speech carefully and practicing it aloud are probably the best ways to improve oral presentation.

Fears about delivering a speech are closely related to nonverbal communication. The role of the rhetor is one that puts pressure on a speaker, threatening social relationships and demanding responsibility and commitment. Apprehensions about communication are appropriate responses to such demands. Experience, practice, and preparation are excellent ways to cope. You can also reduce fear and increase effectiveness by the way you prepare the scene and present your material and yourself.

Summary Outline: A Checklist for Oral Delivery

I. First, prepare the scene.

    A. Judge how formal the occasion ought to be, and then

        1. Arrange the seating.

        2. Arrange the lighting.

        3. Decide on using a table or lectern.

        4. Set up and check out all audiovisual aids.

II. Second, present yourself.

    A. Dress for comfort and, to avoid distraction, wear an outfit to fit your role.

    B. Situate yourself comfortably before you begin to speak.

    C. Move with purpose and for emphasis; avoid distraction.

    D. Look directly at all of your audience.

    E. Speak with variety and dynamism.

    F. Speak slowly enough to be understood.

III. Third, present your materials.

    A. Use visual aids with care.

        1. Display them so that they can be seen easily by all the audience.

        2. Explain all displays in your speech.

        3. Look at the audience, not at the visual aid.

        4. Don't turn a visual aid into competing rhetoric.

    B. Use notes effectively.

1. Type or print your notes on cards.
2. Hold them in one hand at chest level for easy sight and movement.

If your rhetorical act is written, you need to move from the detailed notes to a complete first draft, typed or written with adequate margins and double-spaced so that corrections are easy to make. Struggle to complete a first draft even if you discover some problems along the way. The whole act will help you clarify your purpose and indicate what kinds of changes are needed. As with a speaker, concern yourself with the clarity of supporting materials. At this point, read to simplify. Shorten sentences and simplify sentence structure. Change terms that seem confusing or ambiguous. Check syntax and punctuation so they are correct and help the reader to understand. Read for repetition and redundancy. Unlike a listener, a reader can reread, check an earlier paragraph, and stop to think. For this reason, you should edit to eliminate repetition although you need to keep transitions. Check to be sure that no part of the argument is unstated and, thus, unclear.

A second draft is now in order. When it is completed, check it for syntax, punctuation, and spelling. Now polish for forcefulness and accuracy. Consider terms that are more vivid, precise, and explicit. Read the draft in its entirety again and mark sections that seem less clear and forceful than you wish. Now try for a final draft that is as polished as you can make it. At this point, your instructor's comments should help you revise once again to produce a finished essay, news or feature story, or editorial.

Space does not permit a detailed exploration here of suggestions for editing and polishing. However, what I have written about selecting a topic, narrowing it to a specific purpose, researching the subject, organizing the material, taking notes, and preparing notes for yourself for a final presentation applies equally to speaking or writing a rhetorical act. Also, a strategy report is equally useful for oral and written rhetoric.

At this point you, the rhetor, have the preliminaries to produce your first rhetorical act and to do it with some competence.

■   ■   ■

EXERCISES

1. Prepare a five- to seven-minute speech to alter perception that includes an excerpt from a novel, a short story, or a poem as a major piece of evidence.

2. Prepare a 1,500-word essay that applies a fable, tale, myth, or story to a current problem; use such stories as Aesop's fables, Greek or Roman mythology, or the fairy tales of Hans Christian Andersen or the Grimm brothers.

3. Prepare a speech or essay that combines detailed personal experience with research from secondary sources in order to explain something, for example, to lessen the controversy around an issue or to demystify a process.

4. Prepare a speech or essay to intensify beliefs already held by the audience by providing detailed information. Look at the sermon at the end of Chapter 8, as an example of this kind of effort.

STRATEGY REPORT

For each rhetorical act, prepare a written strategy report to be turned in at the time of your presentation. The report makes explicit at least part of the process you go through in preparing for rhetorical action. As such, it is not an end in itself, but a tool for learning. It should help make you aware of the choices that you make in initiating rhetorical action.

The strategy report has seven parts, some of which can be quite short:

1. Purpose
2. Persona (role) and tone
3. Audience
4. Outline
5. Source sheet
6. Strategies
7. Special remarks

1. Purpose: First, try to define the rhetorical purpose of your speech in terms of the general response you seek from the audience: to alter perception, to explain, to formulate belief, to initiate action, or to maintain belief or action. Recall that each of these purposes is related to assumptions you are making about what your audience knows, feels, and believes.

Second, try to state as briefly and precisely as you can what you would like the audience to know, feel, believe, or do when you are finished. In other words, indicate what you would consider an ideal response from your audience.

2. Persona (role) and tone: A speaker or writer assumes a persona or role in relation to the audience, and the "tone" of the language reflects her or his attitude toward the subject and relationship to the audience. Indicate whether you will speak as a peer or as an expert, and if you will shift roles during the act. Similarly, indicate whether your tone will be relatively impersonal and objective (appropriate for an expert, for instance) or personal and conversational (appropriate for a peer) or ironic (appropriate for a skeptic).

3. Audience: Discuss whether the exposed audience is your target audience and whether it includes agents of change. If there are discrepancies between those exposed and those you seek to reach or who can act (and if there are not, why rhetoric?), discuss some specific obstacles you face from this audience in transforming them into an ideal audience. Consider how you might appeal to them to play a role that would lead them to respond as you desire.

4. Outline: With some practice, most students have little difficulty in making outlines. Look at the examples in Chapter 9, and be sure that your outline is in complete sentences, particularly as it expresses your thesis and your main points. Leave a wide margin on the left in order to label what you are doing at each point, such as kinds of evidence, transitions, organizational patterns, and strategies. Use the margin for an abbreviated descriptive analysis of your own rhetoric.

5. Source sheet: In preparing for a speech or essay, your personal experience and your imagination are important sources from which to draw material and shape it for your audience. But almost no one's personal experience is so broad or insight so penetrating that she or he cannot benefit from the knowledge in secondary sources or the challenge of responding to the ideas of others.

For each rhetorical act, provide a list of annotated sources, that is, sources for which you write a short paragraph describing the nature of each and telling what you used it for.

Sources may be of four types. Use all these types in rhetorical acts throughout this course so you become familiar with different kinds of resources.

a. Popular sources: Mass circulation newspapers and magazines are popular sources. Articles in *TV Guide* or *Newsweek* or your local newspaper are intended for general audiences. They provide useful evidence and often stimulate thinking.

b. Specialized sources: Periodicals intended for limited audiences of specialists are specialized sources. They present articles by experts for specialists, and they analyze more thoroughly topics that are discussed generally or superficially in popular sources. In the *Quarterly Journal of Speech, Signs, Foreign Affairs,* or the *Monthly Labor Review,* for example, you can gain greater understanding, gather data, and verify claims made in popular sources. You should learn to do research that takes you beyond the *Readers' Guide to Periodical Literature.*

Note: A distinction between popular and specialized sources can be made, in many cases, between books written for the mass market and those written by specialists for a specialized audience.

c. Interviews: The world is full of all kinds of experts, and you should take the opportunity to talk to those available in your area on your subject. Such interviews, including the person's credentials, should be listed as part of your source materials.

d. Personal experience: You may have direct knowledge of your subject that goes beyond the ordinary. If you have such experience, and it is relevant to your subject, cite your own expertise and describe its nature. Be reminded, however, of the importance of testing your experience against data gathered by others and the opinions of experts.

Cite your sources in proper bibliographic form. Here are examples for a periodical and a book:

Lang, Susan S. "Sick Building Syndrome Linked to Fibers." *Human Ecology Forum* 22, no. 1 (Winter 1994):4.

Clotfelter, Charles T., and Philip J. Cook. *Selling Hope: State Lotteries in America.* Cambridge, MA: Harvard University Press, 1989.

If your source is an interview with an expert or personal experience, simply make a note of the nature of the interview or the experience. For example:

On October 20, 1992, I interviewed Diana Lisak, an assistant professor of psychology at the University of Massachusetts, Boston. She discussed research on the motivational factors underlying male sexual aggression, including examples from studies of 15 unreported rapists and 15 control subjects, that she believes suggest the importance of child-rearing practices in understanding the motivations of rapists.

From September 1987 to September 1989, I was a volunteer for the Sexual Violence Program at the University of Minnesota.

As a result of my training and of my experience, I have detailed knowledge of the incidence of rape on a large urban midwestern university campus and personal experience of the impact of rape, including acquaintance rape, on undergraduate women students' lives.

6. Strategies: It may take you only a sentence or two to describe your purpose, your persona and tone, and your audience, but it will take you several paragraphs to describe your strategies adequately. In this section, discuss the means you will use to achieve your purpose and the choices you will make to overcome the obstacles you face. Your statement should have two parts.

First, given your subject and purpose, how is your audience likely to respond? Explore the rhetorical obstacles of complexity, cultural history, cost, control, and reasons why the audience might be hostile or indifferent to your subject or to what you propose. (See Chapters 3 through 6.)

Second, discuss specific choices you made to create your audience, to transform the exposed audience into the target audience and agents of change. Specifically, discuss your choice of perspective, evidence, organizational patterns, introductory and concluding remarks, appeals to needs or values, and statements made to indicate your relationship to the subject. Your strategies should reflect the ways in which you have adapted materials for your audience in order to achieve your purpose.

7. Special remarks: Use this section to discuss anything you believe significant that does not fit into the other sections. It may be that you have no special remarks, but many rhetorical acts are unusual, and you may need this section to talk about elements you believe are unique or out of the ordinary.

SOURCES

Fowler, H. W. *A Dictionary of Modern English Usage,* 2d ed. rev. by Ernest Gowers. New York: Oxford University Press, 1987. Provides useful pointers on grammar and style, punctuation, spelling, and pronunciation.

Hacker, Diana. *A Writer's Reference,* 3d ed. Boston: Bedford Books of St. Martin's Press, 1995.

MLA Handbook for Writers of Research Papers, Theses, and Dissertations. New York: Modern Language Association of America, 1977.

Strunk, William, Jr. Revised by E. B. White. *The Elements of Style,* 3d ed. New York: Macmillan, 1979. A most readable, basic work on usage, composition, and style.

Turabian, Kate L. *A Manual for Writers of Term Papers, Theses, and Dissertations,* 6th ed. Chicago: Univ. of Chicago Press, 1987.

Index